Th

TRAINS

OF THE WORLD

Brian Hollingsworth

MBI Publishing Company

This edition first published in 2000 by
MBI Publishing Company,
729 Prospect Avenue, PO Box 1, Osceola,
WI 54020-0001 USA

MBI Publishing Company books are also
available at discounts in bulk quantity for
industrial or sales-promotional use. For
details write to Special Sales Manager at
Motorbooks International Wholesalers &
Distributors, 729 Prospect Avenue, PO
Box 1, Osceola, WI 54020-0001 USA.

Library of Congress Cataloging-in-
Publication Data Available

ISBN 0-7603-0891-8

Printed in Slovenia

Credits

Project Manager: Ray Bonds
Designed by: Interprep Ltd
Color reproduction by:
Studio Technology

The Author

Brian Hollingsworth, M.A., M.I.C.E., is a former civil engineer with Britain's Great Western Railway. He was director of the Romney, Hythe and Dymchurch Railway, and civil engineering advisor to the Festiniog Railway. He has owned a fleet of one-fifth full size locomotives, and a full size LMS "Black Five" Class 4-6-0 which has been operated for tourists and rail enthusiasts in Yorkshire, England. He is the author of more than a dozen books on various aspect of railways and locomotives.

Other Contributors

Chris Bushell is Editor of *Railway Directory*, was a journalist with the monthly *Railway Gazette*, and was formerly Editor/Co-Editor of *Jane's Urban Transport Systems*. He has been writing about railways and public transport for more than thirty years.

Ken Harris is Editor of *Jane's World Railways*, author of *World Electric Locomotives* and has contributed to various technical railway journals. **Arthur Cook** was a staff member of British Rail, before retiring to write many technical articles on trains and railway systems, particularly modern rail power.

Contents

Introduction

Commentators on the growth of air transport often point to a rapid pace of technological development which in less than a century took us from the achievements of the Wright brothers to an everyday acceptance of the Boeing 747 and its contemporaries as a means of mass intercontinental travel. Although spread over a longer period – the opening of the line between Liverpool and Manchester in 1830 is often judged a good starting point for the "modern" railway – the development of rail transport has been every bit as impressive, perhaps more so. Its remarkable legacy continues to shape nations, industry and even such everyday issues such as where we choose to live, thanks to the ability of the train to take us to our workplace. Moreover, rail is a highly versatile mode of transport, readily adaptable equally to accommodate 20,000-ton freight trains or the socially desirable rural passenger lifeline.

To meet these demands, rail has continued to expand its frontiers both in terms of speed and power, adapting its capabilities to embrace high-speed passenger operations at 186mph (300km/h) or more and the heaviest freight hauls. At the centre of this process has been nearly two centuries of locomotive development, many of the highlights of which are recorded in this book. For much of this period, it was steam that dominated railway traction, and the reader will see here the great strides made in the development of this form of traction up to the 1950s and 1960s.

One now wonders how a coal-fired steam-operated railway would fit into today's environmental consciousness. Anyone privileged to have visited one of those virtually extinct magnets for lovers of the railway, a large steam locomotive depot, with machines at rest or being prepared for work, will have experienced that special smoky atmosphere which seemed to demand the attention of all the senses. However, such pleasures were lost on those living close to such depots, the largest of which were often located in urban areas. Increasingly discriminating passengers with the choice of other methods of transport also demanded a clean travel environment. If economics had not dictated the end of steam traction, it is likely that in Western Europe and North America at least pressure for greener and cleaner transport might

have heightened its demise.

Today, diesel and electric traction is virtually unchallenged, save for a few surviving pockets of steam in countries like Cuba and China, and many classic early diesel and electric locomotive types have themselves become a focus of attention for those who love railways. Technological developments now enable designers to construct electric locomotives with over 2,000hp (1,500kW) per traction motor, and 6,000hp (4,476kW) diesel machines are now being supplied to North American railroads, as the more recent entries in this directory reveal.

High-speed rail is one of the great achievements of this mode of transport. To judge how far railways have come in 150 years, compare the public anxiety and outcry that greeted the prospect of Liverpool and Manchester Railway steam locomotives trundling along at 35mph (56km/h) against the matter-of-fact way in which millions of passengers annually board ICE, Shin Kansen or TGV high-speed trains in total confidence that their journey will be a safe and pleasing experience.

High-speed technology will continue to develop: France plans a new generation of TGVs capable of 223mph (360km/h) and in both Japan and Germany magnetic levitation (maglev) is being pursued as an alternative to the steel-wheel-on-rail as a means of high-speed surface-bound guided transport. In April 1999 in Japan, the MLX-001 development train achieved a new world record speed of 342.8mph (552km/h) on the Yamanashi test track.

As far ahead as can reasonably be predicted, though, such systems will find only a limited application, not least because of the high associated infrastructure costs. On the everyday railway serving millions of passengers, increased standards of interior accommodation and lower life-cycle costs will continue to be built into new trains, while freight operators will benefit from the availability of locomotives with higher installed power and better adhesion. Consolidation globally of rail vehicle manufacturing capabilities also looks set to lead to increasing levels of design standardization, although it would be perhaps too bold a prediction to suggest that eventually train operators will select from a range of basic models offered by a few manufacturers in the way that airlines do.

Northumbrian 0-2-2

Origin: Great Britain: Liverpool & Manchester Railway (L&M), 1830.
Tractive effort: 1,580lb (720kg). **Axle load:** circa 6,500lb (3t). **Cylinders:** (2)
11 x 16in (280 x 406mm). **Driving wheels:** 52in (1,321mm). **Heating
surface:** 412sq ft (38m²). **Superheater:** None. **Steam pressure:** circa 50psi
(3.5kg/cm²). **Grate area:** circa 8sq ft (0.75m²) **Fuel (coke):** circa 2,200lb (1t).
Water: circa 400gall (480 US) (1.8m³). **Adhesive weight:** circa 6,500lb (3t).
Total weight: 25,500lb (11.5t). **Length overall:** 24ft 0in (7,315mm).

Readers might be surprised that Stephenson's immortal *Rocket* does not
lead this book's cavalcade of locomotives through the ages. The reason for
this is that between *Rocket's* triumph at the Rainhill trials in October 1829
and the opening of the world's first inter-city steam railway on September
15, 1830, there had been as many fundamental changes in steam
locomotive design as were to occur over all the years that were to follow.
Steam locomotives built in the late 20th Century were no further from those
built in 1830 than were those built in 1829 – at any rate in fundamentals. Of
course they got a little bigger and heavier – by a factor of 40 or thereabouts.

Northumbrian, which hauled the opening train on that disastrous opening
day in 1830, had several important things which *Rocket* had not; first, she
had a smokebox in which ashes drawn through the boiler tubes could
accumulate. Second, the boiler was integrated with the water jacket round
the firebox. These two things meant that the locomotive-type boiler, fitted to
99.9 per cent of the world's steam locomotives to be built over the next 150
years, had now fully arrived. The third thing was that the cylinders had now
come down to the horizontal position – the axis of *Rocket's* cylinders were
fairly steeply inclined at 35° to the horizontal and not surprisingly the out-of-
balance forces caused the locomotive to rock badly. Moreover,
Northumbrian's cylinders were fitted in an accessible position, attached to
but outside the wheels although, it is true, still at the wrong end. The
Northumbrian weighed 7.35 tons less tender, nearly double the 4.25 tons of
Rocket and her destructive forces were recognised by the provision of a front
buffer beam complete with leather buffers stuffed with horsehair. Another
quite important improvement was the use of vertical iron plates as the main
frames and a proper tender – rather than a barrel on wheels – was provided.

The features that made *Rocket* a success at the trials were continued in
Northumbrian, but in larger and stronger form. The multi-tubular boiler – that
is to say one which had numerous tubes instead of one big flue for the hot

Right: 1980 replicas of 1829 locomotives. *Rocket* to left, *Sans Pareil* to right

gases to pass through while they exchanged their heat with the water in the boiler. Numerous little tubes have a much greater surface area than one big flue of equivalent size and so heat is passed across to the water at a higher rate; hence such a boiler has high steam raising capacity in relation to its size.

The other important feature of *Rocket* was the blast-pipe, once more something that was fundamental to the success of 99.9 per cent of the steam locomotives ever built. By arranging that the exhaust steam was discharged through a jet up the chimney, a partial vacuum was set up at the chimney end. Air would rush in to fill this vacuum and the only way (it was hoped) it could do so was through the fire grate at the other end of the boiler. Hence there was a situation where the amount of air being drawn through the fire and thus the amount of heat produced would depend on the amount of steam being used. More than anything else, this automatic connection between the amount of heat needed and the amount supplied was what gave the Stephensons, father and son, their triumph.

It also says enough that the boiler fitted to *Northumbrian* came to be known as the locomotive-type boiler. Of all the locomotives described in this book, only one (London & North Eastern No.10,000) had another type of boiler and only one (South African Railways' class "25") failed to have the blast-pipe. This was not through the lack of trying for something better, for many attempts were made to introduce new ideas. But only very few prevailed far enough to enter revenue service

Below: *Northumbrian* **depicted (so far as is known) in new condition.**

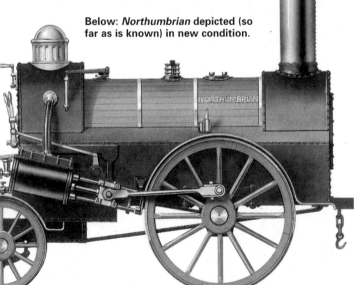

NORTHUMBRIAN

9

at all and, of course, none has managed to topple the Stephenson boiler from its throne whilst steam traction exists. Incidentally, credit for suggesting the multi-tubular boiler was attributed by Robert Stephenson to a Mr Henry Booth treasurer of the L&M Company.

As regards the mechanical part of *Northumbrian*, the principle of having two and only two cylinders outside the frames and directly connected to the driving wheels became more and more the world standard as the years went by. Towards the end of steam this principle became virtually universal, apart from articulated locomotives. Even so, the actual *layout* of *Northumbrian's* machinery had serious draw backs.

Because the driving wheels were at the front, the heavy firebox and the heavy cylinders were at the end where the *carrying* wheels were. There was only a box full of smoke at the other end and yet the driving wheels needed all the weight the track could stand to keep them from slipping. Moreover, when the engine began pulling the force on the drawbar tended to lift the front end of the engine, thereby further reducing the weight available for adhesion.

Another problem arose through the combination of outside cylinders with a short wheelbase. The alternate piston-thrusts tended to swing the engine about a vertical axis so that it proceeded with a boxing motion and in a serpentine manner. It was not until the *Northumbrian* layout was considerably altered by having an extended wheelbase and moving the cylinders to the front that these problems were solved. In the meantime the route of development left the main line for a branch, as we shall see.

A rather dubious feature of *Northumbrian* was the primitive means of reversing. An eccentric – a device to convert rotation to oscillation – was provided on the driving axle in order to move the valve of each cylinder. To reverse the direction of rotation, the eccentric on each side has to be turned nearly 180 degrees relative to the crank. It is easy to leave the eccentrics loose on the axle and provide stops so that they take up the correct position whichever way the wheels turn. The draw-back to this simple and excellent valve gear is that it is difficult to devise an arrangement to move the eccentrics upon the axle while the engine is stationary that is not complicated and inconvenient. Otherwise the locomotive can only be reversed by giving a push.

Both *Rocket* and *Northumbrian* had such an arrangement; one snag was that it could not be used while in motion. This was vividly demonstrated on that opening day. When William Huskisson, MP, stepped out into the path of *Rocket*, Joseph Locke who was driving had no means of *breaking* (to use the spelling of the day) and the famous accident took place. *Northumbrian*

Left: An early replica of *Rocket* before rebuilding.

covered herself with glory in rushing the fatally injured man to medical aid, but to no avail.

Northumbrian is regarded as belonging to the "Rocket" class, seven examples of which had previously been delivered to the Liverpool & Manchester Railway in 1829 and 1830. *Rocket's* immediate successors, *Meteor, Comet, Dart* and *Arrow,* were delivered with the cylinders in an almost horizontal position, while *Rocket* was so altered very quickly. *Phoenix* also had smokebox and so did *North Star. Majestic,* which followed *Northumbrian,* also had all the new features. Only *Rocket's* remains survive, in London's Science Museum, but in fact they come much closer to the later engines than *Rocket* as delivered.

Below: A contemporary engraving of the Stephenson *Northumbrian*. Note the headlights, and the crew's attire.

Planet Class 2-2-0

Origin: Great Britain: Liverpool & Manchester Railway, 1830. **Tractive effort:** circa 1,450lb (660kg). **Axle load:** 11,250lb (5t). **Cylinders:** (2) 11½ x 16in (292 x 406mm). **Driving wheels:** 62in (1,575mm). **Heating surface:** 407sq ft (38m²). **Superheater:** None. **Steam pressure:** circa 50psi (3.5kg/cm²). **Grate area:** 7.2sq ft (0.67m²). **Fuel (coke):** circa 2,200lb (lt). **Water:** circa 400gall (480 US) (1.8m³). **Adhesive weight:** 11,250lb (5t). **Total weight:** 29,500lb (13.5t). **Length overall:** 24ft 4in (7,420mm).

Planet arrived on the Liverpool & Manchester Railway in October 1830, soon after it was opened. The Stephensons had changed two things since they completed *Northumbrian* only a few weeks before. The first one was to put the cylinders at the front end instead of the back. This helped to get a good weight distribution; the drive was on to the rear pair of wheels which supported the heavy firebox, and, moreover, 99 per cent of the world's steam locomotives were to have two horizontal cylinders at the front end.

The second thing which was done was aimed at curing the "boxing" motion which plagued the earlier locomotives. This was achieved by putting the cylinders between instead of outside the wheels and connecting them to the driving wheels by making the main axle in the form of a double crank. Crank-axles continued to present a serious technical problem, not only in themselves but also because the big-end bearings of the connecting rods had to be split - and hence weakened - so that they could be removed and replaced. Even so, some 5 per cent of the world's steam locomotives were to have two inside cylinders and crank-axles; Robert Stephenson & Co. supplied some to British Railways as late as 1953.

Planet was quite successful and many of these engines, some with four coupled wheels, were made both by the Stephensons and by others. Outstanding amongst the imitations was a 2-2-0 called *Old Ironsides,* built in Philadelphia, USA, in 1832 by a Matthias Baldwin. Starting with this first full-size locomotive Baldwin went on to build up the greatest locomotive

manufactory the world has ever known, with a production of 60,000 locomotives during the 130 years of its existence. It is said that Baldwin had such trouble getting payment for his first locomotive that he declared he would build no more! The Stephensons, on the other hand, when they developed *Planet* into their celebrated six-wheel locomotives, decided that this time they would discourage imitators by taking out a patent.

Even so it was *Planet* that finally convinced a sceptical world that a form of reliable mechanical transport had arrived and that the Stephensons were the people to provide it. Soon enough it took them from a humble cottage by the Tyne to being millionaires in the £s of those days, as well as ensuring that their name will be remembered wherever and while railways exist.

Below: A drawing of the *Planet* locomotive of the Liverpool & Manchester Railway, Stephenson's first inside-cylinder locomotive.

Stourbridge Lion 0-4-0

Origin: United States: Delaware & Hudson Canal Company (D&H), 1829
Gauge: 4ft 3in (1,295mm). **Axel load:** 8,624lb (3.9t). **Cylinders:** (2) 8½ x
36in (215 x 914mm). **Driving wheels:** 49in (1,244mm). **Adhesive weight**
15,680lb (7.1t) without tender. **Length overall:** 12ft 10.5in (3,924mm).

Choosing the words with care, it must be stated that August 9, 1829, was
the first day on which a locomotive intended to be used commercially made
a run in America. This event occurred at Honesdale, Pennsylvania, on the
light track of the 4ft 3in (1,295mm) gauge horse-operated tramway which
belonged to the Delaware & Hudson Canal Company and connected the
canal with mines at Carbondale. Horatio Allen, the company's young master
mechanic, who had previously visited England to order the locomotive, later
wrote describing his feelings as follows: "I took my position on the platform
of the locomotive and with my hand on the throttle said, 'If there is any
danger in this ride it is not necessary that the life and limb of more than one
be subjected to danger'. The locomotive, having no train behind it answered
at once to the movement of the hand... soon I was out of sight in the three
miles ride alone in the woods of Pennsylvania. I have never run one since.'

The locomotive was named *Stourbridge Lion*, and was an 0-4-0 built by
Foster & Rastrick of Stourbridge, near Birmingham, England, in what was
then the well-named "Black Country". It weighed over twice as much as had
been promised by the makers when Allen visited them the previous year and
so its effect on the track was such that it was decided not to put the *Lion* into
service as a locomotive. Instead a use was found for it as a stationary engine.
But Allen remained convinced that the future lay with steam, and when his
advice was asked concerning motive power for the South Carolina Railroad
he came down firmly on the side of mechanical power.

Below: *Stourbridge Lion* **as it might have
looked on that memorable day in 1829.
Gross overweight cut short what would surely
have been a successful life on the track.**

STOURBRIDGE LION

Above: D&H replica of the *Stourbridge Lion* now to be seen in Washington at the Smithsonian Museum.

Stourbridge Lion had a sister - an almost identical twin in fact, named *Agenoria*. She was good enough to perform successfully on the Shutt End Railway near Stourbridge in England for over a quarter of a century, so we know that *Lion* would have done well as a locomotive, if allowed to operate. Happily, *Agenoria* has survived and can be seen in London's Science Museum. The most conspicuous difference between the *Lion* and *Agenoria* was that the latter had a much longer smokestack.

The driving mechanism of the Stourbridge twins consisted of what amounted to a pair of single-cylinder beam engines. The beams and linkage effectively reduced the stroke of the cylinders from 36in to 27in. Loose eccentrics engaging with stops fixed to the rear axle worked the valves when running and there was provision to move them by hand for starting.

The design in fact owed much more to William Hedley of *Puffing Billy* fame than to the Stephensons. In 1829 *Puffing Billy* had been running for 16 years and so the *Lion* was built to a well-matured design, the result of a good deal of experience. But it was not to prevail over the direct-drive system which was to be the main feature of some 99 per cent of steam locomotives ever built. Some 120 years were to pass before locomotives with near-vertical cylinders and complicated transmission systems would supersede the *Stephenson* concept. An excellent replica of the *Stourbridge Lion* is kept at the Smithsonian Museum of Science & Technology at Washington, DC.

Best Friend of Charleston 0-4-0 Tank

Origin: United States: South Carolina Railroad (SCRR), 1830. **Gauge:** 4ft 8½in (1,435mm). **Tractive effort:** 453lb (206kg). **Axle load:** 4,500lb (2t) **Cylinders:** (2) 6 x 16in (152 x 406mm). **Driving wheels:** 54in (1,371mm) **Steam pressure:** 50psi (3.5kg/cm²). **Grate area:** 2.2sq ft (2m²). **Water** 140gall (165 US) (0.64m³). **Adhesive weight:** 9,000lb (4t). **Total weight** 9,000lb (4t). **Length overall:** 14ft 9in (4,496mm).

History was certainly made on January 15, 1831, the day when the first full size steam locomotive to be built in the United States went into service. This was *Best Friend of Charleston,* running on the New World's first commercia steam railway, the South Carolina Railroad. This little contraption foreshadowed the building of 170,000 further steam locomotives for service in the USA during the years to come. *Best Friend* was constructed at the West Point Foundry in New York in late 1830. Features included a vertica boiler, a well tank integral with the locomotive, four coupled wheels and two modestly inclined cylinders. It was built at the West Point Foundry in New York to the design of E.L. Miller, who was the engineer of the South Carolina Railroad.

Although, apart from the coupled wheels, none of its principles of design were adopted generally, the locomotive was quite successful, but the next one built for this railroad followed the same principles only as regards mechanical parts – the later version had a horizontal boiler, the first to be built in America. Even so, the original design could handle a train of five cars carrying more than 50 passengers at 20mph (32km/h).

In one rather tragic way, however, the locomotive did contribute to the story of steam traction development. The fireman had become annoyed with the noise of steam escaping from the safety valves and used to tie down the lever which controlled them. One day in June 1831 he did this once too often – and the boiler exploded and he was killed. In due time tamper-proof valves became the rule – people normally need shock before they take action.

Later, the locomotive was rebuilt with a new boiler and re-entered service, appropriately named *Phoenix*. By 1834, the South Carolina Railroad went the whole 154 miles from Charleston to Hamburg, just across the river from the city of Augusta, Georgia. When opened, this was by far the longest railway in the world.

Left: *Best Friend of Charleston*. Some contemporary accounts tell of additional cylinders driving the tender wheels.

Brother Jonathan 4-2-0

Origin: United States: Mohawk & Hudson Railroad River (M&HRR), 1832.
Gauge: 4ft 8^1/2in (1,435mm). **Tractive effort:** circa 1,023lb (464kg). **Axle load:** 7,000lb (3.2t). **Cylinders:** (2) 9^1/2 x 16in (241 x 406mm). **Driving wheels:** 60in (1,524mm). **Boiler:** details not recorded. **Boiler pressure:** circa 50psi (3.5kg/cm²). **Adhesive weight:** circa 7,000lb (3.2t). **Total weight*:** 14,000lb (6.4t). **Length overall*:** 16ft 5^1/2in (5,017mm). *Engine only without tender.

As regards express passenger trains, certainly one of the great benefactors of mankind was John B. Jarvis, who in 1832 introduced the pivoted leading truck or bogie into the locomotive story, an idea suggested to him by Robert Stephenson when he visited England. Although very few particulars have survived, this little 4-2-0, originally known as *Experiment*, was the vehicle used. This pathfinding design of locomotive was built at the West Point Foundry in New York and delivered to the M&HRR.

Amongst the features of the locomotive, one notes that the boiler was rather small (copied from Robert Stephenson's "Planet" type) and that there was room for the connecting rods in the space between the sides of the firebox and the main frames, which were situated outside the driving wheels. These in turn were located behind the firebox, as on a Crampton locomotive.

None of these other features became the norm on the world's locomotives, but as regards express passenger locomotives, the four-wheel bogie certainly is much used. It will be found that all the classes of locomotive described in this book have leading four-wheel bogies according to the principle pioneered with *Brother Jonathan*. Incidentally, *Brother Jonathan* was then an impolite way of referring to the English; no doubt the name was a gesture of triumph at having thrown off any possible continued

Above: A replica of *Brother Jonathan*, alias *Experiment*.

dependence on English technology.

The idea was to provide guidance by having two wheels pressing against the outer rail of curves as near as possible in a tangential attitude. For any particular radius, or even at a kink in the track, the bogie would take up an angle so that the three contact points between wheel and rail on each side would lie correctly on the curve. This was particularly important on the light rough tracks of the time.

This locomotive demonstrated very clearly that the principle was a sound one and for many years thereafter the majority of American locomotives of all kinds had the advantage of this device. *Brother Jonathan* itself was successful in other ways; converted later to a 4-4-0 it had a long and useful life.

Left: *Brother Jonathan*, the first locomotive in the world to have a four-wheel leading truck or bogie.

Tom Thumb 0-2-2

Origin: United States: Baltimore & Ohio Railroad (B&O), 1830. **Gauge:** 4ft 8¹/₂in. (1,435mm). **Tractive effort:** 820lb (372kg). **Axleload:** 5,800lb (2.6t). **Cylinders:** (1) 5 x 27in (127 x 685mm). **Driving wheels:** 30in (762mm). **Heating surface:** 40sq ft (4m²). **Steam pressure:** 90psi (6.3kg/cm²). **Grate area:** 2.7sq ft (0.3m³). **Fuel:** 800lb (0.4t). **Water:** 52 US gall (0.2m²). **Adhesive weight:** 5,800lb (2.6t). **Total weight:** 10,800lb (4.9t). **Length overall:** 13ft 2in (4,013mm). These figures apply to the replica built in 1927.

The first section of the Baltimore & Ohio Railroad had been chartered in 1827. The intention was that it should be a horse worked line, at any rate for the first section from Baltimore to Ellicot Mills near Washington, but after a short length of track had been laid at the Baltimore end a certain Peter Cooper offered to demonstrate the use of steam traction. His *Tom Thumb* locomotive was little more than a toy, with a single-cylinder engine and vertical boiler of which legend states "the boiler tubes were made from musket barrels." The tiny machine pulled a single boat shaped car in which the directors of the Baltimore & Ohio travelled, and the event was staged as a race with a horse-drawn vehicle, on August 28, 1830,

Tom Thumb did fine on the way out but lost the battle on the return trip when the belt driving the fan used to draw the fire broke. Even so, steam won the war because the B&O management decided to become a steam railroad in the future, although as we shall see, vertical-boilered locomotives were used on their railroad for a considerable time.

The replica depicted here was made to entertain the crowds at the Baltimore & Ohio's Centenary Fair of the Iron Horse in 1927. It was constructed in good faith and certainly demonstrated the principles of the original design, but various features of it do not correspond with

Above: The *Tom Thumb* replica on display for the opening of the California Railroad Museum, Sacramento, in 1981.

contemporary accounts of the locomotive which have come to light since.

Thomas Cooper relates how at the last minute he decided that the natural draught of his little vertical boiler would not draw the fire sufficiently. "I screwed a crooked joint on the top of the smoke stack to hold my blower and carried a belt down over a wheel on the shaft," he told the Master Mechanics Association in 1875. In the replica there is no sign of the contrivance attached to the chimney, while the blower is down below on the platform. Amongst other differences it is now found that the original had a conspicuous A-frame to support the cylinder and also the platform was mounted much lower, so that the tops of the wheels protruded through.

The sequel to the run of *Tom Thumb* was that the B&O directors decided to set a competition for American manufacturers only, for the best practical steam locomotive to be decided by trials after the style of those which Stephenson's *Rocket* won at Rainhill, England.

Left: A replica of the *Tom Thumb*, the first steam locomotive to run on the Baltimore & Ohio Railroad, on August 28, 1830.

John Bull 0-4-0 (later 4-2-0)

Origin: Great Britain: Camden & Amboy Railroad, 1831. **Gauge:** 5ft 0in (1,524mm). **Tractive effort:** 765lb (347kg). **Cylinders:** (2) 9 x 20in (228 x 508mm). **Driving wheels:** 54in (1,371mm). **Heating surface:** 300sq ft (28m²). **Steam pressure:** 30psi (2,1 kg/cm²). **Grate area:** 10sq ft (0.9m²). **Adhesive weight:** 44,080lb (20t). **Length overall:** 37ft 0in (11,277mm).

Just as the world now goes to General Motors Electro-Motive Division's plant at La Grange, Illinois, for locomotives, there was a time when it went to the works of George and Robert Stephenson at Newcastle-upon-Tyne, England. The little Camden & Amboy line, an early ancestor of the giant Pennsylvania Railroad, did just that in 1830 for a little 0-4-0 based on the Stephenson's supremely practical "Planet" design. Up until then the portion of the railroad that was open had relied on horse power. The *John Bull* arrived by sea at Philadelphia in mid-1831 and, after a further sea voyage to Bordentown, New Jersey, was erected by the C&A's young Master Mechanic Isaac Dripps. This is someone less-celebrated than he should be, because it was this man who first fitted to a locomotive not only a bell and headlight but the cow catcher or pilot as well. Although only 22 when appointed, he had had a good apprenticeship to Thomas & Holloway, makers of ships' steam engines. Dripps went on to become superintendent of motive power to the Pennsylvania Railroad at Altoona Shops.

John Bull made a demonstration trip on November 12, 1831, but steam operation did not begin on a regular basis for over a year. No doubt the track needed strengthening and improvement, while the locomotive was also modified. The bell which was first put on the *John Bull* is still carried by all North American locomotives today while, until Dripps designed and introduced an oil-burning headlight, which would stand both the vibration and the weather, the only means of lighting the way ahead was a fire in a brazier carried ahead of the chimney. Dripps' pilot was quite different from today's, being carried on its own pair of wheels. It was a primitive kind of

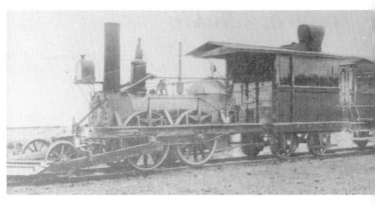

Above and Below: *John Bull*, **built by George and Robert Stephenson of Newcastle, England, in 1831 for the Camden & Amboy Railroad, is now the oldest steam locomotive in the world still in operable state.**

leading truck. The coupling rods with their outside cranks must have given some trouble for they were removed, making the engine into a 4-2-0. The cab now carried was a later addition – the 1830s was not a time when crew comfort was considered very seriously.

One non-Stephenson feature was present, the circular firebox similar to the design used by Edward Bury, locomotive engineer to the London & Birmingham Railway. This item and all the other "Planet" features were very successful and the locomotive ran in service until 1866. It travelled to the Columbian Exposition at Chicago in 1893 under its own steam and, even more remarkably, the oldest operable locomotive in the world celebrated its own 150th anniversary with another run. *John Bull* can be seen in the Smithsonian Museum in Washington, DC.

De Witt Clinton

Origin: United States: Mohawk & Hudson Railroad, 1831. **Gauge:** 4ft 8½in (1,435mm). **Axleload:** 3,526lb (1.6t). **Cylinders:** 5½ x 16in (140 x 406mm). **Adhesive weight:** 6,750lb (3.1t). **Total weight:** 6,750lb (3.1t) without tender. **Overall length** 19ft 8in (5,985mm).

In 1831 steam trains began running on the first section of what was one day destined to become the giant New York Central Railroad. The line in question was the 14 mile (22.5km) Mohawk & Hudson Railroad which ran between Albany and Schenectady. Previous operation had been with horses, but on June 25, 1831 the first steam locomotive was delivered by water up the Hudson River from the West Point Foundry at New York. The locomotive was the *De Witt Clinton*, the third locomotive built by this pioneer locomotive works. The previous locomotives, *Best Friend of Charleston* (previously described), and another locomotive *West Point* had been for the South Carolina Railroad.

De Witt Clinton was designed by John B. Jervis, Chief Engineer of the M&HRR, and like other first attempts it needed some fine tuning. The boiler was domeless and there was a tendency for water to "prime", that is boil over and enter the cylinders; this was corrected by adding a dome. The exhaust pipes also needed some adjustment before they would draw the fire properly. But by August 9, all was ready for the first scheduled run. Five stage coach bodies mounted on railroad wheels were provided, coupled together with chains to form a train. It is said that hundreds wanting to travel were turned away, perhaps it was as well, for the journey was more exciting than comfortable.

The slack action of the chains jerked the cars – particularly the rear ones – violently into motion and upset the passengers a moment after the locomotive had started. Because of the problems with drawing the fire sufficiently to burn coal, wood was being burnt as a temporary expedient.

So red hot fragments poured out of the chimney, the result being

Above: The replica *De Witt Clinton* re-enacting its inaugural trip from Albany to Schenectady on that memorable day in 1831.

more havoc in the form of burn holes in the clothes of the passengers. Even so, it must have been fun doing the journey at a mind-bending speed of 25mph 40km/h) or so (the average speed was reportedly 18mph 28km/h) – watching spectators' horses bolting and, perhaps, being aware that history was being made that day.

The *De Witt Clinton* was very lightly built. The boiler in fact was small enough for there to be room for the connecting rods between it and the timber frame, for the cylinders were mounted at the rear. The performance was excellent and no damage was caused to the wooden rails strapped with iron which formed the track, but the flimsy construction of the locomotive did not help with solving the problem of achieving longevity, for the locomotive was retired a year or two after going into service. A replica was built in 1893 for the World's Columbian Exposition held at Chicago and is now in the Ford Museum at Dearborn.

Left: Replica of the 1831 *De Witt Clinton* M&HRR in the Henry Ford Museum at Dearborn, Michigan.

Grasshopper 0-4-0

Origin: United States: Baltimore & Ohio Railroad (B&O), 1832. **Gauge:** 4ft 8$\frac{1}{2}$in (1,435mm). **Tractive effort:** 4,245lb (1,926kg). **Axleload:** 13,580lb (6.2t). **Cylinders:** (2) 12 x 22in (304 x 558mm). **Driving wheels:** 36in (914mm). **Heating surface:** 204sq ft (19m²). **Steam pressure:** 75psi (5.3kg/cm²). **Grate area:** 11 sq ft (1 m²). **Fuel (coke):** 800lb (0.4t). **Water:** 300 US gall (1.1m³). **Adhesive weight:** 27,160lb (12.3t). **Total weight:** 27,160lb) (12.3t). **Length overall:** 14ft 7in (4,445mm).

With these so-called "Grasshopper" engines and their successors, the vertical-boilered steam locomotive was taken further on the Baltimore & Ohio Railroad than elsewhere. The name came from the form of the driving mechanism, which carried the *Stourbridge Lion* or *Puffing Billy* line a little further. Vertical cylinders raised and lowered beams connected first to a crankshaft which in its turn was geared to a jackshaft. Cranks on the end of this jackshaft drove the wheels by connecting rods, in the manner which many electric locomotives were to follow. It was the movement of the beams which gave the locomotives their name.

The earliest "Grasshoppers" were built by a firm called Davis & Gartner, one of whose founders was watchmaker Phineas Davis who built the vertical-boilered locomotive *York*, and was thus the winner of the B&O locomotive competition held in 1831. His company became official locomotive builders to the B&O and completed their *Atlantic* at the Mount Clare Shops in September 1832. The locomotive was quite successful and regularly made a round trip of 80 miles (128km) daily between Baltimore and the inclines at Parr's Ridge. However, longevity was not yet a feature and together with the second "Grasshopper" called *Traveller*, also completed in 1832, *Atlantic* was retired in 1835. The replica *Atlantic*, currently in the B&O museum, is actually one of the later improved "Grasshoppers" (B&O No.7 *Andrew Jackson*) modified to take on the superficial appearance of the earlier machine.

The first of the new breed was *Arabian*, B&O No.1, delivered in July 1834. By the end of "Grasshopper" production in 1837, 16 had been built. The

Above: Replica Grasshopper *Atlantic* and preserved loco *Tom Thumb* outside the Mount Clare shops, Baltimore, where both were built. This is now the site of the Baltimore & Ohio's Railroad Museum.

details were improved and included such advanced ideas as a fan driven exhaust steam to draw the fire, and a feed-water heater, while later examples were more strongly built. This resulted in a weight which was nearly doubled and was reflected in a life exceeding 50 years, latterly in switching service. Phineas Davis, who originated these engines, was tragically killed in an accident on the railroad in 1836. He gave his name to No.9, amongst the Presidents and other famous men whose names decorated the others. After Davis' death, his company became Gillingham & Winans. No.8 *John Hancock* as well as the much altered No.7 survives in the B&O museum. No.8 also masqueraded for a time as No.3 *Thomas Jefferson*. The details given above refer to this locomotive.

Left: Grasshopper 0-4-0 No. 7 *Andrew Jackson* in disguise as the original *Atlantic* together with replica train of the early-1830s for display at the Baltimore & Ohio's Railroad Museum.

Vauxhall 2-2-0

Origin: Ireland: Dublin & Kingstown Railway, 1834. **Tractive effort:** circa 1,550lb (700kg). **Cylinders:** (2) 11 x 18in (280 x 457mm). **Driving wheels:** 60in (1,524mm). **Steam pressure:** circa 50psi (3.5kg/cm²). **Overall length:** circa 24ft (7,315mm).

George Forrester of Liverpool was a locomotive builder whose name is now hardly known; yet he introduced two fundamental improvements in the mechanism of the steam locomotive, one of which prevailed to the end of steam. The other was also an important move forward.

How *Northumbrian* had two outside cylinders but at the wrong end and how *Planet* had two cylinders at the front but hidden away inside, has already been described. With *Vauxhall,* constructed in 1832 for the Dublin & Kingstown Railway, Forrester built the world's first locomotive with accessible outside cylinders placed horizontally at the leading end. Incidentally, the D&K line was built to the English standard gauge of 4ft 8¹/2in (1,435mm); it was long before the days when the railway gauge in Ireland was standardised at 5ft 3in (1,600mm).

So already the cylinders had reached their final position with this arrangement. Since then it has been applied to most of the world's locomotives built over the subsequent 170 years, even though express passenger locomotives are the ones most prone to being given sophisticated cylinder layouts.

One way in which the Forrester engines differed from modern steam locomotives (except for those built for very narrow gauges) was that the

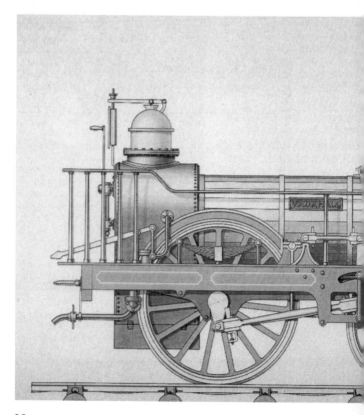

cylinders may have been outside the frames, but the frames were outside the wheels. Separate cranks were provided at the ends of the axles. Even so, in later years this arrangement was much used on locomotives which ran on very narrow gauges, that is, 3ft (914mm) or less.

Forrester's fundamental improvement of the valve gear was also important but as a stepping-stone rather than an arrangement which became much used in the long term. It has been mentioned that the "slip eccentric" valve gear was difficult to reverse from the cab, so Forrester provided a separate eccentric set for each direction for each cylinder – making four in all on the driving axle. The reversing lever could move the eccentric rods (which were set vertically) and engage or disengage the appropriate valve pin by means of V-shaped "gabs" fitted to the ends of the rods. No skill was required as in the previous arrangement, merely enough muscle to move the reversing lever into the appropriate position. But it could not be used while the engine was in motion.

Another feature of the first Forrester locomotives which was not repeated was the substitution of a swing-link parallel motion. This was intended to constrain the joint between the end of the piston rod and the little end of the connecting rod to travel in a straight line, even when the latter was at an angle and therefore trying to force the former out of line.

The Stephensons had previously used a cross-head running between slide-bars for this purpose and this simple arrangement has never been displaced from its throne. The only engine apart from *Vauxhall* in this book which did not have it was the "Turbomotive" and that one only because there were no cylinders!

Wide apart outside cylinders combined with a short wheelbase was not a recipe for steady running and by 1836 these 2-2-0s, as well as others supplied to the Liverpool & Manchester, London & Greenwich and other railways, had been converted to 2-2-2s. Even so, on the opening day in Ireland, 31mph (50km/h) was achieved; passengers were delighted and amazed that they could read and write with ease while moving at this stupendous speed. Few particulars of this pathfinding engine have survived, but the details missing from the specification above would approximate to those of *Planet*.

Left: George Forrester's *Vauxhall* locomotive built for the Dublin & Kingstown Railway in 1834. Note the horizontal outside cylinders at the front end, a mechanical arrangement which most of the world's locomotive engineers followed in time.

Bury 2-2-0

Origin: Great Britain: London & Birmingham Railway (L&B), 1837. **Tractive effort:** 1,386lb (629kg). **Axle load:** 12,600lb (5.7t). **Cylinders:** (2) 11 × 16½in (280 × 415mm). **Driving wheels:** 60¾in (1,546mm). **Heating surface:** 357sq ft (33.2m²). **Superheater:** None. **Steam pressure:** 50psi (3.5kg/cm²). **Grate area:** 7sq ft (0.65m²). **Fuel (coke):** c2,200lb (1t). **Water:** c400gall (480 US) (1.8m³). **Adhesive weight:** 12,600lb (5.7t). **Total weight:** 22,000lb (10.0t). **Length overall:** 26ft 9½in (8,168mm).

Edward Bury had a small engineering works in Liverpool and in 1829 he began work on a locomotive with a view to entering it for the Rainhill trials, but it was not completed in time. In the end he supplied the locomotive, which was called *Liverpool,* to the Liverpool & Manchester Railway during 1830. It had two large coupled wheels 72in (1829mm) in diameter. It had cylinders arranged like *Planet's* but, unlike *Planet,* had frames formed of bars rather than plates. This was a significant innovation, for Bury sold some bar-framed locomotives to America and bar frames for many years became a trademark of engines built on that side of the Atlantic; this went on until bar frames were superseded by cast steel ones. Bury managed to secure the contract for providing locomotives for the London and Birmingham Railway, by far the most important railway to be completed in the 1830s. All 58 of these passenger 2-2-0s had been supplied by 1841.

One problem with these locomotives was their small size and this was a fundamental limitation of the design, rather than something that could be overcome just by a little stretching. Bury considered rightly that pressure vessels should be circular and so his outer firebox was circular in plan and domed on top, attached to a normal cylindrical barrel by circumferential joint. The inner fire-box was D-shaped, with the flat part facing towards the front, to allow the insertion of the tubes at right angles. The trouble was that with the circular shape the length could not be larger than the width. Since the width was also limited, because it had to go between the wheels, the size of the fire (and hence the power output) was strictly limited. Nor could the frames be extended backwards past the round firebox, so a 2-2-2 development would cause some difficulty.

So in 1837 England's first long-distance trunk railway route out of London was opened, using a fleet of locomotives that were under-powered even by the standards of the day. For example, in the same year the London to Bristol railway (then under construction) received a Stephenson 2-2-2 called *North Star* which had double the grate area and double the adhesive weight of a Bury 2-2-0.

The small size and power of these engines had advantages. They were cheap to build and reliable in service – the low stresses on the crank axles brought these always troublesome items more within the scope of the technology of the day. And if heavy passenger trains needed two or three locomotives (or even four) at the head, then so be it. Labour was cheap, while powerful locomotives were expensive as well as relatively untried.

Assuming that Bury was right in thinking like this in 1837 - and there are many subsequent examples in locomotive history - his railway had, certainly fallen behind the times a few years later.

Below: 2-2-0 No.1 of the London & Birmingham Railway, the most important line to have been opened during the 1830s. Edward Bury designed these rather small locomotives which tended to be a little under-powered for express passenger work. Even so, they were cheap and reliable and Bury held on to his principles of little-and-often in locomotive design for many years, in fact until he was forced to resign in 1847. This was soon after the LNWR had been formed from the amalgamation of the Grand Junction and London & Birmingham lines.

Adler 2-2-2

Origin: Germany: Nuremberg-Fürth Railway, 1835. **Tractive effort:** 1,220lb (550kg). **Axle load:** 13,250lb (6t). **Cylinders:** 9 x 16in (229 x 406mm). **Driving wheels:** 54in (1,371mm). **Heating surface:** 196sq ft (18.2m²). **Superheater:** None. **Steam pressure:** 60psi (4.2kg/cm²). **Grate area:** 5.2sq ft (0.48m²). **Adhesive weight:** 13,250lb (6t). **Total weight:** 31,500lb (14.5t) *engine only – tender details not available*. **Length overall:** 25ft 0in (7,620mm).

The first locomotive to be built in Germany was constructed in 1816 but it was unsuccessful, as was a second one built in the following year. It was not until December 7, 1835 that successful steam locomotion was inaugurated in the country, with the opening of the Nuremberg to Fürth railway, known as the Ludwigsbahn, after Ludwig I of Bavaria, who had given his royal assent to the railway in 1834.

The promoter of the railway, Herr Scharrer, tried Robert Stephenson & Co of Newcastle for the supply of material to the line, but Stephenson's prices were considered to be too high, and Scharrer therefore resolved to "buy German". Two Wurtembergers then contracted to supply an engine for the equivalent of £565, "equal to the best English engines and not requiring more fuel". Time passed and Scharrer enquired about the progress of his engine, only to find that the contractors had decamped to Austria. He pursued them there, and was told that the price had doubled. The opening of the railway was approaching, and Scharrer had no alternative but to place an urgent order with Robert Stephenson on May 15, 1835 for a 2-2-2 locomotive, at a price of £1,750 delivered to the line.

Despite the historical importance of this engine, information about it is scanty, even its name being uncertain. Early references are to *"Der Adler"* (The Eagle), but more recently it has dropped the definite article, and is usually known simply as *"Adler"*. Surviving records of the builder do not record details of the engine, but contemporary illustrations show a locomotive resembling the *"Patentee"*, supplied to the Liverpool and Manchester Railway in 1834, developments of which figure largely amongst products of Stephenson's Newcastle works at this period.

In 1830 Robert Stephenson & Co supplied to the L&MR a 2-2-0 named *Planet*, which was notable as being the first engine with inside cylinders and a crank axle. However, the art of forging axles was new, and the combination of the forces from the flanges of the wheels and from the

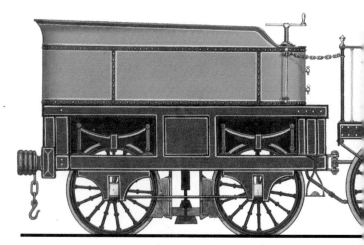

connecting rods soon showed the vulnerability of these delicate forgings. In 1833, therefore, Robert Stephenson designed a 2-2-2 locomotive, in which the driving wheels had no flanges, so that the crank axle was relieved of flange forces. A further advantage of the extra axle was that the axle loading was reduced, a desirable measure, as the axle loading of Stephenson's engines supplied to the L&M had been increasing steadily since *Rocket*, which had been built to the severe weight restrictions which the directors of the railway deemed necessary.

The improvements incorporated in the 2-2-2 were patented, and the first engine to incorporate the patents was named *"Patentee"*. This engine weighed 11.45 tons, but the weight of *"Adler"* was quoted in English sources as 6.6 tons, and in German sources as 14 tonnes, with 6 tonnes on the driving axle. A similar uncertainty applies to the boiler pressure, which has been quoted in an English source as 60lb/sq in (4.2kg/cm^2), and in a German source as 47lb/sq in (3.3kg/cm^2). Amongst details of the engine which are known are that it had 62 copper tubes, and that it had shifting eccentrics. The "Adler" was followed by other engines of similar type from Stephenson's. It remained at work until 1857, when it was sold, without wheels and some other parts, for its scrap value.

In preparation for the centenary of the Nuremberg-Fürth Railway, a working replica of the engine was built at the Kaiserslautern Works of DR. This replica is now in the transport museum at Nuremberg. A second non-working replica was made in 1950 for use at exhibitions. Both are based on contemporary paintings.

Below: Adler was built for the Nuremburg-Fürth Railway in 1835. This was the first railway to be built in what is now known as Germany, but the locomotive was built by the famous firm of Stephenson & Son of Newcastle-upon-Tyne, England.

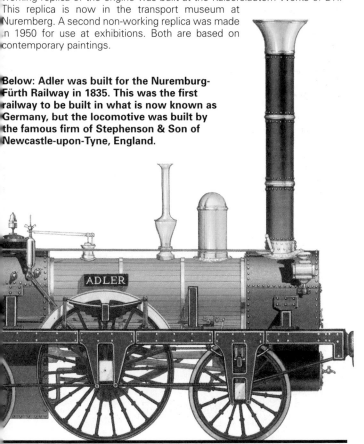

Campbell 4-4-0

Origin: United States: Philadelphia, Germanstown & Norriston Railroad (PG&NRR), 1837. **Tractive effort:** 4,373lb (1,984kg). **Axle load:** 8,000lb (3.6t). **Cylinders:** (2) 14 x 15¾in (356 x 400mm). **Driving wheels:** 54in (1,370mm). **Heating surface:** 723sq ft (67.2m²). **Superheater:** None. **Steam pressure:** 90psi (6.3kg/cm²). **Grate area:** circa 12sq ft (1.1m²). **Adhesive weight:** 16,000lb (7.25t). **Length overall:** 16ft 5½in (5,017mm) *engine only – tender details not known.*

Henry Campbell, engineer to the Philadelphia, Germanstown & Norriston Railroad had the idea of combining coupled wheels, as fitted to *Best Friend of Charleston,* with the leading truck of *Brother Johnathan.* In this way he could double the adhesive weight, while at the same time have a locomotive that could ride satisfactorily round sharp or irregular curves. He patented the idea and went to a local mechanic called James Brooks (not the Brooks who founded the famous Brooks Loco Works of Dunkirk, New York) and he produced the world's first 4-4-0 in May 1837.

Although in fact this locomotive was intended for coal traffic, it has its place here as the prototype of perhaps the most numerous and successful of all passenger hauling wheel arrangements.

The layout of *Brother Johnathan* was followed, the additional driving axle being coupled to the first by cranks outside the frames. The cylinders were thus inside the frames, driving the leading coupled wheels by means of a crank axle, an arrangement which was to become popular on a few railways back in Europe, even if very rarely repeated in America. The high boiler pressure is notable for the time. Whilst this remarkable locomotive demonstrated great potential, the flexibility provided in order to cope with poorly lined tracks was not accompanied with flexibility in a vertical plane to help with the humps and hollows in them. In consequence, Campbell's 4-4-0 was not in itself successful.

Below: The world's first 4-4-0, designed by Henry R Campbell, engineer to the Philadelphia Germanstown and Norriston Railroad. It was built in 1837 by James Brooks of Philadelphia.

Hercules 4-4-0

Origin: United States: Beaver Meadows Railroad, 1837. **Tractive effort:** 4,507lb (2,045kg). **Axle load:** circa 10,000lb (4.5t). **Cylinders:** (2) 12 x 18in (305x457mm). **Driving wheels:** 44in (1, 117mm). **Steam pressure:** 90lb/sq in (6.3kg/cm²). **Adhesive weight:** circa 20,000lb (9t). **Total weight:*** 30,000lb (14t). **Length overall:*** 18ft 11in (2,564mm). *Without tender – boiler and tender details not recorded.*

In 1836, the Beaver Meadows Railroad ordered a 4-4-0 from Garrett & Eastwick, in nearby Philadelphia. The workshop foreman, Joseph Harrison, had become aware of the problems encountered by Henry Campbell in keeping all the wheels of his 4-4-0 pressing on the rail, yet he also remembered 4-2-0 *Brother Jonathan* of 1832 which sat on the rough tracks like a three legged stool on the floor. The saying "right as a trivet" comes vividly to mind, the three legs being, respectively, the two driving wheels and the pivot of the leading bogie or truck. There was also the example of one or two early 4-2-0s by Norris, also of Philadelphia. Harrison had the idea of making his two pairs of driving wheels into a kind of non-swivelling bogie by connecting the axle bearings on each side by a large cast iron beam, pivoted at its centre. The pivots were connected to the mainframe of the locomotive by a large leaf spring on each side.

In this way eight wheels were made to support the body of the locomotive at three points. It was a brilliant notion which solved the problem of running on rough tracks and was the basis of the three-point compensated springing system which was applied to most of the world's locomotives from simple ones up to 4-12-2s.

Hercules was well named and many similar locomotives were supplied. Joseph Harrison was made a partner in the firm which (since Garrett was retiring) became known as Eastwick & Harrison. The famous "American Standard", 4-4-0, of which 25,000 were built for the USA alone, was directly derived from this most innovative engine.

Below: *Hercules,* **designed by Joseph Harrison and built by Garrett & Eastwick of Philadelphia in 1836, marked an important step forward in locomotive development**

Lafayette 4-2-0

Origin: United States: Baltimore & Ohio Railroad (B&O), 1837. **Tractive effort:** 2,162lb (957kg). **Axle load:** 13,000lb (6t). **Cylinders:** (2) 10¹/₂ x 18in (268x457mm). **Driving wheels:** 48in (1,220mm). **Heating surface:** 394sq ft (36.6m²). **Superheater:** None. **Steam pressure:** 60psi (4.2kg/cm²). **Grate area:** 8.6sq ft (0.80m²). **Fuel (coke):** 2,200lb (1t). **Water:** 450gall (540 US, (2m³). **Adhesive weight:** 30,000lb (5t). **Total weight:** 44,000lb (20t) **Length overall:** 30ft 40¹/₄in (9,250mm).

William Norris had been building locomotives in Philadelphia since 1831. Although a draper by trade, after a few years in partnership with a Colonel Stephen Long, he set up on his own and by the beginning of 1836 had produced some seven locomotives. In that year he built a 4-2-0 for the Philadelphia & Columbia Railroad called *Washington County Farmer.* In arrangement it bore some resemblance to *Brother Johnathan* with leading bogie, but the two cylinders were outside the wheels and frames and the valves were on top of the cylinders. The driving wheels were in front of rather than behind the firebox, so increasing the proportion of the engine's weight carried on them.

In this way the final form of the steam express passenger locomotive had almost arrived. *Northumbrian* had the locomotive-type boiler and two outside cylinders; *Planet* had the cylinders at the front while Forrester's *Vauxhall* had cylinders outside and at the front. Bury's locomotives had the bar frames and *Brother Jonathan* had the bogie. Now we find outside cylinders, bar frames and a leading bogie in combination.

In 1827, the Baltimore & Ohio Railroad was the first public railroad for passengers and freight transport to receive a charter. It was opened for twelve miles out of Baltimore in 1830, but for a number of years horses provided haulage power. Steam took over in 1834 in the form of vertical-boiler locomotives, known as the "Grasshopper" type.

The Ohio River was reached in 1842 via a route which then included a series of rope-worked inclined planes, but long before this more powerful locomotives than could be encompassed within the vertical-boiler concept were needed. The B&O management were impressed with Norris' *Washington County Farmer* and asked him to build a series of eight similar engines. The first was *Lafayette* delivered in 1837; it was the first B&O locomotive to have a horizontal boiler. Edward Bury's circular domed firebox and bar frames were there and the engine is said to have had cam-operated valves of a pattern devised by Ross Winans of the B&O. It says enough that later members of the class had the normal "gab" motion of the day.

The locomotives were a great success, giving much better performance at reduced fuel consumption. They were also relatively reliable and

needed few repairs. The same year Norris built a similar locomotive for the Champlain & St. Lawrence Railway in Canada. This was the first proper locomotive exported from America, and the hill-climbing ability of these remarkable locomotives led to many further sales abroad.

The first Old World customer was the Vienna-Raab Railway and their locomotive *Philadelphia* was completed in late 1837. Before the locomotive was shipped it was put to haul a train weighing 200 tons up a 1 in 100 (1 per cent) gradient, a feat then described as the greatest performance by a locomotive engine so far recorded. Railways in Austria were the best customers, but even before 1840 Norris had also sent his 4-2-0s to the Brunswick and Berlin & Potsdam Railways in Germany. A large fleet of 15 went to the Birmingham and Gloucester Railway in Britain, where they had some success in easing the problems involved in taking trains up the 1 in 37 (2.7 per cent) Lickey Incline at Bromsgrove in Worcestershire.

The demand for Norris locomotives was so great that the firm was able to offer the design in a range of four standard sizes. Class "C" had a cylinder bore of 9in (229mm), class "B" 10½in (268mm), class "A" 11½in (292mm), class "A extra" 12½in (318mm). Grate areas were, respectively, 6.4, 7.3, 7.9 and 9.5sq ft (0.6, 0.69, 0.73 and 0.88in²) while engine weights were 15,750, 20,600, 24,100 and 29,650lb (7.1, 9.4, 10.9 and 13.45t).

In his native America, Norris' list of other customers in the 1830s included 27 predecessors of the railroads of the great age of steam, situated in Connecticut, Georgia, Louisiana, Maryland, Massachusetts, New York State, North Carolina, Pennsylvania, Tennessee and Virginia. One of them, the Richmond, Fredericksburg and Potomac Railroad, is even still trading under the same name today. Norris went on to become for a time the largest locomotive builder in the USA, supplying 4-4-0s, 0-6-0s and finally 4-6-0s in addition to the 4-2-0s which made his name.

Below: A typical standard Norris 4-2-0 locomotive is portrayed in this side view. The elementary controls of a locomotive of the 1840s can all be clearly seen. The horizontal handle behind the fire box is the throttle, while the vertical one alongside the firebox controls the "gab" reversing gear. The spring balance pressure gauge is above the firebox together with the whistle. A brake on the engine was regarded as a luxury.

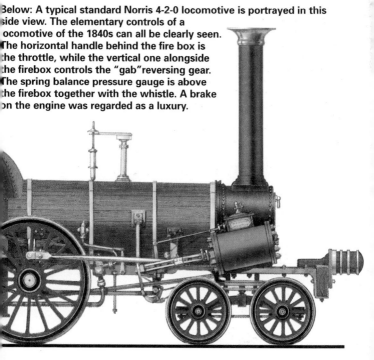

Fire Fly Class 2-2-2

Origin: Great Britain: Great Western Railway (GWR), 1840. **Tractive effort:** 2049lb (929kg). **Axle load:** 25,000lb (11.2t). **Cylinders:** (2) 15 x 18in (381 x 457mm). **Driving wheels:** 84in (2,134mm). **Heating surface:** 700sq ft (65m²). **Superheater:** None. **Steam pressure:** 50psi (3.5kg/cm²). **Grate area:** 13.5sq ft (1.25m²). **Fuel (coke):** 3400lb (1.5t). **Water:** 1,800 gall (2,160 US) (8.25m³). **Adhesive weight:** 25,000lb (11.2t). **Total weight:** 92,500lb (42t). **Length overall:** 39ft 4in (11,989mm).

In 1833 Isambard Kingdom Brunel was made engineer to what he referred as "the finest work in England". He was not one to be a follower and he thought little of what he called contemptuously "the coal waggon gauge". He said, "I thought the means employed was not commensurate with the task to be done..." and accordingly chose a gauge for his railway almost 75 per cent larger than the one employed by the Stephensons. This 7ft 0¼in (2,140mm) gauge was the largest ever employed by any railway in the world.

When it came to locomotive matters the Great Western Railway was truly great, but this was not so at the beginning. Brunel perhaps a little casually had ordered a series of locomotives from various manufacturers; and it was not one of his best efforts. They were given a free hand within certain almost impossible constraints, that is, that the weight of a six-wheeled locomotive should not exceed 10½ tons and that piston speeds should not exceed 280ft per minute (85m per minute) at 30mph (48km/h). The results were totally unsatisfactory and in its earliest days the GWR had only one locomotive upon which it could rely, the fortuitously acquired Stephenson six-wheel "Patentee" locomotive *North Star* which weighed 18.2 tons, over 75 per cent above Brunel's stipulated weight. Even the piston speed at 30mph (48km/h) was over the top at 320ft/min (98m/min).

To take charge of the locomotives Brunel had engaged a young man called Daniel Gooch, a north countryman who had worked with the Stephensons. Following long struggles – often all night – in the running shed at Paddington with the collection of not-too-mobile disasters which formed the GWR locomotive fleet of the time, Gooch eventually was responsible for drawing up plans and specifications for a wholly practical fleet of more than 100 six-wheeled locomotives, based again on Stephenson's

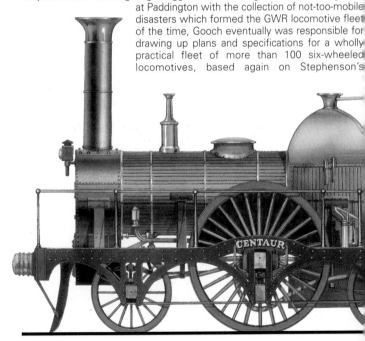

"Patentees", and including 2-4-0s and 0-6-0s for freight work, as well as 2-2-2s for passenger traffic. Boilers, tenders, motion and many other parts were common to all the types – it was standardisation on a scale the world had never seen before. This time the manufacturers were allowed no latitude – as was to be the case so often in future years, there were only two ways to do things – the Great Western Way and the Wrong Way. As well as drawings, templates were issued to the makers; moreover, the builders were responsible for any repairs needed during the first 1,000 miles (1,600km) running with proper loads. Sixty-two of the locomotives were for express trains and these concern us. The first of these to be delivered was *Fire Fly* which came from Jones, Turner & Evans, Newton-le-Willows, Lancashire, in March 1840, to be followed by *Spit Fire, Wild Fire, Fire Ball, Fire King* and *Fire Brand* from the same firm. On March 17, *Fire Fly* took a special train from Twyford to Paddington in 37 minutes for the 30¾ miles (49.5km). The maximum speed was 58mph (93km/h). By the end of 1840, for the opening to Wootton Bassett beyond Swindon, a further 25 of these locomotives were available and a timetable worthy of the name could be issued at last.

The frames were interesting, being of the sandwich type made from thin sheets of iron enclosing a thick in-filling of oak. The "gab" type valve gear was used. This was later altered in most cases to Stephenson's pattern, so allowing for expansive working of the steam. All the locomotives were coke burners and had large domed "gothic" type fireboxes. Both four-wheel and six-wheel tenders were attached to different members of the class at different times; the dimensions given refer to the use of the six-wheel pattern.

There is little doubt that the stability afforded by Brunel's broad gauge tracks with 7ft 0¼in (2,140mm) between the rails, plus the remarkable running qualities of these early standard locomotives, led to locomotive performances unequalled in the world at the time.

During the "Battle of the Gauges" in 1845, one of them, *Ixion*, made test runs on behalf of the broad-gauge faction for the Government's Gauge Commissioners; runs were made from Paddington to Didcot and back. With 60 tons the 53 mile (85km) journey was performed in 63½ minutes with a maximum speed of 61mph (98 km/h), a feat far beyond anything the narrow gauge people could do on their tests between York and Darlington. *Ixion* was the last of these famous locomotives to remain in service, ceasing to run in 1879. The class thus spanned almost 40 years, during which railways grew up as a means of transport. The decision to abandon the broad gauge had been taken, although it was not to disappear finally until 13 years later.

Below: *Centaur* was one of Daniel Gooch's famous standard locomotives, and was built by Nasmyth, Gaskell & Co. of Manchester and delivered in 1841. It ceased work in 1867.

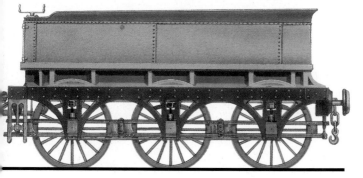

Lion 0-4-2

Origin: Great Britain: Liverpool & Manchester Railway (L&M), 1838.
Tractive effort: 1,836lb (833kg). **Cylinders:** (2) 12 x 18in (305 x 457mm).
Driving wheels: 60in (1,524mm). **Superheater:** None. **Steam pressure:**
50psi (3,5kg/cm²). **Length overall:** 33ft 9in (10,287mm).
(Other details not available).

Whilst not strictly an express passenger locomotive, the locomotive *Lion,*
built for the Liverpool and Manchester Railway in 1838, has several unusual
claims to fame. She was built at a time, almost a decade after the famous
locomotive trials at Rainhill, when locomotive design had begun to settle
down and one could order engines for specific duties with reasonable
confidence. *Lion* came from Todd, Kitson & Laird of Leeds and was one of
a Class of 0-4-2 locomotives named after powerful beasts. It was also a time
when the L&M railway began to manufacture its own motive power, a policy
that has continued through successive owners of the world's first intercity
railway – Grand Junction Railway, London & North Western Railway,
London, Midland & Scottish Railway and British Railways – to this day.

A happy chance led to *Lion* being sold to the Mersey Docks & Harbour
Board in 1859, for use as a shunting engine. Some years later the Board set
her up as a stationary engine. In this guise the engine lasted in commercial
service until 1920, when the LMS railway bought the remains for
restoration. In 1930 *Lion* was run at the centenary celebrations of the
Liverpool & Manchester Railway and afterwards the engine was preserved
to what is now the Merseyside County Museum at Liverpool. *Lion* also ran
in the cavalcade to celebrate the 150th anniversary of the L&M, in 1980, and
is now the world's oldest working locomotive.

Interesting features of the locomotive include the impressive "haycock"

Above: Liverpool and Manchester Railway 0-4-2 _Lion_ still in running order after 140 years.

shape firebox and sandwich frames enclosing the wheels.

Lion has also been a film star, playing the title role in that enchanting frolic called "Titfield Thunderbolt", still a favourite.

Left: 140 years of railway progress. Liverpool & Manchester Railway _Lion_ of 1841 alongside the Advanced Passenger Train.

Beuth 2-2-2

Origin: Germany: Berlin-Anhalt Railway, 1843. **Tractive effort:** 4,120lb (1,870kg). **Axle load:** 20,000lb (9.5t). **Cylinders:** (2) 13.1 x 22.3 in (330 x 560mm). **Driving wheels:** 60¾in (1,543mm). **Heating surface:** 500sq ft (47m²). **Superheater:** None. **Steam pressure:** 78psi (5.5kg/cm²). **Grate area:** 8.9sq ft (0.83m²). **Adhesive weight:** 20,000lb (95t). **Total weight:** *41,000lb (18.5t). **Length overall:** *20ft 2in (6,143mm). *(*Engine only. Tender details not known.)*

August Borsig was a man of immense ability and energy, who built an industrial empire which included an iron works and a large water works. At the time of his entry into locomotive building the 4-2-0-s built by Norris of Philadelphia were being imported by a number of European railways, and Borsig's first products were 15 engines of this wheel arrangement supplied to the Berlin-Anhalt Railway. They closely resembled the Norris products in having bar frames and a large haycock fire-box, but they included a number of improvements due to Borsig.

By 1843 Borsig had incorporated further improvements, some of his own devising and some drawn from English practice. This blending of the practices of America, England and Germany was well illustrated in a 2-2-2 locomotive supplied to the Berlin-Anhalt Railway in 1843 and named *Beuth* in honour of August Borsig's former teacher, Professor Beuth of the Royal Industrial Institute of Berlin.

The equal spacing of the axles gave a better weight distribution than in the Norris 4-2-0s. The design was advanced for its day. The flat side valves above the cylinders were driven by the new Stephenson's link motion, which had

been first applied in 1842. It was actually an invention of an employee of Robert Stephenson, by name William Howe.

Like all great inventions it was very simple. Existing valve gears had separate eccentrics for forward and reverse, and "gabs" or claws on the ends of each eccentric rod which could engage or disengage with the valve spindle as appropriate. Howe's idea was to connect the two eccentric rods by means of a link with a curved slot formed in it. In this slot was a die-block to which the valve spindle was connected. The link now just needed to be raised for one direction of travel and lowered for the other; the arrangement worked very well and the majority of the world's steam locomotives over the next 60 years used it.

It was also possible to use intermediate positions to give cut-off of the steam at an early point in the stroke, to allow more economical working through expansion of the steam. Borsig, however, used an auxiliary slide-valve to control expansion. The fitting of cylinder drain cocks operated from the footplate was an improvement on Norris' engines, in which the drain cocks were operated by levers on the cylinders themselves. The boiler feed pumps were driven by levers attached to the crank pin, and extending back to a position under the cab. As in the Norris engines, bar frames were used. The firebox was elliptical in horizontal section and the upper part formed a capacious steam space. A cylindrical casing on top of the firebox housed the steam pipe and one of the two Salter safety valves. The firebox was finished in bright metal, and the boiler barrel was lagged with wood. The six-wheeled tender had outside frames, and screw operated brakes acted on both sides of all tender wheels.

The locomotive *Beuth* as built for the Berlin to Anhalt Railway in 1843.

"Mud-digger" 0-8-0

Origin: United States: Baltimore & Ohio Railroad (B&O), 1844. **Gauge:** 4ft 8¹/₂in (1,435mm). **Axleload:** 12,925lb (5.9t). **Cylinders:** (2) 17 x 24in (432 x 610mm). **Driving wheels:** 33in (838mm). **Adhesive weight:** 47,000lb (21.3t). **Total weight*:** 47,000lb (21.3t). **Length overall*:** 49ft 10in (6,045mm). *Without tender.

Ross Winans was a horse-dealer who called on the Baltimore & Ohio Railroad in the early days with the idea of selling them motive power. He was not at all put out at finding they had gone over to steam and stayed on to sell and build iron horses instead. He was appointed assistant engineer of machinery in 1831 and four years later, as Gillingham & Winans, took over locomotive building in the B&O Mount Clare shops from Phineas Davis (Davis & Gartner). He completed his predecessors' "Grasshopper" programme, but by 1837 had ready for production his own (patent) design known as "Winan's Crab".

Because of the adoption of horizontal cylinders, the Crabs came one short step closer to conventionality when compared with the Grasshoppers. The separate crankshaft gearing and crankshaft remained however, as well as a vertical boiler. Because of the gearing the cranks turned the opposite way to the wheels, hence the supposedly crab-like gait. Two 0-4-0 crabs, *McKim*

and *Mazeppa*, were built by Gillingham & Winans for the B&O and were delivered in 1838. They gave good service, lasting until 1863 and 1868 respectively.

Out of the Crabs came the relatively enormous 0-8-0 "Mud-diggers". This time (after the first few which did not go to the B&O), a proper locomotive boiler was used, but the layout of the machinery was unchanged, apart from the two extra axles. The first one was appropriately named *Hercules* and there were 13 more, all built between 1844 and 1847.

Seven of the Mud-diggers were rebuilt completely on more conventional lines between 1853 and 1856, losing their names in the process. The remainder soldiered on for many years, the last (No.41 *Elk*) being retired in 1880.

The last of these locomotives to be built (No 49 *Mount Clare*) was rather different from the others. It was built by the B&O itself rather than Winans, had no geared drive and was inside-connected. The cylinders drove on to a jackshaft mounted between the second and third axles. The jackshaft was connected to the wheels by outside cranks and an additional pair of coupling rods. As regards the Mud-digger class as a whole, it was the outside cranks moving so close to the ground - where they were liable to stir up dirt, stones and mud – that produced the evocative name.

Below: 0-8-0 "Mud-digger" class locomotive, built by Gillingham and Winans for the Baltimore & Ohio Railroad, 1844.

John Stevens 6-2-0

Origin: Great Britain: Camden & Amboy Railroad, 1849. **Gauge:** 4ft 8½in (1,435mm). **Cylinders:** (2) 13 x 34in (330 x 863mm). **Driving wheels:** 96in (2,438mm). **Grate area:** 15.2sq ft (11.4m²). **Total weight:** 50,000lb (22.7t).*
Length overall: 29ft 8in (9,042mm).*
*Without tender.

In the 1840s a man called Thomas Russell Crampton had patented a strange type of locomotive which had just one pair of very large driving wheels, the axle of which was mounted behind the boiler. The idea was to keep rotational speed down, while also keeping a very low centre of gravity because the boiler no longer had to be above the wheels. He impressed many railway managers, particularly in Belgium and France, and about 320 locomotives were made to his ideas. In France, the expression "le Crampton" was slang for "le train" over many years.

Robert Stevens, President of the Camden & Amboy Railroad, visited Europe in 1845 and came back enthused with Crampton's thinking. He soon arranged for several similar but even more amazing-looking contrivances to be built by Norris & Co. The first was completed in 1849 and was named after the John Stevens who in 1825 built a small model demonstration locomotive which he ran on a short circular railroad on his estate at Hoboken, New Jersey. Seven 6-2-0s were built in all over the next three years.

Crampton engines were very fast but lacked adhesive weight so they were only really suitable for light trains, and because the trains were fast they were popular and so ceased to be light. Even so these particular examples lasted until the early 1860s, although by then some if not all had been rebuilt into more conventional 4-4-0s.

John Stevens and his companions were intended to burn anthracite but both the grate area and the firebox would have been on the small size even

for bituminous coal. So there were problems of steam generation as well as lack of adhesion. The boiler barrel was no larger in diameter than the wheels of the leading truck and smaller than the amazing smokestack. At the same time, a notable feature was the valve gear operated by a return crank just as in a modem steam locomotive. There were also double valves to control admission and cut-off separately.

As regards looks, nothing quite as bizarre has ever been seen on rails either before or since. The designers may have copied Crampton's principles but they were certainly not followers when it came to matters of detail, possibly influenced by a wish to avoid infringing the Crampton patents. Hidden away were the spiral seams of the boiler barrel, but painfully obvious were those amazing 8ft driving wheels made of wrought iron with a wood in-fill between the spokes! Then there was the connecting rod with wire bracing! And we hardly dare think of that garden shed on top of the boiler as a conning tower for the engineer – even Crampton never thought of that one! Such was the greatest locomotive joke in 170 years of railway history.

Below: Was there ever a more curious looking locomotive than *John Stevens*? But the strange design did incorporate some notable features, and the locos remained in service for more than 20 years.

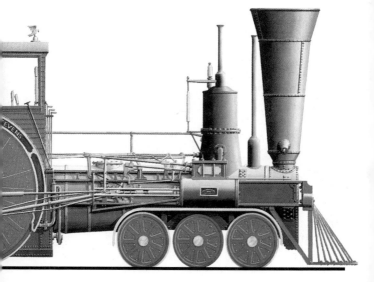

Crampton Type 4-2-0

Origin: France: Eastern Railway (Est), 1852. **Tractive effort:** 5,040lb (2,290kg). **Axle load:** 27,500lb (12.5t). **Cylinders:** (2) 15¾ x 21½in (400 x 500mm). **Driving wheels:** 82¾in (2,100mm). **Heating surface:** 1,059sq ft (98.4m²). **Superheater:** None. **Steam pressure:** 92psi (6.5kg/cm²). **Grate area:** 15.3sq ft (1.42m²). **Fuel:** 15,500lb (7t). **Water:** 1,540gall (1,850 US) (7m³). **Adhesive weight:** 27,100lb (12.5t). **Total weight:** 105,000lb (47.5t). **Length overall:** 41ft 9in (12,728mm).

Thomas Russell Crampton's engines are a legend - the word *Crampton* for a time entered the French language to mean "train" - yet they in no way formed a step forward in the art of locomotive engineering. But they were magnificent.

Crampton was born in August 1816, the same month as Daniel Gooch. He learnt his trade as an engineer under Marc Brunel, father of the Great Western Railway's builder. In due time Crampton joined the GWR himself and worked with Gooch on the design of his celebrated standard locomotives.

In 1842, whilst still working for this company, he applied for a patent for a high-speed express locomotive with a low centre of gravity yet having an adequate size boiler. The problem was the driving axle – if you used big wheels to permit fast running, then the bottom of the boiler had to clear the revolving cranks and had to be mounted high. So that he could set the boiler low and thus keep the centre of gravity also low Crampton put the driving axle *behind* it. The cylinders were outside the wheels and were mounted well back from the front of the engine. It was a very convenient layout as the machinery was all accessible - in fact, in that respect (but little else) the

Above: Eastern Railway of France Crampton 4-2-0 No.80 before restoration as the working museum exhibit we know today.

Cramptons followed the final form of the steam locomotive.

Crampton was working on a broad gauge railway and he must have regarded standard gauge locomotives as having little better stability than the penny-farthing bicycles of the day. In the typical Crampton design illustrated here the height of the centre of the boiler was about the same measurement as the rail gauge, very similar to the same ratio for a conventional design on the 7ft 0¼in (2,140mm) gauge.

He was also concerned about pitching, which affected certain locomotives having a short wheelbase, especially if this was combined with having much of the weight of the engine

Left: Crampton 4-2-0 N0.170 of the French Northern Railway. Note the huge single pair of driving wheels at the back.

concentrated on a single central driving wheel. It could be said that the idea was only dubiously original but even so Crampton got his patent and went into business. It was a case of a "prophet not being without honour save in his own country" and the first engine was the 4-2-0 *Namur* for the Namur-Liége Railway in Belgium. The builders were the little known and long vanished firm of Tulk and Ley of Lowca Works, Whitehaven, and since the Belgian line was not complete when the locomotives was ready, trials were held in Great Britain as well as on the Belgian State Railway. Altogether some 320 Cramptons were built, most of them for various French railways, notably the Northern and Eastern companies. Amongst many notable doings of theirs in that country might be noted the haulage of the last train to leave Paris when it was besieged by the Germans in 1870. Another Crampton belonging to the Eastern Railway and rebuilt with a strange double-barrelled boiler, was responsible for breaking the world speed record – not only for trains but for everything – when No.604 was run at 89.5mph (144km/h) with a load of 157 tons, during trials on the Paris-Laroche main line of the Paris, Lyons & Mediterranean Railway on June 20, 1890.

The main drawback of the Crampton design was the limited adhesive weight which could be applied to the rails; with a single driving axle right at the end of the wheelbase this limitation was a fundamental one. Because of this the success of the Cramptons in handling light trains at high speeds was to some extent self defeating – because of the fast service more people used the trains, more coaches had to be added and the limit of these engines' capacity was soon reached. It is also true to say that, whilst at first sight it would appear that a low centre of gravity would make a locomotive more stable, in fact it is a case where the cure can be worse than the disease. Such locomotives may be less liable to overturn when driven round curves at two or more times the permitted speed, but liability to serious oscillation and consequent derailment from that cause is increased.

Nevertheless, other features made the Crampton engines into sound propositions. Their layout enabled bearings of really adequate size to be

applied to the driving axle and this made for long periods of trouble-free running between visits to the shops. Similar advantage sprung from the fact that a rear wheel of a vehicle tends to run with its flanges clear of the rails on curves, leaving the leading wheels to do the guidance. Hence the small (and cheap) carrying wheels bore the brunt of the flange-wear, leaving the large and expensive driving wheels to last longer.

Crampton was also one of the first locomotive engineers to understand and apply the principles of balancing the reciprocating and revolving weights of a locomotive mechanism. This also contributed to the success of his engines, as did his patent regulator or throttle valve. Crampton had clearly a most original mind, although sometimes his ingenuity outran his good sense. In addition to the well-known Crampton layout which was only secondary in the application, his original patent of 1842 claimed the idea of locomotives with a driving axle *above* the boiler. The first (and almost certainly the last) of these, named *Trevithick* after the builder of the world's first steam locomotive, was built in 1847 by the London & North Western Railway at their Crewe Works. It had 9ft (2,742mm) diameter wheels and presented an exceedingly strange appearance. It was not a success.

Crampton took out a further patent in 1849 to cover locomotives provided with an intermediate shaft, either oscillating or revolving, between the cylinders and the driving wheels or axle. Its application to steam locomotives was brief (but not quite so brief as the underslung boiler) but after Crampton had died in 1888 and the patent had expired the idea found extensive use for the drive mechanisms of early electric locomotives.

The considerable mark which Thomas Crampton made in the world of locomotive engineering is recognised by the preservation of 4-2-0 No.80 *Le Continent,* originally of the Paris-Strasbourg Railway, later the Eastern Railway of France. This beautiful locomotive relic, superbly restored and in working order (but only steamed on great occasions) is usually to be found in the French National Railway Museum at Mulhouse. She is the subject of the vital statistics given at the head of this article.

Below: Crampton 4-2-0 of the Eastern Railway of France as now superbly restored makes one of her rare appearances in steam.

American Type 4-4-0

Origin: United States: Western & Atlantic Railroad (W&ARR), 1855. **Gauge:** Various (see text). **Tractive effort:** 6,885lb (3,123kg). **Axle load:** 21,000lb (9.5t). **Cylinders:** (2) 15 x 24in (381 x 610mm). **Driving wheel:** 60in (1,524mm). **Heating surface:** 98.0sq ft (91m²). **Superheater:** None. **Steam pressure:** 90psi (6.35kg/cm²). **Grate area:** 14.5sq ft (1.35m²). **Fuel:** (wood) 2 cords (7.25m³). **Water:** 1,250 gall (2,000 US) (5.75m³). **Adhesive weight:** 43,000lb (19.5t). **Total weight:** 90,000lb (41t). **Length overall:** 52ft 3in (15,926mm).

The *General* was built by Thomas Rogers of Paterson, New Jersey in 1855 and it is a wholly appropriate example of the most numerous and successful locomotive design ever to have been built. The reason is that Rogers was responsible for introducing most of the features which made the true "American" the success it was. The most significant development, so far as the USA was concerned was the general introduction of Stephenson's link motion, which permitted the expansive use of steam. This was in place of the "gab" or "hook" reversing gears used until then, which permitted only "full forward" and "full backward" positions.

In other aspects of design Rogers gained his success by good proportions and good detail rather than innovation. An example was the provision of adequate space between the cylinders and the driving wheels, which reduced the maximum angularity of the connecting rods and hence the up-and-down forces on the slide bars. A long wheelbase leading truck (in English, bogie) allowed the cylinders to be horizontal and still clear the wheels. This permitted direct attachment to the bar frames, which raised inclined cylinders did not.

To allow flexibility on curves, early examples of the breed inherited flangeless leading driving wheels from their progenitors, but by the late 1850s the leading trucks were being given side movement to produce the same effect. Naturally the compensated spring suspension system giving three-point support to the locomotive was continued. Woodburning was also nearly universal in these early years of the type, and the need to catch the sparks led to many wonderful shapes in the way of spark-arresting smokestacks.

Within two or three years other makers such as Baldwin, Grant, Brooks Mason, Danforth and Hinkley began offering similar locomotives. To buy one of these locomotives one did not need to be a great engineer steeped in the theory of design – it was rather like ordering a car today. One filled in a form on which certain options could be specified and very soon an adequate and reliable machine was delivered.

Below: Typical United States "Standard" 4-4-0 illustrating the elaborate decor that was often applied in the early years of American railroading but which was abandoned in the 1880s.

Above: American Standard 4-4-0 as refurbished to resemble the Central Pacific RR's *Jupiter*, ready to re-enact the completion ceremony of the first transcontinental railroad at the Golden Spike National Monument, in Utah.

Speeds on the rough light tracks of a pioneer land were not high – average speeds of 25mph (40km/h) start-to-stop, implying a maximum of 40mph (64km/h), were typical of the best expresses. Although the 4-4-0s were completely stable at high speeds, the increased power required meant that by the 1880s a bigger breed of 4-4-0 as well as "Ten-wheelers" (4-6-0s) were taking over from the "American".

There was another revolution taking place too. The earlier years of the type were characterised by romantic names and wonderful brass, copper and paint work, but the last quarter of the nineteenth century was a time of cut-throat competition, with weaker roads going to the wall. There was no

question of there being anything to spare for frills of this kind – so it was just a case of giving a coat of bitumen and painting big white running numbers in the famous "Bastard Railroad Gothic" fount on the tender sides.

For most of the second half of the nineteenth century this one type of locomotive dominated railroad operations in the USA. It was appropriately known as the "American Standard" and about 25,000 of them were built, differing only marginally in design. The main things that varied were the decor and the details. They were simple, ruggedly constructed machines appropriate for what was then a developing country, at the same time a leading bogie and compensated springing made them suitable for the rough tracks of a frontier land.

The subject of the specification above is perhaps the most famous of all the 25,000. The *General* came to fame when hijacked by a group of Union soldiers who had infiltrated into Confederate territory during the American Civil War. The idea was to disrupt communications behind the lines, in particular on the 5ft (1,524mm) gauge line 135 miles (216km) long connecting Atlanta with Chattanooga. The Union forces were approaching Chattanooga after their victory at Shiloh and the Confederates were expected to bring up reinforcements by rail. There was a major trestle bridge at a place called Oostenabula and the intention was to steal a train, take it to the site and burn the bridge. A replacement would take weeks to build.

The Union force, twenty in number under the command of a Captain Andrews, having stayed overnight at a place called Marietta and having bought tickets to travel on the train, took over the locomotive at a place called Big Shanty, some 30 miles (48km) north of Atlanta, while the passengers and crew were having breakfast in the depot's eating house. The conductor of the train, whose name was Fuller, gave chase first on a handcart and then on a small private ironworks loco, the *Yonah*.

The raiders' intention was to cut telegraph wires behind them, remove the occasional rail and demand immediate passage at stations they came to in the name of Confederate General Beauregard. A problem Andrews faced was the presence of trains coming the other way on the single line and perhaps the game was lost at Kingston where he had to wait an hour and

twenty five minutes until one divided into two sections had finally arrived.

In the end the *Yonah* arrived there only four minutes after Andrews and the *General* had left. Here Fuller took over another "American" 4-4-0, the *Texas,* and after this Andrews never got enough time to block the track before what had now become a Confederate posse came within rifle range. In the end, after eight hours and 87 miles the *General* expired when it ran out of fuel; the Union group then scattered into the woods. All were later captured and seven of the senior men shot.

Leaving out the human drama for a moment two qualities of the "American Standards" emerge from this affair. First, in spite of the rough track high maximum speeds of around 60mph (100km/h) were reached during the chase and both locomotives stayed on the rails. The second thing was that the range between fuel stops was very short. A full load of two cords of wood fuel (a cord is 128cu ft or 3.62m³) would last for a mere 50 miles (80km).

Both the *General* and the *Texas* (or what purports to be them) have survived. The former, normally in store at Chattanooga, is occasionally run. Oil fuel is used, the tank being concealed under a fake woodpile. The *Texas,* as befits a Confederate conqueror, has an honoured place in Grant Park at Atlanta. Both were converted from the 5ft (1,524mm) gauge of the Western & Atlantic Railroad after the war was over.

The American Civil War was one of the first great wars to be fought using railway transportation, most of which was provided on both sides by this "American" type. The earliest transcontinental railroads were first built and then operated by them; the well-known picture of the last spike ceremony at Promontory, Utah, has placed the Central Pacific's *Jupiter* and the Union Pacific No.119 second only to the *General* on the scale of locomotive fame. It is said that "America built the railroads and the railroads built America"; substitute "American 4-4-0" for "railroad" and the saying is equally true.

The "American" type was a universal loco; the only difference between those built for passenger traffic and those for freight was between 66in (1,676mm) diameter driving wheels and 60in (1,524mm). It also served all the thousands of railroad companies who then operated America's 100,000 miles (160,000km) of line, from roads thousands of miles long to those a mere ten.

The last "American" class in the USA did not retire from normal line service for more than a century after Rogers put the first on the rails in 1852. A few survive in industrial use in the remoter parts of the world even today. Numerous examples are preserved in museums and elsewhere all over North America, a few (a very few) perform on tourist railroads.

Left: Union Pacific's 4-4-0 No. 119, veteran of the Golden Spike ceremony on show at the 1948 Chicago Rail Fair.

Pearson 9ft Single Class 4-2-4

Origin: Great Britain: Bristol & Exeter Railway (B&ER), 1854. **Tractive effort:** 7,344lb (3,330kg). **Axle load:** 41,500lb (18.5t). **Cylinders:** (2) 18 x 24in (457 x 610mm). **Driving wheels:** 106in (2,743mm). **Heating surface:** 1,235sq ft (114.8m²). **Superheater:** None. **Steam pressure:** 120psi (8.4kg/cm²). **Grate area:** 23sq ft (2.15m²). **Fuel:** 4,480lb (2t). **Water:** 1,430gall (1,720 US) (6.5m³). **Adhesive weight:** 41,500lb (18.5t). **Total weight:** 112,000lb (49.7t). **Length overall:** 30ft 9in (9,372mm).

These remarkable tank locomotives were designed for the broad-gauge Bristol & Exeter Railway by Locomotive Superintendent Pearson and eight (running numbers 39 to 46) were built by Rothwell & Co. of Bolton in 1853 and 1854. They were intended specially for working the B&ER's section of the London to Exeter express route, including the famous train "Flying Dutchman", at that time the fastest train in the world. They had the largest driving wheels ever successfully used on a locomotive. The engines were guided by a four-wheel bogie at each end.

As with all locomotives that ran on Brunel's broad-gauge lines, the

Consolidation 2-8-0

Origin: United States: Lehigh Valley Railroad (LVR), 1866. **Gauge:** 4ft 9in (1,447mm). **Tractive effort:** 21,061lb (9,556kg). **Axleload:** 24,200lb (11t). **Cylinders:** (2) 20 x 24in (508 x 609mm). **Driving wheels:** 48in (1,219mm). **Heating surface:** 1,281sq ft (119m²). **Steam pressure:** 130psi (9.1kg/cm²). **Grate area:** 27 6sq ft (2.6m²). **Adhesive weight:** 88,000lb (39.9t). **Total weight:** 100,000lb (45.4t).* **Length overall:** 33ft 10in (10,312mm).*
Locomotive only. Tender details not available.

Locomotives of the 2-8-0 wheel arrangement were built in the USA from 1866 onwards and by 1946 about 24,000 had been supplied to railroads all over the world. Tractive effort varied from 14,000lb (6,352kg) for narrow-gauge examples up to 94,000lb (42,650kg) for one fitted with a booster tender and built for the Delaware & Hudson Railway in the 1920s. They were all intended for freight work, with occasional use hauling passenger trains on steeply-graded lines.

The name "Consolidation", now universally applied to the type, came from the first of some heavy freight locomotives supplied to the Lehigh Valley Railroad in 1866, just as that company had been formed by means of a consolidation of a number of smaller railroads in the area. They were intended

cylinders and motion were inside the frames. Water was carried in the tank at the rear as well as in a well-tank between the frames. Pearson's singles were untypical, though, in that they carried no names, only numbers.

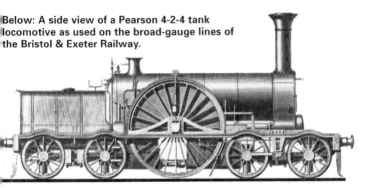

Below: A side view of a Pearson 4-2-4 tank locomotive as used on the broad-gauge lines of the Bristol & Exeter Railway.

to work trains up the Mahoney Hill which had a grade of 2.5 per cent (1-in-40).

To traverse curves easily, the two centre pairs of driving wheels were flangeless. The connecting rods drove on to the third axle, the eccentric rods and links of the Stephenson link motion being shaped and positioned clear of the leading axles. Otherwise the successful US 19th Century recipe for the steam locomotive was applied in its entirety. One important feature which became standard about this time was the casting of each cylinder integral with half the smokebox saddle. When bolted together, a very strong front end was produced.

At this time also, Baldwins had begun making a great effort to standardise parts and fittings as between any particular locomotive and another similar one. It was a pet project of the founder, Mathias Baldwin – who sadly died at the age of 70 in the same year that *Consolidation* was built – and was certainly a major factor in the dominant position in locomotive manufacture that his firm was to reach.

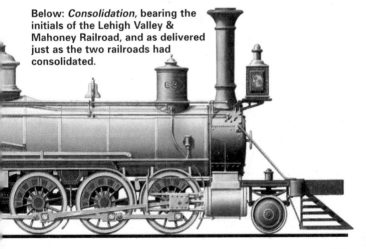

Below: *Consolidation*, bearing the initials of the Lehigh Valley & Mahoney Railroad, and as delivered just as the two railroads had consolidated.

Stirling 8ft Single Class 4-2-2

Origin: Great Britain: Great Northern Railway (GNR), 1870. **Tractive effort:** 11,245lb (5,101kg). **Axle load:** 34,000lb (15.5t). **Cylinders:** (2) 18 x 28in (457 x 711mm). **Driving wheels:** 97in (2,463min). **Heating surface:** 1,165sq ft (108m²). **Steam pressure:** 140psi (9.8kg/cm²). **Grate area:** 17.65sq ft (1.64m²). **Fuel:** 7,500lb (3.5t). **Water:** 2,900 gall (3,480 US) (13m³). **Adhesive weight:** 34,600lb (15.5t). **Total weight:** 145,500lb (66t). **Length overall:** 50ft 2in (15,240mm).

The "Stirling 8-foot single" is considered by many to be the epitome of the locomotive regarded as an art form. The graceful lines set off by lovely paint-and brass-work combine to produce a sight that has few rivals for beauty.

Patrick Stirling, Locomotive Superintendent of the Great Northern Railway, had the first of them built in 1870 at the line's own Doncaster Locomotive Plant. As was the GNR custom, subsequent numbers were allotted at random, but the prototype was actually No.1 and as such enjoyed considerable fame. It was 23 years before the last and 47th of the class was completed.

The domeless boiler was very apparent to the onlooker; it was both unusual for the time as well as being a Stirling trademark. Mechanically the engine was as simple as can be, with outside cylinders but inside valve chests, the slide valves being driven direct by sets of Stephenson's link motion.

In those days, when trains were formed of six-wheel non-corridor coaches, these engines handled all the crack expresses of the line including the famous 10am Kings Cross to Edinburgh express, known then only unofficially as the "Flying Scotsman".

Many authentic recordings were made showing speeds around 75mph (120km/h) with surprisingly heavy loads being hauled by these locomotives, but the coming of such developments as eight-and twelve-wheeled bogie stock, corridor carriages and dining cars spelt their removal to lesser tasks. All had been withdrawn by 1916 except the legendary No.1 which survives at what was the boundary of her home territory at the National Railway Museum at York.

In 1938 Stirling's No.1 was taken out of the museum, restored and used for a publicity stunt in connection with some new rolling stock for the "Flying Scotsman" express. Journalists were invited to Kings Cross for a preliminary run on the Flying Scotsman of 1888, before joining the new luxury train at Stevenage. The event caused a group of railway enthusiasts

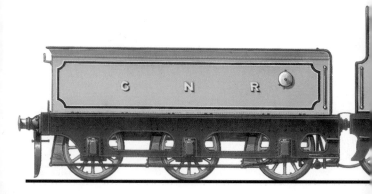

Above: Preserved Stirling No. 1 ready to take part in the Cavalcade celebrating 150 years of main-line railways, August 1975.

known as the Railway Correspondence and Travel Society to charter No.1 and its train of six-wheelers for an excursion from Kings Cross to Cambridge. It was the first occasion that a museum piece main-line steam locomotive was run to give steam enthusiasts pleasure, and was the precedent for such activities starting in earnest after World War II.

Below: Stirling 4-2-2 No.1 of the Great Northern Railway of England, showing the huge single pair of 8-foot diameter driving wheels. Note the domeless boiler and the elegant brass safety valve cover and, on the tender, the gong which was connected to an early form of communication cord. No.1 is preserved in working order.

Duke Class 4-4-0

Origin: Great Britain: Highland Railway (HR), 1874. **Tractive effort:** 12,338lb (5,597kg). **Axle load:** 31,500lb (14.25t). **Cylinders:** (2) 18 x 24in (457 x 610mm). **Driving wheels:** 75½in (1,918mm). **Heating surface:** 1,228sq ft (114m²). **Steam pressure:** 140psi (9.84kg/cm²). **Grate area:** 16.25sq ft (1.51m²). **Fuel:** 9,000lb (4t). **Water:** 1,800 gall (2,160 US) (8m³). **Adhesive weight:** 59,500lb (27t). **Total weight:** 161,500lb (73.5t). **Length overall:** 51ft 3in (15,621mm).

When they were introduced in 1874 the Highland Railway "Duke" class were the most powerful locomotives in Britain. Although a small concern with fewer than 60 locos on its books the HR needed strong engines to take its trains across the mountains. These ten 4-4-0s, built by Dubs of Glasgow and the first design of newly appointed Locomotive Superintendent David Jones, were the forerunners of several other very similar classes. These were the "Lochgorm Bogie" of 1876, the "Clyde Bogie" of 1886 and the "Strath" class of 1889. The celebrated "Skye Bogie" class of 1882 were also very closely related, but with considerably smaller driving wheels. In all, these engines added up to a very competent fleet of 30 locomotives, which profoundly improved speeds and loads on the Highland lines. That famous HR feature, the louvred chimney, intended to throw the exhaust up clear of the cab as well as assist the draughting, appeared for the first time on this class, which also had the graceful double frame arrangement of previous HR locomotives. As befitted a line whose first locomotive chief was Alexander Allan, Allan's straight link valve gear was used.

Another interesting feature was Le Châtelier's counter-pressure brake, by means of which the cylinders could be used to provide the brake force as well as drive the train. The idea was to supplement hand-applied brake-blocks on the long down grades but the equipment never became standard. The principle was very similar to descending a long hill in a motor car by engaging a low gear. The later-fitted front vacuum brake pipe was arranged to fold down to permit the mounting of a wedge-type snowplough. Running numbers were 60 to 69.

Although a ride over the Highland main line was and is one of the finest railway journeys of the world, it has never been one of the fastest. In the early days of David Jones' locomotives the journey from Perth to Inverness 143 miles (230km) took 5¼ hours by the best train, and the continuation on to Wick, a further 162 miles (260km), occupied another 8¼ hours. When this fleet of bogie engines had become established, improvements were made, the timings for the two sections of main line coming down to 4 hours

Right: "Duke" class No. 82 *Fife* passing Welch's Cabin at Inverness en route to the south. The lines to the left lead into the departure platforms of the station. Arriving trains, both then and now, proceed straight on and back into the arrival platforms.

and 6 hours respectively. This occurred in 1890.

One of the problems of the HR was that traffic was either a feast – during the beginning and end of the shooting season for example – or a famine. Foxwell (*Express Trains, English and Foreign,* 1895) records the Euston-Inverness mail train leaving Perth one August morning 1888 with two 4-4-0s and 36 carriages, including horseboxes and saloons from companies all over Britain. Not surprisingly and in spite of a banker being provided for the 18 miles (29km) of 1 in 75 (1.3 per cent) from Blair Atholl to Druimachdar Summit, 22 minutes had been lost against the schedule by the time Kingussie was reached. These 4-4-0s stayed in charge of principal Highland expresses until Peter Drummond's bigger 4-4-0s and 4-6-0s arrived at the turn of the century.

David Jones' predecessor at Inverness was William Stroudley, who introduced to the HR his original, handsome and celebrated livery of yellow ochre, more famous for its use on the London, Brighton & South Coast Railway. The "Duke" class first appeared in this colouring although it was not long before David Jones's own green livery was adopted. The only Highland locomotive which is preserved, "Jones' Goods" 4-6-0 No 103 of 1894, is (incorrectly) decked out in the yellow colour – this being as near as one can get to a preserved Highland 4-4-0. The last "Duke" to survive was the one which gave the class its name. No.67, *The Duke*, later *Cromartie*, ceased work in 1923; the last of the associated classes (No.95 *Strathcarron*) was withdrawn as London, Midland & Scottish No14274 in 1928, well before the age of preservation.

Below: David Jones' "Duke" class 4-4-0, depicted in original livery. Later a more sombre green was adopted.

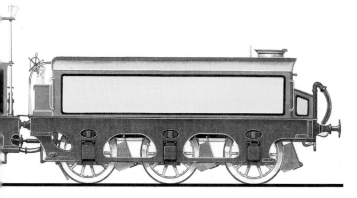

C-16-60

Origin: United States: Denver & Rio Grande Railroad (D&RG), 1882. **Gauge:** 3ft 0in (914mm). **Tractive effort:** 16,800lb (7,623kg). **Axleload:** 13,818lb (6.3t). **Cylinders:** (2) 15 x 20in (381 x 508mm). **Driving wheels:** 37in (939mm). **Heating surface:** 834sq ft (77m²). **Steam pressure:** 160psi (11,3kg/cm²). **Grate area:** 14sq ft (1.3m²). **Fuel:** 12,000lb (5.4t). **Water:** 2,500 US gall (9 5m³). **Adhesive weight:** 50,250lb (22.8t). **Total weight:** 111,600lb (50.6t). **Length overall:** 52ft 52³/4in (17,189mm).

The idea that railroads built on an entirely different and smaller scale should be used not only for small local lines but also for larger operations in difficult country was an attractive one, owing much to the pioneering of the British narrow gauge Festiniog Railway. So when, in the 1870s General William Jackson Palmer set out to build a vast railroad system radiating out of Denver to serve the length and breadth of Colorado, he decided on 3ft gauge.

Even though distracted from his main-line aspirations by the need to serve the booming mining camps of the Territory (as it was until 1876), he had soon taken these narrow tracks to the highest elevation then attained in the USA. Altitude of the line at La Veta pass was 9,400ft (2,865m), reached by a route which included 4 per cent (1-in-25) gradients and 30⁰ (58m radius) curves. Stronger locomotives than the little 2-4-0s, 4-4-0s and 2-6-0s first supplied were then found to be needed.

The solution came when, in 1877, Baldwin delivered to the Denver & Rio Grande their 22nd locomotive, one that was to found a whole dynasty of sturdy iron ponies. This pathfinder was 2-8-0 No.22, *Alamosa*. By the end of 1882, at the height of the silvermining boom, 130 similar locomotives had been delivered, mostly from Baldwin but a few from Grant. Diamond-pattern spark arrestors and other features gave an appearance such that, were trouble to come, one would instantly expect Gary Cooper or John Wayne to ride up out of the woods and put things right.

Most of the 2-8-0s had evocative names – *Roaring Forks, Shoshone, Old Rube, Treasury Mountain, Mosquito Gulch* and *Hardscrabble* were amongst the best. Apart from the narrow gauge the class was entirely orthodox, with slide valves above the cylinders and Stephenson's link motion between the frames. Many similar locomotives were supplied to narrow-gauge railroads at home and abroad. In later years the Denver & Rio Grande Western classified the majority of these locomotives as "C-16" (C - Consolidation; 16 = 16,000lb of tractive effort). There were also 20 of a stretched version known as "C-19".

Development of the system, and thus locomotive acquisition, came almost to a halt when in 1883 the narrow gauge reached Salt Lake City by a circuitous 771-mile (1,240km) route. General Palmer's resources were over-stretched and he effectively lost control of his railroads. Conversion of the

Right: The Colorado Railroad Museum steams and runs its precious No.346 on occasion.

Above: Denver & Rio Grande C16 class No. 278 on display at Montrose, Colorado. Built 1884, retired 1953.

main line to accommodate standard-gauge trains followed in 1889-90. After, much of the narrow-gauge material was sold to other railroads. The "C-16s" and "C-19s" soldiered on with much-rebuilt survivors still active 70 years later.

Many have been preserved, with No.346 *Cumbres* at the Colorado Railroad Museum, as well as Nos.400 *Green River* and 409 *Red Cliff* at Knott's Berry Farm near Los Angeles, both still operable and in "daisy-picking" railroad service.

Above: D&RG C-19 class No.346.

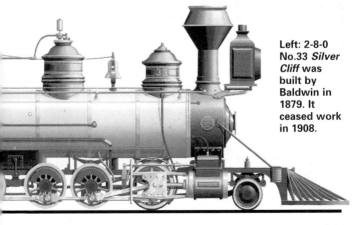

Left: 2-8-0 No.33 *Silver Cliff* was built by Baldwin in 1879. It ceased work in 1908.

Vittorio Emanuele II 4-6-0

Origin: Italy: Upper Italy Railroads (SFAI), 1884. **Tractive effort:** 15,335lb (6,958kg). **Axle load:** 35,500lb (16t). **Cylinders:** (2) 18½ x 24½in (470 x 620mm). **Driving wheels:** 66in (1,675mm). **Heating surface:** 1,720sq ft (124m²). **Superheater:** None. **Steam pressure:** 142lb/sq in (10kg/cm²). **Grate area:** 24sq ft (2.25m²). **Fuel:** 7,700lb (3.5t). **Water:** 2,200gal (2,630US) (10m³). **Adhesive weight:** 106,000lb (48t). **Total weight:** 184,475lb (83.7t). **Overall length:** 54ft 1½in (16,500mm).

The old kingdom of Piedmont, home of Count Cavour, who with King Victor Emmanuel was responsible for ending the Austrian occupation in the north of Italy and going on to create a united Italy, had one of the first important mountain railways in Europe. It connected the capital, Turin, with the port of Genoa, via the Giovi Pass. The 103-mile (165km) line was opened throughout in 1853 after a nine-year construction period.

The problem was the crossing of the Apenines at 1,180ft. (360m) altitude, 14 miles (22.5km) from Genoa. The chosen grade up from the port involved an horrendous 1 in 28½ (3½ per cent). 0-4-0 and 0-6-0 saddle tank locomotives, working in pairs back-to-back with one crew, were used by the Piedmont State Railroads with some success for working the incline.

In 1859 Italy was united and in 1865 the Giovi line became part of the Upper Italy Railroads (SFAI), which concern in 1872 set up the first railway locomotive design office in Italy. The last production of this establishment before the SFAI was absorbed into the Mediterranean System in 1885 was this absolutely remarkable machine, Europe's first 4-6-0, No.1181 *Vittorio Emanuele II*.

It was proposed to use this class for working the new and more sensibly graded Giovi diversion line then under construction, on which (at some cost in extra mileage) the ruling grade would be reduced to 1 in 62 (1.6 per cent). It was opened in 1889, by which time many more 4-6-0s had been completed. By 1896 the class numbered 55. Ansaldo of Genoa, Miani & Silvestri of Milan and Maffei of Munich, Bavaria, shared in the construction.

The locomotives had several unusual features including Gooch's valve gear outside the wheels. The working of this gear is explained in connection with Gooch's "Rover" class 4-2-2s, but here its workings are displayed in full view. The gear is actuated by two eccentrics mounted on a return crank

which in turn has its pivot set in line with the centre of the driving axle. It can be seen that when the reversing rod leading from the cab is moved, the valve rod is raised or lowered, rather than the eccentric rods and link, as in the Stephenson's gear.

The rearward position of the cylinders and the forward position of the short-wheel base bogie and smoke-box will be noted. The designers were concerned that the boiler-tubes would be too long to allow the fire to be drawn properly and to obviate this they recessed the firebox tubeplate into the boiler. This reduced the length of the tubes and increased the firebox volume, thereby forming one of the first-ever applications of a very modern feature known as a combustion chamber. The steam pressure was later raised to 156lb/sq in (11kg/cm^2).

These engines were very successful and could climb the new Giovi line with 130 tons at a steady speed of 25mph (40km/h). The maximum permitted speed, of course, was double that.

These 4-6-0s had another record – the unenviable one of being the first main-line steam locomotives to be displaced from the work for which they were built by a more modern form of traction. The old Giovi line went over to three-phase electric traction at 3,300 volts, 15 cycles (Hz) in 1910 and the diversion line followed in 1914.

Below: The *Vittorio Emanuele II* 4-6-0 as built for the Upper Italy Railroads in 1884. These locomotives worked the famous Giovi incline near Genoa.

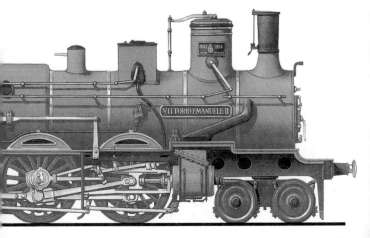

Cog Locomotive 0-4-2T

Origin: United States: Manitou & Pike's Peak (M&PP), 1890. **Gauge:** 4ft 8½in (1,435mm). **Tractive effort:** 22,040lb (10,000kg). **Cylinders, HP:** (2) 10 x 20in (254 x 508mm). **Cylinders, LP:** (2) 15 x 22in (381 x 558mm). **Driving wheels:** 22in (559mm). **Heating surface:** 575sq ft (53m²). **Steam pressure:** 200psi (14.1kg/cm²). **Grate area:** 19sq ft (1.8m²). **Total weight:** 52,700lb (23.9t). **Length overall:** 22ft 7¼ in (6,889mm).

Cog-wheel locomotives are almost as old as steam traction, for in 1812 John Blenkinsop had one built by Fenton, Murray & Woods of Leeds, England, for the Middleton Colliery Railway. This occurred the year before William Hedley built *Puffing Billy*, the world's first really practical steam locomotive. It was soon shown that for normally graded railways the bite of an iron wheel on an iron rail was sufficient and the world then put aside cog railways for half-a-century when this form of traction was used again for mountainous gradients.

The first rack-and-pinion railway which climbed mountains was built in the USA. This was the Mount Washington line of which more later. In 1890 a railroad similar in principle but differing considerably in detail was completed. It ran from Manitou Springs, Colorado, to the 14,100ft (4,302m) summit of Pike's Peak. This altitude is the highest reached by a railway in North America. As regards the rest of the world, the title also applies except for South America. The 8.9 mile (14.3km) line is still open and runs daily (using diesel traction) throughout the season from May to October. The maximum grade is 25 per cent (1-in-4).

To work the line, the Baldwin Locomotive Works supplied in 1890 three six-pinion rack locomotives. The boiler was mounted sloping steeply downwards towards the front so that it would be acceptably level on 1-in-4 gradients. Steam was fed to two pairs of 17in bore by 20in stroke (432 x 509mm) cylinders which drove three double rack pinions mounted on axles separate from the rail wheels as the latter were not driven. There was a separate crankshaft driving the two rear rack pinions directly through gearing with a 1:1 ratio. The leading rack-pinion was driven from the middle one by a pair of short coupling rods.

The arrangement did not prove satisfactory and in 1893 a further locomotive (No.4) was supplied and this had a different arrangement which could be described as an 0-4-2T. Vauclain compound cylinders drove on to a

Below: Manitou & Pike's Peak 0-4-2T cog locomotive as finally rebuilt in 1912.

vertical arm which was also connected, giving a mechanical advantage of 1:1.5, to coupling rods which drove the main axles via outside cranks. The two double rack pinions were mounted on the two main axles, while the rail wheels revolved free. The original locomotives were then rebuilt to this model and one further new one (No.5) was built. No.6, built in 1906 was similar except that, instead of resembling an 0-4-2T, it was effectively a six-coupled 0-6-0T. No.6 had the greater mechanical advantage of 1:1.7 and correspondingly higher tractive effort.

Subsequently, in 1912, the whole fleet was again rebuilt to a uniform design, this time in the M&PP's own shops. A rocking lever, pivoted at the centre and as far distant from the cylinders as possible, replaced the lever arm pivoted at its top and situated between the driving axles. The main driving rods were longer but their angular movement was less, while the mechanical advantage now became 1:1.55.

The M&PP used the Abt rack-and-pinion system, in which a rack consisting of two sets of teeth is mounted between the rails. The position of the teeth are staggered so that as cog teeth come in and out of mesh on one side of the rack, they are fully engaged on the other.

Unlike most other compound locomotives which used the Vauclain principle, the unique arrangement with high-pressure and low-pressure cylinders driving the same crosshead was retained until the use of steam in normal service was ended. Locomotive No.4 has been retained and has recently been restored as a runner, thereby becoming what is thought to be the only operable Vauclain compound. Other steam locomotives from the Pike's Peak line are on show at Colorado Springs (No.1), Golden, Colorado (No.2), and Manitou Springs (No.5).

Below: Preserved M&PP cog locomotive No.4 on display at the Colorado Railroad Museum.

Johnson Midland Single 4-2-2

Origin: Great Britain: Midland Railway (MR), 1887. **Tractive effort:** 14,506lb (6,582kg). **Axle load:** 39,500lb (18t). **Cylinders:** (2) 19 x 26in (483 x 660mm). **Driving wheels:** 93$\frac{1}{2}$in (2,375mm). **Heating surface:** 1,237sq ft (115m^2). **Superheater:** None. **Steam pressure:** 170psi (12kg/cm^2). **Grate area:** 19.6sq ft (1.82m^2). **Fuel:** 8,800lb (4t). **Water:** 3,500gall (4,200 US) (16m^3). **Adhesive weight:** 39,500lb (18t). **Total weight:** 181,500lb (82.5t). **Length overall:** 52ft 7$\frac{1}{2}$in (16,038mm).

The Midland Railway of England was noted for having trains which were fast, frequent and, consequently, light. One reason was certainly the fact that at only one town on the system – Kettering in Northamptonshire – did the company not have to face competition. One result was that the Midland was the last railway in Britain to have a fleet of single-driver locomotives and the only one to build them on into the twentieth century.

The first of the single-wheelers of S.W. Johnson, known colloquially as "Spinners", was constructed at the Company's Derby Works in 1887, after an interval of 21 years during which only coupled engines were made. By 1900, there were 95 locomotives in the class, made up of successive batches which differed slightly in main dimensions. Standardisation was then something the Midland left to newer and brasher railways! The dimensions given above refer to the "115" batch of 1897, considered to be the best.

Their elegance was enhanced by a noble crimson lake livery - which was kept unbelievably clean. In fact, it is said that it was the practice for MR shed foreman to feel behind the *backs* of the wheels with white gloves to find if the engines had been sufficiently groomed to be allowed out in traffic. Trays were placed under the engines when on shed in order to collect any oil drips which might sully the clean floor of a Midland loco depot! In such circumstances it is hardly surprising that the quality of maintenance was very high and this was also a factor in enabling low-powered locomotives to handle the traffic satisfactorily. It was also a factor in permitting all the mechanism - two sets of main motion plus two sets of Stephenson's valve gear - to be tucked away out of sight, but not out of mind so far as the fitters and drivers were concerned.

Another reason for the return of the single-wheeler was the invention of the steam sanding gear, which blew sand under the driving wheels just that

Right: The restored Midland Railway "Johnson Single" 4-2-2 No.673 as it appeared during the crowd-pulling "Rocket 150" celebrations in 1980.

bit more reliably than the gravity sanding previously used. Air sanding would have been just that bit more reliable still but, alas, the Midland showed a preference for the vacuum rather than the air brake and so compressed air was not available on MR locomotives. Good sanding gear was absolutely essential for a single-driver locomotive with limited adhesive weight.

Express trains of seven or eight bogie carriages weighing between 200 and 250 tons were just right for these celebrated locomotives. In dry calm weather heavier loads could be managed and there are records of trains up to 350 tons being handled and time being kept. They were also certainly very speedy, with maxima of around 90mph (144km/h) having been recorded. Another role for these beautiful locomotives was that of acting as pilots to the equally celebrated Midland 4-4-0s.

Before a logical system was adopted, numbers were allocated at random, but after 1907 the "Spinners" class occupied Nos. 600 to 694. Naming, like standardisation in those days, was not a Midland thing but, quite exceptionally, one of the last and twentieth-century batch - the ones with the big bogie tenders heavier than the locomotive - was given the name *Princess of Wales*.

One Midland single has survived; No.118 of the batch built in 1897 was set aside in Derby Works after withdrawal in 1928. Beautifully restored and with a fake wooden chimney now replaced by a proper one, she ran in steam at the Rocket 150 Cavalcade in June 1980.

Below: Midland Railway "Johnson Single" 4-2-2 in all the glory of its superb crimson lake livery.

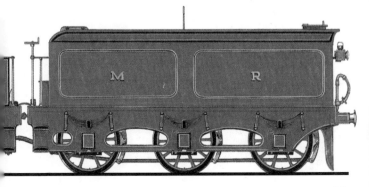

Teutonic Class 2-2-2-0

Origin: Great Britain: London & North Western Railway (LNWR), 1889. **Axle load:** 35,000lb (16t). **Cylinders, HP:** (2) 14 x 24in (356 x 610mm). **Cylinders, LP:** (1) 30 x 24in (762 x 610mm). **Driving wheels:** 85in (2,159mm). **Heating surface:** 1,402sq ft (130m²). **Superheater:** None. **Steam pressure:** 175psi (12.3kg/cm2). **Grate area:** 20.5sq ft (1.9m²). **Fuel:** 11,000lb (5t). **Water:** 1,800gall (2,160 US) (8m³). **Adhesive weight:** 69,500lb (31.5t). **Total weight:** 158,000lb (72t). **Length overall:** 51ft 0¼in (1 5,552mm).

The story of Francis Webb, the London & North Western Railway and the compound locomotive is one of the saddest episodes in the whole of locomotive history. Both the man and the railway were of gigantic stature and with good reason. Not for nothing was the LNWR known as "the Premier Line, the largest joint stock corporation in the World", whilst Webb himself made Crewe Works into a manufacturing unit without a rival in its ability to make everything needed by a great railway, starting with raw material. His superb non-compound 2-4-0s (on which his first three batches of compounds were based) included *Hardwicke* which still survives and runs. This locomotive showed what Webb locomotives were capable of when on August 22, 1895, the last night of the famous Race to Aberdeen, she ran the 141 miles (226km) of hilly road from Crewe to Carlisle at an average speed of 67¼mph (107.5km/h) and with a maximum of 88 (141).

In the late 1870s the idea of compounding was in the air and Webb made up his mind that this was a world that he was going to conquer. He first had a Trevithick 2-2-2 *Medusa* converted to a two-cylinder compound 2-4-0 and then in 1882 came his first three-cylinder compound 2-2-2-0 No.66 *Experiment*. The system Webb adopted was to have two outside high pressure cylinders, 11½in (292mm) diameter driving the rear driving wheels and a great dustbin of a low pressure cylinder 26in (660mm) diameter to drive the front driving axle. There were no coupling rods. Three sets of Joy's valve gear were provided.

Apart from the mechanism of compounding and the three cylinders, the rest of the locomotive was basically a standard LNWR 2-4-0 of which a large number were in use. *Experiment* needed modifications and the first production batch of 29, built in 1883-84, had 13½in (343mm) diameter high pressure cylinders in place of 11½ (292). They were not specially economical and were bad starters - men with pinch bars were needed to give the engines an initial starting movement before they would go. One of the problems was that Webb was an autocrat and anyone who suggested that his beloved compounds were less than perfect was regarded as questioning his superior officer's judgment and hence offering his resignation. So no one told Webb how awful they were even when, inevitably, another 40, the "Dreadnought" class only slightly modified, appeared 1884-88. The only thing his hard-

Below: L&NWR Webb compound 2-4-0 *Jeanie Deans* of the "Teutonic" class.

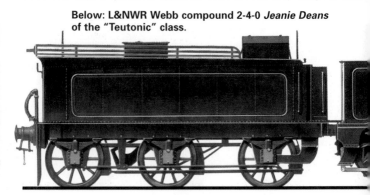

pressed staff could do was to "repair" - actually to renew in more powerful form - the fleet of simple express passenger 2-4-0s. By this means 256 new non-compound locomotives were turned out under the Chief's nose between 1887 and 1901.

In 1889 came the best of the Webb compounds, the ten "Teutonic" class; they are the basis of the drawing on this page and their particulars are listed above. The further modification in this case concerned the valve gear of the inside low pressure cylinder. Its Joy's valve gear was replaced by a "slip eccentric", a gear more familiar to manufacturers of steam toys than to full-size builders. In this arrangement a single eccentric is mounted loose on the driving axle. A pin attached to this eccentric and a stepped collar on the axle is arranged to drive it in one position relative to the crank for forward motion, and in another one for going backwards. The cut-off point of steam admission to the high pressure cylinders could be adjusted in the normal way, using the unusual inverted outside arrangement of Joy's valve gear visible in the drawing above. The arrangement worked well except for one problem; this typically occurred when a locomotive, having first backed on to its train, tried to start. The slip eccentric gear naturally still would be in reverse, but when the driver opened the throttle, the idea was that the two high pressure cylinders would take in the steam and move the train. By the time it had moved forward half-a-revolution of the driving wheels the inside slip eccentrics would have moved round into the forward position; therefore, when the first puff of steam exhausted from a high pressure cylinder into the low, off she would go. Alas, should the engine slip or spin its rear high pressure driving wheels when starting (which, as on all the 2-2-2-0 compounds were not coupled to the front low pressure ones), the low pressure cylinders would still have their valve gear in reverse when they received steam. The result was a stationary locomotive with its two pairs of driving wheels revolving in opposite directions!

Even so, the "Teutonic" locomotives were good once they got going – No.1304 *Jeanie Deans* was famous for regularly working and keeping time on the 2 pm Scottish Express from Euston to Crewe during the whole of 1890s. No.1309 *Adriatic* even starred in that legendary final night of racing in 1895, although her run from Euston to Crewe at an average speed of 63.1mph (102km/h) was not quite as great an achievement as that of her simple equivalent *Hardwicke* on the next stage; still it was certainly a very respectable effort. These ten "Teutonic" class which almost managed to approach simple performance, were the pinnacle of Webb's achievement with his compounds. It says little for the old LNWR that no one could stop him building a further 140 compound express locomotives before he retired in 1903.

Nos. 1-3 B$_o$-B$_o$

Origin: United States: Baltimore & Ohio RR (B&O), 1895. **Type:** Main line electric locomotive. **Gauge:** 4ft 8$\frac{1}{2}$in (1,435mm). **Propulsion:** Direct current at 675V fed via a rigid overhead conductor to four gearless motors of 360hp (270kW) each. **Weight:** 192,000lb (87t). **Max. axleload:** 48,488lb (22t). **Overall length:** 27ft 1$\frac{1}{2}$in (8,268mm). **Tractive effort:** 45,000lb (201kN). **Max speed:** 60mph (96.5km).

The world's first main line electrification was installed on this section of the first public railway in America; it ran through the city of Baltimore and in particular through the 1$\frac{1}{4}$ mile (2km) Howard Street tunnel, adjacent to a new main passenger station at Mount Royal. The tunnel was on a gradient of 1-in-125 (0.8 per cent) and trouble with smoke and steam therein was anticipated. The solution adopted was electrification carried out by General Electric of Schenectady, New York State.

More remarkable than anything was the boldness of the decision - these B&O locomotives were over nine times heavier and nine times more powerful than their nearest rivals. It was upon such an enormous leap forward as this that the success of the whole vast investment in the new line was dependent, because a very different construction would have been necessary for steam traction.

Gearless motors were again used, but not mounted direct on the axle, although concentric with it. Torque was transmitted to the wheels through rubber blocks, this flexible drive was yet another feature many years ahead of its time. Each four-wheeled tractor unit was mechanically quite separate, although two were permanently coupled to form one locomotive. There were three double locomotives in all.

Above: An about-turn indeed, as modern steam propels retired electric at the B&O centennial fair in 1927.

The locomotives were quite successful and had no problems hauling 1,630t (1,800 US tons) trains up the gradient. The load including the train's steam engine, which did no work in the tunnel. Trouble was encountered with corrosion of the unusual conductor arrangements; a brass shuttle ran along a Z-section overhead rail, the shuttle being connected to the locomotive by a one-sided tilted pantograph. A conventional third rail mounted outside the running rails replaced this amazing overhead conductor rail system as early as 1902.

These locomotives stopped work in 1912, but one was laid aside for many years – in fact, until B&O's centennial "Fair of the Iron Horse" in 1927, at which it was exhibited. Alas, scrapping followed and so the first-ever main-line electric locomotive is no longer to be seen. Electric traction continued in use on the B&O using more modern power until 1952 when electric locomotives of the self-generating type – that is, the all too familiar diesel – took over.

Left: Pioneer main line electric locomotive, commissioned in 1895 to work the Baltimore & Ohio's Howard Street tunnel.

No. 382 4-6-0

Origin: United States: Illinois Central Railroad (ICRR), 1896. **Gauge:** 4ft 8¹/₂in (1435mm). **Tractive effort:** 21,930lb (9,950kg). **Axleload:** 36,923lb (16.8t). **Cylinders:** (2) 19¹/₂ x 26in (495 x 660mm). **Driving wheels:** 69in (1,752mm). **Heating surface:** 1,892sq ft (176m²). **Steam pressure:** 180psi (12.7kg/cm²). **Grate area:** 31.5sq ft (2 9m²). **Fuel:** 18,000lb (8 2t). **Water:** 5,000 US gall (18.9m³). **Adhesive weight:** 100,700lb (45.7t). **Total weight:** 205,550lb (93.3t). **Length overall:** 60ft 3in (1 8,364mm).

The most famous of all railroad songs tells the story of John Luther Jones who, one night in April 1900 at Memphis, Tennessee, "mounted to the cabin with his orders in his hand, on his farewell trip to the Promised Land." His locomotive, Illinois Central No.382, was a 4-6-0 which in reality would only be called (as she was in the song) a "six-eight wheeler" by a Swiss. This accident would not really have been remarkable enough to go down to posterity were it not that Wallace Saunders, a labourer at the locomotive depot at Canton, Missouri, which was Casey's intended destination made up the celebrated ballad often attributed to "anon". In those days train wrecks had the frequency, and consequently the status, that automobile accidents have today, so it was news when railroads did not have accidents rather than when they did. In this case the accident occurred at Vaughan, Mississippi, 174 miles (278km) south of Memphis.

The train order system of operation, however satisfactory for a line carrying a few slowish trains, was very susceptible to human failure when used on such an important line as this trunk route from Chicago to New Orleans. The song states that Casey "looked at his watch and his watch was slow". Therefore it might be that, although his train was late by the public timetable, he could have been running ahead of the time set by his orders. Hence the cars he collided with might well have been legitimately still fouling the main track unprotected by a flagman. Since Casey habitually ran like the wind, and since no fixed signals existed, there was no prospect of stopping him and his "Cannonball Express" once his headlight had come into view.

The locomotive, which was very much a standard product of the day, was built by the Rogers Locomotive Works of Paterson, New Jersey. No.382 had

Below: Casey's own locomotive, standard 4-6-0 No.382 in its original form, unsuperheated and with a most ornate cab.

Above: Casey Jones in the cab of ICRR 2-8-0 No.638 just before his death in 1900.

outside slide-valve cylinders, inside Stephenson valve gear and a narrow firebox boiler. Her most unusual feature was a handsome clerestory cab roof. After the accident she was repaired and gave many more years of service. It is said that further men were killed while running her. Later, No.382 was modernised with the original slide-valve cylinders adapted to have piston valves and with outside Baker valve gear replacing the original inside Stephenson's. She gained a superheater but, alas, lost that elegant cab.

Casey was buried at Mount Calvary Cemetery at Jackson, Tennessee, where a memorial was erected to him in 1947, paid for by that pair of incurable railroad romantics (and authors of many evocative books about trains) Lucius Beebe and Charles Clegg. Present at the dedication were Casey's wife Jane, his son Charles (also an Illinois Central employee), his grand-daughter Barbara and most remarkably, Casey's fireman Sim Webb, who had jumped clear just before No.382 struck on that fateful night in Mississippi nearly half a-century earlier.

Class D16sb 4-4-0

Origin: United States: Pennsylvania Railroad (PRR), 1895. **Gauge:** 4ft 8¹/₂in (1,435mm). **Tractive effort:** 23,900lb (10,850kg). **Axleload:** 52,000lb (23.5t) **Cylinders:** (2) 20¹/₂ x 26in (521 x 660mm). **Driving wheels:** 68in (1,727mm). **Heating surface:** 1,400sq ft (130.1m²). **Superheater:** 253sq f¹ (23,5m²). **Steam pressure:** 175psi (12.3kg/cm²). **Grate area:** 33.2sq ft (3.1m²) **Fuel:** 26,000lb (11.8t). **Water:** 4,660gall (5,600US) (21.2m³). **Adhesive weight:** 98,500lb (44.7t). **Total weight:** 281,000lb (127.4t). **Length overall:** 67ft 0in (20,422mm).

By the end of the 19th century the Pennsylvania Railroad had established a reputation for large locomotives, mostly built in its own Altoona shops, and characterized outwardly by the Belpaire firebox, a rarity in North America. Its 4-4-0 locomotives were no exception, and the high water mark of the type was reached with the "D16" class, introduced in 1895. With cylinders 18¹/₂ x 26in (470 x 660mm) and 185psi (13.0kg/cm²) boilers, they were large engines for their day, and their appearance was the more impressive because the firebox was placed above the frames, making the boiler higher than was usual at this period.

Two varieties were built initially, one with 80in (2,032mm) driving wheels for the more level divisions ("D16a"), and the other with 68in (1,727mm) wheels for the hillier parts of the road ("D16"). The "D16a" engines soon established a reputation for high speed, as they were used in competition with the Atlantic City Railroad on the 58¹/₂ mile (94km) "racetrack" between Camden and Atlantic City. On this service one famous driver was credited with covering an eight-mile stretch at 102mph (164km/h). On another occasion the same driver worked a Presidential special over the 90 miles (145km) from Philadelphia to Jersey City at an average of 72mph (116km/h).

The mechanical quality of the design was well demonstrated by engine No.816, which distinguished itself by covering 300,000 miles (483,000km) on the middle division of the PRR in three years and four months, without stopping for other heavy repair. This was a notable feat for its day.

A total of 426 engines were built in five sub-classes of "D16" between 1895 and 1910. Apart from the two driving wheel sizes, their main dimensions were identical as built. With the introduction of Atlantics and then Pacifics in the new century, the "D16s" were displaced from the best trains, but the class was given a new lease of life from 1914 onwards when nearly half of them were modernised in line with the later engines. Slightly

Below. Former PRR Class D16sb (built in 1906) became Long Island Rail No.299, seen in shed at Morns Park, Jamaica, NY, in 1915.

arger cylinders with piston valves were fitted, still with the inside Stephenson's valve gear, and the boiler was given a Schmidt's superheater, with the pressure reduced slightly. Most of the rebuilds were the smaller-wheeled engines, and these became "D16sb" (see the dimensions at the head of this article). In this form they settled down to working numerous branch lines, and three of them were still engaged in this work early in World War II. One of these three, No.1223 built in 1905, was preserved on the Strasburg Rail Road in its native state.

Below: Preserved No.1223, this time with a short train of freight cars near Strasburg, Pennsylvania.

Below: On the Strasburg Railroad D16 4-4-0 No.1223 calls at Groff's Drove in July 1970.

Class S3 4-4-0

Origin: Germany: Royal Prussian Union Railway (KPEV), 1893. **Axleload** 35,000lb (15.6t). **Cylinders, HP:** (1) 18.9 x 23.6m (480 x 600mm). **Cylinders LP:** (1) 26.6 x 23.6m (680 x 600mm). **Driving wheels:** 78in (1,980mm). **Heating surface:** 1,267sq ft (117.7m²). **Superheater:** See descriptive text. **Steam pressure:** 171 psi (12kg/cm²). **Grate area:** 25.0sq ft (2.3m²). **Fuel** 11,000lb (5.0t). **Water:** 4,730gall (5,680US) (21.5m³). **Adhesive weight** 69,000lb (30.9t). **Total weight*:** 112,000lb (50.5t). **Length overall:** 57ft 7in (17,560mm). (*Engine only.)

The passenger engines built by the Royal Prussian Union Railway in the 1880s were 2-4-0s with outside cylinders, but towards the end of the decade the desire for higher speeds and great comfort (and thus greater weight) brought a need for larger locomotives. At that time August von Borries, well known for the system of compounding which bears his name, was locomotive superintendent at Hanover, and the Minister of Public Works sent him on a tour of England and America to study locomotive developments in those countries. Von Borries reported that to carry the larger boiler which would be needed, the engines would need an extra axle, and that the best arrangement would be the American type of 4-4-0. This would give better riding at speed than the existing 2-4-0s with their long front overhang.

In 1890 Henschel built a pair of two-cylinder compound 4-4-0 locomotives to von Borries' design, and in the following year the same firm built four more engines of the same wheel arrangement to the designs of Lochner the locomotive superintendent at Erfurt, two compound and two with simple expansion. A total of 150 engines were later built to the Erfurt simple-expansion design, but experience with these engines convinced the management of the superiority of von Borries' compounds, and in 1892 he produced an improved version of his design. This was the "S3", the "S" denoting "schnellzuglokomotiv", or express engine, and the digit being the serial number of the type from the introduction of this method of classification. The "S3" was highly successful, and in the period from 1892 to 1904 a total of 1,027 engines of this design were built for the Prussian railways, as well as 46 for other German state railways. The engines eventually worked most of the express trains in Prussia. In addition to the "S3"s, a further 424 locomotives were built to the same design, but with smaller driving wheels, and classified "P4".

The bogie was placed symmetrically under the cylinders and smokebox, and with the leading coupled axle set well back to give as long a connecting rod as possible, the layout showed clearly the influence of von Borries

American visit. Outside Walschaert's (Heusinger) valve gear drove slide valves set at an angle above the cylinders. The engines were rated to haul 320 tonnes at 47mph (75km/h) on the level, and 150 tonnes at 31mph (50km/h) on a gradient of 1 in 100 (1 per cent), and they established a reputation for economy in coal consumption and for smooth riding.

By its sheer size the "S3" class earns a notable place in locomotive history, but it is also important as being the first class to which steam superheating was applied. The need for superheating comes from a physical phenomenon – that water evaporates to steam at a definite temperature dependent on the prevailing pressure; thus at the working pressure of the "S3", 171 psi (12kg/cm.²), the temperature is 370°F (197°C). With water present in the boiler, the steam temperature cannot exceed that of the water. When steam is drawn from the boiler it carries some particles of

water with it, and when the steam comes into contact with the comparatively cool metal of the valves and cylinders, it loses that, and further particles of water form by condensation. Much of the work done on the piston is by the steam expanding after the valve has closed. Water has no capacity for expanding, and its presence in the cylinder is therefore a loss; it has been heated to the temperature in the boiler to no effect.

If the steam can be heated after it has left the boiler, and is no longer in contact with the mass of water there, the particles of moisture in the steam can be evaporated, making the steam dry. Still further application of heat causes the temperature of the steam to rise, and it becomes superheated. The main advantage of superheated steam is that if it is cooled slightly on making contact with the cool cylinder walls, no condensation occurs until all the superheat has been removed. Superheating is thus a means of eliminating condensation in the cylinder, and thereby making better use of the heat in the steam.

The attractions of superheating had been known to engineers for many years, but it was not until the 1890s that practicable designs of superheater were produced, by far the most important being those designed by Dr Wilhelm Schmidt of Kassel. The various schemes produced had in common that, after leaving the boiler, the steam flow was divided between a number of small tubes, known as "elements", by a distribution box or "header". After being heated in the elements, the steam was collected in another header, and passed through the main steam pipes to the cylinders. In Schmidt's first design, known as the flame tube superheater, a number of the boiler tubes were replaced by a large tube 17.5in (445mm) in diameter, and the elements were inserted into this tube. It was intended that the tube should be sufficiently large for flames to reach the elements (flames from the firebox die out quickly on entering a small tube).

Schmidt found an enthusiastic supporter of his ideas in Robert Garbe, who was chief engineer of the Berlin division of the Prussian railways. With Garbe's support the flame tube superheater was fitted to two 4-4-0 locomotives, an "S3" and a "P4". The "S3" was completed in April 1898 and made its first trial trip on the thirteenth of that month, a notable date in locomotive history. Although the results were encouraging, trouble was experienced with distortion of the large flame tube. Schmidt therefore

produced two more designs, in one of which the bundle of elements was housed in the smokebox, and in the other of which a number of the boiler tubes were replaced by tubes slightly larger, and each element made a return loop in one of these tubes.

In 1899 two new "S3" locomotives were fitted with the smokebox superheater, and they were also given piston valves in place of slide valves. With the combination of superheater and well-proportioned piston valves, these engines contained the essential ingredients of the final phase of development of the steam locomotive.

One of these two engines was exhibited at the Paris Exhibition of 1900, and attracted considerable attention. In service a reduction in coal consumption of 12 per cent was achieved compared with a standard "S3", but it was recognised that the temperature of the gases in the smokebox was too low for a very high degree of superheat to be attained, and that the scope for further development lay in the design with the elements in smoke tubes. However, increasing the temperature of the steam brought the need for improved lubricating oils, and whilst the problems of lubrication were being solved, many engines of class "S3" were fitted with smokebox superheaters.

The intensive development work needed to perfect superheating was largely due to the genius of Schmidt, and in little more than ten years after the first application of the smokebox superheater, the smoke tube design was virtually a standard fitting for large new locomotives; it was first applied to a Belgian Class 35 Caledonian type 4-6-0 in 1903. For a modest outlay, and with little increase in weight, an improvement in coal consumption of up to 20 per cent was obtained, and, equally important in some countries, a similar economy in water. For many engineers the superheater was an alternative to compounding, as it gave a fuel economy similar to that obtained by compounding, but without the mechanical complications of the compound. Others regarded superheating as an extra advantage to be added to that of compounding. Over a period of years after the fitting of the first superheater, both these points of view were apparent on the Prussian railways, and after a succession of superheated simple engines, a four-cylinder compound 4-6-0 was built.

A total of 34 of the "S3" locomotives survived to be incorporated in the stock of German State Railway in 1924.

Left: A Prussian class "S3" 4-4-0, the 5,000th locomotive built by the engineering firm of Borsig for the Prussian railways.

Class Q1 4-4-0

Origin: Great Britain: North Eastern Railway (NER), 1896. **Tractive effort:** 16,953lb (7,690kg). **Axle load:** 42,000lb (19t). **Cylinders:** (2) 20 x 26in (508 x 660mm). **Driving wheels:** 91¼in (2,315mm). **Heating surface:** 1,216sq ft (113m²). **Superheater:** None. **Steam pressure:** 175psi (12.3kg/cm²). **Grate area:** 20.75sq ft (1.93m²). **Fuel:** Coal, 11,200lb (5t). **Water:** 4,000 gal (4,800 US) (18m³). **Adhesive weight:** 77,000lb (35t). **Total weight:** 206,000lb (93.5t). **Length overall:** 56ft 3in (17,145mm).

A racing locomotive! Not just a fast-running locomotive that sometimes went very fast, but one that was specially and uniquely built for the competitive racing of public trains. The intention was to get a trainload of passengers from London to Scotland before a rival one running on a competing line. The East Coast and the West Coast companies had raced each other day after day in 1888 from London (Kings Cross and Euston) to Edinburgh and night after night in 1895 from London to Aberdeen. During the racing the regular timing of about 12 hours was reduced to 8hrs32min from Euston and 8hrs40min from Kings Cross. To put these figures in perspective, the present night trains from Kings Cross take just short of 10 hours for the 525 miles (840km). On the whole in 1895 the West Coast had just the best of it and so their rivals were determined to obtain revenge. How seriously that matter was taken is illustrated by the fact that the North Eastern Railway, otherwise the staidest of companies and which ran the racing trains over (mostly) straight and level tracks from York to Edinburgh, ordered some specially-designed inside-cylinder 4-4-0s to be ready for a resumption of hostilities in 1896. In the event, a derailment at Preston on the West Coast route which, although not connected with the racing, was attributed to high speed, made the competitors lose their taste for the fast running and accordingly only two of the five (Nos.1869 and 1870) ordered were ever completed. They were known as the Q1 class.

Wilson Worsdell's approach to the problem was to connect quite conventional boiler, cylinders and motion to very large driving wheels which at 7ft 7¼in (2,315mm) were some of the largest ever provided on a coupled engine. Huge wheels might well have meant a very bizarre appearance but the proportions were worked out in such a way as to produce one of the most beautiful designs ever to run on the rails of the world. Unusually for the time, a large and comfortable cab with side windows and clerestory roof was provided for the comfort of their crews. The slide valves were placed on top of the cylinders and were driven by rocking shafts and Stephenson valve gear. The usual NER Westinghouse air brakes were fitted.

Above: North Eastern Railway class "Q" 4-4-0. These engines were similar to the racing "Q1" class with normal-size wheels.

When it was apparent their exceptional services were not going to be needed, the two racers joined their normal-wheeled sisters of Class Q on normal top express passenger work. This continued until the coming of Atlantics in 1903 displaced them on the heaviest trains. A favourite turn was the Newcastle-Sheffield express, which had a remarkable scheduled start-to-stop timing of 43 minutes for the 44 1/4 miles (71km) from Darlington to York, at 61.7mph (98km/h) the fastest in the world at that time. Speeds in excess of 80mph (128km/h) were needed to keep time.

In spite of being non-standard, both survived until 1930, long enough to become London & North Eastern class D18 after the amalgamation of 1923; they kept their original numbers although the green livery and polished metalwork had been replaced by plain black long before.

Below: North Eastern Railway "Q1" class 4-4-0 built in 1896 for the railway races.

Claud Hamilton Class 4-4-0

Origin: Great Britain: Great Eastern Railway, 1900. **Tractive effort:** 17,100lb (7,757kg). **Axle load:** 41,000lb (18.5t). **Cylinders:** (2) 19 x 26in (483 x 660mm). **Driving wheels:** 84in (2,134mm). **Heating surface:** 1,631sq ft (151m²). **Superheater:** None. **Steam pressure:** 180psi (12.7kg/cm²). **Grate area:** 21.3sq ft (2m²). **Fuel (oil):** 715gall (860 US) (3.25m³). **Water:** 3,450gall (4,150 US) (16m³). **Adhesive weight:** 82,000lb (37.5t). **Total weight:** 213,000lb (97t). **Length overall:** 53ft 4³/₄in (16,276mm).

A new century was not yet three months old on the day when a really superb 4-4-0 locomotive, named *Claud Hamilton* after the chairman of the company and appropriately numbered 1900, emerged from the Great Eastern Railway's Stratford Works. Although its inside-cylinder layout was typical of the century that had gone, the large cab with four big side windows and many other features were way ahead of their time. Some of them, such as the power-operated reversing gear and water scoop, were still waiting to be adopted generally when the last steam locomotive for Britain was built 60 years later. Even energy conservation was considered, because the first "Claud"s burned waste oil residues instead of coal; these were available from the company's oil-gas plant. Other equipment very up-to-date for the day included an exhaust steam injector and a blast-pipe with variable orifice. Two sets of Stephenson's valve-gear filled such space as was left after two sets of main motion had been accommodated between the frames. Before 1914, the livery of polished metal and royal blue was as magnificent as any applied to any steam locomotive anywhere at any time.

The "Claud Hamilton" class has a complicated history. Eventually 121 of these engines were built between 1900 and 1923. Up-to-date features such as enlarged boilers, superheaters and piston – instead of slide–valves were gradually introduced on successive batches, culminating in the ten "Super-Claud"s of 1923. As these improvements were introduced on new construction, most earlier locomotives of the class were rebuilt to conform. The original "Claud"s suffered several rebuildings and in due time most of them emerged as one or other of the last two sub-classes of "Super-Claud" The latest of these varieties of rebuilding, done under the auspices of the London & North Eastern Railway, reverted to the round-topped firebox of the original No.1900, while intermediate construction and re-construction provided for a Belpaire firebox.

Using the LNER classification system, the details are given in the accompanying table.

Below: The glorious royal blue, brass and copper livery of the "Claud Hamilton" 4-4-0s of the great Eastern Railway of England was one of the finest ever used.

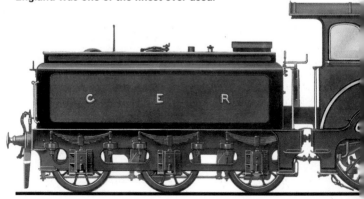

During their days as the prime express locomotives of the GER, the original "Claud"s could handle a 14-car "Norfolk Coast Express" non-stop from the Liverpool Street terminus in London to North Walsham. The schedule provided for hauling loads up to 430 tons and running the 130 miles (208km) in 159 minutes, quite an amazing feat for so small a locomotive.

The coming of 4-6-0s in 1913 meant that the top timetable trains of East Anglia were no longer handled by these famous engines. The top assignment of all, however, remained with them for many years, for no heavier locomotives were permitted to run on the line serving Wolferton, the station for Sandringham House, a favourite Royal residence. The frequent Royal Trains from London to Sandringham were handled by either of two specially painted "Royal Claud"s. In the 1930s these superbly-kept engines were a reminder – even if green rather than blue – of the days when Great Eastern engines were indeed a sight for sore eyes.

On railway nationalisation day, January 1, 1948, there were 13 "Dl5/2"s, 16 "D16/2"s and 88 "D16/3"s. The class just failed to achieve a 60-year working life and also by a sad chance just failed to be represented in preservation. One was so set aside at Stratford works but, alas, was only marked on one side to be spared the torch. Inevitably the foreman of the cutting up gang approached the line of locomotives from the other side. So, unfortunately, these famous engines are now but a memory in the minds of their admirers.

LNER class	Description	Number built new	Number of rebuilds	Length of service
D14	Original "Claud Hamilton" as described above	41	0	1900-1931
D15	Belpaire fireboxes introduced	66	9	1903-1933
D15/1	Superheaters introduced	4	70	1911-1935
D15/2	Extended smokebox	0	80	1914-1952
D16/1	Larger boilers ("Super-Claud")	10	5	1923-1934
D16/2	ditto	0	40	1926-1952
D16/3	Coupling-rod splashers removed. Round top boilers again	0	104	1933-1958

Class 500 4-6-0

Origin: Italy: Adriatic System (RA), 1900. **Axle load:** 32,500lb (14t). (14.5t). **Cylinders, HP:** (2) 14³/₄in x 25in (370 x 650mm). **Cylinders, LP:** (2) 23 x 25in (580 x 650mm). **Driving wheels:** 75¹/₂in (1,920mm). **Heating surface:** 1,793sq ft (166.6m²). **Superheater:** fitted later. **Steam pressure:** 200psi (14kg/cm²). **Grate area:** 32sq ft (3m²). **Fuel:** 9,000lb (4t). **Water:** 3,300 gall (4,000 US) (15m³). **Adhesive weight:** 98,000lb (44.5t). **Total weight:** 221,000lb (100t). **Length overall:** 79ft 2in (24,135mm).

Even as early as 1825, at the time the Stockton & Darlington Railway was opened, the direction in which a locomotive went and the position from which it was driven had been established. The chimney of *Locomotion*, the S&D's original locomotive, came first in front, while the driver and fireman did their work at the other end of the boiler, that is, to the rear, where the controls and firehole door were situated. Behind them again came the tender which carried supplies of coal and water. Almost all steam locomotives built since then have followed this arrangement.

Questioning what almost seems a natural law is a hard thing to do, but there were some original minds who did so. One was Giuseppe Zara, locomotive engineer of the Italian Adriatic System (Rete Adriatica or RA), in charge of the design office at Florence. He decided that it would be best to have the driver in front and to that end produced a 4-6-0 with the boiler and cylinders reversed on the frames. Coal was carried in a bunker on one side of the firebox, which itself was above the bogie rather than between the driving wheels. The tender trailed behind the chimney and of course carried water only.

The advantages claimed were, first, that the lookout was excellent, as good as that of any electric or diesel locomotive today. Second, the exhaust was discharged some distance behind the cab and this reduced the smoke menace in tunnels, so far as the crew were concerned.

There were four compound cylinders with an unusual arrangement. The two high-pressure cylinders were on one side, set at 180 degrees to one another; while the low-pressure pair were similarly arranged on the other. Each pair was set at 90 degrees to the pair on the other side, as in a normal locomotive. A single valve and valve chest each side, driven by sets of outside Walschaert's valve gear, controlled the admission of steam into each pair of cylinders. A number of locomotives in Italy had this arrangement of compounding, known as the Plancher system after its inventor. One drawback was that it was difficult to equalise the work done between the high-pressure and the low-pressure cylinders. The result was that a sideways swinging motion was liable to occur.

The prototype was exhibited at a meeting of the International Railway Congress held in Paris. A detail that impressed R.M. Deeley of the Midland

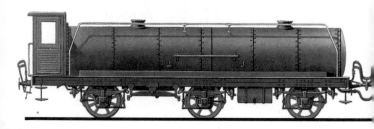

Above: Italian "300" class back-to-front express engine.

Railway was the arrangement whereby a small opening of the regulator admitted live steam to the low-pressure cylinders, essential for starting. When the regulator was opened a little further, the locomotive changed over automatically to compound working. Deeley adopted this arrangement in his successful Midland compounds, but Zara did not use it for his remaining 42 "cab-forward" locomotives, preferring an independently worked valve instead. One reason might have been that it was desirable to use this valve to equalise the work done between the high-and low-pressure cylinders. Normally this would be a pious hope, but in the case of a Plancher compound it would coincide with making the ride more comfortable, since the high-and low-pressure cylinders were on opposite sides of the locomotive. There was therefore some prospect of drivers actually bothering to make this adjustment.

Whilst in France, tests were run with the prototype and 78mph (126km/h) was reached with a 130-ton train. Back at home these strange locomotives, which had become Italian State Railways 670.001 to 670.043 after the railways were nationalised in 1905, successfully worked express trains in the Po Valley for many years. They finally ceased work in the early 1940s. Most were later superheated, becoming class 671 when this was done.

Below: This strange back-to-front steam locomotive was designed for the Italian Adriatic system at the turn of the century. Guiseppe Zara was the engineer responsible.

Class Q 4-6-2

Origin: New Zealand Government Railways (NZGR), 1901. **Gauge:** 3ft 6in (1,067mm). **Tractive effort:** 19,540lb (8,863kg). **Axle load:** 23,500lb (10.5t). **Cylinders:** (2) 16 x 22in (406 x 559mm). **Driving wheels:** 49in (1,245mm). **Heating surface:** 1,673sq ft (155m²). **Superheater:** None. **Steam pressure:** 200psi (14kg/cm²). **Grate area:** 40sq ft (3.72m²). **Fuel:** 11,000lb (5t). **Water:** 1,700 gall (2,000 US) (7.7m³). **Adhesive weight:** 69,500lb (31.5t). **Total weight:** 165,000lb (75t). **Length overall:** 55ft 4¹/₂in (16,872mm).

The year 1901 was marked by the construction of the first of a famous type – arguably *the* most famous type – of express passenger locomotive, which was to go on being built until the end of steam. And it was not one of the great railway nations which was responsible for conceiving the idea (and to whose order it was built) but tiny New Zealand. A.W. Beattie, Chief Mechanical Engineer of the Government Railways, wanted a locomotive with a big firebox capable of burning poor quality lignite coal from South Island mines at Otago.

American manufacturer Baldwin suggested a "camelback" 4-6-0 with a wide firebox above the rear coupled wheels, but the New Zealander proposed a 4-6-0 with the big firebox carried by a two-wheel pony truck, making a 4-6-2. The 13 engines were quickly completed and dispatched across the Pacific Ocean; and in this way a name was given to thousands of locomotives yet to be built. In due time the word "Pacific" entered that dialect of the English language used for describing railways.

A feature which was also to appear on most of the world's steam locomotives built after this time was the type of valve gear used on these engines. Most of the steam locomotives described in this book have Walschaert's valve gear. The invention was not new – a Belgian engineer called Egide Walschaert had devised it back in 1844 and a German called Heusinger had reinvented it since – but this application marked its entry into general use outside continental Europe. The gear gave good steam distribution but the main advantage lay in its simplicity, as well as in the fact that it could conveniently be fitted outside the frames in the position most accessible for maintenance. In this case the gear was arranged to work outside admission piston valves, which piston valves themselves were in the forefront of steam technology at the beginning of the century.

It should be said that this class of engine came closer than ever before to the final form of the steam locomotive. Only two fundamental improvements were still to be applied generally – inside admission piston valves in place of outside, and superheating.

After some minor modification the "Q" class gave long and faithful service, the last of them not ceasing work until 1957.

Above: Commissioning photo of Class "Q" prior to entering service on the South Island main line in 1901.

Left: The splendid New Zealand Government class "Q" 4-6-2 No.343 as running in 1956 when nearing the end of more than 50 years service to this 3ft 6in gauge railway system which had adopted US practice for its locomotives.

Below: NZGR class "Q " – she was the world's first class of Pacific locomotive when built in USA in 1901.

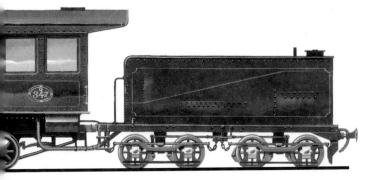

Class E3sd 4-4-2

Origin: United States: Pennsylvania Railroad (PRR), 1901. **Tractive effort:** 27,400lb (12,400kg). **Axleload:** 64,500lb (29.3t). **Cylinders:** (2) 22 x 26in (559 x 660mm). **Driving wheels:** 80in (2,032mm). **Heating surface:** 2,041sq ft (190m²). **Superheater:** 412sq ft (38m²). **Steam pressure:** 205psi (14.4kg/cm²). **Grate area:** 55.5sq ft (5.2m²). **Fuel:** 34,200lb (15.5t). **Water:** 5,660gall (6,800US) (25.7m³). **Adhesive weight:** 127,500lb (58t). **Total weight:** 363,500lb (165t). **Length overall:** 71ft 6in (21,640mm).

In the 19th Century the standard American passenger engine was the 4-4-0, but towards the end of the century the type was reaching the limit of size which was possible on eight wheels, and train loads were still increasing. A move to ten wheels was inevitable, and there were two attractive alternatives, 4-6-0 and the 4-4-2 or Atlantic. The former could have a greater adhesive weight, but the grate was restricted by the need to fit between the rear coupled wheels. The Atlantic had more restricted adhesive weight, but could have a very large grate. For the Pennsylvania Railroad the Atlantic was the obvious choice. The road was already laying exceptionally heavy rails, which could accept a very high axle load, whilst the locomotives had to be able to burn coal of moderate quality in great quantities.

In 1899 Altoona works produced its first two Atlantics, and they exploited the wheel arrangement to the full, with an adhesive weight of 101,600lb (46.1t) and a grate area of 68sq ft (6.3m²), more than twice that of the largest PRR 4-4-0. However, a third engine had a more modest grate of 55.5sq ft (5.2m²), and it was this size which became standard for all subsequent Atlantics, as well as for many other engines of the same period. With this engine the pattern was set for the construction of 576 more Atlantics, all having the same wheel diameter, boiler pressure and grate area.

Although the basic dimensions were common to all the engines, successive improvements were made. The three prototypes had Belpaire tops to the fireboxes, in accordance with established Pennsylvania practice, but the next two batches, totalling 96 engines, had the more usual round-topped firebox. Thereafter the Belpaire box reappeared, and was used on all subsequent engines. The two batches mentioned above differed only in their cylinder diameter, class "E2" having 20.5in (521mm) cylinders, and class "E3" 22in (559mm), the intention being to use the "E3"s on heavier work. All these engines had slide valves, but in the next series, starting in 1903, piston valves were used, at first with Stephenson's valve gear, but from 1906 with Walschaert's.

By 1913 a total of 493 engines had been built, all having a boiler with a maximum diameter of 65.5in (1,664mm). By that time the Pacific was well established on the railway, and it seemed that the heyday of the Atlantic had passed. However, Axel Vogt, the Chief Mechanical Engineer, was still averse to incurring the expense of six-coupled wheels if four would suffice, and in 1910 he built a further Atlantic with another type of boiler, having the same grate area as the earlier Atlantics, but a maximum diameter of 76.75m (1,949mm), almost as large as the Pacifics, and with a combustion chamber at the front. The new engine, classified "E6", developed a higher power than the existing Pacifics at speeds above 40mph (64km/h). Two more "E6"s were then built, but with superheaters, and this made the performance even more impressive, and it was possible to increase the cylinder diameter to 23.5in (597mm).

After four years of intensive development work, a production batch of eighty "E6"s were built, having a number of changes from the prototypes, including longer boiler tubes. These engines were built at great speed between February and August 1914, that is, in the same year that the first of the famous "K4"s Pacifics was built. These engines took over the principal express workings on all the less hilly parts of the system, and during World War 1 they achieved prodigious feats of haulage for four-

**Above: a Pennsylvania Railroad class "E2" 4-4-2 at speed
with a New York-Chicago express.**

oupled engines. When large numbers of production "K4"s Pacifics
appeared after the war, the "E6"s engines settled down to work on the less
busy routes, mainly in New Jersey.

The smaller Atlantic soon established a reputation for high speed, but
their full potential was realised in 1905 when the Pennsylvania Special was
accelerated to an 18-hour schedule from Jersey City to Chicago, giving an
overall average speed of 50.2mph (80.1km/h), with an average of 57.8mph
(92.9km/h) over the 189 miles (304km) from Jersey City to Harrisburg. It
was on the first westbound run to this schedule that "E2" No.7002 was
credited with exceeding 120mph (193km/h), but the claim was based on
dubious evidence. On this service the "E2" and "E3" engines kept time
with up to eight wooden coaches, totalling about 360 (short) tons, but with
the introduction of the heavier steel stock, double heading became
common.

The "E6s" engines were able to handle trains of 800-900 tons on the
New York-Philadelphia-Washington trains, but it was on lighter trains that
they produced their most spectacular performances. Their greatest
distinction was to haul the Detroit Arrow between Fort Wayne and Chicago,
or in 1933 this was the world's fastest train, with a start to stop average of
75.5mph (121.4km/h) over the 64.1 miles (103km) from Plymouth to Fort
Wayne and 75.3mph (121.1km/h) over 123 miles (198km) from Fort Wayne
to Gary. On this service they hauled five or six steel coaches, weighing 300
to 350 tonnes.

Over the years many of the earlier Atlantics were modernised with
superheaters and piston valves, making them into modern engines for light
duties. Five of them survived until 1947, and one of them, by now classified
"E2sd", was preserved. It was renumbered to 7002, thus purporting to be
the engine of the 1905 record. The "E6s" engines survived well into the
1950s, and one of them, No.460, has been preserved. This engine had
achieved fame by hauling a two-coach special from Washington to New
York carrying news films of the return of the Atlantic flyer Lindbergh. The
train averaged 74mph (119km/h); the films were developed en route and
shown in New York cinemas before those carried by air.

Saint Class 4-6-0

Origin: Great Britain: Great Western Railway (GWR), 1902. **Tractive effort:** 24,395lb (11,066kg). **Axle load:** 41,500lb (19t). **Cylinders:** (2) 18¹/2 x 30in (470 x 762mm). **Driving wheels:** 80¹/2in (2,045mm). **Heating surface:** 1,841 sq ft (171m²). **Superheater:** 263sq ft (24.4m²). **Steam pressure:** 225psi (15.8kg/cm²). **Grate area:** 27.1 sq ft (2.52m²). **Fuel:** 13,500lb (6t). **Water:** 3,500 gall (4,200 US) (16m³). **Adhesive weight:** 125,000lb (56t). **Total weight:** 251,000lb (114t). **Length overall:** 63ft 0¹/4in (19,209mm).

When, shortly before the turn of the century, a not-so-young man called George Jackson Churchward found himself heir apparent to William Dean Chief Locomotive Engineer of the Great Western Railway, he (Churchward) had already decided that there would have to be very great changes when he took over. Corridor trains and dining cars, as well as the demand for faster schedules meant a whole new express passenger locomotive fleet, for even by nineteenth century standards the then current GWR locomotives were both heterogenous and unsatisfactory. Whilst Churchward was number two under an ageing chief at the Swindon Factory, he was able to test his ideas by causing to be built a number of very strange designs indeed. Because so many peculiar oddments already existed – such as 4-4-0s converted from standard gauge 0-4-4s(!), themselves converted from the broad gauge on its abolition in 1892 – they attracted little attention.

But 1902 was the year when a big outside-cylinder 4-6-0 No.100 (later 2900), tactfully named *Dean* (later *William Dean*), saw the light of day. By the standards of the locomotive aesthetics of the period it was one of the strangest looking locomotives of all, though to those few who knew about the design and appearance of the typical North American Ten-wheeler No.100 was totally familiar, despite being disguised by ornate Victorian brass and paint work. This reflected Churchward's friendship with A.W. Gibbs Master Mechanic (Lines East) of the Pennsylvania Railroad.

The layout of the American Ten-wheeler prototype was followed exactly. Both cylinders and valve chests were mounted outside the frames in the most accessible possible position; the Stephenson's valve gear inside the frames drove the inside-admission valves via transverse shafts and pendulum cranks. With some refinement the arrangement was used by Churchward and his successors on some 2,000 locomotives. The frame arrangement for Churchward's standard locomotives was a compromise between USA and British practice. Plate frames were used for the main portion in which the driving wheels were held, but the cylinders were in true Yankee style, each together with one half of the smokebox saddle, the front of the locomotive being carried on a short length of bar frame. The domeless boiler had less of the USA and more of Churchward than the engine part

Above: "Saint" class No.2937 Clevedon Court. The "Courts" were the last batch of the "Saints" built in 1911.

about it (but very little previous GWR practice); however, some time was to elapse before the design of this component became fully developed.

At this time Churchward was about to take full charge, not only (as on most British railways) of the building and repairing of locomotives, but also of their running. He would sit round a drawing board together with its incumbent, the incumbent's boss and the Chief Draughtsman and they would discuss the job in question. If doubts arose over manufacture, an expert from the works – the foundry foreman, maybe – would be sent for. If it was a point about the locomotive in service, then the running superintendent would come over. Perhaps Churchward would ask what others did about the problem, in which case the Record Office would quickly produce a book or periodical tabbed to indicate the relevant page. The result was that before long the GWR possessed a locomotive fleet that in many ways had few rivals the world over.

Below: No.2902 *Lady of the Lake* as depicted here retains the straight foot-plating of the original members of the class.

It was a far cry from the ways of some of the autocratic, self-important and "know-all" characters who occupied the chief's chair on a number of other British lines in those days. Churchward did it all, not by cleverness, but simply by listening to others and then applying that rarest of qualities, common sense. Churchward took some time to make up his mind whether to have as his best express power the 77 two-cylinder "Saint" class 4-6-0s derived from *William Dean*; or whether the four-cylinder contemporary "Star" class 4-6-0s of similar speed and power, of which there were 6? before Churchward retired in 1921, would be the better. He finally decided on the latter and it does seem, to this writer at least, that this is one of the very few times when the judgment of one of our greatest locomotive engineers could be seen to be at fault.

The jump from the first-line express power of 1892, the graceful 4-2-2 "Dean Single" to *William Dean* of 1902 involved the following increases in the various measures of power; tractive effort – 20 per cent; cylinder stroke - 25 per cent (the bore was the same); heating surface - 35 per cent; steam pressure - 12 per cent; grate area - 30 per cent; adhesive weight - 204 per cent. In addition to these shocks, there was that arising from the full side nudity of exposing wheels, cylinders and motion.

Although the locomotives came to be known as the "Saint" class, 32 had been built before the first Saint name appeared, No.2911 *Saint Agatha* 1907. Following on *William Dean*, in 1903 there came a second prototype (No.98, later 2998 *Ernest Cunard*) and then in the same year another (No. 171, later 2971, *Albion*). No. 171 was turned out temporarily as a 4-4-2 in order to make direct comparison with a French de Glehn compound 4-4-2 No. 102 *La France*, which had been imported as an experiment. The first production batch of 19 (Nos.172-190, later 2972-90) appeared in 1905, and some of these also had a short period as 4-4-2s; they were named after characters in Sir Walter Scott's Waverley novels. In May 1906 Nos.2901-? were built, later named after Ladies. No.2901 well named *Lady Superior* was the first British locomotive to have a modern superheater, in this case of the Schmidt pattern and all had been given superheaters (now Swindon design) by 1912.

In the 20 genuine Saints which followed in 1907, the austere straight lines of the running boards were mitigated by providing the curved drop ends so much a characteristic of most GWR locomotives built since that time. Finally in 1911 came 25 Courts, a superheated from the outset and with further improvements. Cylinder diameter was increased by 1/2in and more obviously, the very characteristic "topfeed" fittings either side of the safety valves on the domeless boiler were added. These came to be very much a GWR trademark.

Churchward's boilers were his greatest triumph and the best among them was this No.1, which was not only fitted to the 77 Saints but also 74 "Star" 4-6-0s, the 3 "Frenchmen" 4-4-2s, 330 "Hall" 4-6-0s, "Grange" 4-6-0s and 150 "28XX" 2-8-0s.

Amongst the No.1 boiler features were measures to avoid the damage to boiler plates etc. caused by delivering relatively cold feed water straight into the hot boiler water, as was normal before his day. By placing the non-return feed valves (clack valve is the technical term) on top of the boiler and directing the delivery forward, the feed water flowed to the front of the barrel via a series of trays which collected impurities deposited as the water gathered heat. There, now fairly hot, the feed water mixed with that already in the boiler without detriment.

In due time the whole "Saint" class (except the prototype) was brought up to the standards of the last ones to be built. In building these later Churchward finally decided on the two-cylinder versus the four-cylinder question because at the last minute he cancelled the final five Courts, ? continued to build four-cylinder "Star" locomotives. Further development of the GWR express passenger locomotive was all based on the "Star" layout, yet the "Saint" was a remarkable engine and able to match anything in the way of performance which its complex four-cylinder sisters could produce.

Above: Going and coming. Two views of "Saints" at work. The upper photograph shows that they were far from neglected even in British Rail days. As these views show, most of the "Saints" were altered to have the curved foot-plating of the later batches of these path-finding locomotives.

In 1925 No.2925 *Saint Martin* was fitted with 72in (1,828mm) diameter wheels in place of 80½in (2,045mm). Tractive effort was increased in proportion and maximum speed was very little affected. In this form and described as the "Hall" class, a further 330 "Saint"s were built, most of which went on until dieselisation.

A particularly pleasing feature was the exceptional precision with which all these later engines were built and repaired. This was the main contribution of Churchward's successors, who saw to it that Swindon had the kit – the Zeiss optical setting out apparatus was one item – to achieve dimensional accuracy higher than was normal practice elsewhere. The story that British Railways' standards of fits and tolerances for a locomotive when it was new corresponded to Swindon's standards when they considered it as worn out, was not entirely apochryphal.

No.2920 *Saint David* was the final survivor of the Saints proper when withdrawn in 1953.

No. 2400 0-6-6-0

Origin: United States: Baltimore & Ohio Railroad (B&O), 1903. **Gauge:** 4ft 8¹/₂in (1,435mm). **Tractive effort:** 96,600lb (43,829kg). **Axleload:** 61,325lb (27.8t), **Cylinders, HP:** (2) 22 x 32in (558 x 812min). **Cylinders: LP:** (2) 32 x 32in (812 x 812min). **Driving wheels:** 56in (1,422mm). **Heating surface:** 5,586sq ft (519m²). **Steam pressure:** 235psi (16.5kg/cm²). **Grate area:** 72.2sq ft (6.7m²). **Fuel:** 30,000lb (13.6t). **Water:** 7,000 US gall (26.5m³). **Adhesive weight:** 335,104lb (152t). **Total weight:** 477,500lb (216.7t). **Length overall:** 67ft 2in (20,470mm).

Anatole Mallet was a Frenchman who took out a patent in 1884 for a locomotive with the front part hinged. He seems to have had in mind using the idea mainly in connection with small tank engines intended for sharply curved local and industrial railways. The idea that his patent should be the basis of the largest, heaviest and most powerful locomotives ever built would have seemed strange, but so it was.

The Baltimore & Ohio Railroad had a problem in taking heavy trains up the Sand Patch incline, 16 miles (26km) long, graded at 1 per cent (1-in-100). There were sharp 7° curves (250m radius), and this limited the number of driving wheels which a straight unhinged locomotive could have. The idea was to replace the two 2-8-0 helpers necessary for a 2,000-ton train by a single locomotive. Looking at the problem with hindsight the answer now seems obvious, but at the time the proposal to introduce a relatively untried idea from Europe must have seemed bold to the point of rashness. Anyway, the B&O management took their courage in both hands and went to the American Locomotive Co for the first ever US Mallet compound. It was a turning point in US locomotive history.

This No. 2400 launched another innovation as far as the USA was concerned – one which was to affect locomotive practice even more than the Mallet arrangement, for this pathfinding machine was the first significant US locomotive to have outside Walschaert valve gear. One set worked the inside-admission piston valves of the rear high-pressure cylinders and another had the slightly different arrangement appropriate to slide valves

Below: The Great Northern Railway was an early Mallet user from 1906 on, as exemplified by this L class 2-6-6-0.

which are inherently outside-admission.

This simple, accessible and robust mechanism, which produced excellent valve events, was very soon to become the standard valve gear for most North American locomotives. Another feature to become standard later was the steam-powered reversing gear. With four valve gears, the effort required was too great for a manual arrangement. Later, the mechanism of straight two-cylinder engines became so massive that power-reverse became general on all except the smallest.

The Mallet principle could be described as building a normal locomotive with a powered leading truck, for the frame of the rear high-pressure engine has the boiler attached rigidly to it. The large low-pressure cylinders can if required be placed in front of the smokebox, and thereby they can be freed of any restrictions on their size. The pivoting arrangements for the front engine are relatively simple, with a hinge at the rear and a slide at the front.

No.2400, known affectionately as "Old Maude", never had any sisters, but she numbered her descendants in thousands. They included virtually without exception all the world's largest strongest, and most powerful reciprocating steam locomotives ever built.

Above: Baltimore & Ohio compound 0-6-6-0 No.2400 was the first Mallet articulated locomotive in the USA.

Above: By 1916 Baltimore & Ohio was building 2-8-8-0s much more powerful than No.2400, such as this EL-2 class articulated.

Class S 1-D₀-1

Origin: United States: New York Central & Hudson River Railroad (NYC&HR), 1904. **Type:** Electric passenger locomotive. **Gauge:** 4ft 8½in (1,435mm). **Propulsion:** 660V direct current collected from under-contact third rail supplying four 550hp (410kW) frame-mounted gearless traction motors with armatures on the axles. **Weight:** 142,000lb (64.4t) adhesive, 200,500lb (91t) total. **Max. axleload:** 35,500lb (16.1t). **Overall length:** 37ft 0in (11,277mm). **Tractive effort:** 32,000lb (145kN). **Max. speed:** 70mph (113km/h).

A major development in electric traction occasioned by a collision between two steam trains – such was the electrification of New York Central's Grand Central terminal in New York and the surrounding lines. The smoke nuisance in this major city location had long brought criticism upon the railway, but it was the 2-mile Park Avenue tunnel on the approach lines which constituted an operating hazard. At busy times the tunnel was choked with smoke, and sighting of signals was impeded. After several collisions in the tunnel, the climax came in January 1902, when a train ran past a red signal and collided with a stationary train, causing 15 deaths.

The New York Legislature thereupon passed an act prohibiting the use of steam south of the Harlem River after July 1, 1908. Since 1895 the Baltimore & Ohio had operated the Baltimore Belt line with electric traction including the Howard Street tunnel, so the legislation was not unreasonable, but it had the additional effect of forcing the issue of a major rebuilding of the terminal station.

The railroad adopted the third-rail system at 660V dc with under-contact current collection, and General Electric was appointed contractor. The great pioneer of electric traction, Frank Sprague, was one of the engineers to the project, and for commuter services on the electrified lines Sprague's multiple-unit system of control was applied to 180 cars. For haulage of long-distance trains, GE's engineer Asa Batchelder designed a 1-Do-1 locomotive of massive proportions, which incorporated a number of novelties of his devising. The principal feature of the design was the use of bi-polar motors with the armature mounted on the axle and the two poles hung from the locomotive frame. The continuous rating was 2,200hp, and the short-term rating of 3,000hp gave a starting tractive effort of 32,000lb (145kN), which enabled the locomotive to accelerate a train of 800 US tons at 1 mile per second per second (0.45m/s²), and maintain 60mph (97km/h) with 500 tons.

Right: Sixty years on, Class S No.133 is still good for service in NYC's Bronx yard, New York, in November 1966.

The locomotives were fitted with Sprague's multiple-unit control, so that they could operate in pairs with one driver, and they were the first locomotives to be so equipped.

The frames were outside the wheels to allow room for the armatures. The body had a central cab with a good all-round view, and with little more than the air compressors above floor level, the cab was very roomy. Other equipment was housed in the end hoods, including an oil-fired train-heating boiler.

The prototype locomotive, No.6000, was completed late in 1904, and was tested exhaustively on a 6-mile (9.6km) stretch of the NYC main line near the GE works at Schenectady, which was electrified for the purpose. The test included side-by-side comparative runs with the latest steam engines, in which the steam engine usually gained an early lead, but was then overtaken and handsomely beaten by the electric.

The success of No. 6000 was followed by orders for 34 similar locomotives, classified "T", which were delivered in 1906. One of them hauled the first electrically worked train from the partially completed Grand Central Station in September 1906. Full electric working was instituted in 1907, but unfortunately three days later a train hauled by two "T" class locomotives derailed on a curve, causing 23 deaths. Although the cause of the derailment was not established definitely, the locomotives were rebuilt with end bogies, thus becoming 2-Do-2, and they were reclassified "S".

In regular service the electric locomotives showed savings in operating and maintenance costs compared with steam varying between 12 per cent in transfer service to 27 per cent in road service. In 1908-09 a further 12 locomotives were delivered. The entire class survived through half-a-century of service, ending their days on switching and empty coaching stock working. No.6000 went to a museum after 61 years' service. Some of the class were still at work for Penn Central in the 1970s.

Left: The prototype 1-Do-1 electric locomotive, as built for the New York Central & Hudson River Railroad in 1904.

Class P 4-4-2

Origin: Denmark: Danish State Railways QSB), 1907. **Axle load:** 40,000lb (18t). **Cylinders, HP:** (2) 14$\frac{1}{4}$ x 23$\frac{1}{2}$in (360 x 600mm). **Cylinders, LP:** (2) 23$\frac{1}{2}$ x 23$\frac{1}{2}$in (600 x 600mm). **Driving wheels:** 78m (1,980mm). **Heating surface:** 2,072sq ft (192.5m²). **Superheater:** None. **Steam pressure:** 785psi (13kg/cm²). **Grate area:** 34.5sq ft (3.20m²). **Fuel:** 13,500lb (6t). **Water:** 4,650gall (5,550 US) (21m³). **Adhesive weight:** 80,000lb (36t). **Total weight:** 262,500lb (119t). **Length overall:** 60ft 9in (18,515mm).

It could be argued that flat Denmark was uninteresting locomotive country. Nevertheless, Danish steam engines were both distinctive and handsome – and none more so than the "P" class Atlantics, introduced in 1907. Nineteen came from the Hannoversche Maschinenbau AG of Hanover, Germany (Hanomag) and in 1910 a further 14 from Schwartzkopff of Berlin. The second batch was designated "P-2" and had larger cylinders (14$\frac{1}{2}$ and 23$\frac{1}{2}$ x 25$\frac{1}{4}$in – 360 and 600 x 640mm) and higher boiler pressure (213lb/sq in – 15kg/cm²)

They were four-cylinder compounds, with the low-pressure cylinders outside the frames and with a single piston-valve spindle serving both high and low pressure valves on each side. Heusinger's (Walschaert's) valve-gear was used, but out of sight inside the frames instead of in the usual position outside. All cylinders drove on the rear coupled axle, the inside ones were raised and their axis sloped downwards towards the rear so that the inside connecting rods would clear the leading coupled axle. Maximum permitted speed was 62mph (100km/h).

Visually the Danish 4-4-2s were very striking; the chimney was adorned with the Danish national colours – red, yellow, red – and there were such details as that near-complete circle described by the injector pipe on the side of the boiler before homing on to the clack valve.

Denmark was a pioneer in the adoption of diesel-electric traction and the first diesel-electric express trains went into service as long ago as 1935 They were known as the "Lyntog" Lightning trains and, whilst there was n threat to steam haulage of heavy expresses, the Atlantics found that the duties on fast light trains were affected. For this reason between 1943 an 1955 a number were converted to rather close-coupled 4-6-2s at DSB Copenhagen shops. The boiler was lengthened by adding an additional ring while the original wide firebox was replaced by a narrow one the same siz as that belonging to the class "R" 4-6-0s. The original cylinders and motic were retained but new wheels of lesser diameter (68in – 1,727mm) wer provided. The new engines were redesignated class "PR".

The forty-year long process of replacing Danish steam with diesel pow

came to fruition in the end, but a little before this time the last 4-4-2 was withdrawn. This was No 912 in 1968. Denmark is full of steam-lovers and their enthusiasm is recognised by the preservation of two of these superb 4-4-2s (Nos.917 and 931 - the latter is displayed in the museum at Odense) and one (No.908) as rebuilt into a Pacific.

Left: Pre-war view of a Danish State Railways' class "P" 4-4-2, showing the clean lines before air brakes.

Above and below: Danish State Railways class "P" 4-4-2. These striking machines were the mainstay of Danish passenger services from 1910 to 1935.

No. 9 4-6-0

Origin: United States: Nevada-California-Oregon Railroad (NCO), 1909. **Gauge:** 3ft 0in (914mm). **Tractive effort:** 17,800lb (8,076kg) **Axleload:** 23,966lb (10.9t). **Cylinders:** (2) 16 x 20in (406 x 508mm). **Driving wheels:** 44in (1,117mm). **Steam pressure:** 180psi (12.7kg/cm²). **Fuel (oil):** 2,400 US gall (9.1m³). **Water:** 5,000 US gall (18.9m³). **Adhesive weight:** 65,360lb (29.7t). **Total weight:** 165,150lb (74.9t). **Length overall:** 53ft 11in (16,433mm).

By reason of its chance survival, in its later years this small locomotive achieved considerable fame and, indeed, remains virtually intact to this day. Its origins lie in the 1880s when narrow-gauge disease spread across into the far west from Colorado. The route of the Nevada-California Oregon Railway was constructed between 1880 and 1912. It ran 235 miles (378km), generally northwards, from Reno, Nevada, via Alturas in California to Lakeview, Oregon, incorporating the earlier Nevada & Oregon and Nevada & California railroads as well as other lines. Most of the mileage came into the hands of Southern Pacific by purchase in 1926 and was quickly altered to standard gauge.

NCO No.9 was one of four small oil-burning 3ft gauge ten wheelers delivered by Baldwin between 1907 and 1911. They pursued a busy but uneventful existence for 15 years or so until their new owner widened the gauge. However, SP had another narrow-gauge line not far away which had been effectively in its hands since 1900. The Carson & Colorado Railway ran from Mound House, Nevada, nearly 300 miles (483km) southwards to Keeler, California and the best of the NCO engines were moved there after 1928. By 1943 all but the southernmost 70 miles of the C&C had been abandoned or widened.

The remaining narrow-gauge tracks ran through the remote Owens Valley which, though once prosperous, had become desolate following the abstraction of its water to supply the city of Los Angeles. Even so, once World War II was over, the fame of the slim gauge steam operations attracted hundreds of railfans who came both individually and by special excursions. Two of the 4-6-0s, Nos.8 and 9, plus an ex-NCO 2-8-0 (No.18) soldiered on down the years. No.9 was the last steam locomotive to run, not only on the narrow-gauge but on the whole Southern Pacific system. This was in 195? during a period of standby duty beginning in 1954 when a narrow-gauge diesel locomotive arrived. In 1960 the line was finally abandoned.

An unconventional feature of all three locomotives was the semicircular tender, partitioned for oil and water supplies. Otherwise Nos. 8 and 9 followed normal turn-of-the-century practice. No.18 (supplied to NCO in 1911) was more modern, having outside Walschaert valve gear. It says enough of the fame of the line that three of its steam locomotives have survived – No.8 at Carson City, Nevada, No.18 at Independence, California, and No.9 at Bishop, California.

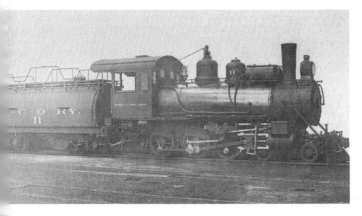

Above: NCO No.11 went to the Southern Pacific Coast Railroad in 1928, and then did war service in Hawaii.

Below: Unusual narrow-gauge survivor, former NCO 4-6-0 No.9 with its curious semi-circular tender.

Class 640 2-6-0

Origin: Italy: State Railways (FS), 1907. **Tractive effort:** 24,810lb (11,256kg). **Axle load:** 33,000lb (150 cylinders: (2) 21^1/4 x 27^1/2in (540 x 700mm). **Driving wheels:** 72^3/4in (1,850mm). **Heating surface:** 1,163sq ft (108m²). **Superheater:** 361sq ft (33 5m²). **Steam pressure:** 171 psi (12kg/cm²). **Grate area:** 26sq ft (2.42m²). **Fuel:** 13,300lb (6t). **Water:** 3,300gall (3,940US) (15m²). **Adhesive weight:** 98,000lb (44 5t). **Total weight:** 197,970lb (89.8t). **Overall length:** 54ft 2^3/8in (16,530mm).

When the Italian State Railways was formed in 1905, one of the first tasks undertaken by the Chief Mechanical Engineer of the new organisation, Guiseppe Zara, was the design of a standard range of locomotives. The class "640" 2-6-0 appeared in 1907 and the first batch was built by Schwartzkopff of Berlin. Production continued until 1930 and 188 in all were built. The majority were constructed by Italian builders. The class also included 15 rebuilt from class "630" two-cylinder compounds. Class "630" was originally intended as the standard class, but the advent of superheating meant that they were superseded by the "640".

The reason why 2-6-0s have not often hauled the world's great trains is that the two-wheel leading pony trucks have been suspect for a fast running locomotive. Most express engines have four wheel bogies, yet a 2-6-0, say, has a higher proportion of adhesive weight in relation to total weight. With

---

Class H4 4-6-2

Origin: United States: Great Northern Railway (GNR), 1909. **Gauge:** 4f 8^1/2in (1,435mm). **Tractive effort:** 35,690lb (16,193kg)*. **Axleload** 55,400lb (25.1t). **Cylinders:** (2) 23^1/2 x 30in (597 x 762mm). **Driving wheel:** 73in (1,854mm). **Heating surface:** 3,177sq ft (295m²). **Superheater:** 620sq ft (57.6m²). **Steam pressure:** 210psi (14.75kg/cm²). **Grate area:** 53.3sq ft (495m²). **Fuel:** 28,000 (12.7t). **Water:** 8,000 US ga (30.3m²). **Adhesive weight:** 151, 200lb (68.6t). **Total weight:** 383, 750l (174t). **Length overall:** 67ft 3in (20,498mm). *45,511lb (20,643kg) wit booster.

The Great Northern Railway was the northernmost US transcontinenta route to be completed between the Mississippi River and the Pacifi Ocean. The GN section of the route ran 1,829 miles (2,926km) from S Paul to Seattle, and before all-steel equipment arrived in the 1920s, 4-6-2 were adequate as haulage units, with some assistance in the mountain But it must not be thought that in the days when timber-bodied equipmer

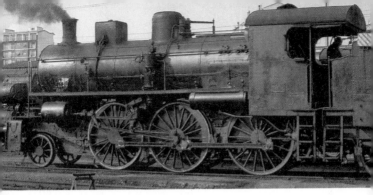

Above: Italian State Railways' class "640" 2-6-0 No.640.004 at Allessandria Locomotive Depot in June 1972.

the Zara truck, called in Italy the Italian bogie, the leading coupled wheels are allowed about 3/4in (20mm) of side-play in their axleboxes, spherical journals and bushes are provided on the crank pins and coupling rods so that the coupling of the wheels will still work properly when the wheels are not in line The leading pony wheels are mounted in a truck which also carries the leading axle, in such a way that both the pony wheels and the leading driving wheels play a part in guiding the locomotive round a curve. The 2-6-0s and 2-6-2s dominated steam express passenger operations in Italy ever after.

---

was used on the "Oriental Limited" the train lacked anything in the way of luxury for its riders. The best food in America was to be found on the trains and certainly the Great Northern was no exception to this rule.

Delivery from the Baldwin Locomotive Works in 1909 of 20 new superheated "H4" class Pacifics coincided with running the "Oriental Limited" through from Chicago via the Burlington's route to St Paul. A further 25 came from Lima in 1913. Superheating was soon to become universal and this class was an early example of the technique. The arrangement used involved elements in the smokebox rather than in flue tubes and so was less efficient but still very creditable. The "H4s" burnt coal but some were later converted to oil-burning.

So all the elements had come together of the style of steam locomotive that would sweep the world. Cast frames, cylinders integral with the smokebox saddle, wide firebox, superheater, compensated springing with three point suspension, inside-admission piston valves and Walschaert valve gear proved an unbeatable combination. Steam locomotives recently in production in China are, as regards principles of design, exact copies.

Below: GNR received Class "H4"s between 1909 and 1913.

de Glehn Atlantic 4-4-2

Origin: France: Northern Railway, 1910. **Axle load:** 39,231lb (17.8t) **Cylinders, HP:** (2) 13^1/2 x 25^1/4in (340 x 640mm). **Cylinders, LP:** (2) 22 × 25^1/4in (560 x 640mm). **Driving wheels:** 80^1/4in (2,040mm). **Heating surface:** 1,485sq ft (138m^2). **Superheater:** 420sq ft (39m^2). **Steam pressure:** 228psi (16kg/cm^2). **Grate area:** 33.4sq ft (2.75m^2). **Fuel:** 15,000lb (7t). **Water:** 5,070gall (6,080 US) (23m^3). **Adhesive weight:** 78,500lb (35.6t) **Total weight:** 264,500lb (120t). **Overall length:** 59ft 10^1/2in (18,247mm).

In spite of his name – partly French and partly German – Alfred de Glehn was born an Englishman, yet he rose to be Director of Engineering of the Société Alsacienne de Constructions Mécaniques at Mulhouse in the 1870s while still under 30. Together with Gaston du Bousquet of the Northern Railway of France he developed a system of compounding for steam locomotives which stood the test of time. In France a majority of twentieth-century express passenger locomotives were de Glehn compounds.

One major factor in its success was the fact that French locomotive drivers were not promoted from firemen but instead were trained as mechanics. In fact, the actual word used was *mechanicien*. This meant that the man in charge on the footplate could be expected to know the reasons for the complexities of a compound's controls and act accordingly to get the best results.

The de Glehn system was certainly complicated from the driver's point of view – there were *two* throttles and *two* sets of reversing gear, as well as intercepting valves, to control the working. The locomotives could be set to work in five modes as shown in table 1.

In the A position of the intercepting valve, the exhaust from the HP cylinders was delivered to the receiver and steam chest of the LP cylinders. A safety valve set to blow off at 85lb/sq in (6kg/cm^2) in this vessel limited the pressure applied on the LP side.

In the B position, this connection was closed and the HP exhaust sent direct to the blast pipe. Settings IV and V were used only to move the engine under light load, or in an emergency if some problem developed in the LP or HP engines respectively. Setting III could boost the pressure on the LP side up to the 85lb/sq in (6kg/cm^2) to which the receiver safety valve was set.

Of course in addition to choosing the correct setting, it was necessary to select the correct combination of cut-offs by adjusting the two independent reversing gears. With all these alternatives to think of, the move from running a simple engine to driving a compound could be likened to moving up from strumming a guitar to conducting a whole orchestra!

Du Bousquet and de Glehn began their co-operation in connection with some very successful compound 4-4-0s produced during the 1890s, but their lasting place in the hall of fame was assured when Northern Railway Atlantic No.2.641 was exhibited at the Paris Exhibition of 1900. Outside bearings on the leading bogie and inside ones on the trailing wheels gave

TABLE I

Mode	Purpose	Nominal tractive effort developed	
I	Normal	16,171lb	(7,337kg)
II	Starting	24,069lb	(10,921kg)
III	Boost	19,194lb	(8,709kg)
IV	LP Isolated	11,125lb	(5,048kg)
V	HP Isolated	12,944lb	(5,873kg)

TABLE II

Mode	HP Throttle	LP Throttle	Intercepting Valves
I	Open	Shut	A
II	Open	Shut	B
III	Open	Open	A
V	Shut	Open	B

TABLE III

Country	Railway	Number ordered
France	Eastern Railway	2
France	Paris-Orleans	14
France	Midi Railway	34
France	French State Railway	9
Britain	Great Western Railway	3
Prussia	Royal Union Railway	79
USA	Pennsylvania BR	1
Egypt	State Railways	10

Below: De Glehn four-cylinder compound 4-4-2 of the Northern Railway of France complete with more modern bogie tender.

an unusual look, but the 4-4-2 was certainly a good-looking example of the locomotive builders' art and the engine was the first of a class of 32 built for the Northern Railway.

The inside LP cylinders were in line with the front bogie wheels and drove the leading coupled axle whereas the outside HP pair were in the familiar position above the rear bogie wheels and drove the rear pair of coupled wheels. The arrangement had a slight objection in that the both sets of cylinders were attached to the frames at a point where the frames were weakened by a circular cut-out to clear the bogie wheels, but otherwise the only difficulty was the servicing and repair of two complete sets of mechanism in the limited space between the frames. Both bogie and six-wheel tenders were used.

In spite of these drawbacks (which could be lived with) the performances of the Atlantics, on such trains as the boat trains between Paris and Calais on some of the hardest schedules in the world, were remarkable. The economy in coal consumption was considerable and the money so saved was welcome, but this was not the only advantage. The Atlantic had begun to approach the point where the performance was limited not by the capacity of the locomotive, but by the capacity of the man who shovels in the coal. It follows that a locomotive which had better thermal efficiency could also produce more power. And so it proved; trains of 270 tons weight hauled by a 4-4-2 were expected, say, to climb the 1 in 200 (0.5per cent) incline 13 miles long between St. Denis and Survilliers at an average speed above 62.5mph (100km/h).

Orders followed for similar machines, not only from all over France but also from many foreign countries. The tally was as shown in table III.

Some of these were of a slightly enlarged design and others differed quite markedly in details of layout, but all followed the same basic principles. The French railway systems went on to build many classes of 4-6-0, 2-8-2, 4-6-2, 4-8-2 and other types to this basic compound design, while the Great Western Railway of England based all their future express passenger designs on the same mechanical layout, but with four simple cylinders.

As elsewhere in the world, all-steel carriages and more spacious

Above: Nord de Glehn 4-4-2 No.2.670 as restored for the National Railway Museum du Mulhouse, France.

accommodation raised train weights to a point where a minimum of six coupled wheels were required, so the de Glehn 4-4-2s vanished between the wars. Northern Railway No.2.670 has survived and is displayed superbly restored in the National Railway Museum at its own city of origin, Mulhouse in Alsace.

Left: Northern Railway of France de Glehn 4-4-2 No. 2.674. These four-cylinder compounds were outstanding.

BESA Class 4-6-0

Origin: India: Indian Railways, 1905. **Tractive effort:** 22,590lb (10,250kg). **Axle load:** 39,500lb (18t). **Cylinders:** (2) 20^1/2 x 26in (521 x 660mm). **Driving wheels:** 74in (1,880mm). **Heating surface:** 1,476sq ft (137m^2). **Superheater:** 352sq ft (32.7m^2). **Steam pressure:** 180lb/sq in (12.7kg/cm^2). **Grate area:** 32sq ft (3.0m^2). **Fuel:** 16,800lb (7^1/2t). **Water:** 4,000gall (4,800 US) (18m^3). **Adhesive weight:** 118,000lb (54t). **Total weight:** 273,000lb (124t). **Length overall:** 62ft 3^1/4in (18,980mm). (These dimensions refer to later examples with Walschaert's valve gear, outside valves and superheater.

More British than anything that ran in Britain, this archetypal Mail Engine gave over 75 years of service. This is the British Engineering Standards Association "Heavy Passenger" 4-6-0, introduced in 1905.

The railways of India were developed mainly by private enterprise under a concession system whereby the then British Government of India guaranteed a modest return on investment in return for a measure of control, as well as eventual ownership. The government felt that one of their perquisites was to set standards and, having made rather a mess of the gauge question, made up for it with an excellent job of setting out a range of standard designs for locomotives.

The decision to do this was the result of representations made by the British locomotive manufacturers. At a time when there was an explosion of demand for steam locomotives, they found it difficult to cope efficiently with orders for small batches of similar locomotives which differed only in minor detail.

For the broad (5ft 6in-1676min) gauge there was a "Standard Passenger" 4-4-0, a "Standard Goods" 0-6-0, a "Heavy Goods" 2-8-0 and, finally, a "Heavy Passenger" 4-6-0, all of which were successful enough to be still in use 75 years after the designs were conceived. The "Heavy Passenger" 4-6-0s were still being supplied in 1950, well after independence, while the 4-4-0s operate still in Pakistan.

State-owned railways such as the North Western obeyed without question, but some of the others were slower to abrogate their independence in such a sensitive matter as locomotive design. However, the qualities of the standard product in due time spoke for themselves. Of course, it was still possible to specify alternatives in the way of accessories, even if one had to accept the fundamental features of the design.

The first BESA 4-6-0s were solid hunks of sound engineering, bigger when introduced than almost anything that ran in the same country. Their closest relations at home seem to have been some 4-6-0s built in 1903 for the

Below: Some of the Indian Railways' surviving "BESA" 4-6-0s have bogie tenders instead of the six-wheel variety originally provided.

Glasgow & South Western Railway by the North British Locomotive Co. of Glasgow. NBL were to supply the first standard 4-6-0s to India.

Down the years many more were built there and at the Vulcan Foundry at Newton-le-Willows as well as by Robert Stephenson & Co. A few came from Kitson of Leeds and, shortly after World War I, some were made by William Beardmore of Glasgow, better known for marine engineering than for locomotives. Early examples were non-superheated with outside cylinders, inside slide-valves and Stephenson's valve gear but, early on, outside Walschaert's gear, outside piston valves and superheaters were adopted. The boilers had Belpaire pattern fireboxes. Between the wars a few small batches were turned out with poppet valves. Some later examples had bogie tenders instead of six-wheeled.

When the all-India locomotive numbering system was adopted in 1957 there were 387 broad-gauge 4-6-0s still running in India. More existed in Pakistan, both East (now Bangladesh) and West. All but a very few were either built to the BESA design or close to it. The new running numbers ran from 24,000 to 24,470; the few gaps were for some 4-4-2s and a few non standard 4-6-2s and 4-6-0s.

The BESA 4-6-0s stayed in top-line work even after their successors, the India Railway Standard (IRS), XA and XB 4-6-2s had arrived in the mid 1920s, because of unsatisfactory qualities amongst the new arrivals. The great success of the BESA designs seems to lie in the fact that they were taken from British practice as it existed, with the difference that both average and maximum speeds in India were 25 per cent lower than at home while loads were about the same. This more than compensated for rougher working conditions; one notes, for example, that in dusty areas, locomotives ran hot so frequently that pipes were provided to trickle cold water on to vulnerable bearings! One factor in the good performance offered by the older engines lay in the extra $9\frac{1}{2}$in (240mm) of space available for the firegrate between the wheels compared with similar engines in Britain, because of the broad gauge track.

Even so, the coming of the post-war 4-6-2s as well as diesels and electrics did spell out the beginning of the end for the BESA 4-6-0s. By 1980 the number in use had fallen to about 100, but they could still be found at work on passenger trains. And if the importance of trains can be measured by the amount of humanity packed into or clinging on to them, then those in question are important indeed. However, they are a far cry from the days when the 'Imperial Indian Mail', hauled by one of these locomotives, provided luxury accommodation for 32 persons only – and their bearers (servants), of course – for the 1,230 mile (1,968km) journey from Bombay to Calcutta.

Below: The condition of 4-6-0 No.24280, supplied by the North British Loco Co. in 1915, belies its age, approaching 70 years.

Class P8 4-6-0

Origin: Germany: Royal Prussian Union Railway (KPEV), 1906. **Tractive effort:** 26,760lb (12,140kg). **Axle load:** 39,000lb (17.75t). **Cylinders:** (2) 22.6in x 24.8m (575 x 630mm). **Driving wheels:** 68.9in (1,750mm). **Heating surface:** 1,542sq ft (143.3m²). **Superheater:** 634sq ft (58.9m²). **Steam pressure:** 170.6psi (12kg/cm²). **Grate area:** 27.8sq ft (2.58m²). **Fuel:** 11,000lb (5.0t). **Water:** 4,700gall (5,700 US) (215m³). **Adhesive weight:** 114,000lb (52t). **Total weight:** 172,500lb (78.50. **Length overall:** 61ft 0in (18,592mm).

At the beginning of the century the Prussian state railways were faced with a problem which other railways were to meet in the next ten years – was the newly invented superheater an alternative to, or an adjunct to compounding? Since 1884 the railway had built both simple and compound locomotives, compounds predominating for express passenger work and simples for secondary passenger work. Construction of non-superheated compounds continued until 1911, but in the meantime some other new types had been introduced with superheaters and simple expansion. One of these was a mixed-traffic 2-6-0, Class "P6", of which 272 were built between 1903 and 1910. However, the 63in (1,600mm) driving wheels of these engines were found to be too small for the speeds that had been intended, and there were difficulties with weight distribution.

In 1906 an enlarged design, a 4-6-0 with wheels of 69in (1,750mm) was introduced. It was originally envisaged that this new engine would have a permissible speed of 68mph (110km/h), and that it could undertake express passenger work on the hilly parts of the system. Unfortunately the first engines of the type proved to be unreliable and unpopular, and suffered many failures in service.

The solution to the problems included a reduction in the cylinder diameter and adjustments to the weight distribution between the axles, but it was also decided that the motion and valve gear was unsuitable for speeds in excess of 62mph (100km/h), and the engines were rated as secondary passenger and mixed traffic engines, with the classification "P8". Thus a locomotive which originally had been intended for express passenger work on a limited part of the Prussian system became the most widely used and popular mixed-traffic engine ever built, serving eventually over much of Europe

Like many of the most successful and popular steam engines, the "P8"

Below: In due time the "P8" class 4-6-0s of the Prussian railways became class "38" of The German State (now Federal) Railways whose smart red-and-black colours are depicted here.

Above: Class "38" 4-6-0 No.38.3635 at the head of a German Federal Railways local train at Lippstadt.

was simple in layout, and initially at least, elegant in outline. The round-topped boiler, with a long narrow firebox, was well proportioned, and although at least two variants of boiler were fitted in due course, the basic shape was not changed. In addition to Dr Schmidt's superheater, the engines also had long-travel piston valves, which he recommended as an adjunct to his superheater. The combination of superheater and piston valves, with a well-proportioned Walschaert's valve gear, gave the engines an efficiency which approached the highest that was ever to be attained with simple expansion. Their load rating was 700 tonnes on the level at 50mph (80km/h) and 300 tonnes on 1 in 100 (1 per cent) at 31mph (50km/h).

Once the initial snags had been cleared from the "P8", it was built in large numbers, its axle load permitting its use over much of the Prussian system. It was also built in small numbers for the state railways of Oldenburg, Mecklenburg and Baden as well as for export. Although nominally a secondary passenger engine, it took a full share in express passenger work on which speed was limited to 62mph (100km/h).

At the end of World War I, by which time 2,350 "P8"s had been built for the KPEV, Germany was required to hand over large numbers of locomotives as reparations, and 628 "P8"s were allocated to other countries. The Belgian railways had been particularly badly affected, and they received 2,000 locomotives, of which 168 were "P8"s. These engines

survived a second invasion by the Germans, and, adorned with an elegant lipped chimney, they lasted until the end of steam in that country in 1966.

The loss of "P8"s was partly made good by building more of them, the last being completed in 1928. On the German State Railway the engines became class 38. Under the German State ownership and later there was much reboilering of the engines, but the alterations which affected their appearance were the fitting of full-depth smoke deflectors, feedwater heaters and other external fittings.

World War II saw the "P8"s spreading into Eastern Europe as the Germans moved east, and this resulted in an even wider distribution than before. They worked in Czechoslovakia, Greece, Jugoslavia, Poland, Roumania and Russia, and many of them remained in those countries. In several countries they were modified externally in accordance with national practice, but the basic design was rarely altered. Eventually a total of 3,438 "P8"s were built in Germany, and about 500 in other countries. In addition the Polish railways, which acquired a large number of genuine "P8"s, built 190 engines in which a larger boiler, with wide firebox, was mounted on a "P8" chassis.

After World War II a nominal total of 2,803 "P8"s remained in Germany, but many of them were unserviceable. On the formation of the DB and DR (in West and East Germany respectively) the engines were divided between the two systems. On both railways the full-depth smoke deflectors were mostly replaced by the post-war variety. Although difficulties with steaming had never been a weakness of the "P8" class, some of the DR engines were fitted with Giesl exhausts.

Two of the DB engines were converted to quasi tank engines by coupling them to four-wheeled tenders by a coupling which was designed to permit running in both directions. In addition a number of engines were equipped for push-and-pull working with the original tenders. However, the spread of dieselization made rapid inroads into the "P8" class, and by 1968 the total was down to 73, mostly working south of Stuttgart. The rate of withdrawal then slowed, and the last engine survived until January 1975, three years after the last of them on DR had been withdrawn. However, engines of the class remained at work in other countries, and several were still at work in

Above: Royal Prussian Union, "P8" class 4-6-0 in its latter days as class"38"on the German Federal Railways.

Poland and Roumania in 1979, 73 years after the introduction of the class. Eight are preserved at various sites in Germany

It is interesting to note that, although the "T8" was built to the Continental loading gauge, the general layout and dimensions were very similar to some 1,500 British 4-6-0s, although the ancestry of the British engines was independent of that of the German ones. The valve events of the "P8" were almost identical with those of the LMS Class 5 Stanier 4-6-0 "Black Fives".

Left: "P8"class 4-6-0 of Prussian design but hauling behind it a train belonging to the Roumanian State.

DD1 2-B+B-2

Origin: United States: Pennsylvania Railroad (PRR), 1909. **Type:** Electric passenger locomotive. **Gauge:** 4ft 8¹/₂in (1,435mm). **Propulsion:** Direct current at 600V fed via outside third rail (or by overhead conductors and miniature pantographs at places where third rail was impractical) to two 1,065hp (795kW) motors, each driving two main axles by means of a jackshaft and connecting rods. **Weight:** 199,000lb (90.2t) adhesive, 319,000lb (145t) total. **Max. axleload:** 50,750lb (23t). **Overall length:** 64ft 11in (19,787mm). **Tractive effort:** 49,400lb (220kN). **Max. speed:** 80mph (129km/h).

The Pennsylvania Railroad gained entry to New York City and its new Pennsylvania Station by single-track tunnels, two under the Hudson River and four under the East River, and for the operation of these tunnels electrification was essential. The third-rail system at 650V was chosen, and between 1903 and 1905 three experimental four-axle locomotives were built, two B-Bs at the Pennsy's Altoona shops and a 2-B by Baldwin. The B-Bs had a separate motor for each axle, whilst the 2-B had a single 2,000hp (2,680kW) motor mounted on the main frame midway between the coupled axles. The motors of both types of locomotive drove through quills, an early version of the drive which was to be used a quarter of a century later on the "GG1" electrics.

Test were made to determine the forces exerted on the rails by the two types of locomotive and by the most recent steam designs, and it was found that the 2-B, with its higher centre of gravity, exerted less than half the force of the B-B, with its low-slung motors. However, the force due to the 2-B was still twice as great as that from the heaviest steam engine. The next two electric locomotives therefore had the 2-B wheel arrangement, but to give the required power each one comprised two units permanently coupled back-to-back, giving the combined wheel arrangement 2-B-B-2. The important change in design from the experimental locomotive was in the drive to the axles, which incorporated a jackshaft mounted in bearings in the main frame of the locomotive, with connecting rods from the motor to the jackshaft and from the jackshaft to the driving wheels. The technical problems with the quill drive were left for solution at a later date.

With 72in (1,829mm) driving wheels, each half of the unit resembled the chassis of an express 4-4-0 steam locomotive. This similarity to steam design was apparent in a number of early electric engines, for example in Prussia, but unusually for such designs the Pennsylvania's was highly successful. It was capable of 80mph (129km/h), and there was no

appreciable clanking of the rods. Maintenance costs were very low, and were helped by the design of the body. The whole casing could be removed in one unit to give access to the motors and control equipment. This feature was repeated in all subsequent PRR electric designs. A small pantograph was fitted to allow overhead current collection on complicated trackwork.

The first two rod-drive units appeared in 1909-10, the individual half-units being numbered from 3996 to 3999. They were followed in 1910-11 by a further 31, numbered from 3932 to 3949 and from 3952 to 3995. The Pennsylvania classified its steam locomotives by a letter, denoting the wheel arrangement, followed by a serial number, letter "D" denoted 4-4-0. For electrics the road used the same system, the letter being doubled when appropriate, so that the 2-B+B-2, being a double 4-4-0, was a DD. The main production batch of 31 units was classified "DD1", and the two prototypes "odd DD".

The Pennsylvania Station project required seven years, from 1903 to 1910, for its execution, and electrification then extended from Manhattan Transfer, near Newark, New Jersey, to the carriage yards at Sunnyside, Long Island, a total of 13.4 route miles (21.5km). At Manhattan Transfer the change was made to or from steam for the 8.8 miles (14.2km) between there and Pennsylvania Station. The heaviest gradient on the descent to the tunnels was 1-in-52 (1.93 per cent).

The "DD" locomotives worked all the express passenger services on this section of line until 1924 when newer types began to appear, but they continued to share the work until 1933 when overhead electrification reached Manhattan Transfer from Trenton, and the remaining section into Pennsylvania Station was converted to overhead. Third-rail current collection was retained between Pennsylvania Station and Sunnyside, because the Long Island Rail Road used this system.

After 1933 "DDs" continued to work empty trains between Pennsylvania Station and Sunnyside for many years. After the arrival of newer power in 1924, 23 of the "DD1s" were transferred to the Long Island Rail Road, and these remained in service until 1949-51.

The "DDs" were a landmark in electric locomotive design, with exceptionally high power and unusual reliability for their day, but at the same time their design was conservative. Simplicity of design and the flexibility of the "double 4-4-0" chassis contributed greatly to their success.

Below: Class DD1 electric loco for Pennsylvania Station-to-Manhattan Transfer traffic.

4500 Class 4-6-2

Origin: France: Paris-Orleans Railway (P-O), 1907. **Axle load:** 39,000lb (17.5t). **Cylinders, HP:** (2) 16.5 x 25.6in (420 x 650mm). **Cylinders, LP:** (2) 25.2 x 25.6in (640 x 650mm). **Driving wheels:** 743/4in (1,900mm). **Heating surface:** 2,100sq ft (195m²). **Superheater:** 684sq ft (63.5m²). **Steam pressure:** 232psi (16kg/cm²). **Grate area:** 46sq ft (4.27m²). **Fuel:** 13,500lb (6t). **Water:** 4,400gall (5,280US) (20m³). **Adhesive weight:** 117,000lb (53t) **Total weight:** 301,000lb (136.5t). **Overall length:** 68ft 2¹/₂in (20,790mm).

(These dimensions refer to the superheated version of the class before rebuilding by Chapelon.)

If the number of express passenger locomotives to be included in this book was reduced to a single one then this locomotive might well be the choice It was by a short head the first Pacific to *run* in Europe (not the first to be built – some were built in Britain for Malaya earlier the same year) and later became not only the most powerful but also the most efficient 4-6-2 ever to run in Europe. It was also certainly the most technically advanced Pacific but also, of course, somewhat complex.

One hundred "4500" Pacifics were built between 1907 and 1910 mostly by French builders but rather strangely including a batch of 30 (Nos.4541-70) by the American Locomotive Co of Schenectady, USA. There were also another 90 of class "3500" which were identical except for wheels 4in (100mm) smaller in diameter. The "3500"s were constructed between 1909 and 1918.

All these Paris-Orleans 4-6-2s were four-cylinder de Glehn compounds. An interesting feature was the trapezoidal grate which was wide at the back in the usual manner of Pacific grates. At the front, however, it was narrow and sat between the frames. Later, examples were delivered with superheaters and some had them fitted later. The high-pressure cylinders had piston valves while the low-pressure ones had balanced slide valves. They were competent but not specially remarkable machines in those days, capable of cylinder horsepowers of around 2000.

In the 1920s the replacement of wooden carriages by steel began to show up the inadequacies of the Pacifics, yet a commitment to electrification absorbed totally any resources there might have been for new construction.

Below: Paris-Orleans Railway 4-6-2 No.4546 shown as restored to original condition for display at the French National Railway Museum at Mulhouse, Alsace.

Right: French National Railways 4-6-2 No.231E23, as rebuilt by Chapelon from the original 1907 Paris-Orleans Railway design.

A young man called André Chapelon, who had an appointment as development engineer on the Paris-Orleans Railway, proposed a drastic rebuilding and in 1926, persuaded his superiors – against their better judgement – to put the work in hand in accordance with his ideas. Changes in the administration meant further patient persuasion but eventually in 1929 the transformed No.3566 took the road. A new era in steam traction had begun; there was a 25 per cent increase in power production for the same amount of steam, while the boiler improvements which made more steam available took the possible cylinder horsepower up to 3,700, an 85 per cent increase over the originals.

Chapelon achieved this apparent miracle after a careful analysis of the shortcomings of the original design. He considered the whole process of producing steam power from cold water to exhaust steam and took the following measures to improve it:
(a) Pre-heating the feed-water with waste heat from the exhaust.
(b) Provision of extra heating surface in the firebox, using flattened vertical ducts known as thermic syphons.
(c) Provision of a superheater 24 per cent larger in size and of a more efficient (but also more complicated) design.
(d) Much larger steam pipes to improve steam flow.
(e) Poppet valves to give quicker and larger openings to steam and exhaust, replacing the existing high-pressure piston valves and low-pressure slide-valves.
(f) An improved exhaust system giving greater draught with less back pressure. This took the form of a double chimney.

The existing Walschaert's valve gears were retained to work the oscillating camshafts of the poppet valves.

The P-O announced that No.3566 had hauled 567 tons from Poitiers to Angoulême, 70.1 miles (113km), start-to-stop at an average speed of 67.3mph (107.7km/h); a 1 in 200 (0.5 per cent) gradient was climbed at 77.5mph (124km/h). This was a performance unprecedented in France and caused a sensation in the world of locomotive engineering.

To cover requirements on the P-O, thirty-one further "3500" 4-6-2s were rebuilt. As electrification proceeded, some of the originals became surplus, and other railways in France could not wait to get their hands on these miracle locomotives. Twenty were rebuilt for the Northern Railway and later 23 for the Eastern. Later on a further 20 were built new for the Northern.

In 1932, sixteen further locomotives of the "3500" series were given a rather less drastic rebuilding, in which poppet valves were not provided, but instead a form of twin piston valve head was used. This gave double the amount of port opening for a given amount of movement and was known as the Willoteaux valve after its inventor, an assistant of Chapelon's.

During the same year one of the remaining unsuperheated "4500" class 4-6-2s was rebuilt into a 4-8-0 at Tours. The intention was to provide a locomotive with one-third more adhesive weight, more suitable for the gradients of the line to Toulouse, altogether steeper than those en route to Bordeaux. A different boiler was needed, having a narrow firebox to fit between the rear driving wheels and one based on those carried by the Northern 4-6-2s was used.

Otherwise the recipe was as before, except that some improvement in detail enabled 4,000 cylinder hp to be developed. Eleven more were rebuilt in 1934 and in 1940 a further twenty-five "4500" were rebuilt for the PLM (now South-Eastern Region SNCF) main line, designated class "240P". This time a mechanical stoker was fitted.

Dimensions etc. of these engines which differed substantially from the originals were as follows:

Axle load: 44,000lb (20t). **Cylinders LP:** (2) 25.2 x 27.2in (650 x 690mm). **Heating surface:** 2,290sq ft (213m²). **Superheater:** 733sq ft (68m²). **Steam pressure:** 290psi (20.4kg/cm²). **Grate area:** 40sq ft (3.75m³). **Fuel:** 26,500lb (12t). **Water:** 7,500gall (9,000US) (34m³). **Adhesive weight:** 177,500lb (80.5t).

The sort of achievement that these 4-8-0s were capable of included the surmounting of Blaisy-Bas summit between Paris and Dijon with 787 tonnes at 59mph (94¹/₂km/h) minimum after several miles at 1 in 125 (0.8 per cent). During the war the "240P" had to manage 28 coaches and could reach 53mph (85km/h) on the level with this load. Alas, after the Paris-Lyons line was electrified in 1952, proposals to use these engines elsewhere in France foundered, for reasons which have never been adequately explained.

Above: Calais Maritime Station. Chapelon 4-6-2 No.231E39 has just arrived from Paris with the "Golden Arrow" express. The connecting steamer is on the right.

In the 1960s the remaining Pacifics of Paris-Orleans design had become concentrated – much to the delight of their many British admirers – at Calais. Their effortless performances with heavy boat trains up, say, the 1 in 125 (0.8 per cent) climb to Caffiers between Calais and Boulogne will long remain in the memory.

In 1956 some tests were made of the behaviour of electric locomotive pantograph current collectors at high speeds, and 110.6mph (177km/h) was

reached by 231E19 pushing an equivalent of 220 tons. This was the highest speed achieved by these engines.

Against this was the sad fact that, economical as the Chapelons were in respect of coal consumption, in overall terms they were more expensive to run than the fleet of simple rugged 2-8-2s – the 141R class-supplied from North America at the end of World War II. These could also manage, say, 850 tons on a 1 in 125 (0.8 per cent) gradient at over 52mph (84km/h), even if you would not describe the performance as effortless. So in the end at Calais as elsewhere in France, simple engines out-lasted even these superb compounds. No.231E22 is displayed at the Mulhouse Museum and No.231E41 is being restored at St Pierre-les-Corps. Unrebuilt Paris-Orleans No.4546 is also preserved.

Left: A Paris–Orleans 4-6-2 rebuilt into a 4-8-0 (No.240P2) for the Paris-Lyons Mediterranean main line in 1940.

Fairlie 0-6-6-0

Origin: Mexico: Mexican Railway (FCM), 1911. **Tractive effort:** 58,493lb (26,533kg). **Axle load:** 46,000lb (21t). **Cylinders:** (4) 19 x 25in (483 x 635mm). **Driving wheels:** 48in (1,219mm). **Heating surface:** 2,924sq f (272mm²). **Steam pressure:** 183psi (12.9kg/cm²). **Grate area:** 47.7sq f (4.43m²). **Fuel:** 20,000lb (9t). **Water:** 3,500 gall (4,200 US) (16m³). **Adhesive weight:** 276,000lb (125t). **Total weight:** 276,000lb (125t). **Length overall** 50ft 7³/₄in (15,435mm).

The Mexican Railway ran 264 miles (426km) from the port of Vera Cruz or the Atlantic Ocean to Mexico City, at an altitude of 7,349ft (2,240m). The summit of the route is at Acocotla, 8,320ft (2,536m), but in 108 miles (174 km) the line climbs to 8,050ft at Esperaza. The maximum gradient is a hideous 1 in 22 (4.5 per cent) and the sharpest curve is 325ft radius or 17¹/₂ degrees. Before electrification came in 1923, this superbly scenic but very difficult railway had not unexpectedly something rather special in the way of motive power.

The "Fairlie" articulated locomotive was invented by an English engineer called Robert Fairlie in 1864 and foreshadowed the majority of locomotives (other than steam) in service today by having a generator for the working fluid – steam in Fairlie's case, electricity in modern times – as part of the locomotive body; the body being carried on two power bogies which provided the traction. All the axles were therefore driven, so the total weight was available for adhesion, yet the whole vehicle remained extremely flexible. The arrangement made the locomotive an excellent proposition for sharply curved steeply graded mountain lines. Even so, "Fairlies" were never as popular as the "Garratt" or "Mallet" articulated locomotive types and their application for this British owned Mexican line was certainly their greatest both as regard size of individual locomotives and their success as haulage units.

The first "Fairlie" came to Mexico in 1871 and by 1911, a total of 49 had been delivered, of which 18 were still in service in 1923 when electrification made them finally redundant. The last and largest of them was a batch of three supplied by Vulcan Foundry in 1911, carrying running numbers 183 to 185. The advantage of the "Fairlie" is best summed up by comparison with a typical British main-line locomotive of the day. Compare, for example, these Mexican Railway locomotives with a LNWR type. For a penalty of 29 per cent in weight and 5 per cent in axleload, one obtained an 114 per cent

increase in grate area, 220 per cent more adhesive weight and 190 per cent more tractive effort. The "Fairlie"s were the most powerful locomotives built in Britain up to this time.

Although the speeds of trains on the Mexican Railway's inclines were severely restricted by traction limitations going up, and to 8mph (13km/h) for safety reasons coming down, the "Fairlie"s had excellent riding and tracking qualities at high speeds. This was inadvertently discovered on one or two occasions when runaways occurred; speeds estimated at up to 70mph (113km/h) were achieved on sharp curves without derailment. The motion of these locomotives was quite conventional, with outside piston valve cylinders and Walschaert's valve gear. On the other hand the double boilers were very unusual indeed. The boiler barrels at both ends were nearly similar, but the firebox in the centre was common to both barrels. One big dome in the usual position for one half of the boiler (normally the uphill end) collected the steam for all four cylinders.

The expense involved in this double boiler was almost certainly the main reason why the "double Fairlie" articulated locomotive was never widely used. It is true there were some problems with the flexible pipes and joints which fed the steam from the boiler to the powered bogies, but experience and the improvement of details would have solved them. In fact this is just what has happened on the one railway left in the world that has "double-Fairlie" steam locomotives still in use, the Festiniog Railway in North Wales. Their 40 ton 0-4-4-0 tanks, are, however, a far cry from the 123-ton Mexican monsters.

"Single Fairlie"s, however, went into quite extensive use. These locomotives had a normal boiler, a leading power bogie and a trailing un-powered bogie behind the firebox. An ability to negotiate absurdly sharp curves was the property that appealed and many (under various names, for Fairlie's patent was not recognised in the USA) were used on urban railways, particularly elevated lines which had to negotiate city street corners. But "single Fairlies" were only, as it were, half of what was a good idea.

Below: A Mexican Railways "Fairlie" locomotive of the batch supplied by the Vulcan Foundry in 1911.

Class S 2-6-2

Origin: Russia: Ministry of Ways of Communication, 1911. **Tractive effort:** 30,092lb (13,653kg). **Axle load:** see text. **Cylinders:** (2) 22$\frac{1}{2}$ x 27$\frac{1}{2}$in (575 x 700mm). **Driving wheels:** 72$\frac{3}{4}$in (1,850mm). **Heating surface:** 2,131sq ft (198m^2). **Superheater:** 958sq ft (89m^2). **Steam pressure:** 185psi (13kg/cm^2). **Grate area:** 51sq ft (4.72m^2). **Fuel:** 40,000lb (18t). **Water:** 5,000gall (6,000 US) (23m^3). **Adhesive weight:** see text. **Total weight:** 370,500lb (168t). **Overall length:** 77ft 10$\frac{1}{2}$in (23,738mm).

This handsome design of express passenger locomotive either was just or was just not the most numerous in the world. Construction continued over a period of 40 years, usage over more than 60 and certainly its numbers were the largest in the hands of one administration. Compared with British locomotives, Russian ones can be four feet (1,200mm) higher and two feet (600mm) wider, in terms of weight, though, in steam days locomotive axles could be loaded at most with two tons less each. So there was no temptation towards (or even the possibility of) filling the huge space available with inaccessible ironmongery.

In both Czarist and Communist Russia, steam locomotive design was in the hands of university professors and they studied and tried out many fascinating theoretical possibilities – more thoroughly, perhaps, than elsewhere. But when it came to actual usage out on the road, then these learned gentlemen seemed always to reach the conclusion that Old Geordie (Stephenson) had got it right and the simplest answer was the best.

Another characteristic in which the old regime was far ahead of its time was standardisation; this continued as did locomotive classification, without even a wriggle, over that great watershed in human history the Russian Revolution. In 1955, Britain had, for example, some 20 classes of express passenger locomotives ten or more strong, while the Soviet Union had a mere four; this out of a fleet intended for such traffic approximately the same in number. These class "S" (written "C" in Russian script) 2-6-2s were a standard design ordered by the Ministry of Ways of Communication for general usage amongst the many independent railways. The "S" stood for the Sormovo works at Nijni Novgorod where the class was built. About 900 were turned out before the Revolution.

Very little needs to be said of the design which took very early on the standard final form of the steam locomotive, having two cylinders, Walschaert's valve-gear, wide firebox, superheater and compensated springing. The fulcrum points of the latter could be altered to bring extra weight on to or off the driving wheels. For running on lines which had inadequate permanent way, the maximum axle-load could be quickly changed from 18 tonnes to 16 tonnes by a simple adjustment, at the cost of reducing the adhesive weight from 54 to 48 tonnes.

Below: The standard Russian passenger locomotive, the class "Su" 2-6-2.

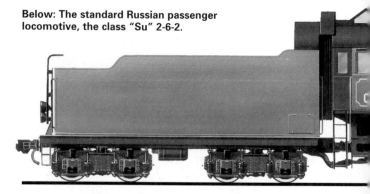

Above: Class "Su" 2-6-2 No.100-85 outside Sormovo works. This example is equipped for burning oil fuel.

A modified and enlarged version known as class "Su", was first produced at the Kolomna Works near Moscow in 1926. This sub-class, of which about 2,400 were built during the next 15 years, is the basis of the particulars and of art-work below. The "u" stood for *usilenny* which means "strengthened"; in Russian script "Su" is written "Cy". The cylinders, wheelbase and boiler were enlarged but, interestingly, the boiler pressure was kept at the same modest level. The adoption of high boiler pressure was so often (like the substitution of diesel for steam 40 years later) a costly matter of "keeping up with the Jones's".

The extra cost of a high-pressure boiler is considerable, especially as regards maintenance, while even its theoretical advantages are dubious. Of course, some railways had to adopt high-pressures in order to obtain sufficient tractive effort with the largest cylinders that could be squeezed into a tight loading gauge, but Soviet Russia was not one of them. Those university owls again!

After World War II, production was restarted at Sormovo Works (whose location was by then known as Gorki) and continued until 1951, by which time some 3,750 "S" class had been built. Variations included some built in 1915 for the standard gauge Warsaw-Vienna line known as sub-class "Sv" (Cb). There was also a "Sum" (Cym) group, having a system for pre-heating the air used in combustion. A Scotsman named Thomas Urquhart introduced successful oil-burning locomotives to Russia in 1880, since when it became commonplace. Many "S" class used this form of firing.

No. 7 2-4-4T

Origin: United States: Bridgton & Saco River Railroad (B&SR), 1913. **Gauge:** 2ft 0in (609mm). **Tractive effort:** 10,072lb (4,570kg). **Axleload:** 21,340lb (9.7t). **Cylinders:** (2) 12 × 16in (304 × 406mm). **Driving wheels:** 35in (889min). **Steam pressure:** 180psi (12.7kg/cm²). **Fuel:** 3,000lb (1.4t). **Water:** 1,000 US gall (3.8m³). **Adhesive weight:** 38,800lb (17.6t). **Total weight:** 69,700lb (31.6t). **Length overall:** 34ft 7³/4in (10,650mm).

This tiny locomotive from a tiny railway was nevertheless a pathfinder. It seems she was the first in the world to be restored for use as an instrument of pleasure after being withdrawn from normal commercial use.

The Baldwin Locomotive Works in 1913 delivered No.7 to the 2ft gauge Bridgton & Saco River Railroad up in Maine. The locomotive followed the Forney style with the addition of a lead truck, making a 2-4-4T type, and had slide valves actuated by Walschaert's valve gear, vacuum brakes and an unsuperheated boiler. These features all helped by their simplicity to give this elegant little iron foal qualities of usefulness and reliability, leading to a long life and finally to survival beyond the end of the age of steam.

In 1930 the 35-mile B&SR had become the 27-mile Bridgton & Harrison, but traffic was miniscule and by the end of the decade abandonment was clearly not far off. On days when the train was not operating regularly, the manager would put on a special for a few dollars to satisfy visiting railfans. One group even went some way towards raising funds to buy the line. In the event, a scrap merchant put in a bid which the fans could not match.

In 1941 No.7 (plus sister No.8 and a number of passenger and freight cars) was bought by a cranberry grower from Massachusetts called Ellis D. Atwood. As the war ended, Atwood began building a railroad on his farm. It

was formed as a circuit 5¹/₂ miles (8.8km) in length, the dykes between the cranberry bogs providing a ready-made alignment on which he and his men could spike down the secondhand rails he had bought.

The idea was that the line should provide essential transport for the estate and only on high days and holidays be a pleasure line for himself and his friends. But it was not to be. People for miles around started to clamour for invitations, and soon enough the idea of opening the Ellis D. Atwood Railroad (Edaville for short) to the public was born. Monday, April 7, 1947 was the day when the golden spike was ceremonially driven, since when Edaville - and railway preservation round the world - has gone from strength to strength. The only sour note is that, after two changes of ownership, Edaville had to move - its presence inconvenienced modem methods of cranberry farming.

Below: Edaville's No.7, forerunner of so many steam locomotives now preserved round the world. Baldwin was the builder in 1913.

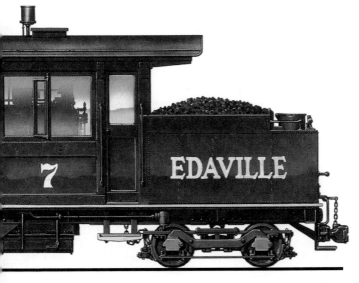

Class 231C 4-6-2

Origin: France: Paris, Lyons and Mediterranean Railway (PLM), 1912. **Axleload:** 40,500lb (18.5t). **Cylinders, HP:** (2) 17.3 x 25.6m (440 x 650mm). **Cylinders, LP:** (2) 25.6 x 25.6in (650 x 650mm). **Driving wheels:** 78.7m (2,000mm). **Heating surface:** 2,185sq ft (203m²). **Superheater:** 694sq ft (65m²). **Steam pressure:** 228psi (16kg/cm²). **Grate area:** 45.7sq ft (4.3m²). **Fuel:** 11,000lb (5t). **Water:** 6,160gall (7,400 US) (28m³). **Adhesive weight:** 122,000lb (55t). **Total weight:** 320,500lb (145.5t). **Length overall:** 65ft 7in (20,000mm).

French engineers were early converts to the creed of compounding, and in no other country was compounding pursued more enthusiastically or successfully. Nevertheless, from time to time right up to the last steam designs, occasional doubts entered the minds of French engineers, and a batch of simple expansion locomotives appeared, but the outcome was always a strengthening of the orthodox doctrine.

The Pacifics of the PLM illustrated this process. Between 1890 and 1907 the railway ordered 845 locomotives, of which 835 were compounds, and in the period 1905 to 1907 construction of compound Atlantics and 4-6-0s was in full swing. But in 1907 the first European Pacific appeared, and in 1909 the PLM produced two prototype locomotives of that wheel arrangement, one simple and one compound. Apart from the recurrent desire to ensure that the mechanical complications of the compounds were really justified there was a further reason for this particular digression into simple expansion. Compound expansion enables a higher proportion of the energy in the steam to be converted into work during expansion, but to get the full benefit of the greater expansion in the compound it is necessary to use a high steam pressure, and high pressure brings higher boiler maintenance costs. At this time there was a new attraction for engineers – the superheater – which offered the possibility of improving the thermal efficiency sufficiently for simple expansion to be acceptable, and with it the possibility of using a lower boiler pressure.

The two PLM Pacifics put this problem to the test, for the compound engine used saturated steam but the simple engine was superheated. The compound had the de Glehn layout of cylinders, with the outside high pressure cylinders set well back over the rear bogie wheels, but the simple engine had the four cylinders in line, as in the PLM Atlantics and 4-6-0s. The in-line arrangement gave a much more rigid assembly than the de Glehn arrangement. Apart from the differences in cylinders, motion and boiler already mentioned, the two engines were as far as possible identical, but the compound worked at 227psi (16kg/cm²) and the simple at 171 psi (12kg/cm²).

In 1911 the two engines ran comparative trials, and the superheated engine developed higher powers and used 16 per cent less coal than the

Left: The locomotive for the "Flèche d'Or" (Golden Arrow) express backs down from Calais depot to Calais Maritime station.

Right: "The Flèche d'Or" (Golden Arrow) hauled by a long-serving, efficient, ex-PLM "231C" 4-6-2.

Left: A Paris, Lyons and Mediterranean Railway compound 4-6-2, depicted in SNCF days, receives attention from its crew.

compound. A natural step would have been to try superheating *with* compounding, but at that time it was not found possible to build a superheated compound within the weight restrictions. Thus 70 more simples were ordered in 1911, but by the following year the design problems of the superheated compound had been overcome, and 20 were built, differing from the prototype in having all four cylinders in line, as in the simple engines. Uncertainty still prevailed, and 20 more simples were next built, but then in 1913 a careful comparison was made between the two varieties of superheated design, and the compound returned a 25 per cent lesser coal consumption and better performance. The issue was finally settled, and the PLM built no more simple Pacifics, the existing simple engines were in due course converted to compounds.

In 1921 a further 230 Pacifics were ordered, and in 1931 55 more, making a total of 462. Successive batches incorporated improvements, mainly to the exhaust arrangements and to the boiler proportions, but the basic layout remained unchanged. Improvements continued to be made, and later still Chapelon's ideas on steam passage and boiler proportions were incorporated in an engine which was rebuilt with a boiler having 284psi (20kg/cm^2) pressure. A scheme to apply this boiler widely was initiated, but the incorporation of the PLM into the SNCF resulted in 30 engines only receiving this treatment, the last of them in 1948, but 284 engines received a more modest treatment on Chapelon lines. By this time the sub-divisions of the class were very complicated.

The PLM Pacifics had long and distinguished lives, and the quality of their performance responded directly to the improvements which were made to them, but they never achieved the levels of the Chapelon rebuilds of the Paris-Orleans Pacifics. As electrification displaced them from the PLM main line from 1952 onwards, they spread to other regions. Withdrawal began in the 1950s, but many of the boilers were not worn out, and there was thus a good supply of spare boilers, with which some of the engines were maintained in service until 1969.

Four engines were retained for preservation, including 231K22, a rebuild with partial Chapelon improvements, which is at Steamtown, Carnforth, Lancashire.

Class 60-3 Shay B-B-B

Origin: United States: Sierra Nevada Wood & Lumber Co, 1913. **Gauge:** 3ft 0in (914mm). **Tractive effort:** 36,150lb (16,402kg). **Axleload:** 19,666lb (8.9t). **Cylinders:** (3) 11 x 12in (279 x 304mm). **Driving wheels:** 32in (812mm). **Heating surface:** 881 sq ft (82m²). **Superheater:** 189sq ft (18m²). **Steam pressure:** 200psi (14.1kg/cm²). **Grate area:** 23sq ft (2.1m²). **Fuel (oil):** 1,200 US gall (4.5m³). **Water:** 3,000 US gall (11.4m³). **Adhesive weight:** 118,000lb (53.5t). **Total weight:** 118,000lb (53.5t). **Length overall:** 50ft 2in (15,290mm).

The story of the Shay – a locomotive like nothing else on earth – is also the story of the Lima Locomotive Works of Lima, Ohio. Before 1880 it was just the Lima Machine Works, but in that year they built their first locomotive, a strange steam-driven flat car to the designs of a veteran logging man called Ephraim Shay. The first Shays had vertical boilers but later examples had locomotive-type ones. These were offset to one side of the centre-line in order to balance the two - or three-cylinder in-line steam engine with vertical cylinders mounted on the other side. This drove the axles via longitudinal shafts fore and aft, universal joints and bevel gears.

The basic Shay had two two-axle trucks but further powered trucks driven in the same way could be added at the rear. Three-truck Shays were common and four-truck ones were also built.

Because it had all wheels driven and because there was the maximum amount of flexibility along its wheelbase, and also because of its simplicity and robustness, the Shay pulled useful loads and held to the rails on crazy temporary tracks in forests which were being felled. It was also ideal for any steeply-graded and sharply-curved railroad. Over the next 65 years a total of 2,771 were sold, most of them in the first 35 or so. Their popularity was a clear indication of their usefulness and efficiency. The last one was delivered in 1944 by which time Lima had become a prestigious supplier of giant high-powered locomotives.

A valuable but by no means obvious feature was the short, fat, heavily tapered boiler barrel which minimised the change in water level at the firebox end for different inclinations. This meant that Shays could run off and on to 10 per cent (1-in-10) grades without trouble. Their flexibility meant they could negotiate 76° (23m radius) curves with serious kinks and wildly varying cross levels without derailing. In addition, they were available straight out of Lima's catalogue in all gauges and in sizes from 320,000lb total weight down to 50,000lb or less. They could burn coal, oil or forest waste and were easy and

Below: This oil-fired three-truck Shay, built in 1913, was originally produced for the Sierra Nevada Wood and Lumber Co.'s logging railroad.

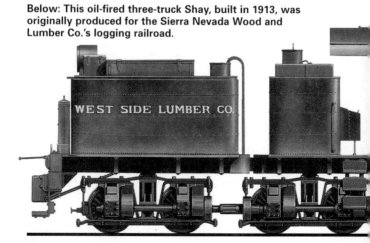

cheap to maintain in primitive workshops. Perhaps one should add that, flat out at 12mph or so, they sounded like the "Overland Limited" setting alight the prairies at 90mph.

The example depicted here is the West Side Lumber Company's three-truck Class "60-3" Shay No.15, supplied by Lima, originally to the Sierra Nevada Wood & Lumber Company in 1913 as their No.9. West Side had one of the largest logging railroads with over 60 miles of main route based on Toulomne, California, where No.15 is preserved. Shays still run on several tourist railroads, notably at Cass, West Virginia; Tacoma, Washington State; Georgetown, Colorado; at Fish Camp and at Felton in California.

Right: A Shay in untypically clean and polished condition, ready to take a trainload of tourists on the Roaring Camp & Big Trees RR, Felton, California.

K4 Class 4-6-2

Origin: United States: Pennsylvania Railroad (PRR), 1914. **Gauge:** 4ft 8¹/₂in (1,435mm). **Tractive effort:** 44,460lb (20,170kg). **Axle load:** 72,000lb (33t) **Cylinders:** (2) 27 x 28in (686 x 711mm). **Driving wheels:** 80in (2,032mm) **Heating surface:** 4,040sq ft (375m²). **Superheater:** 943sq ft (88m²). **Boiler pressure:** 205psi (14.4kg/cm²). **Grate area:** 70sq ft (6.5m²). **Fuel:** 36,000lb (16t). **Water:** 10,000gall (12,000 US) (46m³). **Adhesive weight:** 210,000lb (96t). **Total weight:** 533,000lb (242t). **Overall length:** 83ft 6in (25,451mm)

The famous "K4" 4-6-2s were introduced in 1914 and were the mainstay of steam operations until after World War II. There were 425 of them, built over a period of 14 years, and they followed a series of classes of earlier 4-6-2s introduced previously. The Pennsy was normally exceedingly conservative in its locomotive engineering and its Pacific era was ushered in by a single prototype ordered from the American Locomotive Company in 1907, later designated class "K28". By 1910 the railroad felt it knew enough to start building some of its own and in a short time 239 "K2"s were put on the road. In 1912, quite late in the day really, superheating was applied to these engines.

In 1913, the company went to Baldwin of Philadelphia for 30 "K3" 4-6-2s. These were interesting in that they were fitted with the earliest type of practical mechanical stoker, known as the "Crawford" after its inventor, D.F. Crawford, Superintendent of Motive Power (Lines West). This had been in use on the Pennsylvania Railroad since 1905 and by 1914 nearly 300 were in operation – but only 64 on 4-6-2s. Later designs of stoker used a screw feed, but the principle used in the Crawford was to bring forward the coal by means of a series of paddles or vanes, oscillated by steam cylinders, which were feathered on the return stroke like the oars of a rowing boat. The coal was fed into the firebox at grate level, unlike later types of stoker which feed on to a platform at the rear, for distribution by steam jets.

In addition, there was a further Alco prototype supplied in 1911, larger than the "K28" and designated "K29". There was also the "K1" class, which was an "in house" project, designed but never built.

The prototype "K4" Pacific appeared in 1914; it was considerably larger than the "K2" class, having 36 per cent more tractive effort and 26 per cent more grate area at a cost of a 9 per cent increase in axle loading. The design owed as much to that Apex of the Atlantics, the "E6" class 4-4-2 as to the earlier 4-6-2s.

The prototype "K4" was tested at Altoona soon after it was built, but few changes were needed as a result for the production version. The oil headlight and wooden pilot (cow-catcher) were not, however, repeated. By 1923, after more than 200 "K4"s had been built, power reverse replaced the

Below: One of the famous "K4" class 4-6-2s of the Pennsylvania Railroad. Between 1914 and 1928 425 were built, mostly at the road's own Altoona shops.

hand-operated screw reversing gear of earlier engines. In due time the latter were converted, foreshadowing a date (1937) when hand reversing gear would be illegal for locomotives with over 160,000lb (72.7t) adhesive weight. The same edict applied to the fitting of automatic stokers to locomotives of such size and many (but not all) "K4"s were fitted with them during the 1930s. Before then the power output had been severely limited by the amount of coal a man could shovel. The last five "K4"s had cast steel one-piece locomotive frames. Another interesting box of tricks that also became general in the 1930s, was the continuous cab signalling system. A receiver picked up coded current flowing in track circuits and translated this into the appropriate signal aspect on a miniature signal inside the cab.

One could see signs of Pennsy's conservatism, for example, even in the later "K4"s the ratio of evaporative heating surface to superheater size was as low as 4.3, instead of the 2.2 to 2.5, more typical of the passenger locomotives which other North American railroads were using in the 1930s. There was also the modest boiler pressure, three-quarters or less of what was used elsewhere.

Running numbers were allocated at random between 8 and 8378, although the last batches built during 1924-28 were numbered in sequence from 5350 to 5499. All were built at the PRR's Juanita shops at Altoona, Pennsylvania except Nos.5400 to 5474 of 1927 which came from Baldwin.

There were a few "specials" amongst the "K4" fleet. Two engines (Nos.3847 and 5399) were fitted with poppet valve gear thermic syphons in the firebox, and improved draughting; so equipped they could develop over 4000hp in the cylinders instead of the 3000hp typical of a standard "K4". A number of other engines (designated class "K4sa") had less drastic treatment with the same end in view; in this case the firebox and exhaust improvements were accompanied by larger piston valves, 15in (381mm) diameter instead of 12in (305mm). One engine (No.3768) was fully streamlined for a while; a number of others were partly streamlined and specially painted to match certain streamlined trains. Many types of tender were used, including a few which were so big they dwarfed the engine, but held 25 tons of coal and 23,500 US gallons (107m³) of water.

Remembrance Class 4-6-4 Tank

Origin: Great Britain: London, Brighton & South Coast Railway (LBSCR), 1914.
Tractive effort: 24,180lb (10,991kg). **Axle load:** 44,000lb (20t). **Cylinders:** (2)
22 x 28in (559 x 711mm). **Driving wheels:** 81in (2,057mm). **Heating surface:**
1,816sq ft (167.7m²). **Superheater:** 383sq ft (35.6m²). **Steam pressure:**
170psi (11.9kg/cm²). **Grate area:** 26.7sq ft (2.48m²). **Fuel:** 8,000lb (3¹/₂t)
Water: 2,700gall (3,250 US) (12m³). **Adhesive weight:** 126,000lb (55t). **Total
weight:** 222,000lb (97t). **Length overall:** 50ft 4³/₄in (15,361mm).

Those great trains of the world which were hauled throughout their journeys
by tank locomotives were few and far between. One such was the immortal
"Southern Belle", the all-Pullman express which ran non-stop several times
a day over the 51 miles between London's Victoria Station and Brighton
Specially associated with this train was a group of seven 4-6-4 or "Baltic"
tank locomotives, the most powerful motive power ever owned by the
London Brighton and South Coast Company.

Previously, the express trains between London and the south coast had
been hauled by a fleet of 4-4-0s, 4-4-2s, and 4-4-2Ts, supplemented by two
4-6-2Ts. The new 4-6-4s were to some extent a stretched version of the
latter and were known as class L. Their designer Colonel L. B. Billinton was
instructed to produce locomotives capable of running the "Belle" and other
fast trains such as the "City Limited" to an accelerated timing of 45 or 50
minutes instead of the even hour. In fact, the 60 minute timing was never
improved upon, even by the "Southern Belle's" successor, the electric
"Brighton Belle" which replaced the steam train after 1933, but the addition
of third-class Pullman cars to the previously all-first formation made the train
an increasingly harder haulage proposition.

Conventional practice of the day was followed in most respects but the
valve gear arrangement was interesting. Outside Walschaert's valve gear
was used, actuating inside piston valves between the frames via rocking
levers; all this in spite of having the cylinders themselves outside the
frames. One reason for this unusual arrangement was the wish to have
similar cylinders to the 4-6-2Ts plus the need to provide a well tank between
the frames under the boiler, which the existence of valve motion there
would preclude. There had in fact been trouble including a derailment,
whose cause had been attributed to the swishing of water in half-full tanks
plus the high centre of gravity. This occurred soon after the prototype,
No.321 *Charles C Macrae* first entered service in April 1914. The solution
was on similar lines to the extra dummy funnels on some steamships of the
day, that is, adopted so as not to spoil the appearance. It consisted of

Above: 4-6-4T No.B333 (later 2333) *Remembrance* **at Victoria Station, London in 1930. This was the Southern Railway's War Memorial locomotive and bore special plaques on the side tanks to that effect for many years.**

making all but the bottom 15 inches of the side tanks into dummies in order to lower the centre of gravity of the locomotive. The modifications were successful and speeds as high as 75mph were quite frequently run without any further problems.

A second locomotive (No.328) was completed just before war broke out and five further examples (Nos.329-333) in 1921-22. Two more received names at that time – No.329 became *Stephenson*, while No.333 was chosen to be the War Memorial for the company's servants killed in the war and so was named *Remembrance*. The later examples of the class were never fitted with the feed-water heaters and steam-operated feed pumps which, unusually in British practice, were fitted to the earlier ones for a time after they were new.

After electrification in 1933, the Southern Railway converted the 4-6-4 tanks into 4-6-0s known as class N15X in which guise they had a long and honourable career on the less exacting longer distance services of the bigger system, lasting well after 1948 into British Railways days. That this was considered worthwhile doing demonstrates more than any words the excellent qualities of these extremely handsome locomotives. The last survivor (LB&SCR No.331, SR No.2331, BR No.32331) was withdrawn in July 1957.

Below: "Remembrance" class No. 329 *Stephenson* **is here depicted in its original LB&SCR umber livery. These famous tank locomotives handled the legendary "Southern Belle" all-Pullman express which ran several times a day between Victoria Station, London, and Brighton until 1933.**

Class E 2-10-0

Origin: Russia: Imperial Russian Government, 1917. **Gauge:** 5ft 0in (1,524mm). **Tractive effort:** 51,500lb (23,367kg). **Axleload:** 39,644lb (18t). **Cylinders:** (2) 25 x 28in (635 x 711mm). **Driving wheels:** 52in (1,320mm). **Heating surface:** 2,594sq ft (241m²). **Superheater:** 569sq ft (53m²). **Steam pressure:** 180psi (12.7kg/cm²). **Grate area:** 64.7sq ft (6m²). **Water:** 7,000 US gall (26.5m²). **Adhesive weight:** 180,200lb (81.8t). **Total weight:** 232,600lb (105.5t). **Length overall:** 72ft 9in (22,174mm).

The story of this huge class of locomotive, over 3,000 strong, is almost incredible. The Imperial Russian Government, hard pressed for transport in the war with Germany, in 1915 ordered 400 big 2-10-0s from North American builders. Alco, Baldwin and the Canadian Locomotive Co shared the order and later, after some modifications had been made to the design, a further 475 were built. They became Russian Class "E", with sub-classes designated for the first 400 as "Ef' (Baldwin), "Es" (Alco) and "Ek" (Canadian). The subsequent 475 were all classified "E1 ".

Some became Japanese property and were converted to standard gauge (1,435mm) when that country took over the South Manchurian Railway from Russia. Consequently this group later came into the hands of Chinese National Railways where they were classified "DK2" ('DK' stands for Decapod), and until very recently some of them were still in use. Further orders were placed, but before they were completed the Russian revolution and the separate peace with Germany precluded delivery of the last 200. Eventually, they went to various US roads – the Erie had 75, Seaboard 40, Frisco 21, and 22 other lines had lesser quantities. This followed gauge conversion which involved little more than fitting new tyres to the driving wheels.

During World War II, the Soviet government was again facing major transport problems, and under lend-lease they asked for further large helpings of these rugged but rather out-of-date machines. Accordingly, 2,110 were supplied by Alco and Baldwin from 1944 onwards.

Locomotive classification was one thing that survived unchanged through the turmoil of the revolution and so the new engines became Class "Ea"; later various modifications led to sub-classes "Em" (modified leading driving axleboxes) and "Emb" (feed-water heaters plus the "Em" modification). A few that remained unshipped after the Cold War began are believed to have been scrapped. One is recorded as having been sold to a short line, the Minneapolis, Northfield & Southern RR, with 75 miles (121km) of route in Minnesota.

Below: Preserved St. Louis San Francisco Railroad 2-8-0 originally built for Russia, at Kirkwood, Mo., in 1963.

Some of these locomotives were to be seen in use in the eastern part of Russia on switching duties until very recently, long after the official demise of steam in the Soviet Union. They seemed to have two qualities which were valued in that country. First, they had the rugged reliability of a familiar long-proven design, and secondly, there was a boost to the Communist system because officials could use them to demonstrate that the rival capitalists had made zero progress in the 20 years since the revolution.

800 2-10-10-2

Origin: United States: Virginian Railroad (VGN), 1918. **Gauge:** 4ft 8½in (1,435mm). **Tractive effort:** 176,600lb (80,127kg). **Axleload:** 61,700lb (28t). **Cylinders, HP:** (2) 30 x 32in (762 x 812mm). **Cylinders, LP:** (2) 48 x 32in (1,219 x 812mm). **Driving wheels:** 56in (1,422mm). **Heating surface:** 8,605sq ft (799m²). **Superheater:** 2,120sq ft (197m²). **Steam pressure:** 215psi (15.1kg/cm²). **Grate area:** 108.7sq ft (10.1m²). **Fuel:** 24,000lb (10.9t). **Water:** 13,000 US gall (49.2m²). **Adhesive weight:** 617,000lb (279.9t). **Total weight:** 898,000lb (407.4t). **Length overall:** 99ft 8in (30,368mm).

Until 1918, Mallet articulated steam locomotives with more than 16 driving wheels had been fairly conspicuous by their lack of success. The Virginian Railroad, which had faced serious haulage problems in the Appalachian Mountains, had been persuaded by Baldwin to have a Triplex 2-8-8-8-4, similar to those which were a failure on the Erie. Although attempts were made to give the new locomotive a better steam-raising capacity so as to satisfy the vast appetite of the three sets of machinery, it was not long before she was divided in two. So with one new boiler the VGN got two new locomotives, a 2-8-8-0 and a 2-8-0, both of which gave good service, but not in the way intended.

Nevertheless, the problem of hauling VGN's immense coal drags down to tidewater at Norfolk, Virginia, which first involved climbing the notorious 2.11 per cent (1-in-47) incline from the main collection point at Elmore, West Virginia, to Clark's Gap summit, remained unsolved. In 1917, with swollen wartime traffic round their necks, the management decided to have another go and ordered a batch of huge 2-10-10-2s from the American Locomotive Co. The dialogue between builder and customer was no doubt made more meaningful by the traumatic experiences of the recent past.

Be that as it may, the results were excellent. Small tenders made the "800s" less impressive than they actually were but their vital statistics were huge. For example, 4ft diameter low-pressure cylinders were the largest ever used on a locomotive. Their adhesive weight was 14 per cent greater than that of a Union Pacific "Big Boy" and the tractive effort 40 per cent greater when live steam was admitted to the low-pressure engine at starting. Naturally, power output was much lower, as one might expect from a machine intended for low-speed operation, but these iron mammoths did all that was expected of them and gave 30 years of good service to their owners. When working on their intended task, it was customary to have a 2-8-8-2 at the head of a 5,500 ton train, well able to handle this load other

than on the 2.11 per cent (1-in-47) grade. Two 2-10-10-2s then pushed from the rear and the whole caravan moved upgrade noisily but steadily at some 5½mph (9km/h). It must have been one of the greatest sights and sounds in railroading.

The 800s were interesting in that the high-pressure cylinders had conventional piston valves, but the huge, low-pressure ones used old-fashioned slide valves. These were quite adequate for the lower temperatures involved on the L.P. side, while being easier to keep steamtight.

They are also thought to be the only successful class of locomotives in the world with as many as 20 driving wheels. Certainly the Mallet principle was never carried further than with these giants, although the size and power of articulated locomotives with few coupled wheels would in the end be even greater.

It is perhaps true to say that the problem of Clark's Gap was ameliorated rather than solved by the "800s". A few years later a real solution was found when this hilly stretch of line was the subject of an electrification scheme The 2-10-102s were then given useful but less heroic work to perform elsewhere on the system and survived until the 1940s. Alas, none has been preserved.

Below: Almost a centipede! The Virginian Railroad's Mallet compound articulated 2-10-10-2 steam locomotives pushed coal drags up to Clark's Gap, Va.

Class EP-2 "Bi-polar"
1-B-D-D-B-1

Origin: United States: Chicago, Milwaukee, St Paul & Pacific Railroad, (CM St P&P), 1919. **Type:** Express passenger electric locomotive. **Gauge:** 4ft 8¹/₂in (1,435mm). **Propulsion:** Direct current at 3,000V fed via overhead catenary to twelve 370hp (275kW) gearless motors mounted directly on the axles. **Weight:** 457,000lb (207t) adhesive, 530,000lb (240t) total. **Max. axleload:** 38,500lb (17.5t). **Overall length:** 76ft 0in (23,165mm). **Tractive effort:** 123,500lb (549kN). **Max. speed:** 70mph (112km/h).

When the Chicago, Milwaukee, St Paul & Pacific Railroad was opened to Tacoma, Washington State, in 1909 (through passenger service did not begin until 1911) it was the last railway to reach the West Coast from the east. As a newcomer, then, the company had to try harder, and one of the ways in which it did this was to work the mountain crossings by the clean new power of electricity

Catenary wires mounted on timber poles started to go up five years after the line was opened, and early in 1917 electric working began over the Rocky Mountain and Missoula divisions, between Harlowton and Avery, Montana, a distance of 438 miles (705km). Many miles of 100,000V transmission lines had to be built through virgin territory from hydro-electric power plants to rotary substations along the right-of-way. By 1919 the 230-mile (370km) Coast Division from Othello to Tacoma, Washington State, had been electrified also.

Electrification measured by the hundreds of miles was something quite new in the world, and the North American railroad top brass watched with bated breath for the results. Technically, they were totally satisfactory: much heavier loads could be worked than with steam, energy costs were lower, faster running times – and hence better productivity – could be achieved. The system was reliable and one could have been forgiven for thinking that other railroads would quickly follow. Alas, the enormous costs involved proved too frightening at a time when railroads were beginning to feel the effects of competition from road transport. So, with one notable exception, in the USA main line electrification schemes were confined to shortish lengths of line.

The Milwaukee Railroad itself went bankrupt in 1925, and this caused a further ebb of confidence, although it was claimed that the onset of

**Below: The Chicago, Milwaukee, St Paul & Pacific Railroad's
Class EP-2 "Bi-polar" one of the most impressive locomotives of any
form of traction ever to have been built.**

Above: "Bi-polar" No. E-2 as preserved at the National Museum of Transport, St Louis, Missouri.

bankruptcy was *delayed* rather than *caused* by the $24 million spent on electrification.

The original passenger locomotives (Class "EP1"), delivered from 1915 onwards by The American Locomotive Co and General Electric, were the same as those for freight except that they had higher gearing and oil-fired train-heating boilers. They were formed as twin units, permanently coupled, of the 2-Bo-Bo+Bo-Bo-2 wheel arrangement and produced 3,440hp (2,570kW) for a weight of 288 tons. Their plain "box-car" style belied their ability to pull and go in an unprecedented manner. Thirty freight and 12 passenger locos were supplied.

When the wires were going up over the Cascade mountains in 1918, something more exotic was proposed; the result was these legendary "Bi-polars", created by General Electric. The name arose from using two-pole motors. The reason for this lay in a desire to simplify the mechanics of an electric locomotive. The ultimate in simplicity is to put the armatures of the motors actually on the driving axles, thereby doing away altogether with gearing, but it is then necessary to cater for vertical movement. Hence there can only be two poles, one on each side in a position where the critical air gap between poles and armature is not affected by vertical movement. The price of doing it this way is that the power of each motor is limited, partly because it runs at the low speed of the wheels and partly because two-pole motors are less powerful than those with a more usual number of poles anyway.

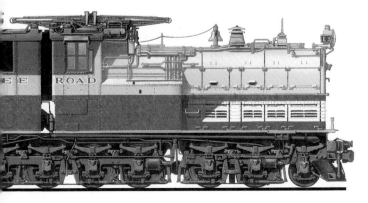

The result was that, for a power output virtually the same as the "EP1s", the "EP2s" had half as many more driving wheels. The body was articulated in three parts, connected together by the four-axle trucks. All this made for a lot of locomotive, but the effect of size on the public was nothing compared with the impact of very impressive styling. The electrical equipment was contained in round-topped bonnets at each end of the locomotive and this simple change was what gave these engines that little extra the others hadn't got.

The designers were sensible enough to put the train-heating boiler, fuel and water tanks – all items that do not mix well with electricity – in the separate centre section. All things considered, the Cascade Division in 1918 found itself in possession of a reliable class of five locomotives that could haul 900t (1,000 US tons) trains up the long 1-in-45 (2.2 per cent) grades at 25mph (40km/h), as well as hold them back coming down. Some rather fine publicity stunts were arranged showing a "Bi-polar" having a tug-of-war with two big steam engines (a 2-6-6-2 and a 2-8-0) on top of a huge trestle bridge. The electric had no difficulty in pulling backwards the two steam engines set to pull full steam ahead.

Ten more passenger engines (Class "EP3") were delivered in 1921 by rival builders Baldwin and Westinghouse, and these were more orthodox. Even so, 20 per cent more power was packed into a locomotive with only half the number of driving wheels, the wheel arrangement being 2-C-1 + 1-C-2. Their appearance was fairly box-like, although not quite as severe as that of the "EP1s".

So the "Bi-polars" were out-classed as well as outnumbered by nearly five-to-one soon after they were built, yet these legendary locomotives demonstrated very clearly the value of cosmetics, because they are the ones remembered and regarded as epitomising this longest amongst North American electrification schemes. The great engines gave excellent service, though, and soldiered on through the years. In the late 1950s they were moving the road's crack "Olympian Hiawatha" luxury express over the 438 miles (705km) of the Rocky Mountain Division in 10hr 40min, compared with 15 hours scheduled when the electrification was new.

Some modem electric locomotives of even greater power, built for the USSR but undeliverable on account of the so-called "Cold War", became available at this time. These "Little Joes" as they were known, were further nails in the coffins of the now ageing "Bi-polars". In spite of a rebuild in 1953 which included the addition of multiple-unit capability, all five were taken out of service between 1958 and 1960. One (No. E2) is preserved at the National Museum of Transport in St Louis, Missouri, but the others went for scrap.

In 1973, all electric operations on the Milwaukee came to end, a favourable price for scrap copper being one of the factors. The escalation in the price of oil which followed might have saved the day, although the existence of the whole railroad was soon to be in jeopardy, there being just too many lines in the area. It was no surprise, then, when in 1980 all transcontinental operations over the one-time electrified tracks ceased, and most have now been abandoned.

Left: A "Bi-polar" in service under the 3,000 volt catenary wires of the Chicago, Milwaukee, St Paul & Pacific Railroad.

No. 24 2-6-2

Origin: United States: Sandy River & Rangeley Lakes Railroad (SRRL), 1919. **Gauge:** 2ft 0in (609mm). **Tractive effort:** 10,085lb (4,576kg). **Axleload:** 5,400lb (7.0t). **Cylinders:** (2) 12 x 16in (304 x 406mm). **Driving wheels:** 33in (838mm). **Steam pressure:** 170psi (12kg/cm²). **Fuel:** 6,000lb (2.7t). **Water:** 2,000 US gall (7.6m³). **Adhesive weight:** 42,000lb (19.1t). **Total weight:** 91,000lb (41.3t). **Length overall:** 44ft 7in (13,589mm).

The Prairie or 2-6-2 wheel arrangement was first tried in any quantity around the turn of the century. It bore the same relationship to the 2-6-0 Mogul type as the 4-4-2 Atlantic bore to the 4-4-0 American standard. You could say that it was a Mogul with a much larger firebox, and hence more power without additional tractive effort. So it was eminently suitable for lines in the "wide open spaces" of the Mid-West, hence the name Prairie. But intense competition and a rapidly expanding economy meant a continuous search for increased productivity, and so the Prairie was quickly superseded by larger 4-6-2 Pacifics and 2-8-2 Mikados. So for main-line use the 2-6-2 was quickly eclipsed. It did however, find a niche on the short lines and by-ways of the US railroad system.

We have seen how the state of Colorado caught the 3ft version of narrow-gauge disease in the last decades of the 19th Century. Equally notable was the 2ft epidemic that swept the state of Maine at the same time. It resulted in construction of seven little narrow-gauge railroads, four of which were later consolidated into one system, which then became little only in respect of distance between the rails. This was the Sandy River & Rangely Lakes Railroad – a 46-mile main line with 60 miles of branches plus 16 locomotives and hundreds of freight cars. It interchanged traffic at Farmington, Maine, with the Maine Central Railroad. The narrow-gauge line eventually became the property of this "big brother", although never formally incorporated into it.

The Sandy River's last locomotive (and the fifth 2-6-2 on the line) was this No.24 delivered by Baldwin in 1919. It is a reflection on the ways in which little railroads could "design" their locomotives, that the superintendent would just jot down a few measurements for the builders to work to and send them off to Philadelphia. The tender tanks on the Sandy River line were typically 84in wide (even that was rather wide for a 24in gauge) but the boss's careless handwriting led to Baldwin building one 8ft 4in wide. Not surprisingly, this overgenerous water cart overbalanced (unfortunately on a

trestle) and had to have a slice taken out of its middle. But this tiny hunk of locomotive engineering was very soundly built – Walschaert valve gear, an unsuperheated boiler and slide valves making an excellent combination for ease of maintenance. "Piston valves wear out, slide valves wear in" is the saying, whilst a little extra fuel consumption would hardly be noticed on such a small machine.

No. 24 survived until the Sandy River line was abandoned in 1935. A railfan actually bought her for $250 (would this be the first ever purchase of a full-size locomotive for preservation by a private individual?) but, alas, problems of storage and finance forced him two years later to let the engine go for scrap. But memories of No.24 linger on in model form, while the railroad itself surely sets a record in the number of pages of print published per mile of railroad abandoned.

Above: 2-6-2 No.24, the last locomotive supplied to the Sandy River & Rangeley Lakes RR.

Below: Sandy River & Rangeley Lakes Railroad No.24, supplied by Baldwin in 1919, ceasing work once the two-foot gauge line was taken up and sold for scrap in 1936.

Class A1 4-6-2

Origin: Great Britain: Great Northern Railway (GNR), 1922. **Tractive effort**
29,385lb (13,333kg). **Axle load:** 45,000 (20.5t). **Cylinders:** (3) 20 x 26m (508
x 660mm). **Driving wheels:** 80in (2,032min). **Heating surface:** 2,930sq f
(272m²). **Superheater:** 525sq ft (49m²). **Steam pressure:** 180ps
(12.6kg/cm²). **Grate area:** 41.25sq ft (3.8m²). **Fuel:** 1,800lb (8t). **Water**
5,000gall (6,000 US) (22.7m³). **Adhesive weight:** 134,500lb (61t). **Tota**
weight: 332,000lb (151t). **Length overall:** 70ft 5in (2,146mm).

The month of April 1922 was a milestone in the history of the railways o
Great Britain for that was the month in which the first member of the firs
whole class of Pacific locomotive went into service. Few designs can match
the record of these engines and their derivatives. Seventy-nine were to be
built between 1921 and 1934 and they were originally class-designated with
great appropriateness "A1".

The Great Northern Railway 4-6-2s were the work of a man called Nige
Gresley (later Sir Nigel Gresley) who became Locomotive Superintendent o
the GNR in 1911. Gresley was very much what would now be called a
"systems" engineer – by this one means that he was more a master o
concepts than of detail.

The concept represented by these famous 4-6-2s was that, overall, a "big
engine" (that is, one with ample capacity for the job in hand) was the mos
economical type. This in spite of the fact that it might cost more to build
The first ten "A1"s cost an average of £8,560 as against £6,840 for the firs
ten Great Western Railway "Castle" 4-6-0s. The thinking behind the desigr
was also difficult to fault in that Gresley recognised that simplicity was the
steam locomotive's greatest asset. At the same time he realised the
importance of having perfect balance of the reciprocating forces. The
minimum number of cylinders to achieve this was three and, whilst this
meant one cylinder and set of motion between the frames, Gresley adopted
a "derived" valve gear which meant that there was no more mechanism to
crowd out the limited space available there.

Gresley was also an artist and his locomotives were aesthetically very
pleasing – and, as will be related, they went as well as they looked. He
decked them out in a really attractive livery and gave them evocative names,
most being taken from racehorses. They rightly hold their place of honour ir
any locomotive hall of fame.

In contrast, they were beset with bad details. A stiff "all-or-nothing"
throttle combined with the absence of any compensating levers between
the rear pony truck and the driving wheels made them liable to slipping their
wheels at starting. Rails needed changing because of wheelburn every few
weeks at places where Gresley's 4-6-2s habitually started heavy trains from
rest! A tendency for the large-ends of inside connecting rods to run hot

Right: Flying Scotsman wakes the echoes for a trainload of admirers. The colour change in the smoke from white to black indicates that a round of firing is in progress.

seemed quite endemic – yet those of other companies never gave more than occasional trouble. There were also such unforgivable things as lubricator pipes which, if they broke, could only be replaced by lifting the boiler off the frames. Another problem was drifting steam obscuring the view of signals.

Certainly one cause of these shortcomings was that Gresley in 1923 became Chief Mechanical Engineer of the London & North Eastern Railway (LNER), an amalgamation of the Great Northern, Great Eastern, North Eastern, Great Central, North British and other smaller companies. He removed himself to London and became remote from locomotive development at Doncaster. Gresley has always been given the credit for certain changes to the Pacifics' valve gear made in 1926 which greatly improved their coal consumption at small cost. It has only recently come to light that Gresley was not only not responsible for initiating the changes but furthermore they were devised in the teeth of his opposition.

The situation arose in 1925 when an elegant but smaller and highly decorated 4-6-0 called *Pendennis Castle* from the rival Great Western Railway was tried out on the LNER. She did everything the big Pacifics could do with easy mastery and burned 10 per cent less coal, as well as

Below: Flying Scotsman as running before conversion from class 'A1" to class "A3" but after the attachment of a corridor tender for long non-stop runs.

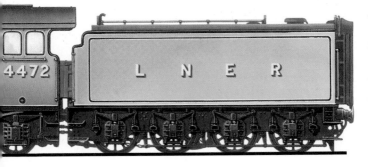

creating a profound impression whilst doing it.

Why the "Castle" was so good was a bit of a puzzle to the LNER men, but suspicion rested on the detailed geometry of the Walschaert's valve gear. Some minor alterations to the Pacific's valve gear were tried but the results were inconclusive. After this, rather than lose face by asking for a set of drawings, a cloak-and-dagger operation was mounted while another "Castle" was on hand at Darlington after taking part in the Stockton & Darlington Railway Centenary celebrations later the same year. All the motion was secretly measured and through the enterprise of Bert Spencer, Gresley's Technical Assistant at Kings Cross, some new geometry was worked out and applied to No.2555 *Centenary*. The results were amazing – not the 10 per cent saving in coal which the "Castle" had achieved against the other Pacifics, but twice as much.

After a preliminary period of disbelief, Gresley took a ride on *Centenary*, expressed himself converted and issued instructions for all his Pacifics to be altered as they went through shops. The savings in coal amounted to around 1$\frac{1}{2}$ tons on a run from Kings Cross to Newcastle and in fact enabled runs of this length to be worked without engine change. About the same time, boilers designed for a higher working pressure of 225psi (15.75kg/cm^2) were introduced, in some cases combined with a reduction of cylinder diameter. Engine weight rose by some six tons, axle load by two tons. Locomotives fitted with these boilers were designated class "A3" instead of "A1" and sometimes as "Super-Pacifics".

The longest non-stop journey in the world was run by these locomotives, over the 392$\frac{3}{4}$ miles (632km) from London to Edinburgh each peacetime summer beginning in 1928. Special corridor tenders were built and attached to certain selected locomotives to enable crews to be changed en route. Pullman-type vestibule connections and automatic 'buck-eye' couplings to match those on standard LNER corridor carriages were provided at the rear of these tenders.

In 1935 No.2750 *Papyrus* made a high-speed run from London to Newcastle preparatory to the introduction of the "Silver Jubilee" express with a 240 minute schedule. The 268 miles (432km) were run off in an amazing net time of 230 minutes, an average of 69.9mph (112.5km/h). Coming back, 108mph (174km/h) was touched at Essendine north of

Peterborough, a speed believed to be still a world record for an unstreamlined steam locomotive. The streamlined version of the Gresley Pacific came into service to run this new highspeed train. This was the event that displaced the non-streamlined 4-6-2s from their prime position on the East Coast main line, but they had no problem in keeping time on the streamliners when called upon to do so in an emergency.

World War II brought 24-coach trains to the East Coast main line and the "A3" as well as the few remaining "A1"s performances on these and on freight trains were a vindication of their brilliance as a concept, although lower standards of maintenance emphasized their detail weaknesses.

After the war, during which Gresley had died, efforts were made to overcome these troubles. Some success was achieved but progress was somewhat hampered by the deaf ear which the main works were liable to turn towards suggestions from the running sheds, however sensible. The "A3"s appearance was slightly changed when the smoke problem was effortlessly solved (after 25 years of fiddling with it) by the fitting of German pattern smoke deflectors either side of the smokebox but even in the 1960s all were easily recognisable as running mates of the original "A1" class which first saw the light of day 40 years before.

The prototype itself had been rebuilt into what was virtually a new design and one other had been withdrawn in 1959. Otherwise the class remained intact until 1962, still on prime express passenger work, and performing better than ever with the double chimneys which had been fitted 1958-60. The last to go was British Railways No.60041 *Salmon Trout* in December 1965.

In 1934 the running numbers had been (in chronological order) 4470-81, 2543-99, 2743-97, 2500-08. The second of two post-war re-numberings had left them as 102-112, 44-100, 35-43 (4470 no longer belonged to this class). In 1948 British Railways had added 60,000 to the numbers so that they became 60035 to 60112.

Happily, a certain Alan Pegler purchased the most famous locomotive in the class (and perhaps in the world), the immortal *Flying Scotsman*. After adventures which have included journeyings as far as the west coast of America, this grand engine is stationed at the Steamtown Museum, Carnforth, and performs with great regularity and panache on main-line steam-hauled special trains.

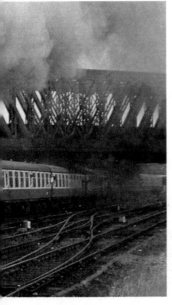

Left: Preserved ex-London & North Eastern Railway class "A3" 4-6-2 *Flying Scotsman* leaves York for the south with an enthusiasts' special.

Castle Class 4-6-0

Origin: Great Britain: Great Western Railway (GWR), 1923. **Tractive effort:** 31,625lb (14,182kg). **Axle load:** 44,500lb (20.25t). **Cylinders:** (4) 16 x 26in (406 x 660mm). **Driving wheels:** 80$\frac{1}{2}$in (2,045mm). **Heating surface:** 2,049sq ft (190m^2). **Superheater:** 263sq ft (24.4m^2). **Steam pressure:** 225psi (15.8kg/cm^2). **Grate area:** 30.3sq ft (2.81m^2). **Fuel:** 13,500lb (6t). **Water:** 4,000gall (4,800 US) (18m^3). **Adhesive weight:** 133,500lb (60t). **Total weight:** 283,500lb (129t). **Length overall:** 65ft 2in (19,863mm).

When Churchward of the GWR produced his first "Saint" largely based on rugged American practice, he also obtained from France a four-cylinder de Glehn compound, later named *La France*. This elegant French lady was put through her paces and compared with the two-cylinder design. Whilst there was not sufficient advantage to justify the complication of compounding, it did seem that the easier running of the compounds' sophisticated mechanical layout was something worth examining further. Hence the building in 1906 of a four-cylinder simple 4-4-2, with the same "No.1" boiler as the "Saint" class, to make direct comparison between a two-cylinder and a four-cylinder mechanism. This 4-4-2 was No.40 (later 4-6-0 No.4000) *North Star*.

The advantages of four-cylinders were, first, that the reciprocating parts could in principle be arranged to be perfectly in balance, whereas the balancing of a two-cylinder locomotive was always a compromise. Second, the forces in the various rods and guides which transmitted the piston force to the wheels would only be half those in the two-cylinder machine. The disadvantages, of course, were the extra costs involved in making nearly twice as much mechanism and also that the moving parts inside the frames would be difficult to reach.

This was compounded in the case of Churchward because, having decided very sensibly to use the same set of Walschaert's valve gear for both the cylinders on one side of the locomotive, he displayed a strange reluctance to expose this gear to the vulgar gaze. Hence the mechanism between the frames became very complex indeed. *North Star* herself in fact had a peculiar "scissors" valve gear, whereby the drive on each side was taken from the cylinder crosshead on the other. This slightly mitigated the complexity between the frames, but there was a problem with R M Deeley of the Midland Railway over patent rights.

Two more French compounds had to be obtained before the simple versus compound issue was finally determined, but construction of "Star" locomotives proceeded to the quantity of eleven in 1907. A batch of ten called Knights followed in 1908, ten Kings (not to be confused with the

Above: "Castle" class 4-6-0 No. 5094 *Tretower Castle* at speed with a Bristol to Paddington express. These superb locomotives were the mainstay of GWR express services.

"King" class of 1927) in 1909 and ten Queens in 1910 and 1911. The year 1913 brought five Princes, 1914 fifteen Princesses and finally there came twelve Abbeys in 1922-23. But all were known generally by the class name of "Star".

By now Churchward had retired and his successor as Chief Mechanical Engineer, Charles Collett ordered his staff to work out the details of a "Star" enlarged to take advantage of an increase in the permitted axle load from 18$\frac{1}{2}$ to 20 tons. It had been hoped that the Swindon No.7 boiler, recently introduced for the big "47xx" class mixed traffic 2-8-0s, would suit but the design incorporating it became too heavy. In the end a new No.8 boiler was designed especially for the "Castle" class, with very happy results indeed. The rest of the locomotive was pure "Star" with an extra inch on the diameter of the cylinders; visually, the slightly larger (but still exiguous) cab with its side windows made an impact on those who worshipped each separate Great Western rivet. The first "Castle", No.4073 *Caerphilly Castle*

Below: The Great Western Railway honoured its builder with this "Castle" class locomotive in 1935 livery.

appeared in August 1923 numbered consecutively after the last "Star" No.4072 *Tresco Abbey*.

The second "Castle" No.4074 *Caldicot Castle*, was put through a series of coal consumption tests. Afterwards Collett presented a paper to the World Power Conference in which he announced that the result was an overall figure of 2.83lb of coal per drawbar-horsepower-hour. This was received with a certain scepticism by other locomotive engineers who had been apt to give themselves a pat on the back if they got down anywhere near 4lb. Certainly the GWR was then far ahead of its rivals; a major factor was the design of the valves and valve gear, which enabled very short cut-offs to be used; hence expansive use of steam gave most of the advantages of compounding without the complications.

The tenth "Castle" No.4082 *Windsor Castle*, was new when King George V and Queen Mary visited the Swindon Factory in 1924; no doubt the name was held back until then. His Majesty personally drove the engine from the station to the works and a brass plaque was added to the cab side commemorating the fact. No.4082 carried this for many years but not all her days for by an unhappy chance she was under repair when King George V died in 1952. The insignia of No.4082 were quickly transferred to No.7013 *Bristol Castle*, which assumed the identity of this Royal engine for the funeral train. It was perhaps a trifle naïve of the authorities to think they would not be found out, but the row which GWR fans raised in the national press – the differences were easily spotted – was a major embarrassment to the then infant (and hated) British Railways.

This time the successive batches kept to the same generic name for the class – fortunately the stormy past of Great Western territory meant that there was an adequate supply of fortified houses therein. Even so, there were a few exceptions such as the 15 converted "Star"s (actually two Stars, one Knight, two Queens and ten Abbeys) and there was a group named after noble Earls, the result of complaints from some aristocratic gentlemen that their names had been given to some rather small and old-fashioned engines. In World War II twelve were given names of famous aircraft and

three gentlemen by the names of *Isambard Kingdom Brunel, Sir Daniel Gooch* and *G.J Churchward* amongst others also were remembered.

At the time of its introduction the "Castle" class was the most powerful locomotive design in the country, although far from being the largest. Those sceptical of this claim were convinced during exchange trials in 1925 and 1926 during which a "Castle" was proved to have an economical mastery with something to spare – over the hardest schedules the LNER or LMS had to offer, whereas those companies were unable to field a candidate which could do the same on the GWR. The "Castle" class handled the "Cheltenham Flyer" which for some years was the fastest train in the world with a 65 minute schedule for the 77$\frac{1}{4}$ miles (124km) from Swindon to Paddington Station, London. A run with this train on June 6, 1932 with *Tregenna Castle* in 56$\frac{3}{4}$ minutes, an average speed to start-to-stop of 81.7 (131.5km/h), was also a world record for some time after it was accomplished.

The "Castle" class was capable of handling heavy trains. The famous "Cornish Riviera Limited" could load up to 15 of the GWR's 70ft carriages on the by no means easy road from Paddington to Plymouth on a schedule which averaged 55mph (88km/h) for the 225.7 miles. For many years this was the longest non-stop run in the country. It is true that carriages were slipped at three points en route but on the last stretch gradients of up to 1 in 37 (2.7 per cent) were encountered.

The last and 171st "Castle" No.7037 *Swindon* appeared in 1950, by which time a few of the earliest had already been withdrawn. The 171 included those fifteen which were converted from "Star"and one (No.111 *Viscount Churchill)* which had originally been that odd-man-out amongst GWR locomotives, Churchward's 4-6-2 *The Great Bear.* These older "Castles" were the first to go.

During the years 1957 to 1960, some time after the GWR had become part of British Railways in 1948, a number of the "Castle" class were modernised with larger superheaters and double chimneys. The results were excellent, but the dieselisation which immediately followed prevented the improvements having any beneficial effect on train working.

Withdrawal began in earnest in 1962 and the last "Castle" ceased running in normal service in July 1965. But this was not to be the end of their history, and it is a measure of the esteem and affection in which they were held that seven have been preserved. The Science Museum had room for one only modern steam engine to illustrate the best in British locomotive engineering and they chose No.4073 *Caerphilly Castle.* This steam locomotive is also the only modern one to appear on a British postage stamp.

Three preserved "Castles" are currently in working order, No. 7029 *Clun Castle* at the Birmingham Railway Museum, No.5051 *Drysllwyn Castle* at the Great Western Society's Didcot Steam Centre, and, so far away and in such a remote part of Australia that its best address is latitude 20°45'S longitude 116°10'E, is No.4079 *Pendennis Castle.*

Left: Preserved Castle class No.7029 Clun Castle. This locomotive is kept at the Birmingham Railway Museum and is used on mainline enthusiast specials.

No.1 B₀-B₀

Origin: United States: American Locomotive Co (Alco), 1924. **Type:** Diesel-electric switching locomotive. **Gauge:** 4ft 8½in (1,435mm). **Propulsion:** Ingersoll-Rand 300hp (224kW) 6-cylinder four-stroke diesel engine and GEC generator supplying current to four nose-suspended traction motors geared to the axles. **Weight:** 120,000lb (54.4t). **Max. axleload:** 30,000lb (13.6t). **Length:** 32ft 6in (9,906mm).

The story of compression-ignition railroad motive power in this book begins with the first diesel-electric locomotives of more than very modest power to be commercially successful in public service. They were the result of co-operation between three well known specialist manufacturers; Ingersoll-Rand of Phillips, New Jersey, produced the diesel engine, General Electric of Erie, Pennsylvania, the electric equipment, and the American Locomotive Company (Alco) of Schenectady, New York, the locomotive body and running gear. Both the principles of design and the configuration are the same as those used for the majority of today's locomotives. The difference is that for the same size and weight GE today could offer 1,000hp (746kW) instead of 300hp (224kW).

The diesel engine in the form in which it is now universally used is much less the work of Doctor Rudolph Diesel, of Germany, than of a Briton called Ackroyd-Stuart. In the 1880s he demonstrated an internal combustion engine in which the fuel was injected into the cylinder at the end of the piston stroke. This engine was turned into a practical proposition by Richard Hornsby & Co., of Grantham, England, later Ruston & Hornsby. Dr. Diesel's engine, demonstrated in 1898, used a high compression ratio typical of present day engines to obtain a big increase in thermal efficiency, but the fuel had to be injected by a blast of compressed air at some 1,000psi (65kg/cm²). This involved heavy ancillary equipment.

In 1896 a small diesel locomotive, the first in the world and which one might more reasonably call an Ackroyd-Stuart locomotive, was built at Hornsbys. It was used for shunting purposes in the works. The first recorded use of a compression-ignition locomotive in public service seems to have occurred in Sweden, when a small railcar with a 75bhp (56kW) engine and electrical transmission was put into service on the Mellersta & Södermanlands Railway in 1913. Of course, this was hardly a greater output than would nowadays be installed in a medium sized family car, and went no distance towards proving the diesel engine as suitable for rail traction.

Experiments with a diesel engine driving an air compressor and feeding compressed air to a normal steam locomotive engine and chassis were not

successful, although the scheme was a simple one. The use of hydraulic fluid as a transmission medium has been reasonably satisfactory, but by far the majority of diesel locomotives ever built have, and have had, electric transmissions. A diesel engine drives an electric generator or alternator which feeds current to the motors of what amounts to an electric locomotive.

Because this concept of a diesel locomotive involved building, to start with, an electric locomotive complete with traction motors and control gear, and then adding to that a diesel-driven generator to supply current to the electric locomotive, it was not only expensive but complex. Furthermore, electrical equipment is not happy living in close company with the vibration and oil-mist which surrounds even the best-maintained diesel engines. Accordingly, in most places and for many years, diesel locomotives – however economical they might be as regards fuel consumption and however efficient operationally – led rather unfulfilled and unhappy lives.

In respect of these drawbacks, the consortium took their courage in both hands and built a demonstrator early in 1924 by Ingersoll-Rand and General Electric. This machine put in over 2,000 hours showing off its abilities in various railroad yards and industrial premises. A feature of this unit was the spectacular all-round visibility available via seven large windows at each of the rounded ends.

This trial locomotive led to a batch of five locomotives being built later that year for stock; 26 units in all were produced during the years 1924 to 1928. Customers included the Baltimore & Ohio (1), Central of New Jersey (1), Lehigh Valley (1), Erie (2), Chicago & North Western (3), Reading (2), and Delaware, Lackawanna & Western (2). The remainder went to industrial buyers. There were also a few twin-engined models supplied, generally similar but longer and of twice the power. Seven were produced between 1925 and 1928. The railroads which had them were the Long Island and the Erie with two each, and the Great Northern with one. The others went to industrial customers. The weight was 200,000lb (90.7t) and each of the two engine- generator sets fitted were similar to those of the single-engined type.

Whilst the claim of commercial success was true in the sense that the makers did not lose money, it was not so for the buyers. All these customers had operations for which steam traction could not be used for some extraneous reason such as fire-risk or legislation, and so a more costly form of power was necessary. Amongst them was that famous ordinance whereby steam locomotives were excluded from New York City. Useful experience was gained which eased the general introduction of diesel traction a quarter century later. It says enough, perhaps, of the technical success of these locomotives that, unlike so many firsts, they stood the test of time. Indeed, some were still giving service 35 years later although, like the legendary Irishman's hammer, they had no doubt acquired a few new heads and a few new handles in the meantime. Two units survive, one in the Baltimore & Ohio Railroad Museum at Baltimore, Maryland and the very first, Central of New Jersey No.1000, at the National Museum of Transport in St Louis, Missouri.

Left: This was the first diesel-electric locomotive to be a commercial success. It was used for switching, from 1924 until it was scrapped in the 1950s.

K-36 2-8-2

Origin: United States: Denver & Rio Grande Western Railroad (D&RGW) 1925. **Gauge:** 3ft 0in (914mm). **Tractive effort:** 36,200lb (16,425kg) **Axleload:** 39,558lb (17.9t). **Cylinders:** (2) 20 x 24in (508 x 609mm). **Driving wheels:** 44in (1,117mm). **Heating surface:** 2,107sq ft (196m²) **Superheater:** 575sq ft (53m²). **Steam pressure:** 195psi (13.7kg/cm²). **Grate area:** 40sq ft (3.7m²). **Fuel:** 16,000lb (7.3t). **Water:** 5,000 US gall (18.9m³) **Adhesive weight:** 143,850lb (65.3t). **Total weight:** 286,500lb (130t) **Length overall:** 68ft 3in (20,802mm).

The last proper steam railroad in the USA! For almost a decade from 1960 to 1968 the remaining Denver & Rio Grande Western 3ft gauge trackage in Colorado and New Mexico was just that. But eight years as the surviving one-thousandth of 250,000 miles of steam railroading was not the only reason why these 250 miles (402km) of lines attracted the attention of a railfan-infested nation to an unparalleled degree. If General Motors' Electro-Motive Division had finally been ousted by the traditional products of Lima, Baldwin, Alco, Roanoke and others, the Rio Grande narrow-gauge would have still made it to the top. It had the lot.

There were trestles, wyes, balloon loops, 10,000ft (3,000m) summits, deserts, snowsheds, 4 per cent (1-in-25) grades, mixed-gauge track, timber-lined tunnels, rotary snowploughs, open-platform passenger cars, steam pile-drivers, wooden gons and boxcars; not to speak of a fleet of vintage Alco and Baldwin mikes which, although bearing external signs of having been rolled down mountainsides on occasion, still had internals that could produce exhaust sounds of unmatched crispness and precision. And those whistles! When the five chimes echoed round the mountains of Colorado, every eagle for miles left its nest in alarm.

For a long time, oil finds near Farmington, New Mexico, generated enough freight traffic to keep the line open. At the same time the prospects were not good enough to justify widening the gauge to standard or to dieselise. It was remarkable that this delicate balance between modernisation and abandonment was maintained for so long. For this we all must be grateful, because when the end of freight operation came in 1968, railroad preservation had become fashionable and the states of Colorado and New Mexico bought the best 64 miles (103km) to run as a museum-piece tourist railroad. The preserved section, known as the Cumbres & Toltec Scenic Railroad, runs from Antonito, Colorado to Chama, New Mexico. With the mountain trackage came 124 cars of various kinds and, most important of all, nine narrow-gauge 2-8-2s of classes "K-36" and "K-37".

The "K-36" 2-8-2s ("K" indicates a 2-8-2; "36" means 36,000lb of tractive

effort) were the third class of narrow-gauge Mikado supplied to the Rio Grande. The squat "K-27" "Mud-hens" of 1903 came first, followed in 1923 by 10 speedy "K-28" "Sports Models" from Alco, intended for passenger work. Three "K-28s" survive in tourist train-service on the Durango to Silverton line, also in Colorado. The 10 much larger "K-36s" came from

Baldwins in 1925 and were entirely standard products of their day, apart from exceptional size and power for the slim gauge. The boilers and cylinders were the same as those of a typical 2-8-0 made for standard gauge. With outside frames and cranks, the distance between the cylinder centre lines would be the same for the two gauges. Seven of the 10 built have been preserved, one on the Silverton line. They are rated to haul 232 tons on a 4 per cent (1-in-25) grade.

When further similar locomotives were needed a year or two later, the Rio Grande produced the "K-37" class "in-house" from some surplus standard gauge 2-8-0s, new frames and wheels being the only substantial pieces of hardware required. The old boilers, cabs, tender bodies, cylinders and most smaller fittings could be re-used. Although three have survived, boiler inspectors have been a little chary of certifying their boilers, dating from as early as 1902, for the hard work expected of locomotives working on the magnificent route of the Cumbres & Toltec Scenic Railroad.

Right: A Denver & Rio Grande Western "K-36" 2-8-2 takes on water at Alamosa, Colorado.

Below: Denver & Rio Grande Western "K-36" 2-8-2 No.481. Note the large snowplough on this classic narrow-gauge loco.

Class 01 4-6-2

Origin: Germany: German State Railway (DR), 1926. **Tractive effort:** 35,610lb (16,160kg). **Axle load:** 44,500lb (20.25t). **Cylinders:** (2) 23.6 × 26.0in (600 × 660mm). **Driving wheels:** 78.7in (2,000m). **Heating surface:** 2,661sq (247.3m²). **Superheater:** 915sq ft (85.0m²). **Steam pressure:** 228psi (16kg/cm²). **Grate area:** 47.5sq ft (4.41m²). **Fuel:** 22,000lb (10.0t). **Water:** 7,500gall (9,000 US) (34m³). **Adhesive weight:** 130,500lb (59.2t). **Total weight:** 240,000lb (109t) (without tender). **Length overall:** 78ft 6m (23,940mm). *(These dimensions etc. refer to engines with copper fireboxes other than the first 10.)*

In 1922, when the German railways were under government control, a Central Locomotive Design Section was set up under Dr R P Wagner, an engineer trained on the KPEV, but having a wide knowledge of railways in other countries. After the establishment of the German State Railway in 1922, Wagner's team prepared a scheme for standard locomotives, much influenced by Prussian practice, but taking into account that, in some parts of the country, the engines would have to burn coal of a lower quality than that to which the Prussian engines were accustomed, and that they would have to work in more mountainous country than the North German plain which dominated the KPEV locomotive designs.

The standard classes therefore had larger grates than their Prussian predecessors, and in the engines with trailing carrying wheels, there was a clear space under the firebox for the entry of air and the removal of ashes as had been provided, largely under the influence of Maffei of Munich, in the modern passenger engines of the southern German states.

Until this time the maximum axle loading permitted in Germany had been 18 tonnes, but a programme of upgrading of track and bridges to take 20-tonne axle loads had been put in hand, and the first of the new locomotives to be built were two classes of Pacific designed to this increased axle load, and designated "01" and "02 ". The specification required the engines to haul 800 tonnes at 62mph (100km/h) on the level, and 500 tonnes at 31mph (50km/h) on a 1 in 100 (1 per cent) gradient; the maximum speed was to be 74.6mph (120 km/h).

Of the 139 Pacifics which DR inherited from the railways of the southern states, all but 10 were four-cylinder compounds. It was originally intended that the standard locomotives should all have two cylinders, but in deference to the representatives of the states other than Prussia on the central design committee, the new Pacific was produced in two versions, Class "01 with two cylinders and Class "02" with four compound cylinders. Ten engines of each type were built, and were divided between three locomotive depots for comparison. Trials of the two classes showed a small advantage in fuel consumption to the compounds, but the advantage was

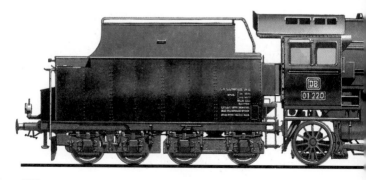

Above: German "01" class 4-6-2 No.012204-4. The final figure is a check digit for use with a computer system.

considered to be offset by the increased costs of maintaining the latter, and the "01' was adopted as standard for future construction. The use of two cylinders only in the largest passenger class was a clear break with former German practice.

Although the basic layout of the "01" was simple, much of the detailed work was complicated, and there was a full range of auxiliary equipment, including a feedwater heater, with a distinctive heat exchanger buried in the smokebox ahead of the chimney. The use of a round-topped firebox was a reversion from recent Prussian practice, and, at a time when engineers in

Below: A German Federal Railways class "01" 4-6-2, used for handling the principal steam express trains in Germany.

many countries were building boilers with a forward extension of the firebox (the so-called "combustion chamber"), Wagner made the front of his firebox almost straight, as he considered that the extra maintenance cost of the combustion chamber was not justified. It was also unusual for a boiler of this size to have a parallel barrel.

The general appearance of the engines owed much to Prussian practice, but with various parts attached to the outside of the boiler for accessibility, there was a distinct North American touch. Of the three apparent domes, the first housed the feedwater inlet, the second was the sand box, and the third housed the regulator. Like the final Prussian designs the engines had bar frames. The long gap between the trailing coupled axle and the trailing carrying axle resulted in the carrying axle having a slightly greater axle load than any of the coupled axles.

The detailed design of the engines was undertaken by Borsig of Berlin, and the first engines were built by that firm and by AEG. Slow progress with upgrading lines for 20-tonne axle loads inhibited the rapid construction of "01"s, but by 1938 a total of 231 had been built, to which were added a further 10 by the rebuilding of the "02" compounds.

Experience with the first engines resulted in later engines having the cylinder diameter increased from 25.6m (650mm) to 26.0in (660mm). The boiler tubes were lengthened, with a corresponding shortening of the smokebox, and later still steel fireboxes were used in place of copper. Improved braking and larger bogie wheels were introduced as part of a programme for increasing the maximum speed of the class to 80.8mph (130km/h).

In the meantime, in 1930, a slightly smaller version of the "01", designated "03", was introduced for lines still limited to an 18-tonne axle load, and 298 of these were built up to 1937.

Until 1937 the speed limit of most lines in Germany was 62mph (100km/h), so it was not until the general raising of the maximum speed to 75mph (120km/h) in 1937 that the "01" and "03" had full scope as express engines. However, by 1937 there were already 58 runs daily in Germany, booked at start-to-stop speeds of 60mph (97km/h) or more, and the majority of these were worked by the "01" or "03".

When further express engines were built from 1939 onwards, the

Below: This picture shows one of the smaller German class "03" 4-6-2s, No.032180-2. Note the small post-war "Witte" pattern smoke deflectors and, again, the computer check digit.

Above: A German Federal Railways class "01" 4-6-2 makes a fine show crossing a wide-span girder bridge.

continued acceleration of passenger trains made it necessary for them to have a maximum speed of 93mph (150km/h), and following experience with the "05" 4-6-4 locomotives, the new engines were given full streamlining and three cylinders. These engines were classed "01^{10}" and "03^{10}", and 55 of the former and 60 of the latter were built between 1939 and 1941; but for the war, the totals would have been 250 and 140 respectively. Apart from two experimental Pacifics made in West Germany in 1957 these were the last new steam express locomotives to be built in Germany.

After the partition of Germany 171 locomotives of class "01" came into the stock of DB in West Germany and 70 into the stock of DR in East Germany. Of these 55 of the DB locomotives and 35 of the DR locomotives were rebuilt. The remaining locomotives on DB received the post-war "Witte" smoke deflectors, in place of the full-depth deflectors. Another alteration which affected the appearance of many of the engines was the removal of the sloping plates which connected the side running plates to the buffer beam. The unrebuilt engines on DR retained their original appearance. The last of the DB engines was withdrawn in 1973, but several of the DR engines were still at work in 1981, after being returned to regular service because of the shortage of oil. With their rebuilt sisters they were the last express steam engines at work in Europe.

There was one other German Pacific to be mentioned, which had an unusual history. As part of the experimental work on high-speed steam trains, a streamlined three-cylinder 4-6-6 tank was built in 1939. Like the Class "05" 4-6-4 it had driving wheels 90^{1}/$_{2}$in (2,300mm) in diameter, and was designed for a maximum speed of 108mph (175km/h) it was used between Berlin and Dresden. This engine came into DR ownership, and in 1960 parts of it, together with some parts of an experimental high-pressure 2-10-2 locomotive, were used to produce a high-speed Pacific for testing new rolling stock and making brake tests. The all-welded boiler was identical to that used in rebuilding the former Prussian Class "P10" locomotives, DR Class "39". The engine was partially enclosed in a streamlined casing of distinctive shape, with a shapely chimney. The designed speed of the engine was 100mph (160km/h), but it was operated well above this speed into the 1970s, being the last steam engine in the world to exceed the magic speed of 100 miles per hour.

King Arthur Class 4-6-0

Origin: Great Britain: Southern Railway (SR), 1925. **Tractive effort:** 25,320lb (11,485kg). **Axle load:** 45,000lb (20.5t). **Cylinders:** (2) 20^1/$_2$ x 28m (521 x 711mm). **Driving wheels:** 79m (2,007mm). **Heating surface:** 1,878sq ft (174.5m^2). **Superheater:** 337sq ft (31.3m^2). **Steam pressure:** 200psi (14.1kg/cm^2). **Grate area:** 30sq ft (2.8m^2). **Fuel:** 11,000lb (5t). **Water:** 5,000gall (6,000 US) (22.7m^3) **Adhesive weight:** 134,500lb (6t). **Total weight:** 310,500lb (141t). **Length overall:** 66ft 5in (20,244mm).

These Knights of the Turntable got their romantic names from the Arthurian legends and this veiled an extreme ordinariness.

No doubt the same applied to King Arthur's knights themselves, but in both cases this was no detriment to – indeed it would enhance – the service they gave.

In 1923 Richard Maunsell was made Chief Mechanical Engineer of the Southern Railway newly formed by amalgamating the London & South Western, London, Brighton & South Coast and South Eastern & Chatham Railways. His own SECR locomotive affairs were getting into good shape, but he understandably had doubts about the foreigners. The LSWR ran long-distance expresses to the west country and the front runners in its fleet were twenty 4-6-0s called the "N15" class. Simplicity was the theme of their design with two big 22in x 28in (559 x 711mm) cylinders, outside valves and valve gear, and a parallel boiler with a round-top firebox. Since the LSWR did not have water troughs, big bogie tenders were attached. They ran well but by SECR standards not brilliantly, and Maunsell set about making some improvements to be incorporated in a further batch.

Cylinders on the new locomotives had valves and valve gear which gave events of the kind that had made the "E1" class 4-4-0s such a success on the SECR. More direct steam passages and larger superheaters were used and the ashpan redesigned to improve combustion. A young man called John Elliot, in charge of Public Relations on the SR – a post in which at that time there was plenty of scope – suggested the names and in February 1925 No.453 *King Arthur* left the ex-LSWR works at Eastleigh, to be followed in March by *Queen Guinevere*, *Sir Lancelot* and eight other knights. Associated names like *Excalibur*, *Camelot* and *Morgan le Fay* were given to the 20 older locomotives, which also had some of the new technical features applied to them.

At the same time 30 more were ordered from the North British Locomotive Co. of Glasgow while the following year a final 14 were built at Eastleigh. These latter were intended for the Central (ex-LBSCR) section of the SR and had smaller 3,500 gallon six-wheel tenders. So there were now, all told, 74 of the "King Arthur" class and they handled most of the principal SR express passenger assignments until Maunsell's first "Lord Nelson" class arrived in 1927.

Above: In British Rail days, ex-Southern Railway "King Arthur" No.30804 *Sir Cador of Cornwall* leaves Bromley, Kent, with a London to Ramsgate train.

The line on which *King Arthur* and his knights rode most often and most nobly into battle was the switchback road beyond Salisbury to Exeter. No.768 *Sir Balin*, travelling eastwards one day in 1934 was observed to regain 6 minutes on a 96-minute schedule with 420 tons, 65 tons more than the maximum laid down for the timing. On this day the maximum speed reached was $86^1/2$mph (139km/h) at Axminster but speeds of 90mph (145km/h) and over were not uncommon.

Perhaps the most remarkable run with one of these engines occurred in 1936 when No.777 *Sir Lamiel* regained $17^1/2$ minutes in covering the $83^3/4$ miles (134km) from Salisbury to Waterloo in $72^3/4$ minutes an average speed start-to-stop of 69.2mph (111 km/h) with a load of 345 tons.

It is thus appropriate that the "King Arthur" allocated to the National Railway Museum and subsequently restored to running order was this same No.777. The "King Arthur" class started to be withdrawn well before steam locomotive preservation became a mania, so none was preserved privately. The saying "happy is the land that has no history" applied to the class, since apart from playing general post with types of tenders, their owners found the "King Arthur" locomotives good enough to remain virtually as they were built, right to the end.

Below: "King Arthur" class No.772 *Sir Percivale* depicted in the livery adopted by the Southern Railway in 1938, when a brighter green was substituted for the olive green of the 1920s.

A-6 4-4-2

Origin: United States: Southern Pacific (SP), 1927. **Gauge:** 4ft 8$\frac{1}{2}$in (1,435mm). **Tractive effort:** 41,360lb (18,766kg).* **Axleload:** 33,000lb (15t). **Cylinders:** (2) 22 x 28in (558 x 711mm). **Driving wheels:** 81in (2,057mm). **Steam pressure:** 210psi (14.8kg/cm²). **Grate area:** 49,5sq ft ,(4.6m²). **Fuel (oil):** 2,940 US gall (11.1m³). **Water:** 9,000 US gall (34.1m³). **Adhesive weight:** 62,0001b (28.1t). **Total weight:** 465,900lb (211.4t). **Length overall:** 78ft 8$\frac{1}{2}$in (23,990mm). *29,860lb (13,094kg) without booster.

These delightfully elegant and simple locomotives have a very complex history, not being made any easier to understand by the fact that their owner ran three separately-administered railroad establishments. There was Southern Pacific proper upon which the 75 4-4-2s built between 1902 and 1911 were numbered in chronological order from 3000 to 3074. Then, from time to time, some of them ran with different numbers on SP de Mexico or on the Texas & New Orleans (the "Cotton Belt") Railroad. Both Mexico and Texas had hostile legislation concerning "foreign" railroads on their territories and SP had to set up these nominally independent railroads to operate therein.

Further complications arise because the 4-4-2s were divided into five classes ("A-1" to "A-6" but not "A-4"). On top of that each class – following various rebuildings – included differences as great or greater than between the separately-designated classes. The most obvious variations lay in the type of tender fitted; tubular "Vanderbuilt" tanks of various sizes, ordinary "box" pattern tenders as well as those with semicircular tanks could all be found on the 4-4-2s.

The illustration shows the "A-6" class of 1925, which was the last word as regards 4-4-2s on SP. The "A-6s" were produced in SP's own shops at Sacramento and Los Angeles by rebuilding four of the 51-strong "A-3" class built by Alco and Baldwin between 1904 and 1908. They took the numbers (No.3000-3003) of older 4-4-2s of Class "A-1" which had started life as Vauclain compounds and had by then been scrapped. Seven other members of the "A-3" class were given similar treatment but were not reclassified. One of these latter machines, No.3025, is the sole survivor of the 4-4-2s and can be seen at Traveltown Museum in Burbank, Los Angeles, California.

The great strength of the 4-4-2 steam locomotive lay in the big deep and wide firebox which it was possible to provide above the small rear carrying wheels; the great weakness, of course, lay in the limited adhesion possible with only four driving wheels. This problem was overcome by equipping the rebuilds with booster engines driving the rear wheels. At the same time, the new "Delta" pattern cast-steel trailing trucks, which were needed to house this device, meant that the trailing wheels were converted from inside bearings to outside, and this had advantages too. Boosters were popular on the SP, being

Below: The class A-6 4-4-2s were produced in 1925 by rebuilding in Southern Pacific's own shops a number of older class A-3 4-4-2s which had been built in 1904-1906.

Above: Southern Pacific rebuilt class A-4 4-4-2 No.3025 on display at Traveltown, Burbank. Note below-centre position of headlight, an SP trademark.

fitted also to over 300 4-8-2s, 2-8-4s, 4-8-4s, 2-10-2s and 4-10-2s.

The addition of a booster was the most important alteration made to the rebuilt Atlantics and it added 11,500lb (5,218kg) to the nominal tractive effort. It cut out automatically above 10mph (16km/h). In this guise the 4-4-2s could play their part in running SP's crack high-speed "Daylight" expresses and two (3000-1) were painted in the special orange and black livery used on those trains. When loads exceeded the maximum permitted to a 4-8-4, a 4-4-2 would be attached as a helper on steeply-graded sections of the main coast line between Los Angeles and San Francisco.

A 4-4-2 on its own was assigned to the "Sacramento Daylight" on the independent section of its run. This was a portion of the "San Joaquin Daylight" which connected Los Angeles and San Francisco. Although the large driving wheels of the "A-6s" were a little smaller than the full 7ft of the "A-1s", they were totally adequate for the fast running necessary to keep time with these trains.

The rebuilding had involved improvements to the ports, passages and valve timing, quite apart from the substitution of Walschaert for Stephenson valve gear, thereby making it possible for the A-6s to run adequately fast to keep to schedule on such smartly-timed trains.

Class A 4-8-4

Origin: United States: Northern Pacific Railroad (NP), 1926. **Gauge:** 4ft 8¹/₂in (1,435mm). **Tractive effort:** 61,600lb (27,950kg). **Axle load:** 65,000lb (29.5t). **Cylinders:** (2) 28 x 30in (711 x 762mm). **Driving wheels:** 73in (1,854mm). **Heating surface:** 4,660sq ft (433m²). **Superheater:** 1,992sq ft (185m²). **Steam pressure:** 225psi (15.8kg/cm²). **Grate area:** 115sq ft (10.7m²). **Fuel:** 48,000lb (22t). **Water:** 12,500gall (15,000 US) (58m³). **Adhesive weight:** 260,000lb (118t). **Total weight:** 739,000lb (335t). **Overall length:** 105ft 4³/₈in (32,125mm).

The King of wheel arrangements at last! It needed 96 years for the 0-2-2 to become a 4-8-4, because all at once in 1927 4-8-4s quickly appeared on several railroads. But by a photo-finish the Northern Pacific's class "A" 4-8-4 was the first and hence the type-name Northern was adopted. The Canadian National Railway, whose first 4-8-4 appeared in 1927, made an unsuccessful play for the name Confederation. Delaware, Lackawanna & Western put forward Pocono for their version. Other early members of the 4-8-4 Club – eventually to be over 40 strong in North America alone – were the Atchison, Topeka & Santa Fe and South Australia, the first foreign member.

The genesis of the 4-8-4 lay in the imbalance between possible tractive effort and grate area of its predecessor the 4-8-2. The Northern Pacific Railroad had a special problem in that its local coal supplies - known rather oddly as Rosebud coal – had a specially high ash content; hence the need for a big firebox and a four-wheel instead of a two-wheel truck at the rear.

And when we say a big firebox, we mean a *really* big one – measuring 13¹/₂ x 8¹/₂ft (4 x 2¹/₂m) – exceeding that of any other line's 4-84s. Northern Pacific themselves found their first Northerns so satisfactory they never ordered another passenger locomotive with any other wheel arrangement, and indeed contented themselves with ordering modestly stretched and modernised versions of the originals – sub-classes "A-2", "A-3", "A-4" and "A-5" – right up to their last order for steam in 1943.

The originals were twelve in number and came from the American Locomotive Co of Schenectady. Apart from those enormous grates they were very much the standard US locomotive of the day, with the rugged features evolved after nearly a century of locomotive building on a vast scale. A booster fitted to the trailing truck gave a further 11,400lb (5,172kg) of tractive effort when required at low speeds.

The next 4-8-4 to operate on NP was another Alco product, built in 1930 to the order of the Timken Roller Bearing Co to demonstrate the advantages of having roller bearings on the axles of a steam locomotive. This "Four

Below: Northern Pacific Railroad class "A-5" 4-8-4 No.2680 built by Baldwin 1943. Note the "centipede"fourteen wheel tender.

Above: One of the 1938 build of "A-3"s
No.2664 eases a freight past the small
depot at Manitoba Junction, Minn.

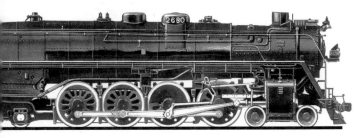

Aces" (No.1111) locomotive worked on many railroads with some success as a salesman. The NP was particularly impressed – not only did they buy the engine in 1933 when its sales campaign was over but they also included Timken bearings in the specification when further orders for locomotives were placed. On NP No.1111 was renumbered 2626 and designated "A-1".

Baldwin of Philadelphia delivered the rest of the Northern fleet. The ten "A-2"s of 1934 (Nos.2650-59) had disc drivers and bath-tub tenders, and the eight "A-3"s of 1938 (Nos.2660-67) were almost identical. The final two batches of eight and ten respectively were also very similar; these were the "A-4"s of 1941 (Nos.2670-77) and the "A-5"s of 1943 (Nos.2680-89). These last two groups may be distinguished by their 14-wheel Centipede or 4-10-0 tenders of the type originally supplied for Union Pacific.

This final batch is the subject of the art-work on the previous pages. The amount of stretching that was done may be judged from the following particulars.

Tractive effort: 69,800lb (31,660kg). **Axle load:** 74,000lb (33.5t). **Driving wheels:** 77in (1,956mm). **Steam pressure:** 260psi (18.3kg/cm). **Fuel:** 54,000lb

24.5t). **Water:** 21,000gall (25,000 US) (95m³). **Adhesive weight:** 295,000lb 134t). **Total weight:** 952,000lb (432t). **Overall length:** 112ft 10in (34,391mm). Other particulars are sensibly the same as the "A" class.

Northern Pacific had begun well by receiving a charter from President Abraham Lincoln in 1864 to build the first transcontinental line to serve the wide north-western territories of the USA. Through communication with the Pacific coast was established. in 1883. By the time the 4-8-4s began to arrive it had established itself under the slogan "Main Street of the North West", and connected the twin cities of St Paul and Minneapolis with both Seattle and Portland.

The flag train on this run was the North Coast Limited, and the 4-8-4s assigned to it, after taking over from Chicago Burlington & Quincy Railroad power at St Paul, ran the 999 miles to Livingston, Montana, without change of engine. This is believed to be a world record as regards through engine runs with coal-fired locomotives. No doubt it was made possible by using normal coal in a firebox whose ash capacity was designed for the massive residues of Rosebud lignite.

Below: Biggest of the giants – "A-5" class 4-8-4 No.2685 starts "The Alaskan" out of Minneapolis in June 1954.

P-1 4-6-4

Origin: United States: Wabash Railroad (WAB), 1925. **Gauge:** 4ft 8¹/₂in (1,435mm). **Tractive effort:** 44,244lb (20,074kg). **Axleload:** 72,009lb (32.7t) **Cylinders:** (2) 26 x 28in (660 x 711mm). **Driving wheels:** 80in (2,032mm) **Heating surface:** 4,225sq ft (393m²). **Superheater:** 1,051sq ft (98m²) **Steam pressure:** 220psi (15.5kg/cm²). **Grate area:** 71sq ft (6.6m²). **Fuel** 35,840lb (16.3t). **Water:** 12,000 US gall (45.4m³). **Adhesive weight** 1,196,390lb (542.8t). **Total weight:** 582,680lb (264.4t). **Length overall:** 87ft 5in (26,644mm).

The Wabash Railroad Company had headquarters in St Louis and its tracks extended to Chicago, Kansas City, Omaha, Toledo and Detroit. With a route length of 4,000 miles, the Wabash was one of those medium-size lines which led a charmed life in spite of serving an area far too well provided with railroads. Its survival depended on the personal touch – that little extra bit of devotion on the part of the staff which made Wabash freight or passenger service just that critical amount better than its competitors. The personal touch was all that was available for the Wabash had for long been unable to afford much in the way of new equipment. Until dieselisation, the work was all done with a steam fleet which by the end of the war had no units less than 14 years old and included a high proportion built before World War I.

An urgent need for passenger locomotives in 1943 led to the rather drastic step of rebuilding six "K-5" class 2-8-2s into the road's first and only 4-6-4s, Class "P-1". A further "P-1" was produced in 1947 from a "K-4" 2-8-2. This remarkable piece of locomotive surgery was done in the Wabash Shops at Decatur, Illinois.

The original 2-8-2 locomotives were built by Alco in 1925 and, in accordance with the fashion of the moment, had a three-cylinder arrangement. The rebuilds had only two cylinders, three instead of four main axles, much larger driving wheels, two-axle instead of single-axle rear trucks, and roller bearings instead of plain ones. The boilers would also no doubt have needed renewal after 20 years service, so not too much of the originals could have been used.

One might wonder about the need for smallish, but fast new passenger engines in the middle of a war. The reason seems to lie in the fact that many Wabash passenger trains were light yet the only locomotives available to work them (apart from 40-year-old Class "J-1 4-62s) were the large "M1" and "0-1" 4-8-2s and 4-8-4s supplied in 1930-31. Even these had 70in (1,778mm) drivers – rather small for passenger services. So a batch of modest-sized rollerbearing 4-6-4s with high driving wheels, produced by

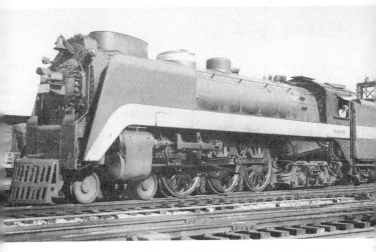

Above: Ready to go with the "Cannonball"! A blue-and-white 4-6-4 of the Wabash Railroad at St. Louis, Missouri, in 1946.

rebuilding (in theory at least) some hard-to-maintain oldish 2-8-2s, would release bigger locomotives for freight and troop movements. At the same time the War Production Board's ban on new passenger locomotives would remain unbroken and the maintenance burden would be relieved by the up-to-date features of the rebuilds. Hence, benefits all round in a totally satisfactory way and the "Wabash Cannonball" would run to time.

The "P-1s" were semi-streamlined in a particularly handsome way, while the striking blue and white livery suited such excellent trains as the *Blue Bird* and *Banner Blue* between St Louis and Chicago. However, an obsolescent fleet of steam locomotives, expensive to run and to maintain, showed up badly against the diesel alternative. So all too soon after production of the last "P-1", the Wabash was to become an all-diesel line. Regrettably, none of these fine locomotives has been preserved.

Below: The Wabash Railroad produced these notable express passenger locomotives in 1943 by conversion from 2-8-2s.

Class S 4-6-2

Origin: Australia: Victorian Government Railways (VGR), 1928. **Tractive effort:** 41,100lb (18,643kg). **Axle load:** 53,000lb (24t). **Cylinders:** (3) 20½ x 28in (521 x 711mm). **Driving wheels:** 73in (1,854mm). **Heating surface:** 3,121 sq ft (290m²). **Superheater:** 631 sq ft (59m²). **Steam pressure:** 200psi (14kg/cm²). **Grate area:** 50sq ft (4.7m²). **Fuel:** 18,500lb (8.5t). **Water:** 13,000gall (15,500 US) (59m³). **Adhesive weight:** 158,000lb (72t). **Total weight:** 497,500lb (226t). **Length overall:** 85ft 6in (26,060mm).

These big 4-6-2s were built by the Victorian Railways in 1928 for the principal trains between Melbourne and the New South Wales border at Albury, on the way to Sydney. Their heavy axle load precluded running elsewhere on the VGR and only four were constructed. They were one of the very few classes of steam locomotives in Australia to have three cylinders. The valves of the outside cylinders were actuated by Walschaert's valve gear, while the inside valve was driven via a set of Holcroft-Gresley two-to-one derived gear, as used on the British London & North Eastern Railway. Out of sight, however, were a set of totally un-British cast-steel bar frames. Streamline shrouds were added in 1937; in combination with a blue livery the addition matched a set of new all-steel coaches for the "Spirit of Progress" express. The big 12-wheel tenders dated from this time and enabled the 192 mainly level miles (307km) from Melbourne to Albury to be run non-stop in 220 minutes, an average speed of 52mph (83km/h). Fairly modest as this might seem, diesel traction today has only meant 8 minutes less journey time. They were early victims of dieselisation, being displaced from the "Spirit of Progress" train in 1952; all had been withdrawn by 1954.

Above: "S" class 4-6-2 No.S302 *Edward Henty* heads the air-conditioned "Spirit of "Progress" on the Melbourne - Albury run.

Below: Victorian Government Railways "S" class 4-6-2 No.S300 before streamlining.

9000 4-12-2

Origin: United States: Union Pacific Railroad (UP), 1926. **Gauge:** 4ft 8½in (1,435mm). **Tractive effort:** 96,650lb (43,852kg). **Axleload:** 60,000lb (27.2t). **Cylinders:** (2) 27 x 32in (685 x 812mm). (1) 27 x 31in (685 x 787mm). **Driving wheels:** 67in (1,701mm). **Heating surface:** 5,853sq ft (544m²). **Superheater:** 2,560sq ft (238m²). **Steam pressure:** 220psi (15.5kg/cm²). **Grate area:** 108sq ft (10m²). **Fuel:** 42,000lb (19.1t). **Water:** 15,000 US gal (56.8m³). **Adhesive weight:** 355,000lb (161.1t). **Total weight:** 782,000lb (354.8t). **Length overall:** 102ft 7in (31,267mm).

Several times in this book the crossing of the Continental Divide by the Union Pacific Railroad will receive mention. The reason lies in the outstanding locomotive power needed to work ever-increasing tonnages over the grades involved. In the 1920s, traffic was being handled by 2-10-2s and 2-8-8-0 compound Mallets. The latter had adequate tractive effort but speeds above 25mph (40km/h) were not then possible with the Mallet arrangement, while the 2-10-2s had limited adhesion.

The idea of a 12-coupled engine was made possible by using the then new lateral-motion device developed by the American Locomotive Company. This arrangement enabled a long-wheelbase locomotive to negotiate sharp curves. Very few 12-coupled classes of steam locomotive then existed; apart from one or two singletons there were 24 narrow-gauge Class "61" 2-12-2Ts in Java, 44 of Class "59" 2-12-0s in Wurttemburg, Germany, and 10 0-12-0Ts in Bulgaria. Union Pacific had in mind something very much bigger than any of these. In fact the first 4-12-2 when it appeared from Alco in 1926 was well over double the weight of its nearest 12-coupled rival.

The three-cylinder arrangement was adopted because otherwise the piston thrusts involved with a two-cylinder design would be greater than was considered feasible at the time. Tests indicated that No.9000 could take the same loads as the Mallets at very much higher speeds and with much lower coal consumption. Production was put in hand at once and by 1930 the world's first and last class of 4-12-2s totalled 88.

Some of the 9000's more unusual features did cause some trouble. Much was hoped for from the conjugated motion for the centre-cylinder which, being rugged, simple and accessible, had apparently all the attributes. But, as also was found in Britain (its country of origin), the motion needed careful maintenance. There were two reasons – first, wear of any of the pins or

Below: Unique as a wheel arrangement, these 4-12-2s were also the longest non-articulated locos ever built.

Above: Front-end clutter adds to the
impressive proportions of the prototype
Class 9000, built by Alco in 1926.

bearings led to over-travel of the valve, and this in turn led to the middle cylinder doing more than its share of the work, often with dire results. The situation was particularly severe on the centre big-end bearing. A few engines were provided with separate third sets of Walschaert's gear set between the frames to operate the valves of the inside cylinder. This was driven from a second return crank mounted on the crankpin of the fourth axle on the right-hand side of the locomotive.

In order to encourage that 30ft 8in (9,347mm) of fixed wheelbase to perform as a contortionist, the leading and trailing coupled wheels were allowed 1in (25mm) sideplay either side of the centre line. The first locomotive originally had the centre (third) pair of driving wheels flangeless, but later examples had thin flanges. The sideplay was controlled against spring pressure, but no other devices such as spherical joints in the side rods were provided. The arrangements were entirely successful, so much so that the class as a whole would see steam out a quarter of a century later although they were soon to be displaced from prime assignments and to other parts of the system by some greatly improved Mallet-type articulateds – the "Challengers" – introduced a few years later.

Only one of these unique locomotives is preserved; this is No.9004 at the Transportation Museum at Los Angeles.

Below: No.9032 of UP's unique class of 4-12-2s pauses at Topeka, Kansas, on a midsummer day in 1952.

Above: Ready for its next crack at the formidable Sherman Hill (40 miles of 1-in-66), Class 9000 No.9013 waits at Cheyenne in May 1953.

Royal Scot Class 4-6-0

Origin: Great Britain: London Midland & Scottish (LMS), 1927. **Tractive effort:** 33,150lb (15,037kg). **Axle load:** 46,000lb (21t). **Cylinders:** (3) 18 × 26in (457 x 660mm). **Driving wheels:** 81in (2,057mm). **Heating surface:** 1,851 sq ft (172m²). **Superheater:** 367sq ft (34.1m²) **Steam pressure:** 250psi (17.6kg/cm²). **Grate area:** 31.25sq ft (2.90m²). **Fuel:** 20,000lb (9t) **Water:** 4,000gall (4,800 US) (18m³). **Adhesive weight:** 137,000lb (62t) **Total weight:** 312,500lb (142t). **Length overall:** 64ft 11in (19,787mm).

The "Royal Scots" were another notable class of locomotive that managed more than thirty years on top express work, although a rebuilding which left little of the originals intact halfway through their lives perhaps detracts a little from this achievement. In the mid-1920s the then rather new LMS Railway had to face the fact that there was no locomotive capable singly of hauling the principal train, the 10a.m. Scottish Express from London to Edinburgh and Glasgow, shortly to be known as the "Royal Scot". An ex-LNWR 4-6-0 and 4-4-0 combination would take the train from Euston to Carnforth, while two Midland 4-4-0s would take it on over the hills from there.

A Great Western "Castle" class 4-6-0 was borrowed and demonstrated very effectively in October 1926 that better things were possible. It is said that the LMS made enquiry for 25 "Castles" to be built for the summer service of 1927 but, more practically, the biggest locomotive factory in Britain was given a design-and-build contract for 50 large 4-6-0 express locomotives. The contract with the North British Locomotive Co. (NBL) of Glasgow was not signed until February 1927 and, whilst the first locomotive did not quite go into service in time to help with the summer trains that year, all the "Royal Scot" class were in service by the end of November.

Three cylinders were provided, each with its own set of Walschaert's valve gear and a parallel-barrel boiler with a Belpaire firebox as big as the loading gauge would allow. The locomotives had no technical innovations but were representative of the best practice of the day. In consequence they took to the job they were designed for with the minimum of trouble – and at the same time became much admired by both professionals and the enthusiasts.

Of the 50 locomotives, 25 were given names of regiments and 25 the names of early locomotives. Subsequently, though, all the locomotives were named after regiments of the British Army.

A few minor problems had to be overcome, one was that the piston valves leaked when worn, to an extent that increased steam consumption by nearly half before repairs became due. An accident at Leighton Buzzard in 1931 was attributed to smoke beating down and obscuring the driver's view of signals – this led to the rapid fitting of large smoke deflector plates

Above: No.46103 *Royal Scots Fusilier* in British Rail colours sets out with the "Thames-Clyde Express". Note the horse box coupled next to the tender.

at the front end, using the pattern developed on the Southern Railway. During the previous year a further 20 "Royal Scot" class had been built, at the old Midland Railway works at Derby; this time the names included a few non-Army titles such as *The Royal Air Force, The Girl Guide* and *The Boy Scout*.

The period was notable for experiments aimed at improving the thermal efficiency of the steam locomotive by increasing the pressure and hence the temperature of the steam. Although it is by no means the only factor involved, steamships and steam power stations use much higher steam temperatures

Below: No.6129 *The Scottish Horse* shown in the LMS postwar livery.

and produce much higher efficiencies, so the prospects were there.

The LMS therefore commissioned from NBL a further "Royal Scot"-like 4-6-0, but with a Schmidt-pattern boiler which generated steam at 1,800psi (and at 325 degrees C) and used that steam to generate more steam, (at 900psi) in a separate circuit (steam pressure 126 and 63kg/cm^2). This new steam was fed to three compound cylinders (one high-pressure, two low-pressure) that were fairly conventionally arranged, except that the feed to the two low-pressure cylinders was supplemented by a steam supply at 250psi (17.5 kg/cm^2) from yet another compartment in the complex steam generating system.

The locomotive was No.6399 and named *Fury*. Steam at 325 degrees C is very nasty stuff indeed, and when a fire tube burst while *Fury* was on test at Carstairs in February 1930, one man was killed and another seriously injured. After this accident the locomotive was laid aside.

In 1933 the LMS sent a "Royal Scot" locomotive – which changed names with *Royal Scot* for the occasion – to North America, complete with rolling stock, for exhibition at the Chicago World Fair. The train was also exhibited at many places, including Montreal, Denver, San Francisco and Vancouver, on an 11,000-mile (17,700km) tour which followed.

By this time a new locomotive chief had arrived on the LMS scene. William Stanier came from the Great Western Railway, the reputation of which line as the leader in British locomotive practice was then at its zenith. Four things that he did directly affected the "Royal Scot" class. First, he finally eliminated axlebox troubles by initiating a new design of bearing based on GWR practice, which reduced the incidence of "Royal Scot" hot boxes from some 80 to seven annually. Second, he had all the class fitted with new and larger tenders with high curved sidesheets, as used on the other types of locomotive being introduced on the LMS. Third, he took the carcase of *Fury* and rebuilt it into a new locomotive called *British Legion*. The rebuild differed from the others in having a taper-barrel boiler, thereby foreshadowing the shape of things to come. The fourth item was the advent of the Stanier 4-6-2s, which had the effect of displacing the "Royal Scot" class from the very highest assignments.

The effects of well over a decade of hard steaming now began to be felt

and in the normal course of things new boilers would be needed, plus other repairs so extensive that the costs would approach that of renewal. The decision was taken to rebuild all the class with taper-barrel boilers of a new pattern, thereby bringing the "Royal Scot" class into line with all Stanier's designs. The rebuilding included new cylinders, in many cases new frames and even new wheel centres, only the tenders, cabs and nameplates remained.

The first rebuilt "Royal Scot" (No.6103 *Royal Scots Fusilier*) appeared in unlined black livery in 1942, while the last did not come out until 1955. One alteration, fairly insignificant as far as the locomotives were concerned but significant to their public, was the change from the high-pitched Midland Railway whistle to a low-pitched hooter of Caledonian Railway origin, which in Stanier's time was fitted to new LMS locomotives.

The rebuilding was a great success. The new engines stood up to all the abuse of high speed running, heavy loads and wartime neglect better than the originals, and then after the war covered themselves with glory. In the locomotive trials which took place in 1948, shortly after the nationalisation of the main line railways, "Royal Scot" representatives performed particularly well.

Although these trials were mounted with great attention to detail by the mechanical side of the railway, there is much evidence in the voluminous report issued afterwards that the results were invalidated by lack of co-operation on the part of the operating authorities and the staff. For example, comparative coal-consumption figures based on a run from Carlisle to Euston of the "Royal Scot" express which included 27 signal checks and stops could be of little use. Such things happened on many of the test runs due to thoughtless controllers allowing a slower train to occupy the line in front.

One thing that did emerge, however, was that the "Royal Scot" 4-6-0s could handle any express train in Britain with something to spare, more economically and just as ably as the bigger and more costly 4-6-2s of nominally much greater power. This surprised many observers, but it is perhaps an indication of the point that these trials were never intended to be taken seriously, and that the one valid conclusion that could be drawn from them, that 4-6-2s could do no more when fired by hand than 4-6-0s, was totally ignored.

The 70 "Royal Scots" disappeared in a very short time once dieselisation was undertaken. The first withdrawal was BR No.46139 (ex-LMS No.6139), *The Welch Regiment* in October 1962. The last ceased work in January 1966, when BR No.46115 *Scots Guardsman* was set aside for preservation. A Mr. Bill acquired her and she is at present on show at the steam centre at Dinting, near Manchester; No.6115 had been out on the main line on various occasions including the Rocket 150 Cavalcade at Rainhill in May 1980. No.6100 *Royal Scot* is also preserved, and can be seen at Alan Bloom's steam centre at Bressingham.

**Left: Preserved Royal Scot
No.6115 Scots Guardsman
approaching Chinley with an
enthusiast special in
November 1978.**

Class J3a 4-6-4

Origin: United States: New York Central Railroad (NYC), 1926. **Gauge:** 4ft 8½in (1,435mm). **Tractive effort:** 41,860lb (19,000kg). **Axleload:** 67,500lb (30.5t). **Cylinders:** (2) 22½ x 29in (572 x 737mm). **Driving wheels:** 79in (2,007mm). **Heating surface:** 4,187sq ft (389.0m²). **Superheater:** 1,745sq ft (162.1m²). **Steam pressure:** 265psi (18.6kg/cm²). **Grate area:** 82sq ft (7.6m²). **Fuel:** 92,000lb (41.7t). **Water:** 15,000gall (18,000 US) (68.1m³). **Adhesive weight:** 201,500lb (91.5t). **Total weight:** 780,000lb (350t). **Length overall:** 106ft 1in (32,342mm).

Some locomotive wheel arrangements had a particular association with one railway; such was the 4-6-4 and the New York Central. In 1926 the Central built its last Pacific, of Class "K5b," and the road's design staff, under the direction of Paul W Kiefer, Chief Engineer of Motive Power, began to plan a larger engine to meet future requirements. The main requirements were an increase in starting tractive effort, greater cylinder power at higher speeds, and weight distribution and balancing which would impose lower impact loads on the track than did the existing Pacifics. Clearly this would involve a larger firebox, and to meet the axle loading requirement the logical step was to use a four-wheeled truck under the cab, as was advocated by the Lima Locomotive Works, which had plugged engines with large fireboxes over trailing bogies under the trade name of Super Power. As the required tractive effort could be transmitted through three driving axles, the wheel arrangement came out as 4-6-4. Despite the Lima influence in the design, it was the American Locomotive Company of Schenectady which received the order for the first locomotive, although Lima did receive an order for ten of them some years later. Subsequent designs of 4-6-4s took over the type-name Hudson applied to these engines by the New York Central.

Classified "J1a" and numbered 5200, the new engine was handed over to the owners on February 14, 1927. By a narrow margin it was the first 4-6-4 in the United States, but others were already on the production line at Alco for other roads. Compared with the "K5b" it showed an increase in grate area from 67.8sq ft (6.3m²) to 81.5sq ft (7.6m²), and the maximum diameter of the boiler was increased from 84in (2,134mm) to 87⅝in (2,226mm). The cylinder and driving wheel sizes were unchanged, so the tractive effort went up on proportion to the increase in boiler pressure from 200psi (14.1kg/cm²) to 225psi (15.8kg/cm²). The addition of an extra axle enabled the total weight on the coupled axles to be reduced from 185,000lb (83.9t) to 182,000lb (82.6t), despite an increase in the total engine weight of 41,000lb (22t). Improved balancing reduced the impact loading on the rails compared with the Pacific.

The engine had a striking appearance, the rear bogie giving it a more balanced rear end than a Pacific, with its single axle under a large firebox. At

Below: Standard Hudson or 4-6-4 of Class J3. The NYC had 275 locomotives of this type in passenger service and they monopolised the road's express trains for 20 years.

Above: Nearing the end of its career as a mile-a-minute express locomotive, Class J3a No.5449 at East Albany NY in 1952.

the front the air compressors and boiler feed pump were housed under distinctive curved casings at either side of the base of the smokebox, with diagonal bracing bars. The boiler mountings ahead of the cab were clothed in an unusual curved casing.

No.5200 soon showed its paces, and further orders followed, mostly for the NYC itself, but 80 of them allocated to three of the wholly-owned subsidiaries, whose engines were numbered and lettered separately. The latter included 30 engines for the Boston and Albany, which, in deference to the heavier gradients on that line, had driving wheels three inches smaller than the remainder, a rather academic difference. The B&A engines were classified "J2a", "J2B" and "J2c", the suffixes denoting minor differences in successive batches. The main NYC series of 145 engines were numbered consecutively from 5200, and here again successive modifications produced sub-classes "J1a" to "J1e". Amongst detail changes were the substitution of Baker's for Walschaert's valve gear; the Baker's gear has no sliding parts, and was found to require less maintenance. There were also changes in the valve setting.

From their first entry into service the Hudsons established a reputation for heavy haulage at high speeds. Their maximum drawbar horsepower was 38 per cent more than that of the Pacifics, and they attained this at a higher speed. They could haul 18 cars weighing 1,270 tonnes at an average speed of 55mph (88km/h) on the generally level sections. One engine worked a 21-car train of 1, 500 tonnes over the 639 miles (1,027km) from Windsor

(Ontario) to Harmon, covering one section of 71 miles (114km) at an average speed of 62.5mph (100.5km/h).

The last of the "J1" and "J2" series were built in 1932, and there was then a pause in construction, although the design staff were already planning for an increase in power. In 1937 orders were placed for 50 more Hudsons, incorporating certain improvements and classified "J3". At the time of the introduction of the first Hudson, the NYC, like the German engineers of the time, were chary of combustion chambers in fireboxes because of constructional and maintenance problems, but by 1937 further experience had been gained, and the "J3" incorporated a combustion chamber 43in (1,092mm) long. Other changes included a tapering of the boiler barrel to give a greater diameter at the front of the firebox, raising of the boiler pressure from 225psi (15.9kg/cm²) to 275psi (19.3km/cm²) (later reduced to 265psi), and a change in the cylinder size from 25 x 28in (635 x 711mm) to 22½ x 29in (572 x 737mm). The most conspicuous change was the use of disc driving wheels, half the engines having Boxpok wheels with oval openings, and the other half the Scullin type with circular openings.

The final ten engines were clothed in a streamlined casing designed by Henry Dreyfus. Of all the streamlined casings so far applied to American locomotives, this was the first to exploit the natural shape of the locomotive rather than to conceal it, and the working parts were left exposed. Many observers considered these to be the most handsome of all streamlined locomotives, especially when hauling a train in matching livery. Prior to the building of the streamlined "J3"s, a "J1" had been clothed in a casing devised at the Case School of Science in Cleveland, but it was much less attractive than Dreyfus' design, and the engine was rebuilt like the "J3"s; while two further "J3"s were given Dreyfus casings for special duties.

The "J3"s soon showed an improvement over the "J1"s both in power output and in efficiency. At 65mph (105km/h) they developed 20 per cent more power than a "J1". They could haul 1,130 tonne trains over the 147 miles (236km) from Albany to Syracuse at scheduled speeds of 59mph

Below: J1 4-6-4 No.5280 hauling the "Empire State Express" at Dunkirk, NY, in February 1950.

Above: The streamlined version of New York Central's famous J3 Hudsons. The designer of the casings was Henry Dreyfus.

(95km/h), and could reach 60mph (96km/h) with a 1,640 tonne train. The crack train of the NYC was the celebrated 20th Century Limited. At the time of the building of the first Hudsons this train was allowed 20 hours from New York to Chicago. This was cut to 18 hours in 1932 on the introduction of the "J1e" series, and in 1936 there was a further cut to 16½ hours. Aided by the elimination of some severe service slacks, and by the "J3" engines, the schedule came down to 16 hours in 1938, which gave an end-to-end speed of 59.9mph (96.3km/h) with 900-tonne trains, and with seven intermediate stops totalling 26 minutes. On a run with a "J3" on the Century, with 940 tonnes, the 133 miles (214km) from Toledo to Elkhart were covered in a net time of 112½ minutes, and the succeeding 93.9 miles (151km) from Elkhart to Englewood in 79½ minutes, both giving averages of 70.9mph (114km/h). A speed of 85.3mph (137km/h) was maintained for 31 miles (50km), with a maximum of 94mph (151km/h). The engines worked through from Harmon to Toledo or Chicago, 693 and 925 miles (1,114 and 1,487km) respectively. For this purpose huge tenders were built carrying 41 tonnes of coal, but as the NYC used water troughs to replenish the tanks on the move, the water capacity was by comparison modest at 18,000 US gallons (68.1m³).

Eventually the engines allotted to the subsidiaries were brought into the main series of numbers, and with the removal of the streamlined casings in post-war years, the NYC had 275 engines of similar appearance numbered from 5200 to 5474. It was the largest fleet of 4-6-4 locomotives on any railway, and constituted 63 per cent of the total engines of that wheel arrangement in the United States.

Although the Hudson had their share of troubles, they were generally reliable, and the "J3"s ran 185,000 to 200,000 miles (297,000 to 32 1,000km) between heavy repairs, at an annual rate of about 110,000 miles (177,000km).

After World War II the Niagara 4-8-4s displaced the Hudson from the heaviest workings, but as that class numbered only 25 engines, the Hudsons still worked many of the 150 trains daily on the NYC booked at more than 60mph (96km/h) start-to-stop. Despite rapid dieselisation the engines lasted until 1953-6, apart from an accident casualty.

Class Ps-4 4-6-2

Origin: United States: Southern Railway (SR), 1926. **Tractive effort:** 47,500lb (21,546 kg). **Axle load:** 61,000lb (27.25t). **Cylinders:** (2) 27 x 28in (686 x 711mm). **Driving wheels:** 73in (1,854mm). **Heating surface:** 3,689sq ft (343m²). **Superheater:** 993sq ft (92.3m²). **Steam pressure:** 200psi (14.1kg/cm²). **Grate area:** 70.5sq ft (6.55m²). **Fuel:** 32,000lb (14,5t). **Water:** 11,600gall (14,000 US) (53m³). **Adhesive weight:** 182,000lb (81t). **Total weight:** 562,000lb (255.0t). **Length overall:** 91 ft 11⁷/₈in (28,038mm).

Hundreds of classes of Pacific locomotives ran in America; to illustrate them the first choice was the earliest proper 4-6-2, of the Chesapeake & Ohio. Second choice was the Pennsylvania RR class "K4", as the 4-6-2 design built in the largest numbers. This locomotive, our third choice, is without any doubt the most beautiful amongst the Pacifics of America.

The history of the Southern Railway's Pacifics began in World War I, when the United States Railroad Administration, which had taken over the railroads for the duration, set out to design a standard set of steam locomotives to cover all types of traffic. One of these was the so-called USRA "heavy" 4-6-2. Based on this design, the American Locomotive Company built the first batch of 36 Class "Ps-4" 4-6-2s in 1923.

In 1925 President (of Southern Railway) Fairfax Harrison, visited his line's namesake in England and was impressed with its green engines. He determined that his next batch of 4-6-2s would make an equal if not better showing. He naturally chose a style very similar to the English SR except that a much brighter green was used together with gold – the small extra cost paid off quickly in publicity. Coloured locomotives were then quite exceptional in North America. A little later the earlier batch of locomotives appeared in green and gold also.

The 1926 batch of 23 locomotives had the enormous 12 wheel tenders illustrated here, in place of the USRA standard 8-wheel tenders on the earlier engines, and a different and much more obvious type (the Elesco) of feed water heater involving the large transverse cylindrical vessel just in front of the smokestack. Some locomotives from each batch had the Walschaert's gear, others had Baker's. A final batch of 5 came from Baldwin in 1928. These had Walschaert's valve gear and 8 wheel tenders of large capacity. All were fitted with mechanical stokers.

Southern had what it called an "optional equipment policy" whereby drivers were allowed to adorn their locomotives in various ways, ways in fact that were similar to those of 70 years earlier. Eagles could be mounted above the headlights, themselves flanked by brass "candlesticks"; stars were fixed to cylinder heads, brass rings to smokestacks. Some locomotives were named after and by their regular drivers. A lot of this might be considered mere nonsense, but the end effect was that few steam engines anywhere were better maintained.

Of the 64 locomotives built, 44 were allocated to the Southern Railway

Above: One of the Southern Railway's superb "Ps-4 " 4-6-2s in action. This particular loco is the one preserved in the Smithsonian Museum.

proper, 12 to subsidiary Cincinnati, New Orleans & Texas Pacific and 8 to the Alabama Great Southern, although "Southern" appeared on the tenders of all. Running numbers were as follows:
SR proper – Nos. 1366 to 1409. CNO&TP – Nos.6471 to 6482.AGS – Nos.6684 to 6691.

The CNO&TP engines had a device known as a Wimble smoke duct, by which the exhaust which otherwise would issue from the chimney could be led backwards to level with the sand dome and discharged there. The CNO&TP was a line with many timber-lined tunnels and a direct close-up vertical blast would have played havoc with the tunnel linings.

The "Ps-4" class was the last steam passenger locomotive type built for the Southern and they remained in top-line express work until displaced by diesels in the 1940s and 1950s. No.1401 is preserved and is superbly displayed in the Smithsonian Museum, Washington, D.C,

Alas, this involved erecting the display building around the locomotive, thereby preventing its use on special trains for railfans, a Southern speciality.

Below: The glorious green and gold beauty of the livery applied to the Southern Railway (of USA) "Ps-4 " class Pacific is superbly depicted below.

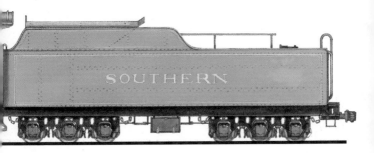

Class 500 4-8-4

Origin: Australia: South Australian Government Railways (SAR), 1928
Tractive effort: 51,000lb (23,133kg). **Axle load:** 49,500lb (22.5t). **Cylinders**
(2) 26 x 28in (660 x 711mm). **Driving wheels:** 63in (1,600mm). **Heating
surface:** 3,648sq ft (339m²). **Superheater:** 835sq ft (77.5m²). **Steam
pressure:** 200psi (14.1kg/cm²). **Grate area:** 66.5sq ft (6.2m²). **Fuel:** 2,4500lb
(11t). **Water:** 7,000gall (8,400 US) (32m³). **Adhesive weight:** 196,500lb
(89t). **Total weight:** 498,000lb (226t). **Length overall:** 83ft 1¹/₂in
(25,641mm).

South Australia is by no means easy locomotive country. For example, when
South Australian Railway's trains leave the capital, Adelaide, for Melbourne,
they have to face a long 1 in 45 (2.2 per cent) climb into the Mount Lofty
ranges. In spite of this their motive power almost eighty years ago was on
the small side. In the early 1920s the latest and largest express passenger
power was the class "S" 4-4-0 of 1894, with 12,700lb (5,762kg) of tractive
effort and 17¹/₂sq ft (1.6m²) of grate area.

The State government was not happy about the state of its 5ft 3in
(1,600mm) gauge railway system and so adopted the idea of inviting a
senior executive from a USA railroad to be the Railway Commissioner. In
due time a certain Mr. W.A. Webb, who hailed from the Missouri-Kansas-
Texas Railroad – the famous "Katy" – arrived in Australia. His plans for SAR
were to include some very large locomotives indeed.

Above and left: Two views of 4-8-4 No. 500 on a special farewell run from Adelaide to Victor Harbour, Victoria, in March 1962, just before withdrawal from service.

The most notable of Webb's two passenger designs were the ten "500" class 4-8-2s, which had over four times the tractive effort of the previous top-line passenger locomotives plus other attributes in proportion! Although typically American in design, these monsters were built in 1926 by the English armaments firm, Armstrong-Whitworth of Newcastle-upon-Tyne. In 1928 the locomotives, apparently still not regarded as sufficiently strong pullers, were further enhanced by a booster giving an additional 8,0001b (3,640kg) of tractive effort. This was accommodated in a four-wheel truck, thereby giving Australia the honour of having the world's first 4-8-4 outside North America; the pony truck had previously had an axle loading of over 22 tons.

Another later addition was a pair of elegant footplate valances bearing the "Overland" motif. This reflected the labours of these magnificent locomotives on "The Overland" express between Adelaide and Melbourne. The 1 in 45 of the Mount Lofty incline could be negotiated at 15mph with 550 tons – this with booster in action. It must have been worth listening to – but then so would be *three* of the "500"s 4-4-0 predecessors on the 350-ton Melbourne express of a few years earlier.

The "500"s and the other Webb classes were not multiplied, mainly because heavy axle-loadings precluded their use on all but the principal main lines. Diesel-electric locomotives appeared in South Australia from 1951 on and in 1955 the first "500" was withdrawn. By 1962 all had gone, except No.504, which is preserved at the Australian Railway Historical Society's museum at Mile End, near Melbourne.

P-7 4-6-2

Origin: United States: Baltimore & Ohio Railroad (B&O), 1927. **Gauge:** 4ft 8^1/$_2$in (1,435mm). **Tractive effort:** 50,000lb (22,686kg). **Axleload:** 68,000lb (30.9t). **Cylinders:** (2) 27 x 28in (685 x 711mm). **Driving wheels:** 80in (2,032mm). **Heating surface:** 3,782sq ft (351m²). **Superheater:** 950sq ft (88m²). **Steam pressure:** 280psi (19.7kg/cm²). **Grate area:** 70.2sq ft (65m³). **Fuel:** 39,000lb (17.7t). **Water:** 11,000US gall (41.6m³). **Adhesive weight:** 201,000lb (91.2t). **Total weight:** 544,000lb (246.8t). **Length overall:** 87ft 10^1/$_2$in (26,784mm).

The Baltimore & Ohio Railroad has used Pacifics for its principal passenger trains since 1906. For the start of through running by B&O, locomotives from Washington to Jersey City in 1927, the eighth class of 4-6-2 was placed in service; these 20 Class "P-7s" were over 50 per cent more powerful than the original Class "P" of 20 years earlier.

This was also the year in which the B&O celebrated the centenary of the granting of its charter with an ambitious "Fair of the Iron Horse" at Baltimore. One of the visitors to the fair was an elegant green and gold 4-6-0 called *King George V* which came from the Great Western Railway of England. The absence of visible plumbing and the stunning livery caused a sensation. As a result, imitation being the sincerest form of flattery, the "P-7" 4-6-2s not only took names from US presidents, but were painted a similar shade of green. It was many years since any B&O engine had been painted anything else but black. Incidentally, the elegant simplicity of the British engine was no triumph of design – the plumbing really was simple. With no air pump, no sandboxes on top of the boiler, no bell, no power reverse, no feed-water pump, and no turbo-generator, anything but a clear outline was impossible. The "P-7s" had all these things, with mechanical stokers and water scoops as well.

The twenty-first "P-7", named *President Cleveland* and completed in 1928, was an experimental locomotive with a watertube firebox and camshaft-driven Caprotti pattern poppet valves, similar in principle to those used in automobile practice. The latter were not a success and were altered to the conventional Walschaert pattern the following year. Unlike the earlier engines, all of which came from Baldwin, this No.5320 was built in the B&O's own Mount Clare shops. Incidentally, the names were allocated in historical order beginning with No.5300 *President Washington*, one loco

Left: Baltimore & Ohio P-7 "President" class 4-6-2 No.5307 crosses the famous bridge at Harper's Ferry, Virginia, in 1952.

sufficing for both presidents named Adams.

The water-tube firebox, while not sufficient of an improvement to displace convention, did remain on the locomotive until 1945. In 1937 one other "P-7" No.5310 *President Taylor* was also treated in this way, with equally inconclusive results. These two locomotives were designated "P9" and "P9b" respectively when running in this condition.

From 1937 to 1940 No.5310 was streamlined, painted blue and renamed *The Royal Blue* for working the train of that name. Because of the difficulty of allocating a specific locomotive to a particular train, the rest of the class were also painted blue and this matched the colour of new B&O trains then being put into service. Soon afterwards, the whole class ceased to carry names and in 1946 a further batch of four was streamlined for running the "Cincinnatian," following a rebuild which included provision which included of cast locomotive beds, roller bearings and bigger 12 wheel tenders.

Left: A "President" class 4-6-2 leans to the curve on this well ballasted stretch of the Baltimore & Ohio Railroad.

G5s 4-6-0

Origin: United States: Long Island Rail Road (LIRR), 1928. **Gauge:** 4ft 8½in (1,435mm). **Tractive effort:** 41,328lb (18,751kg). **Axleload:** 63,000lb (28.6t). **Cylinders:** (2) 24 x 28in (609 x 711mm). **Driving wheels:** 68in (1,727mm). **Heating surface:** 2,855sq ft (265m²). **Superheater:** 613sq ft (57m²). **Steam pressure:** 205psi (14.4kg/cm²). **Grate area:** 55sq ft (5.1m²). **Fuel:** 24,000lb (10.9t). **Water:** 8,300US gall (31.4m³). **Adhesive weight:** 178,000lb (80.8t). **Total weight:** 409,000lb (185.6t). **Length overall:** 70ft 5½in (21,475mm).

These handsome locomotives must represent in this book all those built to carry people to and from the places where they earn their daily bread. Most railroads used superannuated main-line locomotives for this purpose, but the Pennsylvania Railroad. was not one of them, being then in the fortunate position of being able to afford the proper tools for the job.

Pennsy also followed the economical practice of do-it-yourself and 90 of these fine 4-6-0s, designated Class "G5s" were built in 1923, 1924 and 1925 in the road's own Juanita shops. The design owed a great deal to the "E6s" 4-4-2 class of 1910, thereby avoiding some of the expense of new tooling and patterns. An exception was the driving wheels which were 15 per cent smaller than those of the "E6s". Incidentally, the "G" and the "E" stood for the respective wheel arrangements, while "s" stood for "superheated".

The only important feature which was not standard North American practice was the Belpaire firebox. Invented by a Belgian engineer in 1864, the idea was to increase the surface area of the firebox and its internal volume, whilst keeping plenty of room for water to circulate round it. The simplicity of the round-top firebox was lost because the change of section of the boiler made construction more complex. Furthermore, a good deal of additional staying was required, but improved steam generation was thought to make the extra costs worthwhile. Belpaire fireboxes were common in Europe but few other North American railroads used them.

Below: This Long Island G5s 4-6-0 was built in 1929, retired in 1955 and has undergone restoration.

Above: Long Island Rail Road Class G5s 4-6-0 No.38 makes a fine display of smoke at Kings Park, New York, in 1950.

Prosperous Pennsy had an immense freight business which could underpin essentially dubious commuter operations, but an orphan child in the household had no such advantage. This was the Long Island Rail Road, owned by the Pennsylvania, whose whole basis of existence was bringing daily-breaders to and from the city of New York. Between 1924 and 1929, a fleet of 31 "G5s" locomotives, identical to those on the Pennsy proper except that the keystone numberplate on the smokebox was originally replaced by a plain circular one, were built specially for the subsidiary railroad. Most of the shorter-distance Long Island traffic was operated electrically, so the new locomotives took the longer distance runs to the outer extremities of the island.

When diesels took over outside the electrified areas in the 1950s, the "G5s" were retired. One (No.5741) is preserved in the Railroad Museum of Pennsylvania at Strasburg.

No. 9000 2D$_o$-1

Origin: Canada: Canadian National Railways (CNR), 1929. **Type:** Main line diesel-electric locomotive. **Gauge:** 4ft 8½in (1,435mm). **Propulsion:** Beardmore 1,330hp (992kW) four-stroke V12 diesel engine and generator, originally supercharged, supplying direct current to four nose-suspended traction motors geared to the axles. **Weight:** 255,644lb (116t) adhesive, 374,080lb (170t) total. **Max. axleload:** 63,920lb (29t). **Overall length:** 47ft 0½in (14,338mm). **Tractive effort:** 50,000lb (222kN). **Max. speed:** 75mph (120km/h).

The shape of things to come! These two locomotives – which usually worked coupled back-to-back as a pair – were the first main-line diesel units in North America. They were a joint product of the Canadian Locomotive Co and Westinghouse Electric. From all accounts they worked quite well when they were actually working – keeping time easily with 700 US tons on the "International Limited" between Montreal and Toronto, for example, on a schedule which involved an average speed of 44mph (70km/h) including 13 stops, some lengthy. Running costs were absurdly low, and yet the locomotives were not successful.

The problem lay in the difficulties of maintenance. CNR's own maintenance department was almost entirely steam-orientated and so the basic infrastructure was not there. Secondly, the locomotives themselves had all the small faults typical of any unproven piece of equipment. Thirdly, none of the manufacturers involved nor CNR had a stock of spare parts worthy of the name – almost all the parts needed had to be specially made to order, and many hand-fitted thereafter, a process which was both slow and expensive. No progress in dieselisation could be made until a package appeared which included a solution to these problems. This was shortly to happen, as will be seen.

On the other hand, both the overall technology and the concept were good, one or two quite basic shortcomings being easily resolved. For example, in 1931 the engine manufacturer had to replace both crankcases with stronger ones nearly a ton heavier. This perhaps underlined the fact that an engine like the Beardmore, which was excellent in a submarine under the watchful eye of highly-qualified "tiffies" (Engine-room Artificer, 1st class, RN), was less satisfactory under railway conditions. Even so, the specific weight of the Beardmore engine at 24.5lb per hp (15kg/kW) had come a long way from the Ingersoll-Rand engines fitted to switchers a few years earlier, which turned the scales at double that figure. This must be considered against the background of present day North American diesel locomotives, which have engines of specific weights only half that of the Beardmore.

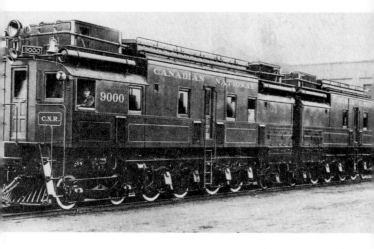

After trials with the locomotive as a twin unit, the two "ends" were operated separately, being then renumbered 9000 and 9001. No.9000 was scrapped in 1939, but during the war No.9001 found a use in the west as a coastal defence train. Its bodywork was altered to give the appearance of a boxcar, as well as a modicum of armoured protection for the crew. After the war, No.9001 worked for a short time in the east but was withdrawn in 1947. Even so, 20 years later, virtually all Canadian trains were to be hauled by locomotives of totally similar concept.

Above and below: The first main line diesel-electric in North America, No.9000, built in 1929, and split into two units for operation following trial running.

Pioneer Zephyr
Three-car train

Origin: United States: Chicago, Burlington & Quincy Railroad (CB&Q) 1934. **Type:** High-speed articulated streamlined diesel-electric train. **Gauge:** 4ft 8¹/₂in (1,435mm). **Propulsion:** Electro-Motive Type 20 1 E 600hp (448kW) inline two-stroke diesel engine and generator feeding two nose-suspended traction motors on the leading bogie. **Weight:** 90,360lb (41t) adhesive, 175,000lb (79.5t) total. **Max. axleload:** 45,180lb (20.5t). **Overall length:** 196ft 0in (59,741mm). **Max. speed:** 110mph (177km/h).

On May 25, 1934 the fastest train between Denver and Chicago (1,015 miles – 1,624km) was the "Autocrat", timed to do the run in 27hr 45min including 40 stops, an average speed of 37mph (59km/h). On May 26 a brand new stainless steel articulated streamlined self-propelled train reeled off the miles between the two cities in just over 13 hours at an average speed of 78mph (125km/h). As the little train triumphantly ran into its display position at the Century of Progress Exhibition in Chicago, US railroading had changed for ever.

Preparation for this triumph had begun in 1930 when mighty General Motors purchased both the Electro-Motive Company and their engine suppliers, the Winton Engine Co. GM concentrated their efforts on making a diesel engine suitable for rail transport. "Softly, softly catchee monkey" was their policy and it was with considerable reluctance that after four years work they agreed to let an experimental engine out of their hands for this *Pioneer Zephyr*. The floodlight of publicity that illuminated its triumph could so easily have lit up a disaster – indeed, electrical faults occurring during the trip, but bravely corrected by the staff whilst the equipment was still live, indicated that it was a very close-run thing indeed.

In some ways, of course, it was a nonsense. Naturally, the manufacturers pressed the view that the whole performance was due to diesel traction when it was really due to a different approach to long-distance passenger movement. Various railroads (notably the Chicago, Milwaukee, St Paul & Pacific and Southern Pacific) were quick to demonstrate that equal improvements were possible with steam, at much lower first cost. Of course, once they had been paid for, running costs of the new trains were much lower than with steam, but overall there was little in it. Incidentally, over one-third of the space available was devoted to the carriage of mail and parcels.

Extra comforts such as air-conditioning, radio reception, reclining seats,

Below: Streamline Zephyr-style trainsets were adopted for many of the Burlington's prestige routes.

grill-buffet and observation lounge were very nice, but significantly little has ever been said about the riding of the *Pioneer Zephyr*. One must unkindly suspect, though, that compared with the heavyweight stock the new train replaced a little was left to be desired. Even so, many other Zephyr trains – but never quite as lightly built as the original – were to go into service on the Burlington. It is true that the self-propelled concept was soon dropped in favour of separate locomotives, but the name is still commemorated today with Amtrak's "San Francisco Zephyr" running daily between Chicago and Oakland (San Francisco). The original little 72-seat train – later enlarged to four cars – ran over 3 million miles in traffic and is today enshrined in Chicago's Museum of Science & Industry.

Left: The diesel era rushes in at an average of 78mph (125km/h). Pioneer Zephyr on its record-breaking run, May 26, 1938.

Class V 4-4-0

Origin: Ireland: Great Northern Railway (GNR (I)), 1932. **Axle load:** 47,000lb (21.5t). **Cylinders:** (3) see text. **Driving wheels:** 79m (2,007mm). **Heating surface:** 1,251sq ft (116m²). **Superheater:** 276sq ft (25.6m²). **Steam pressure:** 250psi (17.6kg/cm²). **Grate area:** 25sq ft (2.3m²). **Fuel:** 13,200lb (6t). **Water:** 3,500gall (4,200 US) (16m³). **Adhesive weight:** 92,000lb (42t). **Total weight:** 232,000lb (105t). **Length overall:** 55ft 3¹/₂in (16,853mm).

Beginning in 1876, the Great Northern Railway of Ireland owned and operated the main line railway connecting Dublin to Belfast. For many years the steel viaduct over the Boyne River 32 miles north of Dublin presented a severe limitation on the size of locomotives but once it was strengthened in 1931, the way was clear for some really powerful express locomotives to use it, and the distinctive Irish Class Vs were among the first.

The five Class V compound 4-4-0s were supplied by Beyer, Peacock of Manchester; the tenders were built by the company at their own Dundalk Works. They were three-cylinder compounds on the Smith principle – similar to those built for the Midland Railway of England. The high-pressure inside cylinder was 17¹/₄in (438mm) diameter, whereas the two outside low-pressure ones were 19in (483mm) diameter; all were 26in (660mm) stroke. Three sets of Stephenson's link motion filled what space remained between the frames. The LP cylinders originally had balanced slide valves but these were soon altered to piston valves as on the HP cylinder.

The new locomotives were used to provide faster train services, including a run over the 54¹/₄ miles (138km) from Dublin to Dundalk in 54 minutes, the fastest anywhere in Ireland at that time. The timing for the 112¹/₂ miles (286km) between Dublin and Belfast was 148 minutes but this included five stops as well as customs examination at the border. In terms of net time this is still the fastest ever scheduled between the two cities; but it lasted only a short time, for the slump combined with a disastrous strike led in 1933 to drastic economies which included decelerations and, in the case of these locomotives, to a reduced boiler pressure.

The simple yet handsome lines of the five compounds were enhanced by the beautiful blue livery and the names *Eagle, Falcon, Merlin, Peregrine* and

Above: Great Northern of Ireland class "VS" 4-4-0 built in 1948 by Beyer Peacock & Co. These locomotives differed from the original batch in having Walschaert's valve gear and being non-compound.

Kestrel. Running numbers were 83 to 87. *Merlin* is preserved and is at present being maintained to running condition under the auspices of the Railway Preservation Society of Ireland.

A further five similar locomotives (Class "VS") with three simple cylinders and Walschaert's valve gear were built in 1948. These were numbered 206 to 210 and were named *Liffey, Boyne, Lagarn, Foyle* and *Erne*, after Irish rivers.

The last "V" class 4-4-0 was withdrawn in 1961 and the last "VS" in 1965; both classes outlasted the GNR which was dismembered in 1958.

Below: One of the original class "V" 4-4-0s built by Beyer Peacock in 1932.

GREAT NORTHERN

GG1 2-C$_o$-C$_o$-2

Origin: United States: Pennsylvania Railroad (PRR), 1934. **Type:** Heavy-duty express passenger electric locomotive. **Gauge:** 4ft 8$\frac{1}{2}$in (1,435mm). **Propulsion:** Medium-frequency alternating current at 15,000V 25Hz fed via overhead catenary and step-down transformer to twelve 410hp (305kW) traction motors, each pair driving a main axle through gearing and quill type flexible drive. **Weight:** 303,000lb (137t) adhesive, 477,000lb (216t) total. **Max. axleload:** 50,500lb (22.9t). **Overall length:** 79ft 6in (24,230mm). **Tractive effort:** 70,700lb (314kN). **Max. speed:** 100mph (160km/h).

The Pennsylvania Railroad devised a keystone herald to underline the position it justifiably felt it held in the economy of the USA. The keystone, displayed both front and rear of these superb locomotives, might equally well stand for the position they held in Pennsy's remarkable passenger operations. Since 1928, PRR had been pursuing a long-considered plan to work its principal lines electrically. The statistics were huge; $175 million in scarce depression money were needed to electrify 800 route-miles (1,287km) and 2,800 track-miles (4,505km) on which 830 passenger and 60 freight trains operated daily.

The medium-frequency single-phase ac system with overhead catenary was adopted. The reason lay in the fact that the dc third-rail system used in New York City was not suitable for long-distance operations and, moreover, since 1913 Pennsy had been gaining experience working its Philadelphia suburban services under the wires on 25Hz ac. Only a corporation of colossal stature could have kept such a costly scheme going through the depression years, but by 1934 impending completion of electrification from New York to Washington meant a need for some really powerful express passenger motive power. There were two contenders for the prototype, the first being a 2-Do-2 which was based on the 2-Co-2 "P5a" class already in use. For comparison, a rather plain articulated locomotive of boxcar appearance and 2-Co-Co-2 configuration was borrowed from the neighbouring New York, New Haven & Hartford.

The latter proved superior, but first a further prototype locomotive was built. The main difference was a steamlined casing, which for production members of the class was stylishly improved by the famous industrial designer Raymond Loewy. Between 1935 and 1943, 139 of these "GG1s" were built; only very recently have they been superseded on prime express work.

Some of the "GG1s" were constructed in-house by the railroad's Altoona shops, others by Baldwin or by General Electric Electrical equipment was supplied by both GE and Westinghouse. The philosophy behind the design was the same as that of the railroad – solid, dependable and above all, well tried. For example, the arrangement of twin single-phase motors, the form of drive, and many other systems were essentially the same as had been in use for 20 years on the New Haven. An interesting feature was the

Above: A GG1 speeds through Glenolden, Pennsylvania, with the Chesapeake & Ohio RR's "George Washington" express.

continuous cab-signalling system whereby coded track circuits conveyed information regarding the state of the road ahead, which was displayed on a miniature signal inside the "GG1" cabs. It was a remarkable tour-de-force for those days, especially considering that the rails also carried the return traction current.

Below: Pennsylvania Railroad Class GG1 electric locomotive in tuscan-red Avery. These noble machines could also be seen in black or dark green.

At this time fortune was smiling on the Pennsy, because low traffic levels during the depression years meant that the physical upheaval of electrification was almost painless, while its completion (there was an extension to Harrisburg, Pennsylvania, in 1939) coincided with the start of the greatest passenger traffic boom ever known, that of World War II. The peak was reached on Christmas Eve 1944 when over 175,000 long-distance passengers used the Pennsylvania Station in New York. It was true that anything that had wheels was used to carry them, but coaches old and new could be marshalled in immense trains which the "GG1s" had no problem at all in moving to schedule over a route which led to most US cities from Florida to Illinois.

In numerical terms, a "GG1" rated at 4,930hp (3,680kW) on a continuous basis, could safely deliver 8,500hp (6,340kW) for a short period. This was ideal for quick recovery from stops and checks. In this respect one "GG1" was the totally reliable equivalent of three or four diesel units 30 or 40 years its junior. It is perhaps telling tales out of school, though, to mention an occasion when brakes failed on a "GG1" and it came through the ticket barrier on to the concourse of Washington Union Station. This was built for people not "GG1s", and the locomotive promptly descended into the basement!

Of the fate of the Pennsylvania Railroad in the post-war years, perhaps the less said the better. It is enough to state that the "GG1" fleet passed piecemeal to the later owners of the railroad, or parts of it – Penn Central, Conrail, Amtrak, and the New Jersey Department of Transportation. At this time it would have been laughable had it not also been tragic how various highly-advertised successors to what were now regarded as relics of a bad past failed to match up to these contemptible museum pieces. But finally, and more recently, the coming of Amtrak's "AEM7" class put an end to the use of "GG1s" on main-line passenger trains.

Conrail also de-electrified the parts of the ex-Pennsylvania lines it inherited on the bankruptcy of Penn Central and so it too had no use for

Above: Superseded at last on main line duties by more modern motive power a string of Amtrak GG1s await the next call to duty.

Above: GG1 No.4835 restored to Pennsy black livery, ahead of two further GG1s and a modern E60P unit in Amtrak colours.

Above: Beautifully restored to its original black livery, GG1 No.4935 also sports full Pennsy regalia.

even a handful of "GG1s". Sadly, on October 28, 1982, the last "GG1" was withdrawn from service by the New Jersey DoT which had a few of these noble machines performing on a humble suburban operation.

Fortunately for rail fans, at least two "GG1s" survive in museums at Altoona and Strasburg, but no longer will it be possible to see one of these mighty people-movers effortlessly in action at 90mph (144km/h) plus, treating a 20-coach passenger train like a sack of feathers.

KF Type 4-8-4

Origin: China/UK: Chinese Ministry of Railways, 1935. **Tractive effort**
36,100lb (16,380kg). **Axle load:** 38,000lb (17.5t). **Cylinders:** (2) 21¼ ×
29½in (540 x 750mm). **Driving wheels:** 69in (1,750mm). **Heating surface**
2,988sq ft (278m²). **Superheater:** 1,076sq ft (100m²). **Steam pressure**
220psi (15.5kg/cm²). **Grate area:** 68.5sq ft (6.4m²). **Fuel:** 26,500lb (12t)
Water: 6,600gall (8,000 US) (30m³). **Adhesive weight:** 150,000lb (68t)
Total weight: 432,000lb (196t). **Length overall:** 93ft 2½in (28,410mm).

Twenty-four of these magnificent locomotives were supplied by the Vulcan
Foundry of Newton-le-Willows, Lancashire, to China in 1935-6. They were
paid for out of funds set aside as reparations for damage done in China to
British property in the so-called Boxer riots of 1910. Although British built as
well as designed by a Briton, Kenneth Cantile, the practice followed was
American – except in one respect, that is, the limitation of axle load to 16½
tons. Twice that would be more typical of United States locomotive.

The typical American locomotive was directly in line with the original
simple Stephenson concept of a locomotive having just two outside
cylinders, but it was very fully equipped in other ways. Hence these "KF"
locomotives, destined for what was in those days and in material things a
rather backward country, had, for example, electric lights, while crews of the
last word in passenger steam locomotives back in Britain had to make do
with paraffin oil. British firemen had to use a shovel to put coal in the firebox
while Chinese ones had the benefit of automatic stokers.

Other equipment included a supply of superheated steam for certain
auxiliaries, and a cut-off control indicator to advise the driver on the best
setting for the valve gear. In the case of some of the locomotives, the
leading tender bogie was fitted with a booster engine; two axles of the six-
wheel truck were coupled, so that the booster drive was on four wheels
The booster gave an additional 7,670lb (3,480kg) of tractive effort while in
operation. These engines were allocated to the Canton-Hankow railway,
while the others were divided between that line and the Shanghai-Nanking
railway. One interesting feature was that the Walschaert's valve gear was
arranged to give only half the amount of valve travel needed. A 2-to-1
multiplying lever was provided to give the correct amount. The piston valves
were 12½in (320mm) in diameter, an exceptionally large size. Running
numbers were 600 to 623.

When locomotive-building firms set out to build locomotives bigger than
were used in their native land they were not always a success, but this case
was an exception, and the class gave excellent service. During the war
years exceptional efforts were made to keep these engines out of the hands
of the Japanese and to some extent the efforts were successful. It has been
reported that 17 out of the 24 survived World War II, which for China lasted
over ten years and was exceptionally devastating.

**Below: 4-8-4 locomotive (later class "KF") as built by the Vulcan
Foundry for the Chinese Ministry of Railways in 1936.**

Right: Chinese class "KF" 4-8-4 locomotive awaiting departure from Nanjing station.

Left: Class "KF" 4-8-4 No.7 at Shanghai in 1981 awaiting shipment back to England for the National Railway Museum.

After the communists gained control, the class was designated "KF" – in Roman not Chinese characters – and renumbered from 1 upwards. The letters KF seem to correspond with the English word Confederation; other class designations of what are now non-standard Chinese types lend support to this supposition. The prime position given to these engines in the re-numbering is some indication of the regard in which they were held.

Dieselisation of the Chinese Railways is proceeding slowly, priority being given to long distance passenger trains. Trains entrusted to these 4-8-4s were early targets for dieselisation and no 4-8-4 has been seen by Western visitors since 1966, although it is reported they were in use in the Shanghai area as late as 1974.

In 1978, the Chinese Minister of Railways, while on a visit to Britain promised one to the National Railway Museum at York, as a prime example of British exports to the world. This was to happen when a "KF" was taken out of use; accordingly in 1981 No.KF7 was shipped from Shanghai back to the country from whence it came.

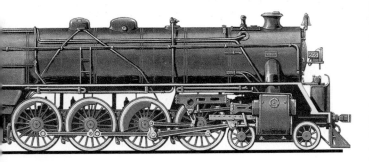

Class A 4-4-2

Origin: United States: Chicago, Milwaukee, St. Paul & Pacific Railroad (CMStP&P), 1935. **Gauge:** 4ft 8¹/₂in (1,435mm). **Tractive effort:** 30,685lb (13,920kg). **Axle load:** 72,500lb (33t). **Cylinders:** (2) 19 x 28in (483 x 711mm). **Driving wheels:** 84in (2,134mm). **Heating surface:** 3,245sq ft (301.5m²). **Superheater:** 1,029sq ft (96m²). **Steam pressure:** 300psi (21kg/cm²). **Grate area:** 69sq ft (6.4m²). **Fuel (oil):** 3,300gall (4,000 US) (15m³). **Water:** 10,800gall (13,000 US) (49.5m³). **Adhesive weight:** 144,500lb (66t). **Total weight:** 537,000lb (244t). **Length overall:** 88ft 8in (27,026mm). (See text below.)

Class F7 4-6-4

Origin: United States: Chicago, Milwaukee, St. Paul & Pacific Railroad (CMStP&P), 1937. **Gauge:** 4ft 8¹/₂in (1,435mm). **Tractive effort:** 50,295lb (22,820kg). **Axle load:** 72,250lb (33t). **Cylinders:** (2) 23.5 x 30in (597 x 762mm). **Driving wheels:** 84in (2,134mm). **Heating surface:** 4,166sq ft (387m²). **Superheater:** 1,695sq ft (157m²). **Steam pressure:** 300psi (21kg/cm²). **Grate area:** 96.5sq ft (9.0m²). **Fuel:** 50,000lb (22¹/₂t). **Water** 16,700gall (20,000 US) (76m³). **Adhesive weight:** 216,000lb (98t). **Total weight:** 791,000lb (359t). **Length overall:** 100ft 0in (30,480mm).

"Fleet of foot was Hiawatha" wrote Longfellow ... Intensive competition for the daytime traffic between Chicago and the Twin Cities of St Paul and Minneapolis was the inspiration for the "Hiawatha" locomotives and trains the fastest-ever to be run by steam. Three railroads were involved in the competition; first, there was the Chicago & North Western Railway; this line had a 408¹/₂ mile (657km) route which its "400" expresses traversed in 400 minutes. The "400"s were formed of conventional equipment of the day, but specially refurbished and maintained. The Chicago Burlington & Quincy Railroad pioneered some stainless steel lightweight diesel-propelled "Zephyr" trains – fairly noisy in spite of their name – over a route 19 miles (30km) longer than the North Western one.

Lastly – and to us most importantly – there was the Chicago, Milwaukee, St Paul and Pacific Railroad, whose management decided to enter the lists with special matching high-speed steam locomotives and trains designed to offer a 6¹/₂ hour timing for the 412-mile (663km) route. For the first time in the history of steam locomotion a railway ordered engines intended for daily

Below: No.3 of the original Class A 4-4-2s built for 100mph (161km/h) running. The striking livery was adopted for the streamline "Hiawatha" trainsets.

Top: Class A 4-4-2 No.1 near Deerfield, Illinois, 1939.

Above: Class F7 No.101 darkens the sky over Milwaukee as it pulls out with Train No.101, the streamlined 13-coach "Afternoon Hiawatha".

operation at 100mph (160km/h) and over.

The American Locomotive Company of Schenectady, New York, responded with two superb oil-fired and brightly coloured streamlined 4-4-2s. They were known as class "A" and received running numbers 1 and

2. In service they earned this prime designation by demonstrating that as runners they had few peers. They could develop more than 3000 horsepower in the cylinders and achieve 110mph (177km/h) on the level. It says enough about that success of these locomotives that they were intended to haul six cars on a 6½-hour schedule, but soon found themselves handling nine cars satisfactorily on a 6¼-hour one. These schedules included five intermediate stops and 15 permanent speed restrictions below 50mph (80km/h).

The design was unusual rather than unconventional; the tender with one six-wheel and one four-wheel truck, for instance, or the drive on to the leading axle instead of the rear one, were examples. Special efforts were made to ensure that the reciprocating parts were as light as possible – the high boiler pressure was chosen in order to reduce the size of the pistons –and particular care was taken to get the balancing as good as possible with a two-cylinder locomotive. Another class "A" (No.3) was delivered in 1936 and a fourth (No.4) in 1937.

Further high-speed locomotives were ordered in 1938 and this time the six 4-6-4s supplied were both usual *and* conventional. This time also the class designation "F7" and running numbers (100 to 105) were just run-of-the-mill. The 4-4-2s were superb with the streamliners but not at all suited to the haulage of heavy ordinary expresses. This restricted their utilisation hence the 4-6-4s which combined heavy haulage powers with high-speed capability. The main concession to speed in the design was the big driving wheels, whilst the main concession to general usage was a change back to coal-burning, in line with most Milwaukee steam locomotives. This in its turn necessitated a high-speed coal hopper and shoots at New Lisbon station, which enabled an "F7" to be coaled during the 2-minute station stop of the "Hiawatha" expresses there. The "F7"s were also very successful

engines, capable of 120mph (193km/h) and more on level track with these trains.

Test running showed that such speeds could be maintained with a load of 12 cars, a load of 550 tons, and this makes the feat an even more remarkable one. There are also reports of maximum speeds of 125mph (200km/h) and it is a great pity that these cannot be authenticated, since if true would be world records. One did occur in 1940: a speed-up and retiming produced the historic fastest start-to-stop run *ever* scheduled with steam power – 81¼mph (130km/h) for the 78½ miles (126km) from Sparta to Portage, Wisconsin. This was on the eastbound "Morning Hiawatha", for by now a second daily run in each direction was operated. Also in 1940 came the "Mid-West Hiawatha" from Chicago to Omaha and Sioux Falls and it was to this train that the 4-4-2s gravitated, although one was usually held in reserve against a 4-6-4 failure on the Twin Cities trains.

Dieselisation came gradually, diesel locomotives made their first appearance on the "Hiawatha" trains in 1941, while steam did not finally disappear from the "Twin Cities Hiawatha" until 1946. The 4-4-2s held on two years longer on the Mid-West train. The last of both types were withdrawn– after a period on lesser workings or set aside – in 1951. It is a matter of considerable regret that none of these record-breaking steam locomotives has been preserved, especially now that the whole Milwaukee Road from Chicago to the Pacific is following them into oblivion.

Even so, models and memories keep these wonderful locomotives alive in the minds of those who admired them in their prime.

Below: Class F7 No.100, which with its sisters and the Class A 4-4-2s, monopolised the prestige "Hiawatha" express of the Milwaukee Road.

Andes Class 2-8-0

Origin: Peru: Central Railway of Peru (FCC), 1935. **Tractive effort:** 36,600lb (16,600kg). **Axle load:** 36,500lb (16.5t). **Cylinders:** (2) 20 x 28in (508 x 71 mm). **Driving wheels:** 52in (1,321mm). **Heating surface:** 1,717sq f (160m²). **Superheater:** 341sq ft (32m²). **Steam pressure:** 200ps (14.1kg/cm²). **Grate area:** 28sq ft (2.6m²). **Fuel:** (oil) 1,465gall (1,760 US (6.7m³). **Water:** 2,650gall (3,180 US) (12m³). **Adhesive weight:** 146,000lb (66t). **Total weight:** 250,000lb (113t). **Length overall:** 61ft 11¹/₄in (18,879mm).

"Highest and Hardest" wrote Brian Fawcett in *Railways of the Andes*. He was describing the Central Railway of Peru – a line in whose service he spent much of his life – which climbed from sea level near Lima to 15,693f (4,783m) altitude at the Galera Tunnel, a bare 99 miles (158km) from Lima en route for the copper mines high up in the mountains. For many years it was said that the necessarily slow passenger service remained invulnerable to air competition, because none of the airlines operating on the Pacific coast had an aircraft which could go as high as the trains!

Most of the climbing; much of it at between 1 in 22 and 1 in 25 (4.5 and 4 per cent), is concentrated in the final 74 miles (118km) to the top; some of the most spectacular engineering in the world takes the trains via six "Z" double-reversals up to the summit. Oxygen is provided for passengers, bu curiously enough steam locomotives become more rather than less efficien as the atmospheric pressure drops. Even so, the task of lifting traffic up this railway staircase was an horrific one and it was only after many years o traumatic experience that a class 2-8-0 was evolved, combining rugged North American design features with the best British Beyer, Peacock workmanship, which could do the job satisfactorily.

A short boiler was essential because of the heavy grades which mean quick alterations of slope relative to water at each zig-zag. On the other hand a narrow firebox between the wheels was no detriment with oil firing and on such gradients it was an advantage that as many as four out of the five

Below: One of the world's hardest-working locos, a Central Railway of Peru "Andes" class 2-8-0 depicted in the company's handsome green livery.

pairs of wheels should be driven. The existence of ample water supplies over the mountain section meant that only a very small quantity need be carted up the mountain – hence the small tender.

The arrangements for sanding were vital because hideous gradients are usually combined with damp rails. Since both gravity and steam sanding gear had been found wanting, the "Andes" class were fitted with air sanding. The quantity of sand carried was also important and on later versions of the class a vast box on the boiler-top held supplies of this vital element in Andean railroading. It also incorporated the steam dome, thereby keeping the sand warm and dry.

By law, a "counter-pressure" brake had to be fitted, but was not normally used because of the damage that was caused to piston and valve rings when it was used. The double-pipe air braking system used avoids the necessity of releasing the brakes periodically during the descent to re-charge the reservoirs – something that might well lead to a runaway in Andean conditions.

As a locomotive that would need to be driven "wide-open" for hour after hour on the ascent, the "Andes" class was very robustly constructed indeed. That the class gave a satisfactory performance on the world's hardest railway is indicated by the fact that the company came back for more, eight times, no less, between 1935 and 1951. Finally there were 29, numbered 200 to 228. Neighbouring railways had some too – the Southern of Peru (under the same ownership) had 20 with slightly larger driving wheels, while the Cerro de Pasco Railroad (which connected with the Central) had a further five. These latter were the last "straight" steam locomotives to be built by the great firm of Beyer, Peacock.

Alas, no longer does steam rule the mountain section, but the 6-hour timing of the old days has not been improved upon. Maybe a 22mph 35km/h) average speed does not seem much but the ascent certainly justified the inclusion of the daily train over the mountain section amongst the Great Trains of the World. No.206 is preserved at Lima.

A4 Class 4-6-2

Origin: Great Britain: London & North Eastern Railway (LNER), 1935
Tractive effort: 35,455lb (16,086kg). **Axle load:** 49,500lb (22.5t). **Cylinders**
(3) 18^{1}/$_{2}$ x 26in (470 x 660mm). **Driving wheels:** 80in (2,032mm). **Heating
surface:** 2,576sq ft (240m^2). **Superheater:** 749sq ft (70m^2). **Steam
pressure:** 250psi (17.5kg/cm^2). **Grate area:** 41sq ft (3.8m^2). **Fuel:** 18,000lb
(8t). **Water:** 5,000gall (6,000 US) (23m^3). **Adhesive weight:** 148,000lb (67t)
Total weight: 370,000lb (170t). **Length overall:** 71ft 0in (21,647mm).

If British railway enthusiasts were to vote for one express passenger
locomotive that they considered to be the best, there is little doubt that this
one would be elected. For one thing, it would be difficult to ignore the
claims of the all-time holder of the world's speed record for steam
locomotives.

The Class "A4" streamlined 4-6-2 came in direct descent from the Class
"A1" or "Flying Scotsman" 4-6-2s. The LNER management had taken note
of a two-car German diesel train called the "Flying Hamburger" which in
1933 began running between Berlin and Hamburg at an average speed of
77.4mph (124km/h) for the 178 miles (285km). The makers were
approached with the idea of having a similar train to run the 268 miles
(429km) between London and Newcastle, but after an analysis had been
done and the many speed restrictions taken into account the best that could
be promised was 63mph (102km/h), that is, 4^{1}/$_{4}$ hours. The train was
surprisingly expensive for two cars, as well. On March 5, 1935, standard
"A3" 4-6-2 (No.2750 *Papyrus*) showed what steam could do by making the
run with a six-coach train in 230 minutes, thus demonstrating that a four
hour timing was practicable.

In this way was born the concept of a streamlined matching locomotive
and train to be called "The Silver Jubilee". The LNER Board authorised the
project on March 28, 1935 and the first of the four streamlined locomotives
No. 2509 *Silver Link* was put into steam on September 5.

The new train, bristling with innovations, was shown to the press on
September 27. Unkind people might compare this with the recent gestation
period of British Railways' celebrated High Speed Train, not dissimilar in
appearance, concept and in degree to which it extended beyond the bounds
of current performance. This was six *years* not six *months*.

On this press trip the British speed record was broken with a speed of
112^{1}/$_{2}$mph (180km/h) at Sandy. The locomotive rode superbly and 25 miles

**Below: Preserved "A4" class 4-6-2 No.4498 *Sir Nigel Gresley* with an
enthusiasts' train.**

Above: An "A4" class 4-6-2 bursts from Gas Works tunnel shortly after leaving Kings Cross station, London, for Scotland.

(40km) were covered at a speed above 100mph (160km/h), those aboard being sublimely unconscious of the terror they were inspiring in the lively-sprung articulated carriages behind. Even so, three days later "The Silver Jubilee" went into public service, achieving an instant and remarkable success. In spite of a supplementary fare, the down run at 5.30 p.m. from Kings Cross, with a first stop at Darlington, 232 1/2 miles (374km) in 198 minutes and due at Newcastle 9.30 p.m., was fully booked night after night.

The new locomotives did not bristle with innovations like the trains, but those they had were important. The internal streamlining and enlargement of the steam passages from the regulator valve to the blastpipe made them particularly free-running, while extra firebox volume in the form of a combustion chamber helped steam production. Evocative three-chime whistles gave distinction to the voice of the "A4"s.

The "A4"s were so good that 31 more were built between 1936 and 1938, not only for two more streamline trains ("Coronation" and "West Riding Limited") but also for general service. A few were fitted with double blastpipes and chimneys and it was with one of these (No.4468 *Mallard)* that on July 4, 1938, the world speed record for steam traction was broken with a sustained speed of 125mph (201km/h), attained down the 1 in 200 (0.5 per cent) of Stoke bank north of Peterborough. Driver Duddington needed full throttle and 45 per cent cut-off and the dynamometer car record indicated that 126mph (203km/h) was momentarily reached. Equally impressive was an occasion in 1940 when No.4901 *Capercaillie* ran 25 level miles (40km) north of York with 22 coaches (730 tons) at an average speed of 76mph (122km/h).

At first a distinction was made between the original "silver-painted" locomotives, those in LNER green with bird names for general service, and those in garter blue livery with Empire names for the "Coronation". Also in blue were *Golden Fleece* and *Golden Shuttle* for the "West Riding Limited". By 1938, blue had become the standard colour and very nice it looked – not only on the streamlined trains but also with the varnished teak of ordinary stock.

After the war, during which the "A4"s had to cope with enormous loads and one (No. 4469 *Sir Ralph Wedgwood)* was destroyed in an air raid on York, they were renumbered 1 to 34, later becoming British Railways Nos.60001 to 60034. In the famous locomotive exchange trials of 1948, the "A4"s proved to be substantially the most efficient of all the express engines tested, but their proneness to failure also showed up on three occasions during the trials.

Although by no means the most recent LNER large express passenger locomotives, they were never displaced from prime workings, such as the London to Edinburgh non-stop "Elizabethan", until the diesels came in the early 1960s. The reliability problem – one serious weakness was over-heating of the inside large-end – was resolutely tackled and to a great extent solved.

Since the last "A4" was withdrawn in 1966, six have been preserved – No.4498 *Sir Nigel Gresley*, No.60009 *Union of South Africa* and No.19 *Bittern* privately; No.4468 *Mallard* is in the National Railway Museum,

Below: London & North Eastern Railway class "A4" 4-6-2 *Empire of India,* one of the batch built in 1937 to work the "Coronation" express

Above: Class "A4" No.2510 *Quicksilver* when new in 1935. Note the footplate valences which were later removed.

No.60010 *Dominion of Canada* is in the Canadian Railway Museum at Delson, Quebec, and No.60008 *Dwight D. Eisenhower* is in the USA at the Green Bay Railroad Museum, Wisconsin. Nos.4498 and 60009 currently perform on special trains, thereby giving a new generation of rail fans just a hint of what these magnificent locomotives were like in their prime.

Below: Class "A4" No.60024 *Kingfisher*. The locomotives of this class, built ostensibly for "general service", were named after birds.

E Series A1A-A1A

Origin: United States: Electro-Motive Division, General Motors Corporation (EMD), 1937. **Type:** Express passenger diesel-electric locomotive; "A" units with driving cab, "B" units without. **Gauge:** 4ft 8½in (1,435mm). **Propulsion:** Two EMD 567A 1,000hp (746kW) 12-cylinder pressure-charged two-stroke Vee engines and generators, each supplying current to two nose-suspended traction motors geared to the end axles of a bogie. **Weight:** "A" unit 212,310lb (96.3t) adhesive, 315,000lb (142.9t) total. "B" units 205,570lb (93.3t) adhesive, 305,000lb (138.4t) total. **Max. axleload:** "A" 53,080lb (24.1t), "B" 51,390lb (23.3t). **Overall length*:** "A" 71ft 1¼in (21,670mm), "B" 70ft 0in (21,340mm). **Tractive effort:** 53,080lb (236kN). **Max. speed:** 85mph (137km/h), 92mph (148km/h), 98mph (157km/h), or 117mph (188km/h) according to gear ratio fitted.
*(*Dimensions refer to the E7 variant of 1945.)*

In 1930 the General Motors Corporation made two purchases which were to have dramatic effects on the American locomotive scene. The first was the Winton Engine Co, a firm specialising in lightweight diesel engines. The second was Winton's chief customer, the Electro-Motive Corporation, an organisation established in 1922 to design and market petrol-electric railcars, which had sold some 500 units in 10 years. With the engine-building facility and the expertise acquired in these purchases, EMD was a major partner in the sensational pioneer streamlined trains introduced in 1934, and in the following year the firm produced its first locomotives. There were four Bo-Bo units with rectangular "boxcar" bodies, each powered by two 900hp (670kW) Winton 12-cylinder Vee engines. Pending the completion of its own plant, EMD had to employ other builders to assemble them.

In 1936 EMD moved into its own purpose-built works at La Grange, Illinois, and work commenced on the next locomotives. These were the first of the "E" series, known also as the "Streamline" series. Like the four earlier locomotives, they had two 900hp Winton engines, but the chassis and body were completely new. The body had its main load bearing strength in two bridge-type girders which formed the sides. The bogies had three axles to give greater stability at high speeds, but as only four motors were needed, the centre axle of each bogie was an idler, giving the wheel arrangement A1A-A1A. The units were produced in two versions, "A" units with a driver's cab and "B" units without. The Baltimore & Ohio was the first purchaser, taking six of each type to use as 3,600hp (2,690kW) pairs. Santa Fe bought eight As and three Bs, and the "City" streamliner roads bought two A-B-B sets for the "City of Los Angeles" and the "City of San Francisco". These latter at 5,400hp were the world's most powerful diesel

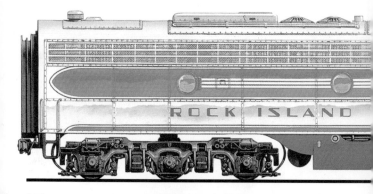

Above: A passenger train of the Gulf Mobile & Ohio RR hauled by EMD E-series units.

locomotives when they appeared in 1937. The B&O units were classed "EA" and "EB", the Santa Fe were "E1A' and "E1B", and the City units "E2A" and "E2B".

All these locomotives were an immediate success, not only by their performance but also by their reliability. The reliability was a striking tribute to the quality of the design, for there had been no demonstrator subsequent to the "boxcar" Bo-Bos. In multiple-unit working it was possible for some maintenance to be done on the road on the easier stretches, on which one engine could be shut down. With servicing assisted in this way, remarkable feats of endurance could be achieved. One of the B&O A-B sets gained national publicity when it completed 365 continuous days of service between Washington and Chicago, covering 282,000 miles (454,000km) at

Below: A 2,000hp E9 cab unit supplied to the Chicago, Rock Island & Pacific Railroad and specially painted in the livery of the line's "Rocket" express trains.

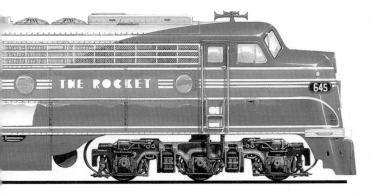

an average scheduled speed of 56mph (90km/h).

Progress at La Grange was rapid. At 900hp the Winton engine was reaching its limit and an EMD engine was therefore developed. Designated 567 (the capacity of a cylinder in cubic inches), it was available in three sizes with 8, 12, and 16 cylinders, giving 600, 1,000 and 1,350hp (448, 746 and 1,007kW). Simultaneously La Grange began to manufacture its own generators, motors and other electrical equipment.

The first all-EMD locomotives were an order from Seaboard Air Line for 14 A and five B units, which appeared from October 1938 onwards. They had two 1,000hp engines and were operated as 6,000hp three-unit 1 "lash-ups" (in the US jargon). These were the "E4s". "EW" and "E5" followed, the former comprising 18 Units for the Sante Fe and the latter 16 for the Burlington.

So far each railroad's order had incorporated some individual variations – hence the different designations – but EMD aimed to gain the maximum benefits from production-line assembly of locomotives, to which end individual variations were to be discouraged. The next series, the "E6" which appeared in the same month in 1939 as the first freight demonstrator, was therefore a standard off-the-shelf unit, with the minimum of options. This was the start of real diesel mass production and 118 units had been built by the time the War Production Board terminated building of passenger locomotives in February 1942.

Construction of passenger locomotives was resumed in February 1945 with the first of the "E7' series. These locomotives benefited from the experience gained from both the "E" and the "F" series freight units. Improvements included a new and larger cooling system for the engine. Externally there was a noticeable difference in that the front of the body was sloped at 800 to the horizontal, as in the "F" series, instead of 700, as in previous "E" series bodies. Apart from this change, there were few differences in external appearance throughout the range of "E" series, and most of them concerned windows and port-holes.

With locomotive fleets rundown by wartime traffic, the railroads were even more eager to acquire passenger diesels, and Electro-Motive Division (as it had now become) settled down to a steady production of "E7s", averaging 10 per month for four years. During this time 428 A units and 82 B units were built so that the "E7" outnumbered the passenger diesels of all other US makers put together. In general it was roads which had fast passenger services on easy gradients which bought "E7s"; for mountain work the all-adhesion "F" series was favourite.

Amongst "E7" buyers were the Pennsylvania and the New York Central. With 60 and 50 units respectively they had the largest numbers of any owner. On the NYC the most thorough comparison ever made between steam and diesel was conducted during October 1946. Two twin "E7" locomotives were tested against six of the new "Niagara" 4-8-4 steam engines working between Harmon, New York, and Chicago, 928 miles (1,493km). The "E7s" averaged 28,954 miles in the month and the 4-8-4s 27,221. Average operating costs per mile were $1.11 for the "E7" and $1.22 for the 4-8-4. However, a succession of coal strikes and then some trouble with the alloy steel boilers of the "Niagaras" ensured that the NYC did not allow its lingering love of steam to interpret the results in favour of the 4-8-4s, but the tests were still encouraging to steam enthusiasts in showing how small was the improvement when the best of steam locomotives, intensively used and adequately serviced, were replaced by diesels. But on most roads the margin was much wider, and there was a handsome saving from diesels, quite sufficient to offset the greater capital cost.

In 1953 the 1,125hp (840kW) 567B engine was available, and this was incorporated in the next series, the "E8". By this time most of the principal passenger services were dieselised, so the impact of the "E8" was less spectacular than that of the "E7". By the time the final version appeared, the "E9" with 1,200hp (900kW) 567C engines, the need for passenger diesels had almost been met, and only 144 units were sold between 1954 and 1963, compared with 457 "E8s".

In the 1960s the American passenger train declined rapidly in the face of air and coach competition, and many of the later "Es" had short lives, being traded in against the purchase of new general-purpose locomotives.

The "E" series instituted the general conversion of the American passenger train to diesel operation, and they eventually saw many of the most famous trains out in their heyday the US had an undisputed world lead in passenger train speeds. Geared for up to 117mph (188km/h), (although few roads operated them above 100mph (160km/h), the "Es" were the fastest diesel locomotives in the world, and yet their construction was rugged and straightforward. In particular they had nose-suspended traction motors, which the heavy North American rails with their close-spaced sleepers seemed able to accept without distress.

In 1980 Amtrak operated the last run of "E" locomotives in multiple and the ranks were very thin by this time. Fortunately the body of the first B&O unit is preserved.

Left: E8A survivor working out its time in push-pull service on Burlington Northern's Chigago area commuter lines.

Galloping Goose railcar

Origin: United States: Rio Grande Southern Railroad (RGS), 1933. **Type:** Home-made gasoline railcar for local passenger, mail and express traffic. **Gauge:** 3ft 0in (914mm). **Propulsion:** Pierce Arrow (later General Motors) gasoline engine driving the centre truck via clutch, manual gearbox, propellor shaft, gearing and chains. **Weights:** 7,200lb (3.25t) adhesive, 14,770lb (6.7t). **Max. axleload:** 3,600lb (1.65t). **Overall length:** 43ft 3in (13,183mm).

Amongst all the famed narrow-gauge railroads of Colorado, the most spectacular, the bravest and the most impecunious was the Rio Grande Southern. It says enough that its 162-mile (260km) route connected terminals only 102 miles apart as the crow flies and that of 47 steam locomotives owned by the company during its 60 years of day-by-day struggle to survive all were acquired second-hand. Typically only two or three were required at a time so the idea was to buy worn-out machines and squeeze just one more drop of service from them before passing them on to even poorer lines.

In 1893, the year after the RGS opened, repeal of the Sherman Silver Purchasing Act of 1892 and the consequent collapse of the silver mining industry put the company in the Bankruptcy Court for three years. After a few years things got better, but in 1929 the line again found itself bankrupt as well as in very poor physical shape. A resourceful man called Victor A. Miller was appointed as receiver and amongst many measures adopted to reduce expenses was construction of these remarkable railbuses made from old motor cars. In his own words:

"A seven-passenger automobile sedan of Pierce Arrow manufacture, model 33, of the year 1926, is spread in the body to the ordinary width of a narrow-gauge car to give a carrying capacity of ten passengers, with the chassis remodelled to fit two four-wheel trucks of 36m gauge. A light metal trailer of box-car character and a capacity in excess of ten tons, running on a third narrow-gauge truck, is permanently affixed to the rear of the automobile."

As regards the name, it must be said that while geese in flight are the most graceful of God's creatures, ground movement is not something they do well. No.1 railbus appeared in June 1931 and was made from an old Buick. It was rather small and No.2 which came out three months later was similar but larger. No.3, also made this way, was a considerable advance on the earlier experiments. It seated 12 people and was the final solution, being sufficiently economical to pay back its cost in a few months. No.4, virtually

Above: Early version of a "Galloping Goose" railcar with box car body preserved at the Colorado Railroad Museum.

a copy of No.3, followed in 1932 and No.5 in 1933. No.6 was used by the roadmaster to move materials and labour, while No.7 was a refrigerated unit provided to haul supplies to Civilian Conservation Corps camps.

Air brakes soon replaced mechanical ones and, aside from their helplessness in coping with frost and snow, the "Galloping Geese" did all that was asked of them and more in hauling mail, passengers and parcels in the mountains. After the war, (during which the RGS was busy with such traffic as the uranium ore used to produce the first atom bombs), surviving Geese Nos. 3, 4, and 5 were rebuilt with new General Motors engines and bigger bus bodies, but still accommodating 12 people. In 1950, after loss of the mail contract, the trailers of the remaining buses (which also included No.7) were rebuilt to seat parties of 20 tourists. Although nearly 2,500 sightseeing passengers had been carried in 1951, the first (and last) year that RGS catered seriously for tourists, it was to no avail and the railroad was abandoned at the end of the year. Through the efforts of their numerous admirers, four of these legendary creatures have been preserved and can be seen at Knott's Berry Farm, Los Angeles; Dolores and Telluride, Colorado, and at the Colorado Railroad Museum, Golden.

Below: Rio Grande Southern RR home-made "Galloping Goose" railcar as adapted for running scenic tours in summer 1951.

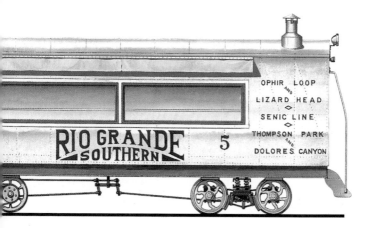

Class 05 4-6-4

Origin: Germany: German State Railway (DR), 1935. **Tractive effort:** 32,776lb (14,870kg). **Axle load:** 43,000lb (19. 5t). **Cylinders:** (3) $17^3/4 \times 26$in (450 × 660mm). **Driving wheels:** $90^1/2$in (2,300mm). **Heating surface:** 2,750sq ft (256m²). **Superheater:** 976sq ft (90m²). **Steam pressure:** 284psi (20kg/cm²). **Grate area:** 51sq ft (4.71m²). **Fuel:** 22,000lb (10t). **Water:** 8,200gall (9,870 US) (37m³). **Adhesive weight:** 127,000lb (56t). **Total weight:** 475,064lb (213t). **Length overall:** 86ft 2in (26,265mm).

In 1931 the general speed limit on the German railways was only 62 miles per hour (100km/hr) but in that year the first of the high-speed diesel railcars was introduced, with a maximum speed of 100 miles per hour (160km/hr), and suddenly Germany leapt from a backward position in world rail speed to be the world leader. However, the twin railcars had limited accommodation, and their immediate popularity was a challenge to the steam engineers to produce a locomotive which could attain similar speeds when hauling a longer train of conventional coaches. It was calculated that a steam locomotive and train having a seating capacity of 50 per cent more could be built for half the cost of a railcar set.

In 1932, therefore, in accordance with normal German practice, private locomotive builders were invited to submit proposals for a locomotive to haul 250 tons at 93mph (150km/h) in normal service, with the capacity to reach 108mph (175km/h) with this load if required. In the meantime wind tunnel work was conducted at the research establishment at Göttingen to determine the possible benefits of streamlining, and it was found that full streamlining of the engine could reduce by 20 per cent the power required to haul 250 tons at 93mph.

From the 22 proposals submitted, a scheme by Borsig of Berlin for a 3-cylinder 4-6-4 was selected. The detailed design, produced under the direction of Adolf Wolff, incorporated standard DRG features as far as possible, but the overall concept of a locomotive to develop very high speeds with limited loads called for a boiler larger than those of the existing Pacifics, but with the possibility of a smaller adhesive weight. The 4-6-4 wheel arrangement was chosen because a bogie at each end was thought necessary for stability at high speed. Aids to high speed included large driving wheels $90^1/2$in (2,300mm) diameter, and very large valves and steam passages. For good balance at speed three cylinders were fitted. The boiler pressure of 284psi (20kg/cm²) was the highest so far used on a conventional German locomotive. Special attention was paid to braking, all axles being braked, with two blocks on all wheels except the leading bogie wheels. Tender was also of record size, with five axles and weighing 86 tons fully loaded. The casing enveloped the engine and tender almost down to rail level, and access to the motion was achieved through roller shutters.

Three engines were ordered, two arranged for conventional coal firing but the third equipped for burning pulverised fuel, and arranged with the cab leading. The first two engines, 05001/2 appeared in March and May of 1935

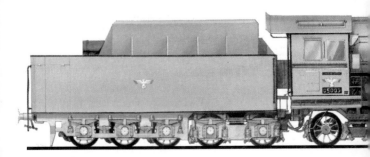

Right: Class "05" locomotive No. 05.001, as built in streamline form, depicted on a run in March 1935 when the speed record for steam was broken.

and in their highly-finished red livery they made a great impression. For more than a year they were subjected to intensive testing, partly on the road and partly on the locomotive testing plant at Grunewald. In the most notable of the road tests, on May 11, 1936, 05002 reached a speed of 124.5mph (199km/h) on the level with a load of 197 tons. On another test run with 169 tons, a speed of 118mph (189km/h) was maintained for 26 miles (42km), requiring an indicated horsepower of 3,409, an exceptional figure at that speed.

In October 1936, 05001/2, working from Hamburg Altona depot, entered regular service on trains FD 23/4 from Hamburg to Berlin and back. For the 178.1 miles (285km) from Hamburg to Berlin Lehrter the time allowed was 144 minutes on the outward journey and 145 on the return, giving average speeds of 74.2 and 73.7mph (118.7 and 117.9km/h) the normal maximum running speed being 94mph (150km/h). These were then the highest speeds by steam in Europe, although allowing for the gradients, the locomotive work required was no heavier than with the LNER "Silver Jubilee". The engines often demonstrated their ability to recover time lost by engineering works.

The war brought these high-speed schedules to an end, and after a period of use on ordinary trains, the engines were laid aside until 1950, when they were rebuilt by Krauss-Maffei of Munich into non-streamlined engines with new boilers. The experimental pulverised fuel firing on the third engine, 05003, was not successful, and it was rebuilt as a conventional engine in 1944/5, but it saw little service until it too was further rebuilt by Krauss-Maffei in 1950. In their rebuilt form the three engines worked for seven years on the fastest steam workings then in force on Deutsche Bundesbahn, but the tide of electrification then overtook them. 05002/3 were scrapped, but 05001 was restored to its original streamlined condition, and in 1961 it was placed in the German National Railway Museum in Nürnberg.

Below: Class "05" locomotive No. 05.003, originally designed for the burning of pulverised fuel, in shop grey finish after rebuilding in normal form.

Class 16E 4-6-2

Origin: South Africa: South African Railways (SAR), 1935. **Tractive effort:** 40,596lb (18,414kg). **Axle load:** 47,000lb (21.3t). **Cylinders:** (2) 24 x 28in (610 x 711mm). **Driving wheels:** 72in (1,830mm). **Heating surface:** 2,914sq ft (271m²). **Superheater:** 592sq ft (55m²). **Steam pressure:** 210psi (14.75kg/cm²). **Grate area:** 63sq ft (5.8m²). **Fuel:** 31,000lb (14t). **Water:** 6,000gall (7,200 US) (27m³). **Adhesive weight:** 134,000lb (61t). **Total weight:** 375,000lb (170t). **Length overall:** 71ft 8¹/₄in (21,850mm).

High-speed locomotives are rare in most of Africa. Driving wheels as large as 60in (1,524mm) diameter were exceptional and larger ones were unknown except in the countries bordering the Mediterranean coast. Most of Africa is narrow-gauge country, it is true, but that is no reason for low speeds, provided the track is well aligned and maintained. During the 1930s South African Railways perceived this fact and, with a view to accelerating such schedules as 30 hours for the 956 miles (1,530km) from Cape Town to Johannesburg (average speed 32mph – 51km/h), they ordered five high speed locomotives from Henschel & Son of Kassel, Germany, to be known as class "16E"; running numbers were 854 to 859.

Driving wheel diameter was increased by 20 per cent compared with the "16 DA" class, which previously had handled such crack expresses as the famous "Blue Train". This involved a boiler centre line pitched very high (9ft 3in – 2,820mm above rail level – 2.6 times the rail gauge of 3ft 6in (1,067mm). This in its turn made necessary a domeless boiler, steam being collected by pipes with their open end placed as high as possible in the boiler barrel. Aesthetically the effect was most imposing and it all worked well too.

The valve gear was interesting, being more akin to that usually found in motor cars than in steam locomotives. As in nearly all car engines, the "16E" class had poppet valves actuated by rotating cams on camshaft. Naturally there had to be a set of valves at each end of each cylinder, steam locomotive cylinders being double acting; in addition, since steam engines

Above: South African Railways' "16E" class 4-6-2 No.858 *Millie* on 'Sunset Limited" at Kimberley.

have to go in both directions without a reversing gearbox, and in order to provide for expansive working, the cams were of some length and coned longitudinally. The camshaft could be moved laterally by the driver, so that the cam followers engaged different cam profiles, and thus caused the poppet valves to open for longer or shorter periods to vary the "cut-off" for expansive working, while a still greater lateral movement reversed the locomotive. The "RC" poppet valve gear gave wonderfully free running and, moreover, its complexities gave little trouble in SAR's competent hands.

On various special occasions (it can now be told) the "16E"s have shown abilities to reach safely and easily – but illegally according to the SAR rule-book – what by African standards were very high speeds indeed. Alas, these locomotives never had an opportunity to demonstrate their high-speed abilities in normal service. South African Railways – the only railway to *fly* into London's Heathrow Airport – has also operated the national airline since its inception and early on it seemed reasonable to encourage anyone in a hurry to travel by aeroplane. So the rail schedules remained unaccelerated and the five handsome "16E"s remained unduplicated. Four of the five were withdrawn in the 1960s and 1970s, but one (No.858) named *Millie*, is kept on hand in order to work special trains for steam enthusiasts. These are very much a speciality of SAR and often last for ten days or so, the train being stabled each night while its occupants sleep on board. The run behind this beautiful engine, polished like a piece of jewellery and at speeds up to above 70mph (110km/h) is always one of the high spots of the trip.

Left: A pair of beautifully polished South African "16E" class 4-6-2s handle a special train for steam enthusiasts.

Royal Hudson Class 4-6-4

Origin: Canada: Canadian Pacific Railway (CPR), 1937. **Gauge:** 4ft 8¹/₂in (1,435mm). **Tractive effort:** 45,300lb (20,548kg). **Axle load:** 65,000lb (29.5t). **Cylinders:** (2) 22 x 30in (559 x 762mm). **Driving wheels:** 75in (1,905mm). **Heating surface:** 3,791sq ft (352m²). **Superheater:** 1,542sq f (143m²). **Steam pressure:** 275psi (19.3kg/cm²). **Grate area:** 81sq ft (7.5m²) **Fuel:** 47,000lb (21t). **Water:** 12,000gall (14,400 US) (54.6m³). **Adhesive weight:** 194,000lb (88t). **Total weight:** 659,000lb (299t). **Length overall** 90ft 10in (27,686mm).

To be both Royal and North American is almost a contradiction in terms but forty years ago, the Canadian Pacific Railway was as much British as it was Canadian. It had been incorporated by an Act of the British Parliament, and its east-most terminal was situated at Southampton, England. It was here in 1939 that King George VI and Queen Elizabeth set sail in the Canadian Pacific liner *Empress of Britain* for a tour of their largest Dominion. Once ashore, their home for much of the visit was a royal train, at the head of which was a new 4-6-4, No.2850, specially turned out in royal blue and silver with stainless steel boiler cladding. The royal arms were painted on the tender and a replica crown was mounted on the running board skirt just ahead of the cylinders; later this crown was affixed to all 45 of CPR's famous 4-6-4s built between 1937 and 1945.

The genesis of these fine locomotives lay in a wish to improve upon the class "G-3" 4-6-2s which before 1931 had been the top-line power of the system, by increasing their steam-raising capacity a substantial amount. A fire-grate 23 per cent larger was possible if the 4-6-4 wheel arrangement was adopted and the boilers of the new locomotives were based on this. But in other ways, such as tractive effort or adhesive weight, the new locomotives were little different to the old. Their class designation was H-1 and the running numbers were 2800 to 2819.

The boilers had large superheaters and combustion chambers (the latter an addition to the firebox volume, provided by recessing the firebox tubeplate into the barrel), as well as front-end throttles which worked on the hot side of the superheater. This enabled superheated steam to be fed to the various auxiliaries. There were arch tubes in the firebox and, necessary with a grate of this size, a mechanical stoker.

The first effect of the new locomotives was to reduce the number of engine changes needed to cross Canada, from fourteen to nine. The longest stage was 820 miles (1,320km) from Fort William, Ontario, to Winnipeg, Manitoba; experimentally a 4-6-4 had run the 1,252 miles (2,015km) between Fort William and Calgary, Alberta, without change.

For five hectic months in 1931 the afternoon CPR train from Toronto to

Above: Ex-Canadian Pacific Royal Hudson Class No.2860 hauls a tourist train on the shores of Howe Sound, BC.

Montreal, called the "Royal York" became the world's fastest scheduled train, by virtue of a timing of 108 minutes for the 124 miles (200km) from Smith's Falls to Montreal West, an average speed of 68.9mph (111km/h). The record was wrested from the Great Western Railway of England, whose "Cheltenham Flyer" then had a timing of 70min for the 77$\frac{1}{4}$ miles

Below: The beautiful red livery of preserved 4-6-4 No.2860 was basically the same as used on these engines in Canadian Pacific Railway days.

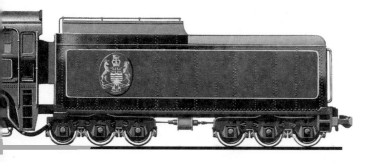

(124km), an average speed of 66.3mph (106.1km/h). The 4-6-4s were normally assigned to this train. Subsequently the GWR dropped 3 minutes from their timing and took back the record.

An interesting feature, later provided on one of the "H-1"s, was a booster engine working on the trailing truck. One of the problems of a 4-6-4 was that only six out of 14 wheels were driven; this was no detriment while running at speed but starting was sometimes affected by the limited adhesion. The extra 12,000lb (5,443kg) of tractive effort provided by the booster came in very handy; the mechanism cut out automatically at 20mph (32km/h).

The 1930s were the period when streamlining was in fashion but when the time came to order some more 4-6-4s, H.B. Bowen, the CPR Chief of Motive Power, decided to compromise. He came to the conclusion that the shrouds which enveloped many contemporary designs made the mechanism inaccessible to an extent which smothered any savings attributable to reduced air resistance. On the other hand, he accepted that the public liked their trains hauled by locomotives which were a little easier on the eye than was then customary.

The result in 1937 was another batch of 30 Hudson type, Nos. 2820 to 2849 designated "H-1c", (the earlier ones had been delivered in two batches of ten, "H-1a" and "H-1b") which had not only softer lines but also sported a superb coloured livery, as our artist has tried to show. Very few mechanical changes needed to be made – although there were certain improvements or changes such as power-operated reversing gear, domeless boilers and a one-piece cast locomotive frame, while boosters were fitted to five of the locomotives. A further ten 4-6-4s, designated "H-1d" were delivered in 1938, while the last batch of five ("H-1e") Nos.2860 to 2864 of 1940, differed from the others in being oil burners. All the "H-1e"s and five of the "H-1d"s had boosters.

The last batch of 4-6-4s were intended to operate in the far west between Vancouver and Revelstoke, British Columbia, where oil firing had been the rule for many years. After the war, when the big Canadian oil fields were being exploited, all the "H-1"s operating over the prairies were also converted. This was made easier by the fact that it was customary to allocate a particular locomotive to a particular depot when they were built and they would then remain there for many years. This unusually stable

Above: A head-on shot of 4-6-4 No. 2860 as preserved and now running on the British Columbia Railway.

approach to locomotive allocation also allowed the booster-fitted locomotives to be rostered for sections of line where their extra push was needed. For example, booster fitted "H-1c"s allocated to Toronto could take the 18-car 1,300-ton "Dominion" express up the Neys Hill incline on Lake Superior's north shore unassisted with booster in operation; otherwise a helper engine would have been an obvious necessity.

Like other lines which had excellent steam power, well maintained and skillfully operated, the Canadian Pacific Railway was in no hurry to dieselise and, in fact, it was not until 1956 that the first 4-6-4 was scrapped. By mid-1960 all were out of service, but five have survived the scrap-men's torches. Standard Hudson No. 2816 is (at the time of writing) at Steamtown, Bellows Falls, Vermont, USA. Of the "Royal Hudson" types, No.2839 has recently been seen in operation in the USA on the Southern Railway, a line which regularly operates special steam trains for enthusiasts. No.2850 is in the Canadian Railway Museum at Delson, Quebec, No.2858 is on display at the National Museum of Science and Technology at Ottawa and, most famous of all, No.2860 works regular tourist trains on the British Columbia Railway between Vancouver and Squamish. No.2860 has visited Eastern Canada as well as steaming south as far as Los Angeles, hauling a show train intended to publicise the beauties of British Columbia.

Left: Original Class H-1 No. 2816 preserved far from home at Steamtown, Vermont.

Class 3460 4-6-4

Origin: United States: Atchison, Topeka & Santa Fe Railway (AT&SF), 1937.
Gauge: 4ft 8¹/2in (1,435mm). **Tractive effort:** 43,300lb (19,640kg).
Axleload: 77,510lb (35t). **Cylinders:** (2) 23¹/2 x 29¹/2in (597 x 749mm).
Driving wheels: 84in (2,131mm). **Heating surface:** 4,770sq ft (443m²).
Superheater: 2,080sq ft (193m²). **Steam pressure:** 300psi (21kg/cm²).
Grate area: 98.5sq ft (9.2m²). **Fuel (oil):** 7,000US gall (26.5m³). **Water:**
21,000US gall (79.5m³). **Adhesive weight:** 211,400lb (96t). **Total weight:**
412,400lb (187t). **Length overall:** 100ft 3in (30,556mm).

A decisive point in favour of diesel traction compared with steam, so it was
said, was that trains could travel that much further without changing
engines. It was convenient to forget the exploit of Atchison, Topeka & Santa
Fe 4-6-4 No.3461, which in December 1937 brought an eastbound
scheduled mail train all the way from Los Angeles to Chicago, a distance of
2,227 miles (3,583km). This still stands as a world record, although it must
be said it was not one which any other single railroad in the USA had the
length of route available to beat.

No.3461 was one of a small class of six 4-6-4s delivered from Baldwin in
1937. These were developed directly from (and numbered in series with) 50
4-6-2s delivered between 1919 and 1922, followed by 10 otherwise similar
4-6-2s in 1927. This "3400" class was typical of its day and included coal-
burning as well as oil-burning examples. They demonstrated very clearly that
this great railway had finally thrown aside the thought of anything with a hinge
in the middle or more than two cylinders. Not that big power was needed for
much of Santa Fe's work; there are hundreds of miles of continuous level or
near-level track between Chicago and Los Angeles as well as the more
famous sections such as the ascents to the Cajon and Raton passes.

But it was considered that higher speeds could be run, and so in the 1930s
the class went into the shops for a rebuild. This included replacing the 74in
(1,880mm) spoked driving wheels with 79in discs, and a higher boiler pressure.

This was the period when Santa Fe's first streamline train – the now
legendary "Super Chief" – was coming into service, and the idea of running
other trains at faster speeds was important. Hence additions to the "3400s"
were 4-6-4s rather than 4-6-2s and they had relatively enormous 84in
(2,137mm) driving wheels, 19 per cent more tractive effort than the 4-6-2s
and considerably bigger grates. Larger tenders were also attached both to
the new 4-6-4s as well as to some of the rebuilt 4-6-2s, and this helped by

**Below: Atchison Topeka & Santa Fe Railway Class 3460 4-6-4 built by
Baldwin in 1937 for long distance passenger trains.**

reducing time spent taking on fuel and water.

The first of the new locomotives was streamlined and became the only Santa Fe steam loco to be so treated. This was No.3460, known colloquially as the "Blue Goose". The others well matched the standard heavyweight equipment used on such trains as the "Grand Canyon" and the "Santa Fe Chief," and could roll them at steamliner speeds over the long level miles of the Mid-West.

Below: Santa Fe 4-6-4 fitted with a fortunately temporary sky-line casing as an attempt to improve locomotive decor.

231-132BT Class
4-6-2 + 2-6-4

Origin: Algeria: Paris, Lyons & Mediterranean Co (PLM), 1937. **Tractive effort:** 65,960lb (29,920kg). **Axle load:** 40,500lb (18.5t). **Cylinders:** (4) 19¹/₄ x 26in (490 x 660mm). **Driving wheels:** 71in (1,800mm). **Heating surface:** 2,794sq ft (260m²). **Superheater:** 975sq ft (91m²). **Steam pressure:** 284psi (20kg/cm²). **Grate area:** 58sq ft (5.4m²). **Fuel:** 24,000lb (11t). **Water:** 6,600gall (7,900 US) (30m³). **Adhesive weight:** 241,000lb (111t). **Total weight:** 47,500lb (216t). **Length overall:** 96ft 6⁷/₈in (29,432mm).

One day in 1907, an engineer by the name of H.W. Garratt visited a firm of locomotive manufacturers in Manchester called Beyer, Peacock. Garratt was then working as an inspector for goods manufactured in Britain for the New South Wales Government, but he came to discuss with them an idea which he had patented for articulated locomotives built to the same basic format as mobile rail-mounted guns. The main result in due time was some hardware in the form of two little 0-4-4-0 compound locomotives, hinged twice in the middle, for far-off Tasmania.

This Garratt layout consisted of taking two conventional locomotive chassis or engine units, of whatever wheel arrangement was preferred, and using them back-to-back as bogies a certain distance apart. A boiler cradle was then slung between them, tanks and fuel bunkers being mounted on the engine units.

The reason for the Garratt's success when compared with rival types of articulated locomotives such as the "Mallet", was mainly due to the elegance of its geometry. For example, when swinging fast round curves, the boiler and cab unit moved inwards like a bowstring in the bow of the curve, thereby countering an overturning effect of centrifugal force.

Another advantage of the Garratt arrangement was that there was no running gear (so vulnerable to grit) immediately under the fire-grate; just lots of room and plenty of the fresh air so necessary to ensure good combustion. More important, the absence of running gear beneath the boiler gave complete freedom in respect of the design of this important component. Although a Garratt gives the impression of great length and slenderness, in fact, the boiler can be relatively short and fat.

Although many were sold for freight and mixed traffic use, the excellent riding qualities of Beyer-Garratts were seldom exploited for express passenger work, until 1927 when a group of 2-6-2 + 2-6-2s – later altered to 4-6-2+2-6-4s – with 5ft 6in (1,676mm) diameter driving wheels, were built for the 5ft 3in (1,600mm) gauge Brazilian San Paulo Railway. With them 70mph (113km/h) was achieved, with excellent stability. In 1931 the Spanish Central Aragon Railway obtained six 4-6-2+2-6-4s with 5ft 9in (1,753mm) driving wheels, and these were equally satisfactory; these latter locomotives were built by Euskalduna of Bilbao under licence.

In 1932 the Paris, Lyons & Mediterranean Company ordered an experimental Garratt-type locomotive from the Franco-Belge Company of Raismes, France, for the Algerian lines. This 4-6-2 + 2-6-4 was successful, both at fast running as well as at climbing over the mountains, to a point where further express Garratts of an improved design were ordered. When the PLM lines in Algeria had been amalgamated with the Algerian State Railways (CFAE) an initial order for 10 was later increased to 29.

Amongst many interesting features of a design which kept wholly to the standard Garratt layout was the Cossart valve gear. This unusual gear drove cam-operated piston valves and enabled the locomotive to use very early cut-offs indeed, in the range of 5 per cent to 7 per cent. If normal valve gears such as Stephenson's or Walschaert's are arranged so they can be linked up to give cut-offs as early as this, it is impossible to arrange the geometry so that the exhaust ports would then open for an adequate fraction of the return stroke. Such a locomotive would experience a checking influence at speed – generally speaking 15 per cent or 17 per cent is the limit with conventional gears, and any more fully expansive working is not possible. The valve gear was operated electrically.

Other equipment included duplicate controls at the rear of the cab for running hind end first, a feed water heater, and a turbofan for ventilating the cab. There were drench pipes to the ashpan and smokebox, a soot blower to clean the boiler tubes on the run, and a recording speedometer. A double chimney and double variable blast-pipe was provided; unusually the two orifices were placed side by side instead of end-on. A coal-pusher assisted in bringing coal forward ready to be fed to the fire. The tanks and bunker were arranged to correspond in shape with the boiler. The ends were streamlined and the result aesthetically most impressive.

On test on the Northern Railway between Calais and Paris, it was found that the engine rode steadily and could develop cylinder horse-power up to 3,000. In service on the Algiers-Constantine main line, which included gradients as steep as 1 in 38$\frac{1}{2}$ (2.6 per cent), the running time for the 288 miles (464km) was reduced from 12$\frac{1}{2}$ hours to 8$\frac{1}{2}$. Between Algiers and Oran the new timing of 7 hours for the 262 miles (422km) represented an acceleration of 2 hours.

Until the war came to Algeria the express Garratts gave good service but, alas, the electrical valve gear did not stand up to the inevitable neglect when the fighting began. Soon after the war there was an opportunity to dieselise and by 1951 these 30 superb locomotives were out of use.

Below: The magnificent class 231-132BT Beyer-Garratt locomotives built in France for the Algerian railways.

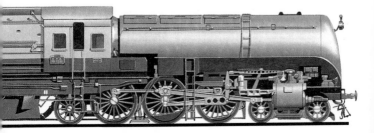

Class I-5 4-6-4

Origin: United States: New York, New Haven & Hartford (New Haven), 1937. **Gauge:** 4ft 8½in (1,435mm). **Tractive effort:** 44,000lb (19,960kg). **Axle load:** 65,000lb (29.5t). **Cylinders:** (2) 22 x 30in (559 x 762mm). **Driving wheels:** 80in (2,032mm). **Heating surface:** 3,815sq ft (354m²). **Superheater:** 1,042sq ft (97m²). **Steam pressure:** 285psi (20kg/cm²). **Grate area:** 77sq ft (7.2m²). **Fuel:** 32,000lb (14.5t). **Water:** 18,000 US gall (68m³). **Adhesive weight:** 193,000lb (87.4t). **Total weight:** 698,000lb (317t). **Length overall:** 97ft 0¾in (29,585mm).

These handsome engines were the first streamlined 4-6-4s in the USA to be delivered. They were also very much an example to be followed in that, firstly, the desire to streamline was not allowed to interfere with access to the machinery for maintenance and, secondly, they followed in all essential respects the simple Stephenson concept.

The New York, New Haven & Hartford Railroad (called the New Haven for short) had its main line from New York to Boston. This had been electrified in stages, beginning as early as 1905 and reaching its greatest extent at New Haven, 72 miles (115km) from New York, in 1914.

There remained 159 miles (256km) of steam railroad from there to the "home of the bean and the cod". Trains such as "The Colonial" or the all-Pullman parlor car express "The Merchants Limited" heavily overtaxed the capacity of the existing class "I-4" Pacifics and, in 1936, after a good deal

of research and experiment, ten 4-6-4s were ordered from Baldwin of Philadelphia. Running numbers were 1400 to 1409.

This "I-5" class with disc driving wheels, roller bearings and Walschaert's valve gear went into service in 1937. They certainly met the promise of their designers in that they showed a 65 per cent saving in the cost of maintenance compared with the. 4-6-2s they replaced and, moreover, could handle 16-car 1,100-ton trains to the same schedules as the Pacific could barely manage with 12.

Another requirement was met in that they proved able to clear the 1 in 140 (0.7 per cent) climb out of Boston to Sharon Heights with a 12-car 840-ton train at 60mph (97km/h). But, alas, the "I-5"s were never able to develop their no doubt formidable high speed capability because of a rigidly enforced 70mph (113km/h) speed limit. For this reason and because the line was infested with speed restrictions, the schedule of the "Merchants Limited" never fell below 171 minutes including two stops, representing an average of 55mph (89km/h). Forty years' "progress" and a change from steam to diesel traction since the days of the "I-5"s has only succeeded in reducing this time to 170mins today.

It is unfortunate that none of the I-5s has been preserved. Incidentally, nor has any other New Haven steam locomotive, except for an old 1863 American Standard 4-4-0, displayed in the State Fair Grounds at Danbury, Connecticut.

Left: The New Haven to Boston section of NH's New York-Boston main line was the stamping ground of the 10 Class I-5 4-6-4s delivered by Baldwin in 1937.

05A 4-8-4

Origin: United States: Chicago, Burlington & Quincy Railroad (CB&Q), 1939. **Gauge:** 4ft 8¹/₂in (1,435mm). **Tractive effort:** 67,500lb (30,626kg). **Axleload:** 77,387lb (35.1t). **Cylinders:** (2) 28 x 30in (711 x 762mm). **Driving wheels:** 74in (1,879mm). **Heating surface:** 5,225sq ft (485m²). **Superheater:** 2,403sq ft (223m²). **Steam pressure:** 250psi (17.6kg/cm²). **Grate area:** 106.5sq ft (9.9m²). **Fuel:** 54,000lb (24.5t). **Water:** 18,000 US gall (68.1m³). **Adhesive weight:** 281,410lb (127.7t). **Total weight:** 838,050lb (380.2t). **Length overall:** 105ft 11in (32,283mm).

The Chicago, Burlington & Quincy Railroad, as its slogan but not its title indicated, served "Everywhere West". In steam days its tracks went far beyond the relatively local implications of its name, serving St Paul, Minneapolis, Kansas City, Omaha, Denver and St Louis. In addition a north-south axis of wholly-owned subsidiary lines connected Billings, Montana, not far from the Canadian border, with Galveston, Texas, on the Gulf of Mexico.

In 1930 Baldwin supplied the Burlington with eight 4-8-4s intended for freight movement and classified "05". Subsequently in 1937 a further 13 of these giants were built. The locomotives were all coal-burners and not specially remarkable, although they did have Baker valve gear. Their one optional complication was a Worthington feed-water heater, as power reverse and mechanical stoker were essential for locomotives of such size and power. In the following years the Burlington's shops turned out 15 "Super 05s" designated "05A". Although they were dimensionally the same, a number of modern features were applied. There were "Box-pok" disc driving wheels in place of spoked, and Timken roller bearings to all axles as well as to the pins of the valve gear. Later on, some of the locomotives were equipped for oil-burning.

Generally, 4-8-4s are regarded as passenger power, but the "05s" were classified as freight locomotives. One reason for this was that the CB&Q was the pioneer of diesel-electric streamlined trains and had been building up its fleet of such trains – the famous "Zephyrs" – ever since 1934. By 1939 all the principal routes were so operated by trains such as the "Denver Zephyr," "Twin Cities Zephyr" and others, so the need for powerful steam passenger locomotives was minimal. The other reason was that Burlington country was largely free from mountain grades. So a 4-8-4 had adequate adhesion for heavy freight haulage. The big firebox intrinsic to the type was needed for the high power output involved in running heavy long-distance trains at high speeds over straight alignments.

All except the first eight of the 36 "05s" and "05As" were built by the Burlington in their own shops at West Burlington, Iowa. Though CB&Q was

Below: A Class "05A" of the Burlington Route. These fine locomotives were intended for freight traffic in spite of their 4-8-4 wheel arrangement.

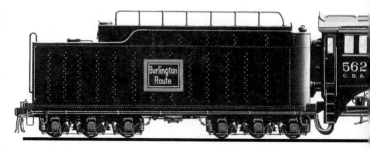

Above: Chicago, Burlington & Quincy "O5A" class 4-8-4 No. 5632 heads a fan trip from Chicago to Denver after normal steam working had ceased.

one of the few US railroads to do this, "do-it-yourself" was common all over the world in the age of steam, when even quite small railways in almost wholly agricultural countries built their own locomotives. The passing of steam has left them completely in the hands of the two biggest of the big corporations.

For a time after complete dieselisation the CB&Q kept an "O5A" (No.5632) in running order for special passenger trains. About 1967 this was ended, but four others are preserved as static exhibits. No.5614 is at St Joseph, Missouri, 5620 at Galesburg, Illinois, 5629 at the Colorado Railroad Museum, Golden and 5631 at Sheridan, Wyoming.

Right: Do-it-yourself was a speciality of the Chicago, Burlington & Quincy Railroad. This "O5A" 4-8-4 was built at the West Burlington shops in 1938, ceasing work in 1960.

Duchess Class 4-6-2

Origin: Great Britain: London, Midland & Scottish Railway (LMS), 1939. **Tractive effort:** 40,000lb (18,144kg). **Axle load:** 52,500lb (24t). **Cylinders** (4) $16^1/2$ x 28in (419 x 711mm). **Driving wheels:** 81in (2,057mm). **Heating surface:** 2,807sq ft (261m²). **Superheater:** 856sq ft (79.5m²). **Steam pressure:** 250psi (17.6kg/cm²). **Grate area:** 50sq ft (4.6m²). **Fuel:** 22,400l (10t). **Water:** 4,000gall (4,800 US) (18m³). **Adhesive weight:** 147,500l (68t). **Total weight:** 362,000lb (164t). **Length overall:** 73ft $10^1/4$in (22,510mm).

The most powerful steam locomotive ever to run in Britain! This was demonstrated in February 1939, when No.6234 *Duchess of Abercorn* was put to haul a 20-coach 605-ton test train from Crewe to Glasgow and back. An authentic recording of an indicated horse-power of 3,330 was made and this power output from a steam locomotive has never been matched in Britain. It occurred coming south when climbing the 1 in 99 (1.01 per cent) of Beattock bank at a steady speed of 63mph (102km/h). This feat was, however, a purely academic one, not because of any limitations on the part of the locomotive but because the power developed corresponded to a coal shovelling rate well beyond the capacity of one man. Two firemen were carried on the occasion of the test run, which certainly equalled anything achieved later with diesel traction before the arrival of the High Speed Train.

It remains a pity that none of the "Duchess" class 4-6-2s were tried with oil firing or mechanical stoking, not so much because a somewhat academic record might then have been pushed higher, but rather that the faster train services which followed dieselisation might have been achieved years earlier with steam.

Incidentally, the "Duchess" locomotives were fast runners as well as strong pullers and even held the British rail speed record for a short period, although it was not an occasion for any pride. This was because in order to obtain the 114mph (182km/h) maximum, steam was not shut off until the train was so close to Crewe that the crossovers leading into the platform and good for only 20mph (32km/h) were taken at nearly 60mph (96km/h). Minor damage was done to the track and much to the crockery in the kitchen car, but the train and the newsmen aboard survived. The practical features of the design which saved the day were a credit to the engineer concerned, but this was cancelled out by a typical disdain for theory, which could so easily have established the point at which steam should have been shut off and the brakes applied so that the safety of the train should not have been endangered.

Completely unshaken by this incident, with the down train, the imperturbable driver J.T. Clarke using the same locomotive then proceeded to take the party back to London in 119 minutes at an average speed of 79.5mph (127km/h) with several maxima over 90mph (144km/h) and the

Above: Ex-London Midland & Scottish Railway 4-6-2 No. 46236 *City of Bradford* **on the down "Royal Scot" in the Lune Gorge near Tebay, Lancashire.**

magic 100 (160) maintained for some distance near Castlethorpe.

Enough has been said to show that the "Duchess" class represented something close to the summit of British locomotive engineering. Simplicity was not the keynote of the design, but sound conventional engineering made these locomotives the success they were. The designer was William Stanier who had come to the LMS from the Great Western Railway in 1932; he was a worthy product of the Churchward tradition and at the age of 52 far from being a young man. He had one great advantage over his predecessors on the LMS – a direct line to Lord Stamp, president of the company, who had recruited him personally over lunch at the Athenaeum Club. Previous locomotive engineers had been dictated to even over such details as axleboxes by the operating department of the railway – and then blamed for the consequent failures.

So Stanier was able without interference to initiate design work on an excellent range of standard locomotives; the results took the LMS from a somewhat backward position into an enviable one so far as their locomotive

Below: No. 46251 *City of Nottingham* **depicted in LMS style British Railways livery but with the streamline pattern tender originally attached.**

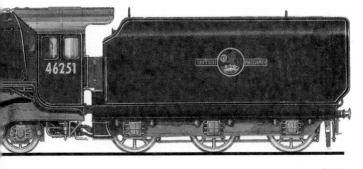

stud was concerned. His first 4-6-2 was the *Princess Royal* which appeared in 1933; her cylinder layout was similar to the Great Western "King" class, except that two more independent sets of Walschaert's valve gear were fitted outside the wheels for the outside cylinders. At first the taper boiler did not steam as well as it should and several quite considerable successive internal alterations had to be made, which were applied new to later "Princess Royal" class locomotives as they came out and retrospectively to those already built. One of these locomotives was the "Turbomotive".

A decision to run a streamlined high-speed express from Euston to Glasgow in 1937 was the opportunity to apply all that had been learnt from the 12 locomotives of the "Princess Royal" class for these 4-6-2s were far larger than anything the LMS had had before. The train and the first of the five new locomotives built for it took the names *Coronation Scot* and *Coronation* respectively.

This time the cylinder layout was moved well away from that of the GWR. The centre lines were inclined upwards at a slope of 1$\frac{1}{2}$ degrees, while the outside cylinders were brought forward from the original position in line with the rear bogie wheel. The outside valve gears were made to work the valves of the inside cylinders as well as the outside by rocker arms just to the rear of the outside cylinders. A similar arrangement had been fitted to No.6205 Princess Victoria. Both wheel and cylinder diameters were slightly larger on the "Coronation" class than on the "Princess Royal" class. An interesting gadget in the tender was the steam coal-pusher which helped the fireman bring coal forward from the back of the tender when supplies at the front got used up.

The boiler was notable for an 11 per cent larger fire grate area and a 133 per cent increase in superheater heating surface, compared with the original *Princess Royal* – although subsequent "Princess Royal" class locomotives had bigger superheaters, none were as large as that. Not many people liked the sausage-shaped streamlined shroud that enveloped the locomotive, but the new blue and silver livery was lovely. The other four locomotives were named after members of the royal family – *Queen Elizabeth, Queen Mary, Princess Alice* and *Princess Alexandra*.

The 6$\frac{1}{2}$-hour schedule of the "Coronation Scot" from London to Glasgow with only a 270-ton load was not too demanding for these great locomotives but, quite aside from this, they were found to be excellent heavy artillery for general express passenger use on this West Coast main line. Accordingly, a further ten were ordered of which only the first five were streamlined. All ten were named after duchesses (in fact, the whole class is now usually referred to by that name) and it was No.6230 *Duchess of Buccleuch* that first demonstrated how extremely handsome these engines

Above: In London Midland & Scottish Railway days and as originally built in streamline form, No.6225 *Duchess of Gloucester* passes Rugby.

were when unclothed.

More streamlined engines of an order for 20 (named after cities) placed before the war were delivered gradually over the war years 1939-43. After 18 of them had been completed construction continued with non-streamlined examples, and in 1945 instructions were issued for the streamline casings to be removed from locomotives fitted with it. This was not completed until 1949 by which time the last and 38th "Duchess" (No.6257 *City of Salford*) had been complete for a twelve-month.

The success of the class is measured by the minimal number of changes that were made over their years of service from 1937, until electric and diesel locomotives took over in 1964. Nos.6256 and 6257 had some modification, but these were more in the nature of experiments than cures for recognised ills. In contrast, the number of livery changes were legion – blue and gold streamline, standard LMS maroon, maroon and gold streamline, plain wartime black, lined post-war black, experimental gray, BR dark blue, BR medium blue, BR green and finally LMS maroon with BR insignia as shown in the painting on the previous pages.

Three have been preserved – No.6229 *Duchess of Hamilton*, in the charge of the National Railway Museum, and currently restored to main line running condition, No.6233 *Duchess of Sutherland* in Alan Bloom's collection at Bress-ingham, near Diss, and No. 6235 *City of Birmingham* in the Birmingham Science Museum.

Left: The second-from-last and considerably modified "Duchess" No.46256 was named *Sir William A Stanier* FRS in honour of her designer.

5001 Class 2-10-4

Origin: Atchison, Topeka & Santa Fe Railway (AT&SF), 1938. **Gauge:** 4ft 8¹/₂in (1,435mm). **Tractive effort:** 108,960lb (49,440kg). **Axleload:** 81,752lb (37t). **Cylinders:** (2) 30 x 34in (762 x 864mm). **Driving wheels:** 74in (1,880mm). **Heating surface:** 6,075sq ft (564m²). **Superheater:** 2,675sq ft (249m²). **Steam pressure:** 310psi (22kg/cm²). **Grate area:** 121sq ft (11.25m²). **Fuel (oil):** 7,100US gall (27m³). **Water*:** 24,500US gall (93m³). **Adhesive weight:** 371,600lb (169t). **Total weight*:** 1,002,700lb (455t). **Length overall*:** 123ft 5in (37,617mm).
*with 16-wheel tender.

The 2-10-4 type got the name "Texas" from a group of locomotives built by Lima for the Texas & Pacific Railroad in 1925. Yet the Atchison, Topeka & Santa Fe Railway had one earlier than that. In 1921 a Santa Fe type (2-10-2) had its rear truck replaced by a two-axle one. The railway got its second 2-10-4 (and its first designed as such) nine years later when new power was needed to hurtle vast freights across Kansas, Oklahoma, Texas and New Mexico along the southern and more easily graded of the two routes that ran southwest from Kansas City and joined at Belen, New Mexico, on the way to Los Angeles.

We have seen how Santa Fe's locomotive department promised itself, after traumatic experiences, never again to order locomotives with more than two cylinders. Within this limitation their own 2-10-2 type was the favourite, but fast running on moderate gradients needs a high power output in relation to tractive effort. This means a high heat input, hence a large grate and a two-axle rear truck to carry its weight, making a 2-10-2 into a 2-10-4.

Because of the Depression the unremarkable prototype 2-10-4 No.5000 delivered in 1930 – built by Baldwin like almost all Santa Fe locomotives – remained a singleton for eight years, although it delivered the goods in a literal sense. In the meantime, however, the specification had grown to give for the first and only time in the history of steam a big-wheeled high-speed locomotive with as many as ten coupled wheels. Another way of getting speed was to cut out the need for fuel and water stops and the huge 16-wheel tender which resulted from this thinking brought the fully-loaded weight to over a million pounds, another record for a two-cylinder steam locomotive. More than 100,000lb of nominal tractive effort is also confined to a handful of examples.

Above: Santa Fe 2-10-4 No. 5022, leased by the Pennsylvania Railroad for its last assignment at Columbus, Ohio, June 1956.

These racing mammoths did all that was expected of them and more, being capable of developing over 6,000hp (4,475kW) in the cylinders. This applied particularly to the second wartime batch (Nos. 5011 to 5035) which had roller bearings as well as larger tenders from the start.

Dieselisation came early to the Santa Fe, the first freight units arriving in 1940. Whilst the 2-10-4s showed up well against them, the older steam locomotives – then in the majority even on Santa Fe – did not. Moreover, in the west there were major problems in finding enough good water for steam locomotives; diesels eliminated much unproductive hauling in of water supplies. So, by the early 1950s, modern 4-8-4s and 2-10-4s were the only steam locomotives operating, and even these had ceased by August 1957.

Happily, four of these giants have been preserved in widely separated locations – No.5011 at St Louis, Missouri; 5017 at Green Bay, Wisconsin; 5021 at Belen, New Mexico; and 5030 especially appropriately at Santa Fe itself.

Left: Prototype 2-10-4 No.5000, known as "Madam Queen" preserved at Amarillo.

Class 12 4-4-2

Origin: Belgium: Belgian National Railways (SNCB), 1939. **Tractive effort:** 26,620lb (12,079kg). **Axle load:** 52,000lb (23.4t). **Cylinders:** (2) 18⁷/8 x 28³/8in (480 x 720mm). **Driving wheels:** 82³/4in (2,100mm). **Heating surface:** 1,729sq ft (161m²). **Superheater:** 678sq ft (63m²). **Steam pressure:** 256psi (18kg/cm²). **Grate area:** 39.8sq ft (3.7m²). **Fuel:** 17,500lb (8t). **Water:** 5,280gall (6,300 US) (24m³). **Adhesive weight:** 101,000lb (45.8t). **Total weight*:** 188,500lb (89.5t). **Length overall:** 69ft 6¹/4in (21,190mm).

(*Engine only without tender.)

Most modern steam locomotives trace their descent more from *Northumbrian* than *Planet*; but here is an exception; and, moreover, one that was good enough for a world record for scheduled start-to-stop speed: Whilst the Belgian class "12" 4-4-2s were totally conventional as regards principles, the layout of their machinery was unusual if not unique – but then what other than original thinking would be expected of a country that produced both Alfred Belpaire and Egide Walschaert?

The concept was to operate frequent lightweight high-speed trains, of three cars only, over the 71 miles (121km) between Brussels and Ostend in the even hour, including a stop at Bruges. Between Brussels and Bruges the timing was to be 46 minutes, giving an average speed of 75.4mph (121.3km/h). The speed limit of this almost level route was specially raised for these trains to 87mph (140km/h). It was decided that four coupled wheels were adequate, whilst the power needed for the high speeds contemplated was best provided by a wide firebox. A leading bogie was certainly desirable and, to avoid oscillations, inside cylinders were preferred, made reasonably accessible by the use of bar rather than plate frames. All this added up to the world's last 4-4-2s as well as the world's last inside-cylinder express locomotives. The tenders were second-hand, with streamlining added, and the locomotives were built by Messrs Cockerill of Seraing, Belgium.

Alas, the high-speed trains only ran for a few months before war broke out in September 1939. One of the 4-4-2s (No.1203) has, however, survived and is preserved at the SNCB locomotive depot at Louvain. The best timing by electric traction today between Brussels and Ostend is 11 minutes longer with one extra stop – an 18 per cent *increase* in journey time when steam gives way to electric traction is possibly yet another record achieved by these remarkable locomotives.

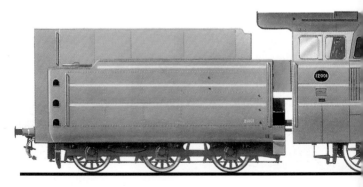

Above: SNCB Class "12" 4-4-2 No.12.004, one of the world's last 4-4-2s.

Above and below: Two views of the Belgian National Railways' class "12" high-speed 4-4-2 locomotives, built in 1938 to haul lightweight expresses between Brussels and Ostend.

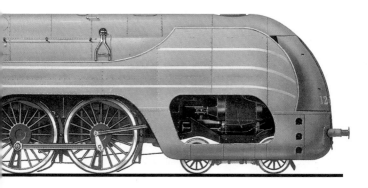

FEF-2 Class 4-8-4

Origin: United States: Union Pacific Railroad (UP), 1939. **Gauge:** 4ft 8½in (1,435mm). **Tractive effort:** 63,800lb (28,950kg). **Axle load:** 67,000lb (30.5t). **Cylinders:** (2) 25 x 32in (635 x 813mm). **Driving wheels:** 80in (2,032mm). **Heating surface:** 4,225sq ft (393m²). **Superheater:** 1,400sq ft (130m²). **Steam pressure:** 300psi (21kg/cm²). **Grate area:** 100sq ft (9.3m²). **Fuel:** 50,000lb (23t). **Water:** 19,600gall (23,500 US) (90m³). **Adhesive weight:** 266,500lb (121t). **Total weight:** 908,000lb (412t). **Length overall:** 113ft 10in (34,696mm).

The origin of the class occurred during the late 1930s, when rising train loads began to overtax the 4-8-2s which were then the mainstay of UP passenger operations. One day in 1937 a "7000" class 4-8-2 had the temerity to demonstrate the lack of steaming power inherent in the type, on a train with UP President William Jeffers' business car on the rear. Even while the party was waiting out on the prairies for rescue, a dialogue by telegram went on with Alco in far off Schenectady, with a view to getting something better.

The result in due course was this superb class of 45 locomotives of which 20, numbered 800 to 819, were delivered in 1938. A further 15 (Nos.820 to 834) with larger wheels and cylinders as well as 14-wheel centipede tenders – instead of 12-wheel ones – came the following year and it is to these that the specifications etc given above apply. This second batch was designated "FEF-2", the earlier ones becoming class "FEF-1". FEF stood for Four-Eight-Four!

A final batch of ten, almost identical to the second one except for the use of some substitute materials, appeared in 1944. These were known as "FEF-3"s and were the last steam power supplied to UP. All the "800"s came from Alco.

The "800"s as a whole followed – like *Northumbrian* 108 years earlier – the standard recipe for success in having two outside cylinders only, the simplest possible arrangement. That king of passenger locomotive wheel arrangements, the "Northern" or 4-8-4, was adopted and misgivings originally felt regarding the suitability of eight-coupled wheels for very high speeds were found not to be justified. The negotiation of curves was made easier by the fitting of Alco's lateral motion device to the leading coupled wheels.

The basic simplicity of so many US locomotives was often spoilt by their designers being an easy touch for manufacturers of complicated accessories. The UP managed to resist most of them with the pleasing result that the locomotives had a delightfully elegant uncluttered appearance, unmarred by any streamline shroud. On the other hand, they rightly fell for such excellent simplifications as the cast-steel locomotive frame, which replaced many separate parts by one single casting. Another example was the use of a static exhaust steam injector instead of a steam-driven mechanical water-pump and feed water heater. A complication

**Above: No. 8444 smokes it up on a railfan special "Extra 8444".
Note enthusiasts at the windows of the train.**

resisted by the UP was the provision of thermic syphons in the firebox; they held the view that on balance these quite common devices were more trouble than benefit. Even so, both common sense as well as Uncle Sam's rules meant power reversing gear and automatic stoking, whilst electric lighting was something that certainly paid off in helping "800" crews to see what they were doing.

Perhaps the most original feature and one which contributed a good deal to the success of the "800"s was the main motion. Aesthetically, the main rods were pure poetry but there was a great deal more to it than that. Because of the speeds and forces involved, current technology was taken beyond the then accepted limits; at the same time, the magnitude of the stresses to which those whirling rods were subject are very different to evaluate with any degree of confidence.

Below: The last steam locomotive built for the Union Pacific Railroad, class "FEF-3" 4-8-4 No.844 (renumbered to 8444 to avoid confusion with a diesel unit).

What a triumph for the designers, then, that these lovely tapered coupling and connecting rods were a resounding success even though frequently moved at revolutions corresponding to running speeds above the 100mph (160km/h) mark. The main principle of the new design was that the pulls and thrusts were transmitted from the connecting rods – and hence to three out of the four pairs of wheels – by separate sleeve bearings instead of via the main crankpins in accordance with convention. The result was that separate knuckle-joints in the coupling rods were replaced by making the centre pair of rods forked at both ends and combining the roles of crank-pins and knuckle-pins.

The results were superb and there are many reports of speeds being run up to the design limit of 110mph (176km/h). After the war there was a period when coal supplies were affected by strikes and, in order to safeguard UP passenger operations, the "800"s were converted from coal to oil burning; a 6,000gall (27m³) tank was fitted in the bunker space. Otherwise only minor modifications were needed over many years of arduous service, a fact which is also much to the credit of the designers.

Normally the 4-8-4s were entrusted with the many expresses formed of the then conventional heavyweight stock, but the new engines' arrival on UP coincided with the introduction of diesel-electric streamline trains on much faster timings. In those early days the new form of motive power was not too reliable and "800" class locomotives frequently found themselves replacing a multi-unit diesel at the head end of one of UP's crack trains. They found no problem in making up time on the tight diesel schedules sufficient to offset extra minutes spent taking on water.

The last service passenger train hauled by an "800" was caused by such a failure; it occurred when in 1958, the last one built took the "City of Los Angeles" over the last stretch of 145 miles (232km) from Grand Island into Omaha. No.844 gained time on the steamliner's schedule in spite of the crew's lack of recent experience with steam. A year later there came a time when all were out of service awaiting scrapping.

Below: Preserved Union Pacific 4-8-4 No.8444 on parade. In addition to outings for the railfans, the loco is used to promote publicity.

Class GS-4 4-8-4

Origin: United States: Southern Pacific Railroad (SP), 1941. **Gauge:** 4ft 8¹/₂in (1,435mm) **Tractive effort:** 71,173lb (32,285kg). **Axle load:** 68,925lb (31.25t). **Cylinders:** (2) 25¹/₂ x 32in (648 x 813mm). **Driving wheels:** 80in (2,032mm). **Heating surface:** 4,887sq ft (454m²). **Superheater:** 2,086sq ft (194m²). **Steam pressure:** 300psi (21.1kg/cm²). **Grate area:** 90.4sq ft (8.4m²). **Fuel (oil):** 4,900gall (5,900 US) (22.3m³). **Water:** 19,600gall (23,500 US) (89m³). **Adhesive weight:** 276,000lb (125.5t). **Total weight:** 883,000lb (400.5t).

The "Daylight" express of the Southern Pacific Railroad was the third of three famous train services worked by matching streamlined express locomotives and coaches over a similar distance. The "Hiawatha" trains of the Milwaukee line between Chicago and the Twin Cities and the "Coronation" of the British London & North Eastern Railway between London and Edinburgh have been described elsewhere. Each of the three trains introduced new standards of speed, comfort and decor, and each train was spectacularly successful in attracting new traffic

The 470-mile route between Los Angeles and San Francisco was much the hardest as well as the longest of the three. For example, there was nothing on either of the other lines to compare with the 1 in 45 (2.2 per cent) gradient of Santa Margharita Hill, north of San Luis Obispo. The "light-weight" 12-car "Daylight" express weighed 568 tonnes, nearly double the weight of the British train – though it must be said that as regards weight hauled per passenger carried, the latter came out at 15 per cent less than the former.

Because of the severe curvature of the line as well as the heavy gradients the 48.5mph (78km/h) average speed of the "Daylight" train was considerably less than that of the other two, although the lessening of running times represented by all three of the new trains were roughly even The gradients encountered by the "Daylight" nicely balanced out with the "Hiawatha" faster running, but certainly the "Daylight" was a far tougher haulage proposition than the British train. The motive power provided reflected this.

Eight-coupled wheels were needed and enabled the resulting "Daylight" 4-8-4 to have (with booster) 124 per cent more tractive effort than the LNER "A4" 4-6-2. As regards grate area, that is, the size of the fire, the increase was 119 per cent. The SP already had fourteen 4-8-4s (class "GS-1"), which came from Baldwin of Philadelphia in 1930. As with the LNER's but unlike the Milwaukee's, the SP's new locomotives (class "GS-2") were from a mechanical point of view based very closely on their immediate predecessors. Of course, the decor was something else again and it gave these four black, silver and gold monsters from the Lima Locomotive Works of Lima, Ohio, an appearance which could hardly be described as less than superb.

Like so many large North American locomotives of the time, the success

Above: An improvement to Class "GS-4" was fitting of fully-enclosed cabs. No.4449 of this batch has been preserved in the full Southern Pacific "Daylight" livery.

Designation	Date	Running Nos	Features
GS-2	1937	4410 to 4415	Driving wheels 73$\frac{1}{2}$in (1,867mm) dia instead of 80in (2,032mm)
GS-3	1937	4416 to 4429	
GS-4	1941-2	4430 to 4457	Fully enclosed cabs began with this batch
GS-5	1942	4458 to 4459	As GS-4 but with roller bearings.
GS-6	1943	4460 to 4469	No streamlining – plain black

of the "Daylight" type was due to the application of the excellent standard of US practice of the day. Amongst a few special features worth recording was one that has almost no steam traction parallel elsewhere, that is the provision of electro-pneumatic brake equipment. With other forms of

Below: One of the original batch (class "GS-2") of Southern Pacific's "Daylight" 4-8-4s as delivered from the Lima Locomotive Works, Ohio, in 1937.

traction, the electro-pneumatic brake is commonplace today, especially for multiple-units. Application of the brakes on a normal air-brake system relies on a pressure change travelling down the brake pipe from the locomotive to switch on the brakes under each successive car. This involves a flow of air towards the driver's brake-valve and in consequence a delay of several seconds occurs before the brakes are applied to the wheels of the rear car. In contrast, with EP braking the signal to apply the brakes goes down the train with the speed of electric current. The thinking was that these few seconds – during which the train would travel several hundred feet – might in the case of a high-speed service be the difference between an incident and a disaster.

The curvature of the route was recognised by the provision of spring-controlled side-play on the leading coupled axle. In this way the wheels could "move-over" on a curve and allow the flange force to be shared between the two leading axles, with benefits to the wear of both rails and tyres. The hilliness of the line gave rise to a series of water sprays to cool the tyres on engine and tender wheels during braking on the long descents. Air sanding gear was provided, fed from a tank under that boiler-top casing which held a full *ton* of sand! With booster cut in, the "GS"s could manage the standard "Daylight" consist on the 1 in 45 grades (2.2 per cent); but if any extra cars were attached a helper was needed.

Although the "Daylight" type held to the simple and world standard concept of a two-cylinder locomotive with outside valve gear, the host of equipment provided did add a certain complexity. There were three turbo-generators, for example, and a feed-water heater and pump as well as injectors. It must be said that virtually all of this complication was made up of items of proprietary equipment each of which, as it were, came in a box and could be bolted on. Such fittings were apt to work well because competition kept the suppliers on their toes; and if problems arose a replacement could be fitted quickly. Even so, an electro-magnetic gadget – inside the boiler! – which sensed foaming and opened the blow-down cock automatically, did not last.

Like most SP steam locomotives, the "Daylight"s were fired with oil –

Above: Last of the GS classes were the unstreamlined GS-6s, of which no. 4466 hauls the "Klamath Express" at Dunsmuir, California, n June 1952.

ndeed, SP were the United States' pioneers in this area – economy being achieved with a device called a "locomotive valve pilot" which indicated to the engineer what cut-off he should set to suit any particular speed and conditions of working.

Streamlined trains, worked by further batches of these magnificently-equipped locomotives, spread to all parts of SP's system and thus served such far distant places as Portland in Oregon, Ogden in Utah and New Orleans. Details of the 60 locos were as shown in the table.

The War Production Board refused to sanction the "GS-6" batch, but on being told that "GS" now stood for "General Service" rather than "Golden State", they accepted the proposal. Of an order for 16, six went to Western Pacific Railroad.

The first "GS" to be withdrawn was No.4462 in 1954 and in October 1958 No.4460 (now displayed at the Museum of Transportation at St Louis, Missouri) brought SP steam operations to a close with a special excursion from Oakland to Reno, Nevada. No.4449 also survived to haul the "Freedom Train" several thousands of miles across the USA in connection with the bi-centennial of independence in 1976. The locomotive is still able to run and has recently been restored to the original superb "Daylight" colours.

Left: Southern Pacific's tough-haulage class "GS-4" 4-8-4 No. 4456 at San Francisco, California, in May 1952.

M3 Yellowstone 2-8-8-4

Origin: United States: Duluth, Missabe & Iron Range Railroad (DM&IR) 1941. **Gauge:** 4ft 8$\frac{1}{2}$in (1,435mm). **Tractive effort:** 140,000lb (63,521kg). **Axleload:** 74,342lb (33.7t). **Cylinders:** (4) 26 x 32in (660 x 812mm). **Driving wheels:** 63in (1,600mm). **Heating surface:** 6,758sq ft (628m²). **Superheater:** 2,770sq ft (257m²). **Steam pressure:** 240psi (16.9kg/cm²). **Grate area:** 125sq ft 11.6m²). **Fuel:** 52,000lb (23.6t). **Water:** 25,000 US gal (94.6m³). **Adhesive weight:** 565,000lb (256.4t). **Total weight:** 1,138,000lb (516.3t). **Length overall:** 126ft 8in (38,608mm).

These fine locomotives are the ones which pulled the heaviest steam-hauled trains ever regularly operated in the world. They belonged not to one of the giant railroads of America but to a smallish concern in remote Minnesota known as the Duluth, Missabe & Iron Range. As the name implies its reason for existence was the transportation of iron ore some 70 miles (112km) to the Lake Superior port of Duluth.

Bulk movement is the task railroads are best suited to, and accordingly the little line prospered well enough to afford good equipment, which in its turn led to even better prosperity. A final stage of steam re-equipment was completed with eight of these superb million-pound-plus locomotives obtained from Baldwins in 1941. A further 10 came in 1943. The 1941 locomotives were designated Class "M3", the 1943 batch as Class "M4" but there were no significant differences between the two except for the use of some substitute material in wartime.

The 2-8-8-4 or Yellowstone wheel arrangement appeared first on the Northern Pacific Railway in 1928, hence a name appropriate to Northern Pacific territory. Use of low-quality coal mined on-line on NP led to these machines having grates as large as 180sq ft (17m²) in area, 20 per cent more than on the Union Pacific Big Boys, but for the DM & IR 10 per cent less would suffice with good Pennsylvania coal in their tenders. Even so, the "M3"s had a tractive effort significantly greater than UP's giants could exert a world record for any non-compound class of steam locomotive and reflecting the requirements of hauling loads three times as great as the "Big Boys" did albeit on an easily-graded railroad.

In steam days, the Missabe moved up to 50 million tons each year, a period reduced by the length of time Lake Superior is frozen over. This implied a need to move over 200,000 tons each day to meet this target. A 2-8-8-4 could haul 190 ore cars with a gross weight of some 18,000 tons, carrying 13,000 tons of ore. Handling trains of this size was made easier by the fact that the railroad on the whole descended from the mines to the lakeside, although local grades of up to 0.3 per cent (1-in-330) faced loaded trains.

No reliance was placed on the locomotive to stop loads of this kind, but the ore cars had special differential systems whereby an extra and larger brake cylinder was automatically brought into operation when the car was loaded with over twice its empty weight of ore. So the 2-8-8-4s would set out with their crews secure in the knowledge that brake force was available proportionate to the immense load behind, on down-grades as steep as 1.4 percent (1-in-70).

Above: A Duluth, Missabe & Iron Range 2-8-8-4 awaiting orders at Proctor Minnesota.

Above: DM&IR 2-8-8-4 No.204 heads a farewell passenger train before retirement.

In spite of excellent track with heavy rail and deep ballast, a major factor in the economical operation of the railroad was strictly enforced: modest speed limits of 30mph (48km/h) for loaded cars and 35mph (56km/h) for empties. "Safety First" was rightly incorporated in the herald displayed on DM & IR tenders. Incidentally, the DM & IR is one of the few railroads in the United States to run left-handed on double-track sections.

Articulation of the "M3"s and "M4"s was based on the Mallet layout as developed by US builders, although a true Mallet, of course, has compound cylinders. Comprehensive equipment included feed-water heaters, recording speedometers, radio and an ample-sized enclosed vestibule cab. Two have been preserved, at Proctor and Two Harbors respectively.

Below: DM&IR 2-8-8-4 No.229, a line example of the huge "M3"s, which were among the greatest steam heavy haulers.

Class J 4-8-4

Origin: United States: Norfolk & Western Railway (N&W), 1941. **Gauge:** 4ft 8¹/₂in (1,435mm). **Tractive effort:** 80,000lb (36,287kg). **Axle load:** 72,000l (33t). **Cylinders:** (2) 27 x 32in (686 x 813mm). **Driving wheels:** 70i (1,778mm). **Heating surface:** 5,271sq ft (490m²). **Superheater:** 2,177sq ft (202m²). Steam pressure: 300psi (21kg/cm²). **Grate area:** 107.5sq ft (10m² **Fuel:** 70,000lb (31.75t). **Water:** 16,700gall (20,000 US) (76m³). **Adhesiv weight:** 288,000lb (131t). **Total weight:** 873,000lb (396t). **Length overal** 100ft 11in (30,759mm).

Around 1940 the Norfolk & Western Railway locomotive chiefs felt that should be possible to have something better than the standard United State Railroad Association's design of 4-8-2 upon which N&W passenge expresses then relied. Very wisely, they accepted that Robert Stephenso had got the thermal and most of the mechanical principles right with th *Northumbrian*, but what needed attention was the cost and time involved i servicing and maintenance. This meant, for example, roller bearings to th axleboxes and throughout the motion, while an unparalleled number c subsidiary bearings, over 200 in fact, were automatically fed with oil by mechanical lubricator with a 24-gallon (110-litre) tank, enough for 1,500 mile (2,400km). Even the bearings of the bell were automatically lubricated!

There was another large lubricator to feed high-temperature oil for th steam cylinders; this is normal but the feeds from this lubricator also ran t the steam cylinders of the water and air pumps and the stoker engine Hence the labour involved in filling separate lubricators at each of these wa avoided. The basic simplicity of the two-cylinder arrangement with Baker' valve gear also had the effect of minimising maintenance costs.

Huge tenders enabled calls at fuelling points to be reduced to a minimum Together with the usual modern US features such as a cast-steel locomotiv frame, all these things added up to a locomotive which could run 15,00 miles (24,000km) per month, needed to visit the repair shops only every 1 months and had a hard-to-believe record of reliability.

One feels that the "J"s were the best of all the 4-8-4s, but that is a matte of opinion; in matters of fact, though, they had certainly the highest tractiv effort and, as well, the class included the last main-line steam passenge locomotives to be constructed in the United States. They were built a follows, all at N&W's Roanoke shops: Nos. 600 to 603, 1941; 604, 1942; 60 to 610, 1943; 611 to 613, 1950.

No.604 had a booster engine on the trailing truck.

Nos.605 to 610 were originally unstreamlined and ran for two years a chunky but attractive locomotives in plain garb.

In spite of having driving wheels which were on the small side for passenger locomotive, speeds up to 90mph (144km/h) were recorded i service and 110mph (176km/h) on test. The latter was achieved with a 1,00 ton trailing load of 15 cars and represented the development of a remarkabl 6,000hp in the cylinders.

With such power and speed capability available, the fact that overa

258

Above: A Class "J" 4-8-4 of the Norfolk & Western Railway climbs into the hills of Virginia with an express passenger train.

peeds were not high reflected the hilly nature of the country served. For xample, the coach streamliner "Powhattan Arrow" needed 15hr 45min for he 676 miles (1,082km) from Norfolk, Virginia, to Cincinatti, Ohio, an verage speed of 43mph (69km/h). Whilst this train was not a heavy one, he overnight "Pocahontas" which carried through cars from Norfolk to :hicago via Cincinatti and Pennsylvania Railroad, could load up to 1,000 tons vhich had to be handled on ruling grades up to 1 in 62 (1.6 per cent).

Norfolk & Western also acted as a "bridge road" and their 4-8-4s hauled imiteds such as the "Tennessean" and the "Pelican" – the original :hattanooga Choo-choos – between Lynchburg and Bristol, on the famous ourneys from New York to Chattanooga and points beyond. No.611 was reserved at the Transportation Museum in Roanoke, Virginia, and was estored to working order in 1982-84.

Below: First of the Class "J" streamliners turned out of Norfolk & Western's Roanoke shops in 1941. The 1943 batch of six Class "J"s were at first not fitted with streamline casing, but all were ubsequently altered to match the superb line of the first five built.

Big Boy 4-8-8-4

Origin: United States: Union Pacific Railroad (UP), 1941. **Gauge:** 4ft 8^1/2i (1,435mm). **Tractive effort:** 135,375lb (61,422kg). **Axleload:** 67,750l (30.7t). **Cylinders:** (4) 23^3/4 x 32in (603 x 812mm). **Driving wheels:** 68i (1,727mm). **Heating surface:** 5,889sq ft (547m^2). **Superheater:** 2,466sq (229m^2). **Steam pressure:** 300psi (21.1kg/cm^2). **Grate area:** 150sq (13.9m^2). **Fuel:** 56,000lb (25.4t). **Water:** 25,000 US gall (94.6m^3). **Adhesiv weight:** 540,000lb (245t). **Total weight:** 1,189,500lb (539.7t). **Lengt overall:** 132ft 10in (40,487mm).

"Big Boy!" This evocative name is applied to what the world knows wer the biggest, heaviest, most powerful and strongest steam locomotives eve built. In the one sense though, the world is wrong because the 25 "Bi Boys" were surpassed (often substantially) in respect of most of th individual attributes mentioned above by other US steam locomotive described in these pages. Yet what the world says is completely correct one considers the overall picture. If a magic figure could be produced whic combined all these individual attributes, then the "Big Boys" would withou doubt be No.1 in the world. Should one go further and add som measurement of success in respect of performance as economic an successful tonnage-moving instruments, then these absolutely magnificer means of locomotion stand amongst those at the very top.

The genesis of the "Big Boys" lay in the recovery of the US econom during the late-1930s from the Depression of 1929 combined with increase spending on defense. In 1940 Union Pacific went, not for the first time, t the American Locomotive Company (Alco) for a locomotive to handle ye heavier trains across the mountainous Wyoming Division betwee Cheyenne, Wyoming and Ogden, Utah. Out of Cheyenne going west th ruling grade was until 1953 1.55 per cent (1-in-65) on the notorious Sherma Hill, with a maximum elevation of 8,013ft (2,443m) at Sherman Summi Eastwards out of Ogden, the crossing of the Wahsatch Mountains involve some 60 miles (96km) uphill, much of it at 1.14 per cent (1-in-88) as the rail climbed from 4,300ft (1,310m) altitude to 7,230ft (2,200m) at Altamont. Th prime object of acquiring the new locomotives was to handle 3,600-to trains unassisted on this latter section using the new locomotives.

A rapid-fire dialogue between UP's excellent mechanical department an Alco's equally experienced design teams led to design work bein completed in an amazingly short time of six months or so. Such was th confidence of UP management in the work done that they ordered 20 locomotives straight from the drawing board. The price was $265,174 each

Legend states firmly that a shopman at Alco chalked the name "Bi Boy!" on the smokebox of an early member of the class. There are tales c UP's efforts to counter it with more solid suggestions such as "Wahsatch' But, whatever its origin, media publicity was such that the "Big Boy" nam was clearly with us for good even before the first one arrived at Omaha earl in September 1941, about a year after the order was placed.

Above: The impressive front end of Union Pacific articulated "Big Boy" 4-8-8-4 No. 4002, built by the American Locomotive Company in 1941.

Below: The mightily impressive "Big Boy" 4-8-8-4, weighing in at almost 540 tons.

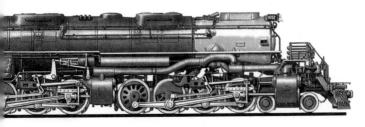

Before this memorable day much preparatory work had to be done including replacement of lighter rails with new 130lb/yd (65kg/m) steel and new 135ft (41m) turntables at Ogden and Green River. Many curves had to be realigned, not so much because these surprisingly flexible monsters could not get round them but rather that excessive overhang might mean contact with trains on adjacent lines. The front of the boiler swung out some 2ft (600mm) sideways from the centre of the track on a 10° (134m) radius curve! In fact, the maximum curvature that could be negotiated was as sharp as 20° (87m) and few locations on main tracks are as sharply curved as that. On good alignments the maximum speed of a "Big Boy" was about 70mph (112km/h).

The engineering of the "Big Boys" was massive but wholly conventional. Such up-to-date features as cast-steel locomotive beds and roller bearings were adopted as a matter of course. All were coal burners except No.4005 which for a time burned oil. They are recorded as developing 6,290 horsepower (4,692kW) in the cylinders, consuming some 100,000lb of water and 44,000lb of coal per hour whilst doing it. As the years went by experience gained allowed loads to be increased. Towards the end of their lives, with the aid of the new line which reduced the grade to 0.82 per cent (1-in-122), the "4000s" were taking 6,000-ton trains up Sherman Hill. It says enough that a "Big Boy" had the unique distinction for a steam locomotive of appearing on the cover of *Time* magazine! Six are preserved at widely spread locations from California to New Hampshire, but none is operable.

Below: UP "Big Boy" 4-8-8-4 at the head of freight extra X4019 conveying Pacific Fruit Express refrigerator cars through Echo Canyon, Utah. In accordance with UP practice, the train number of the extra is also that of the locomotive.

Above: A preserved "Big Boy", six out of 25 of which have been saved for posterity. They are deserving, since they were among the greatest steam locomotives ever built in terms of weight and power, as well as performance.

"Electroliner":
Four-car trainset

Origin: United States, Chicago, North Shore & Milwaukee Railroad (North Shore), 1941. **Type:** High-speed articulated electric interurban train. **Gauge:** 4ft 8½in (1,435mm). **Propulsion:** Direct current at 550V (600/650V post World War II) fed via trolley wire and poles (or 600V on third rail on the Loop) to eight 125hp (200kW) Westinghouse nose-suspended traction motors geared to the driving axles of all except the third of the five Commonwealth cast steel bogies. **Weight:** 171,030lb (77.6t) adhesive, 210,500lb (95t) total. **Max. axleload:** 21,380lb (9.7t). **Overall length:** 155ft 4in (47,345mm). **Max. speed:** 85mph (136km/h) (after World War II.)

At a time when high-speed electric multiple-unit trains seem set to provide the inter-city transport of the future, it is worth considering that the United States has already developed and discarded a huge network, 18,000 miles (29,000km) in extent, of fast interurban electric trains. Some were faster than others but virtually all have now vanished. Some of the longest lasting as well as the fastest and best, ran on the Chicago, North Shore & Milwaukee Railroad. On this line, travellers started their journeys at selected stops on the famous central loop of Chicago's elevated railway – which meant that trains had to be flexible enough to turn street corners on 90ft (27.5m) radius curves. This was achieved by making the cars articulated as well as rather short.

Only a few minutes later they would have to be rolling along at 85mph (135km/h) on the North Shore's excellent main line tracks. In Milwaukee, the trains made their final approach to the city centre terminal on street-car tracks, with all that that involves in control at crawling speeds. It was a superb feat of design to build rolling stock that was able to suit both such a high-speed as well as such a low-speed environment.

The famous trains that did all this so spectacularly had some unusual features, not least the fact that the line's employees had agreed to finance improvements to the line, including the "Electroliners", by taking a wage cut! This was because the trains were a last-ditch attempt to hold off abandonment.

St Louis Car built the trains, using electrical equipment from Westinghouse. They seated 146 and boasted a tavern-lounge car. The two "Electroliner" trainsets were scheduled to make the 88-mile (141km) journey from Chicago to Milwaukee and return five times daily from February 9, 1941 until the flexibility of the motor car finally won out. The last full day on which the North Shore line operated was January 20, 1963.

Above: White flags indicate an "extra" worked by one of the North Shore's "Electroliners".

The "Electroliners" were sold to the Red Arrow lines of the Southeastern Pennsylvania Transportation Authority in Philadelphia. In 1964 they went into service as "Liberty Liners" *Valley Forge* and *Independence Hall*, complete with a vivid maroon, white and grey colour scheme.

Below: The legendary Chicago, North Shore & Milwaukee Railroad "Electroliner" trains consisted of five articulated cars of which the outer two pairs are depicted here. They were financed by employees' pay cuts, staving off closure until 1963.

H-8 Allegheny 2-6-6-6

Origin: United States: Chesapeake & Ohio Railway (Chessie), 1941. **Gauge:** 4ft 8^1/2in (1,435mm). **Tractive effort:** 110,200lb (50,000kg). **Axleload:** 86,350lb (39.2t). **Cylinders:** (4) 22^1/2 x 33in (571 x 838mm). **Driving wheels:** 67in (1,701mm). **Heating surface:** 7,240sq ft (673m²). **Superheater:** 3,186sq ft (296m²). **Steam pressure:** 260psi (18.3kg/cm²). **Grate area:** 135sq ft (12.5m²). **Fuel:** 50,000lb (22.7t). **Water:** 25,000 US gall (94.6m³). **Adhesive weight:** 471,000lb (213.7t). **Total weight:** 1,076,000lb (488.2t). **Length overall:** 130ft 1in (39,653mm).

The most powerful locomotives ever built! And for once this barely needs qualifying in any way, except to say that only prime-movers are included. Several times in this narrative we have discussed the search for ever more economic means of bringing coal across the Allegheny Mountains. This was spurred on by the fight between competing roads, upon which cheap energy and therefore United States' industrial might depended. Just as the USA entered World War II in December 1941, the Lima Locomotive Works delivered to the Chesapeake & Ohio – "George Washington's railroad" – the first of the most super of all their celebrated "super-power" designs. The design involved a unique 2-6-6-6 wheel arrangement and was totally modern and totally successful.

During the traumatic years which followed, 59 more were built, the last batch as late as 1948. The class was designated "H-8" and carried road numbers 1600 to 1659. A further eight were built for the nearby Virginian Railroad.

Power output from a steam locomotive depends on the size of the fire and so the most important feature of the "H-8" was the huge deep firebox made possible by having that six-wheeled rear truck. The area of the grate was 11 per cent less than that of a Union Pacific "Big Boy", but the "H-8" firebox, not being situated above the rear driving wheels, was much deeper. Moreover, West Virginian coal was of better quality than that used on UP. Hence the "H-8"s could steam at higher rates, corresponding to a record drawbar-horsepower just short of 7,500 (10,000kW). However, high horsepower involves high speed as well as a heavy pull, but it was some time before these vast machines – which took their name from the mountains they first conquered – had arrived in sufficient numbers to be used elsewhere and so prove their speed capabilities. About a third of the "Alleghenies" were fitted with steam connections for use on passenger work, on which their ability to reach 60mph (100km/h) was useful.

On the climb from Hinton, West Virginia, eastward up to the 2,072ft (631m) summit at Allegheny tunnel, inclined at 0.57 per cent (1-in-175) two "H8"s, one at each end, could manage an immense train of 140 cars weighing 11,500 US tons. An important feature in this remarkable capability was the high adhesive weight upon which all hauling ability depends. A total

Above: Lifeblood of steam! A Chesapeake & Ohio "H-8" 2-6-6-6 articulated locomotive has its 25,000 gallon tank filled from convenient water crane alongside the tracks.

of 254 tons was carried on the six driving axles, corresponding to an unprecedented axleload of well over 40 tons, a 37 per cent increase over that of their predecessors, the "H-7a" 2-8-8-2s.

This was a world record for any major common-carrier railroad and only made possible because of Chessie's superb well-maintained heavy-duty permanent way. Even so, a great deal of track strengthening and tunnel enlargement had to be undertaken before the weight and bulk of the "H-8"s could be accommodated. The comparatively large driving wheels also helped in preventing rail-head failures – too small wheels carrying too

Below: Equally at home with fast passenger or heavy freight trains, the "H-8"s were the final flowering of steam traction on Chessie.

large loads are liable (in lay terms) to "sink in" and cause shelling-off of the running surfaces.

Every possible well-tried modern feature was applied to the "Alleghenies" in order to improve their efficiency and availability. Cast-steel locomotive beds with integral cylinders, roller bearings on all main axles, Worthington feed-water heaters, Baker valve gear and very sophisticated counter-balancing of the reciprocating parts all contributed. More ancient devices, such as a totally adequate sand supply from four great sandboxes situated each side of the top of the boiler, were not forgotten. Sand could be put just ahead or just behind each driving wheel; there were also steam jets to wash it off, so keeping the train wheels rolling with minimum friction on clean smooth rails.

Also notable was the C&O trademark, known as the "flying pumps", whereby both brake pumps were mounted on the smokebox front. In typical

Below: No diesel fumes in the air yet as Allegheny No. 1648 takes water at Russell, Kentucky, May 1949.

Mallet fashion, the headlight was fixed to the leading articulated engine in order that its beam should follow the line of rails more closely. Unusually the tender had a six-wheel leading truck plus an eight-wheel trailing one; the engine and tender just squeezed on to existing 115ft (35m) turntables.

It is sad but almost incredible to relate that, with the newest "H-8"s a bare four years old, in 1952 the C&O had begun to replace them by diesels. Four years later all 60 has been laid aside. Only two survive. No. 1601 is preserved well outside their territory at the Henry Ford Museum, Dearborn, Michigan, while No. 1604 is in the Transportation Museum at Roanoke, Virginia.

Almost half a century later, with the relative cost of coal and oil changed so considerably, it is scant comfort that a new and much enlarged Chessie, along with other coal-hauling railroads, is reconsidering ordering steam locomotives, as will be related.

Challenger Class 4-6-6-4

Origin: United States: Union Pacific Railroad (UP), 1942. **Gauge:** 4ft 8½in (1,435mm). **Tractive effort:** 97,400lb (44,100kg). **Axle load:** 68,000lb (31t). **Cylinders:** (4) 21 x 32in (533 x 813mm). **Driving wheels:** 69in (1,753mm). **Heating surface:** 4,642sq ft (431m²). **Superheater:** 1,741sq ft (162m²). **Steam pressure:** 280psi (19.7kg/cm²). **Grate area:** 132sq ft (12.3m²). **Fuel:** 56,000lb (25.4t). **Adhesive weight:** 406,000lb (184.3t). **Total weight:** 1,071,000lb (486t). **Length overall:** 121ft 11in (37,160mm).

On virtually all counts this locomotive was the largest, heaviest, strongest and most powerful one which ever regularly handled express passenger trains. Its existence was only possible because it was an articulated locomotive, that is, there was a hinge in the middle.

Articulated locomotives were introduced early in locomotive history, but it was not until the full flowering of the narrow-gauge railway late in the 19th century that they were built in quantity. Many designs were tried, but the most popular was that of Anatole Mallet, a French consulting engineer, Mallet was an early advocate of compounding, and from 1876 a number of two-cylinder compound locomotives were built to his designs. In 1884, to cater for larger locomotives, he proposed an articulated design in which the rear set of driving wheels were mounted in the main frame, which supported the firebox and the rear part of the boiler. The front set of driving wheels were in a separate frame, the rear end of which was hinged to the front of the main frame. The front of the boiler rested on the hinged frame, and as the boiler swung across this frame on curves, a sliding support was needed. The high-pressure cylinders drove the rear set of wheels and the low-pressure cylinders the leading set. High-pressure steam was thus entirely on the rigid part of the locomotive, and hinged steam pipes were needed only for the steam to and from the low-pressure cylinders.

The European engines built to this design were mostly for narrow-gauge railways. However, in 1903 the first American Mallet was built. Here the aim was to get the maximum adhesion, and as there were difficulties in designing a locomotive with six driving axles in a rigid frame, articulation was an attractive proposition at this stage. The American engine was an 0-6-6-0 built for the Baltimore and Ohio Railroad. It was the largest locomotive in the world and thereafter that distinction was always held by an American member of the Mallet family.

More American Mallets followed, at first mainly for banking duties, but then for road work. However, with their huge low-pressure cylinders and the tortuous steam pipes between the cylinders, these engines were unsuitable for speeds above 30-40mph (50-65km/h). Above these speeds oscillations of the front frame developed leading to heavy wear on locomotive and track.

In 1924 the Chesapeake and Ohio Railroad ordered twenty 2-8-8-2 locomotives with four simple expansion cylinders. Although the main reason for this was that the loading gauge of C&O could not accommodate the large low-pressure cylinders of a compound, the change brought the further

Above: "Challenger" class 4-6-6-4 No. 3985 at Cheyenne awaiting restoration to working order in 1981.

benefit that more adequate steam pipes could be provided, and the engines were capable of higher speeds. Some intensive work was needed to develop flexible joints suitable for carrying high-pressure steam to the leading cylinders.

From this time onwards American interest centred on the four-cylinder simple Mallet and successive improvements were made which upgraded the type from banking duties to main line freight work and, eventually, on a few roads, to express passenger work. Amongst changes introduced were longer travel valves and more complete balancing of the moving parts, but most important were the changes made to the connection between the

Below: Union Pacific Railroad "Challenger" 4-6-6-4 depicted in the two-tone grey passenger livery used in the late 1940s.

leading frame and the main frame, and to lateral control of the leading wheels. It was these latter alterations which eliminated the violent oscillations which had limited the speed of earlier Mallets.

The Union Pacific acquired 70 compound 2-8-8-0s with 59in (1,500mm) driving wheels between 1918 and 1924. These were essentially hard-slogging, modest speed engines and in 1926, for faster freight trains, the railroad introduced a class which was remarkable in several respects. It was a three-cylinder 4-12-2 with 67in (1,702mm) driving wheels, and was the first class with this wheel arrangement. It was also one of the few American three cylinder engines and the only one to be built in quantity, a total of 88 being built. They were highly successful, but with their long rigid wheelbase and heavy motion they were limited to 45mph (72km/h), and with growing road competition a twelve-coupled engine was needed capable of higher speeds than the 4-12-2.

Experience with the compound Mallets had led to the decision to convert them to simple expansion and the way was then set for the railroad to make another important step forward in 1936 by ordering 40 simple-expansion 4-6-6-4s with 69in (1,753mm) driving wheels. They were numbered from 3900 to 3939 and designated "Challenger". The leading bogie gave much better side control than a pony truck and the truck under the firebox assisted the fitting of a very large grate. The engines were distributed widely over the UP system and were used mainly on fast freight trains, but the last six of the engines were ordered specifically for passenger work. The most obvious difference between these earlier "Challenger" locomotives and those depicted in the art-work on the previous pages was the provision of much smaller 12-wheel tenders. Much of the coal which the UP used came from mines which the railroad owned.

In 1942 pressure of wartime traffic brought the need for more large engines and the construction of Challengers was resumed, a total of 65 more being built up to 1944. A number of changes were made, notably an enlargement of the grate from 108sq ft (10.0m²) to 132sq ft (12.3m²), cast steel frames in place of built-up frames, and an increase in the boiler pressure to 255psi (17.9kg/cm²) accompanied by a reduction in cylinder size of one inch, which left the tractive effort unchanged.

A less obvious but more fundamental change from the earlier engines was in the pivot between the leading unit and the main frame. In the earlier

engines there were both vertical and horizontal hinges, but in the new engines, following the practice adopted in the "Big Boy" 4-8-8-4s, there was no horizontal hinge. The vertical hinge was now arranged to transmit a load of several tons from the rear unit to the front one, thus evening out the distribution of weight between the two sets of driving wheels, and thereby reducing the tendency of the front drivers to slip, which had been a problem with the earlier engines. With no horizontal hinge, humps and hollows in the track were now looked after by the springs of each individual axle, as in a normal rigid locomotive.

All the engines were built as coal-burners, but in 1945 five of them were converted to oil-burning for use on passenger trains on the Oregon and Washington lines. Trouble was experienced with smoke obstructing the driver's view so these five engines were fitted with long smoke deflectors, and they were also painted in the two-tone grey livery which was used for passenger engines for a number of years, as depicted below.

A favourite racing ground for these monsters was the main line, mostly across the desert, between Salt Lake City, Las Vegas and Los Angeles, where they regularly ran at up to 70mph (112km/h) on passenger trains.

In 1952 coal supplies were interrupted by a strike and a crash programme for further conversions to oil-burning was put in hand, but the strike ended after eight engines had been converted. Rather perversely, in 1950 ten of the original series had been converted back to coal-firing, but in less than a year had been changed yet again to oil. Dieselisation gradually narrowed the field of operation of the "Challengers", but they continued to take a major share of steam working up to 1958 when the delivery of a large batch of diesels rendered them redundant.

The numbering of the Challengers was extremely complicated due to the practice of renumbering engines when they were converted from coal-burning to oil-burning or vice versa. Thus the original engines were renumbered from 3900-39 to 3800-39 and the three batches of the second series were numbered successively 3950-69, 3975-99 and 3930-49, so that 3930-9 were used twice but 3970-4 not at all. Furthermore, eighteen of the second series which were converted to oil-burning were renumbered from 3700-17.

Several other roads bought engines of the 4-6-6-4 wheel arrangement, generally similar to the "Challenger" and they also were used on some passenger work, but it was on the UP that the articulated locomotive had its most important application to passenger work, and a "Challenger" hauling 20 or more coaches was a regular sight. Fortunately one of the engines, No.3985 was preserved as a static exhibit, but in 1981 it was restored to working order, making it by far the largest working steam engine in the world.

Left: Now unchallenged as the biggest working steam locomotive in the world, Union Pacific "Challenger" class 4-6-6-4 No.3985 at the head of a train of steam enthusiasts.

2900 Class 4-8-4

Origin: United States: Atchison, Topeka & Santa Fe Railway (AT&SF), 1944.
Tractive effort: 79,960lb (36,270kg). **Axle load:** 74,000lb (33.5t). **Cylinders**
(2) 28 x 32in (711 x 813mm). **Driving wheels:** 80in (2,032mm). **Heating**
surface: 5,313sq ft (494m²). **Superheater:** 2,366sq ft (220m²). **Steam**
pressure: 300psi (21kg/cm²). **Grate area:** 108sq ft (10m²). **Fuel (oil)**
5,830gall (7,000 US) (26.5m³). **Water:** 20,400gall (24,500 US) (93m³).
Adhesive weight: 294,000lb (133t). **Total weight:** 961,000lb (436t).
Length overall: 120ft 10in (36,830mm).

The Atchison, Topeka & Santa Fe Railway (Santa Fe for short) was remarkable
in that it was the *only* railroad company which connected Chicago with
California. Odder still perhaps that it was named after three small places in the
southern Mid-West, while so many railroads with Pacific in their titles never
got there. Even now it remains as it was in the great days of steam – solvent,
forward-looking and with its physical plant in first-class condition. With a main
line stretching for 2,224 miles (3,580km) across America (or 2,547 miles –
4,100km – if you let the Santa Fe take you as far as San Francisco Bay)
together, once upon a time, with some of the world's finest and most
prestigious passenger services, you might think that the company's steam
power must have been remarkable and you would not be wrong.

Nearly all Santa Fe's steam locomotives came from Baldwin of
Philadelphia. At one time it included briefly such exotic items as 2-4-6-2 and
2-6-6-2 superheated express Mallet locomotives with 73 and 69in (1,854
and 1,753mm) diameter driving wheels respectively. Six of the class of 4·
of the 2-6-6-2s even had *boilers* with a hinge in the middle! Experience with
these and a few other wild ideas brought about a firm resolve to stick to the
Stephenson path in the future and almost without exception all subsequent
steam locomotives built for Santa Fe were "straight" (ie non-articulated)
"simple" (ie non-compound) and with two cylinders only. The results of the
slow-and-steady policy were magnificent.

The Santa Fe main line crossed the famous Raton Pass in New Mexico
with its 1 in 28¹/₂ (3¹/₂ per cent) gradient, as well as the less impossible but
still severe Cajon Pass in eastern California. East of Kansas City across the
level prairies 4-6-2s and 4-6-4s sufficed until the diesels came, but for the
heavily graded western lines Santa Fe in 1927 took delivery of its first
4-8-4s. It was only by a small margin that the Northern Pacific Railroad could
claim the first of the type as its own. These early 4-8-4s (Nos. 3751 to 3764)
were remarkable for having 30in (762mm) diameter cylinders, the largest
both in bore or volume in any passenger locomotive, apart from compounds

This first batch burnt coal, subsequent 4-8-4s being all oil-burners. More
4-8-4s (Nos.3765 to 3775) came in 1938 and a further batch was built in 1941.
The final group (Nos.2900 to 2929) on which the particulars given in this
description are based, were constructed in wartime. Quite fortuitously, they
also became the heaviest straight passenger locomotives ever built, because
high-tensile steel alloys were in short supply and certain parts – in particular
the main coupling and connecting rods – had to be much more massive when

Above: Santa Fe "2900" class 4-8-4. Note the chimney extension in the raised position, the handsome tapered connecting rods and the enormous tender with two eight-wheel bogies. Eight of these magnificent engines survive, but none is now steamable.

designed to be made from more ordinary metal. They managed this feat by a very small margin, but when those immense 16-wheel tenders were included and loaded there were no close rivals to this title. The big tenders were fitted to the last two batches; and as well as being the heaviest

Below: Atchison, Topeka & Santa Fe Railway class "3700" 4-8-4 No.3769 climbing the Cajon Pass, California, with the first part of the "Grand Canyon Limited", in June 1946. Note that the chimney extension is in the fully raised position.

passenger locomotives ever built, they were also the longest.

It must be said that Santa Fe would have preferred diesels to the superb last batch of 4-8-4s, but wartime restrictions prevented this. The company had been early into the diesel game with the now legendary streamlined light-weight de luxe "Super Chief" train, introduced in 1937, as well as the equally celebrated coach-class streamliner "EL Capitan". But forty years ago there were still trains such as the "California Limited", "The Scout" and the "Grand Canyon Limited" and, of course, the original "Chief", still formed of standard equipment. They were often then run in two or more sections each and all needed steam power at the head end.

Apart from the early diesel incursions, these 4-8-4s that totalled 65 ruled the Chicago-Los Angeles main line from Kansas City westwards. It was normal practice to roster them to go the whole distance (1,790 miles – 2,880km – via Amarillo or 1,760 miles – 2,830km – via the Raton Pass); in respect of steam traction these were by far the longest distances ever to be scheduled to run without change of locomotive. Speeds up in the 90-100 mph (140-160km/h) range were both permitted and achieved.

This journey was not made without changing crews. In this respect feather-bedding union rules based on the capacity of the "American" 4-4-0s of fifty years earlier applied and crews were changed 12 times during the 34 hour run. Water was taken at 16 places and fuel nearly as often, in spite of the enormous tenders.

These magnificent examples of the locomotive builder's art were conventional in all main respects. One unusual feature was the "hot hat" smoke-stack extension shown on the picture on the previous page; absence of overbridges and tunnels over many miles of the Santa Fe route meant that this could be raised for long periods with beneficial effect of keeping smoke and steam clear of the cab. Another detail concerned a modification to the Walschaert's valve gear on some of the 4-8-4s. To reduce the amount of swing – and consequent inertia forces – needed on the curved links, an intermediate lever was introduced into the valve rod. This was so arranged as to increase the amount of valve travel for a given amount of link swing.

Santa Fe was generous in handing out superannuated 4-8-4s as not

always properly appreciated gifts to various online communities. These included Modesto and San Bernadino, California, Pueblo, Colorado; Fort Madison, Iowa; Kingsman, Arizona; Alburquerque, New Mexico; and Wichita, Kansas. No. 2903 is displayed in the Chicago Museum of Science and Industry, while No.2925 is still in the roundhouse at Belen, New Mexico. There was a rumour some time ago that Santa Fe might have intentions of entering the steam-for-pleasure business with this locomotive, like neighbour Union Pacific, but nothing appears to have come of the proposal.

Right: The impressive front end of a Santa Fe "2900" class 4-8-4.

Left: Atchison Topeka & Santa Fe Railway class "3700" 4-8-4 No.3787 hauling the streamline cars of the legendary "Chief" express amongst the mountains of the Cajon Pass in California. This train ran daily over the 2,225 miles (3,580km) of Santa Fe metals between Chicago and Los Angeles.

Class U1-f 4-8-2

Origin: Canada: Canadian National Railways (CN), 1944. **Gauge:** 4ft 8¹/₂in (1,435mm). **Tractive effort:** 52,500lb (23,814kg). **Axle load:** 59,500lb (27t). **Cylinders:** (2) 24 x 30in (610 x 762mm). **Driving wheels:** 73in (1,854mm). **Heating surface:** 3,584sq ft (333m²). **Superheater:** 1,570sq ft (146m²). **Steam pressure:** 260psi (18.3kg/cm²). **Grate area:** 70.2sq ft (6.6m²). **Fuel:** 40,000lb (18t). **Water:** 11,500gall (9,740 US) (53m³). **Adhesive weight:** 237,000lb (107.5t). **Total weight:** 638,000lb (290t). **Length overall:** 93ft 3in (28,426mm).

It was in 1923, very soon after the formation of Canadian National Railways, that eight-coupled locomotives were first introduced into passenger service there. This was the original "U1-a" a batch consisting of 16 locos, built by the Canadian Locomotive Company. Then 1924 and 1925 brought the "U1-b" and "U1-c" batches of 21 and five from Canadian and from Baldwin respectively. The latter were for CN's Grand Trunk Western subsidiary in the USA. In 1929 and 1930 there followed five "U1-d" and 12 "U1-e" from Canadian and from the Montreal locomotive works.

Thus in seven years, fifty-nine 4-8-2s, numbered from 6000 to 6058, became available, although by now the class had become overshadowed by the 4-8-4s introduced in 1927, described here. There were also four 4-8-2s acquired by the Central Vermont Railway, another CN subsidiary but one which did not then number or classify its locos as part of the main CN fleet. It did use the CN method of classification, though, so these 4-8-2s were also Class "U1-a". In fact they were rather different in design, having been acquired from amongst a flood of 4-8-2s which the Florida East Coast Railroad had ordered but found itself unable to pay for.

The 6000s performed with *élan* on the then highly competitive express trains between Montreal and Toronto; speeds up to 82mph (131km/h) have been noted with 700 tons or so. Later, the same engines operated well in pool service in conjunction with Canadian Pacific.

In 1944, a further twenty 4-8-2s were delivered from Montreal, of the "U1-f" batch illustrated here. They were brought up-to-date by having cast-steel locomotive frames, disc wheels and other improvements. Some were oil-burners and all had Vanderbilt cylindrical tenders and outside bearings on the leading bogies. Most significant was a major simplification consisting of the replacement of the boiler feed pump and feed-water heater, by a device called an exhaust steam injector. Injectors are usually tucked away tidily under the side of the cab but in this case the device was hung outside the driving wheels, the large pipe which supplied the exhaust steam adding to its conspicuousness.

Like other injectors but more so, exhaust steam injectors are remarkable conjuring tricks in the application of natural laws. It is difficult to believe that exhaust steam at, say 10psi (0.7kg/cm²) could force water into a boiler containing steam and water almost 30 times that pressure. However, an

Left: Canadian National Railways Class "U1-f" 4-8-2 No.6071 depicted at Toronto in April 1952.

arrangement of cones turns a high velocity jet of low pressure steam into a low velocity high-pressure flow of water, which has no difficulty in forcing its way past the non-return clack valves into the boiler.

With just a few exceptions, CN steam locomotives were totally utilitarian, but with these excellent engines, efforts were made to make them good looking too. Side valences, a flanged British-style smokestack, green and black livery, brass numbers and placing the dome and sand container in the same box all contributed to the clean lines. The result is so good that one can almost forgive the designers that bullet nose to the smokebox!

Canadian National is amongst that superior class of railway administrations who offer steam for pleasure, as exampled by the fact that a total of six of these locomotives are preserved. No. 6060 of class "U1-f" does the honours and in addition No.6069 is displayed at Bayview Park, Sarnia, and No.6077 at Capreol, Ontario. Of the elder CN Mountains, No.6015 is at the Museum at Delson, Quebec, No.6039 (Grand Trunk Western) was at Steamtown, Bellows Falls, Vermont, and No.6043 at

Below: Artist's impression of Canadian National Railways class "U1-f" 4-8-2 as built.

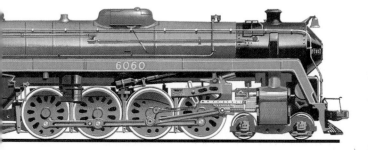

F3 Model B₀-B₀

Origin: United States: Electro-Motive Division, General Motors Corporation (EMD), 1945. **Type:** All-purpose diesel-electric locomotive, "A" units with cab, "B" units without. **Gauge:** 4ft 8½in (1,435mm). **Propulsion:** One EMD 567B 1,500hp (1,120kW) 16-cylinder pressure-charged two-stroke Vee engine and generator supplying current to four nose-suspended traction motors geared to the axles. **Weight:** 230,000lb (104.4t) (minimum without train heating steam generator). **Axleload:** 57,500lb (26.1t). **Overall length:** "A" unit 50ft 8in (15,443mm), "B" unit 50ft 0in (15,240mm). **Tractive effort:** 57,500lb (256kN). **Max speed:** Between 50mph (80km/h) and 120mph (192km/h) according to which of eight possible gear ratios fitted.

The railway locomotive leads a rugged existence, and only the fittest survive. Evolution has thus tended to move in moderate steps, and few successful developments have been sufficiently dramatic to merit the term "revolutionary". One such step was the pioneer four-unit freight diesel, No 103, produced by the Electro-Motive Division of General Motors in 1939. When that unit embarked on a 83,764 mile (134,776km) demonstration tour of 20 major American railroads, few people, other than EMD's Chief Engineer Richard M. Dilworth, ever imagined that it would be possible for the country to be paying its last respects to steam only 20 years later.

Below: A pair of "F3" units as supplied to the Baltimore & Ohio Railroad. The left-hand one is a "cab" or "A" unit while the right-hand one with no driving cab is a "booster" or "B" unit.

BALTIMORE AND OHIO

Above: A short Gulf, Mobile & Ohio Railroad suburban train leaves Chicago behind a single "F"-series diesel-electric locomotive.

Left: "F"-series cab and booster units of the Canadian Pacific Railway on a passenger train at London, Ontario, in January 1983.

By 1939 EMD had some six years' experience of powering high-speed passenger trains by diesel locomotives tailored to suit the customer's requirements. Their ability to outrun the best steam locomotives had gained them acceptance in many parts of the USA, but this was a specialised activity, and even the most diesel-minded motive power officer did not regard the diesels as an alternative to the ten, twelve or sixteen coupled steam locomotive for the heavy grind of freight haulage.

Dilworth had faith in the diesel, and his company shared his faith to the tune of a four-unit demonstrator weighing 912,000lb (414t) and 193ft (58,830mm) in length. Most of the passenger diesels built so far incorporated the lightweight Winton 201 engine, which EMD had acquired, but in 1938 EMD produced its own 567 series of two-stroke Vee engines (numbered from the cubic capacity of the cylinder in cubic inches). The 16-cylinder version was rated at 1,350hp (1,010kW), and this fitted conveniently into a four-axle Bo-Bo layout, with the whole weight thus available for adhesion.

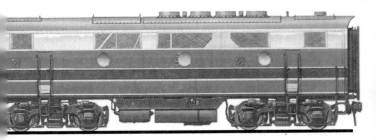

Two such units were permanently coupled, an "A" unit with cab and a "B" or booster unit without; two of these pairs were coupled back-to-back by normal couplings. Multiple-unit control enabled one driver to control all four units, but they could easily be separated into pairs, or, with a little more work, into 1 plus 3. Dilworth reckoned that a 2,700hp pair was the equal of a typical steam 2-8-2 or 2-10-2, and that the full 5,400hp (4,030kW) set could equal any of the largest articulated steam locomotives. As the combined starting tractive effort of his four units was almost double that of the largest steam engine, his claim had some substance. They were geared for a maximum speed of 75mph (120km/h) but could be re-geared for 102mph (164km/h), thereby producing a true mixed traffic locomotive.

The units were built on the "carbody" principle, that is, the bodyshell was stressed and formed part of the load-bearing structure of the locomotive. The smooth streamlined casing was in sharp contrast to the Christmas-tree appearance of most large American steam engines, festooned as they were with gadgets. But this was one of the revolutionary ideas demonstrated by No.103. Bright liveries on the passenger streamliners had attracted great publicity; now there was the possibility of giving the freight locomotive a similar image.

Despite the scepticism of steam locomotive engineers, 20 railroads spread over 35 states responded to EMD's invitation to give No. 103 a trial,

Above: A single "F" cab unit heads a short train on the Denver & Rio Grande Railroad's steeply graded Moffat Tunnel route.

and everywhere it went it improved on the best steam performance by a handsome margin. From sea level to 10,240ft (3,120m), from 40°F below zero (–40°C) to 115°F (46°C), the story was the same. Typical figures were an average speed of 26mph (42km/h) over 98 miles (158km) of l-in-250 grade with 5,400t, compared with 10mph (16km/h) by a modern 4-6-6-4, or an increase in load from 3,800t with a 2-8-4 to 5,100t. The booster units were equipped with steam generators for train heating, and this enabled No. 103 to show its paces on passenger trains. The impression it made on motive power men was profound.

Not least amongst the startling qualities of No. 103 was its reliability. Throughout the 11-month tour no failure occurred, and even when allowance is made for the close attention given by accompanying EMD staff, this was a remarkable achievement.

Production locomotives, designated "FT", followed closely on the heels of the demonstrator, and orders were soon received from all parts of the country. EMD's LaGrange Works was tooled-up for quantity production and over a period of six years 1,096 "FT" units were built, Santa Fe being the biggest customer with 320 units. The War Production Board was

sufficiently impressed by the contribution which these locomotives coul
make to the war effort to allow manufacture to continue with only a shor
break, despite the use of scarce alloys.

By the end of the war the freight diesel was fully accepted on man
railroads, and total dieselisation was already in the minds of some motiv
power chiefs. The first post-war development was production of the 567
engine rated at 1,500hp (1,120kW) to replace the 1,350hp 567A model. Afte
104 interim units designated "F2", there came a four-unit demonstrator c
the "F3" model, with a larger generator to suit the 1,500hp engine, and
number of other improvements based on six years' experience with th
"FTs". Amongst these were automatically-operated cooling fans; the fan
fitted to the "FTs" were mechanically-driven through clutches, and ha
manually-worked shutters. The fireman had a frantic rush to de-clutch th
fans and close the shutters when the engine was shut down, particularly i
severe cold when the radiators would freeze very quickly.

EMD proclaimed the "F3" as "the widest range locomotive in history"
and the railroads seemed to agree, for new sales records were set with
total of 1,807 units sold in little more than two years up to 1949. Railroad
took advantage of the scope which the smooth curved shape offered fo
imaginative colour schemes, and an EMD pamphlet showed 40 differen
liveries in which these locomotives had been supplied.

Simplicity of maintenance, and improvements in the engine to reduce fue
consumption, were two of EMD's claims for the "F3", and these sam
claims were repeated for the next model, the "F7", launched in 1949. Th
main change from the "F3" was in the traction motors and other electrica
equipment. With the same engine power, the new motors enabled 25 pe

ent more load to be hauled up heavy grades. The model was offered with the usual options, including eight gear ratios.

The "F7" proved to be a bestseller too; 49 US roads bought 3,681 "F7s" and 301 "FP7s", the version with train-heating boiler, whilst Canada and Mexico took 238 and 84 respectively. They handled every type of traffic from the fastest passenger trains to the heaviest freight. Measured by sales, the "F7" was the most successful carbody diesel ever. "F7" production ended in 1953, to be replaced by the "F9". The main change was the 567C engine of 1,750hp (1,305kW). By time the US market for carbody diesels was drying up, as "hood" units gained popularity, and only 75 "F9s" were built over a period of three years.

By the 1960s steam had been replaced totally, and manufacturers were now selling diesels to replace diesels. Trading-in old models became popular, and bogies in particular could be re-used. Many "Fs" were replaced in this way as the more powerful hood units became increasingly popular, and the decline of passenger traffic helped the process. Nevertheless some units of the "F" series were still to be found at work in 1999 on short lines and tourist railways, and preserved in museums. Even the Class I railroads maintain a few for powering special trains - BNSF and UP amongst them.

The "F" series, more than any other model, showed that improvements in performance and economies in operation could be achieved in all types of traffic by dieselisation, despite uncertainties about the life which could be expected from a diesel locomotive.

Below: Four General Motors' "F" series units of the Denver & Rio Grande Western RR head the westbound "Western Zephyr".

Niagara Class 4-8-4

Origin: United States: New York Central Railroad (NYC), 1945. **Type:** Express passenger steam locomotive. **Gauge:** 4ft 8½in (1,435mm). **Propulsion:** Coal fire with a grate area of 10sq ft (9.3m²) generating steam at 272psi (19.3kg/m²) in a fire-tube boiler, and supplying it via a superheater to two 25½ x 32in (648 x 813mm) cylinders, driving the main wheels direct by means of connecting and coupling rods. **Weight:** 274,000lb (124t) adhesive, 891,000lb (405t) total. **Axleload:** 70,000lb (32t). **Overall length:** 115ft 5½in (35,192mm). **Tractive effort:** 61,570lb (27,936kg). **Max speed:** 80mph (128km/h).

The New York Central Railroad's speedway from New York to Chicago, was in steam days arguably the greatest passenger railway in the world, in terms of speeds run and tonnage moved. By the 1940s these speeds and loads were beginning to be as much as the famous Hudsons could cope with and the Central's chief of motive power, Paul Kiefer, decided to move on a step. He proposed a 4-8-4 with more than 30 per cent greater adhesive weight and tractive effort than the 4-6-4, together with a fire grate 25 per cent bigger. His aim was a locomotive which could develop 6,000hp in the cylinder for hour after hour and could do the New York-Chicago run day after day without respite.

The American Locomotive Company at Schenectady proposed what was to be the last really new design of passenger locomotive to be produced in the USA. It owed something to the Union Pacific's "800" class; dimensionally, the two designs were very close and, in addition, the design of the 14-wheel Centipede or 4-10-0 tender was certainly based on UP's. The NYC engines had something else unusual for North America, in common with the "800s" - a smooth and uncluttered appearance but with no false streamlining or air-smoothing.

Because the NYC structure gauge only allowed rolling stock to be 15ft 2in (4,623mm) high instead of 16ft 2in (4,928mm) as on the UP, the chimney had to be vestigial and the dome little but a manhole cover. There were other differences, such as Baker's valve gear instead of Walschaert's, but in general the adoption of standard American practice led to similarities.

The foundation of the design was a cast steel integral locomotive frame – nothing else could have stood up to the punishment intended for these engines. Also, as one might expect, all axles, coupling rods and connecting rods had roller bearings. Baker's valve gear has the advantage that it has no slides, so all its moving parts could, as in this case, be fitted with needle bearings. While speaking of the valves, an interesting detail was that the edges of the valve-ports were sharp on the steam side, but slightly rounded on the exhaust side. This eased the sharpness of the blast beats, thereby evening out the draught on the fire.

Although fundamentally of the same design as that fitted to the UP locos, the tender had some interesting differences. The fact that the NYC was one of the very few American railroads equipped with water troughs meant that less water could be carried, leaving more capacity for coal. This enabled the

Above: Heading "The Missourian" from St Louis to New York, "Niagara" No.6018 leans to the curve at Peekskill, New York State.

New York-Chicago run to be done with just one intermediate coaling, while an improved design of power-operated pick-up scoop reduced delays by allowing water to be taken at 80mph (128km/h). Special extra venting avoided bursting the tenders (there had been cases!) when some 1,600cu ft (45m³) of incompressible fluid entered the tank all in a few seconds. Incidentally, the overhang of the tank at the rear was to allow the engines to be turned on 100ft turntables by reducing the wheelbase.

Allocating the number 6000 to a locomotive whose target was that amount of horsepower as well as that number of miles run per week might seem to be tempting providence, but all was well. The prototype had the sub-class designation "Sla", while the 25 production models (Nos. 6001-6025) were known as "Slb", and there was also a single poppet-valve version known as "Slc" (No. 5500). This greatest of steam locomotives got the class-name "Niagara" and when the word is uttered, no steam man worthy of the name ever thinks of a waterfall!. Both targets were achieved

Below: Regarded by many as The Ultimate Steam Locomotive Of All Time - the vast "Niagara" 4-8-4 of the New York Central Railroad.

- 6,700hp on test and an average of 26,000 miles run monthly.

The original idea was that the prototype should be tested and then a production order confirmed, but before work had gone very far instructions were given for all 27 to be put in hand. This was reasonable because in fact the "Niagaras" were very much a standard, if slightly stretched, product of the industry, whereas what really needed attention was the ground organisation to enable the mileage target to be met. And this, of course, could not be tested until a fleet was available.

By an ordinance of the City of New York, steam locomotives were not allowed inside city limits. Trains therefore left Grand Central Station behind third-rail electric locos for Croton Harmon, 32 miles out in the suburbs. It was here, then, and at Chicago that the "Niagaras" were, in their great days, kept in first-class condition for what was without doubt one of the hardest services ever demanded of steam, or for that matter of any motive power.

World records are not achieved without extreme efforts, but excellent organisation allowed quick and thorough servicing. The power production part of the locomotives had to be just-so to give such a remarkable performance out on the road, and to achieve this the fire was first dropped with the engine in steam. Then a gang of "hot men" in asbestos suits entered the firebox – the size of a room – and cleared tubes and flues, and did repairs to the brick arch and grate. Good water treatment ensured that no scale built up in the heating surface, preventing the heat reaching the water inside the boiler. On many railways steam locomotives were allocated one "shed day" each week for these things to be done, but running the 928 miles (1,493km) from Croton Harmon to Chicago or vice versa each night, the "Niagaras" needed to do a week's work in one 24-hour period.

In those days there were 12 daily trains each way just between New York and Chicago - the "Chicagoan", the "Advance Commodore Vanderbilt", the "Commodore Vanderbilt", the "Advance Empire State Express", the "Empire State Express", the "Lake Shore Limited", the "Mohawk", the "North Shore Limited", the "Pacemaker", the "Water Level", the "Wolverine" and, the greatest of all, the 16 hour "Twentieth Century Limited".

Even the most fanatical steam enthusiast would admit that other factors have contributed, but nevertheless the Day of the "Niagaras" did mark a peak. In the late 1990s, the best time by diesel traction over a slightly longer

Above: Smoke and steam fill the air as a New York Central "Niagara" takes a westbound passenger train out of Dunkirk, NY.

variant of this route between New York and Chicago was 17hr 40min, and there was only one daily train.

The "Niagaras" also demonstrated once again that modern well maintained steam power could be more economical than diesel. Alas, in those days, coal supplies controlled by miners' leader John L. Lewis were less reliable than oil supplies; moreover, most of New York Central's steam power was neither modern nor well-maintained. So, having run more miles and hauled more tons in their short lives than most locomotives which run out their term to obsolescence, the "Niagaras" went to their long home. None has been preserved.

Below: Able to produce 6,000hp and run 26,000 miles per month, the superb "Niagara" 4-8-4s of the New York Central RR were regarded by many as the Ultimate Steam Locomotive.

E7 Series A1A-A1A

Origin: United States: Electro-Motive Division. General Motors Corporation (EMD), 1945. **Type:** Express passenger diesel-electric locomotive; "A" units with driving cab, "B" units without. **Gauge:** 4ft 8½in (1,435mm). **Propulsion:** Two EMD 567A 1,000hp (746kW) 12-cylinder pressure-charged two-stroke Vee engines and generators, each supplying current to two nose-suspended traction motors geared to the end axles of a bogie. **Weight:** "A" unit 212,310lb (96.3t) adhesive, 315,000lb (142.9t) total. "B" units 205,570lb (93.3t) adhesive, 305,000lb (138.4t) total. **Axleload:** "A" 53,080lb (24.1t), "B" 51,390lb (23.3t). **Overall length:** "A" 71ft 1¼in (21,670mm), "B" 70ft 0in (21,340mm). **Tractive effort:** 53,080lb (236kN). **Max speed:** 85mph (137km/h), 92mph (148km/h), 98mph (157km/h), or 117mph (188km/h) according to gear ratio fitted.

In 1930 the General Motors Corporation made two purchases which were to have dramatic effects on the American locomotive scene. The first was the Winton Engine Co, a builder specialising in lightweight diesel engines. The second was Winton's chief customer, the Electro Motive Corporation, established in 1922 to design and market petrol-electric railcars, which had sold some 500 units in 10 years. With the engine building facility and the expertise acquired in these purchases, GM's new Electro-Motive Division (EMD) was a major partner in the sensational pioneer streamlined trains introduced in 1934, and in the following year the firm produced its first locomotives. These were four Bo-Bo units with rectangular "boxcar" bodies, each powered by two 900hp (670kW) Winton 12-cylinder Vee engines. Pending completion of its own plant, EMD had to employ other builders to assemble them.

In 1936 EMD moved into its own purpose-built works at LaGrange, Illinois, and work commenced on the next locomotives. These were the first of the "E" series, known also as the "Streamline" series. Like the four earlier locomotives, they had two 900hp Winton engines, but the chassis and body were completely new. The body had its main load-bearing strength in two bridge-type girders which formed the sides. The bogies had three axles to give greater stability at high speeds, but as only four motors were needed, the centre axle of each bogie was an idler, giving the wheel arrangement A1A-A1A. The units were produced in two versions, "A" units with a driver's cab and "B" units without. The Baltimore & Ohio was the first purchaser, taking six of each type to use as 3,600hp (2,690kW) pairs. Santa Fe bought eight "As" and three "Bs", and the "City" streamliner roads bought two "A-B-B" sets for the "City of Los Angeles" and the "City of San Francisco". These latter at 5,400hp were the world's most powerful diesel locomotives when they appeared in 1937. The B&O units were classed "EA" and "EB", the Santa Fe's were "E1A" and "E1B", and the City units "E2A" and "E2B".

All these locomotives were an immediate success, not only by their

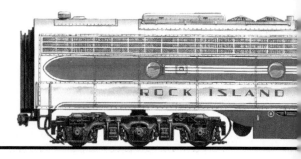

Above: A model "E7" diesel-electric locomotive built to head the streamliners, on a Chicago double-deck commuter train.

performance but also by their reliability. The reliability was a striking tribute to the quality of the design, for there had been no demonstrator subsequent to the "boxcar" Bo-Bos. In multiple-unit working it was possible for some maintenance to be done on the road on the easier stretches, on which one engine could be shut down. With servicing assisted in this way, remarkable feats of endurance could be achieved. One of the B&O "A-B" sets gained national publicity when it completed 365 continuous days of service between Washington and Chicago, covering 282,000 miles (454,000km) at an average scheduled speed of 56mph (90km/h).

Progress at LaGrange was rapid. At 900hp the Winton engine was reaching its limit, and an EMD engine was therefore developed. Designated 567 (the capacity of a cylinder in cubic inches), it was available in three sizes with 8, 12, and 16 cylinders, giving 600, 1,000 and 1,350hp (448, 746 and 1,007kW). Simultaneously La Grange began to manufacture its own generators, motors and other electrical equipment.

First all-EMD locomotives were an order from Seaboard Air Line for 14 "A" and five "B" units, which appeared from October 1938 onwards. They had two 1,000hp engines and were operated as 6,000hp three-unit "lash-ups" (in the US jargon). These were the "E4s". "E3" and "E5" followed,

Below: A 2.000hp E9 diesel-electric cab unit of the Chicago, Rock Island & Pacific RR, specially painted in the stunning livery of that line's prestigious "Rocket" express trains.

Above: An "E8A""cab" unit of the Burlington Northern RR heads a double-deck push-pull Chicago suburban train.

the former comprising 18 units for the Santa Fe and the latter 16 for the Burlington.

So far each railroad's order had incorporated some individual variations – hence the different designations – but EMD aimed to gain the maximum benefits from production-line assembly of locomotives, to which end individual variations were to be discouraged. The next series, the "E6" which appeared in the same month in 1939 as the first freight demonstrator (No. 103), was therefore a standard off-the-shelf unit, with the minimum of options. This was the start of real diesel mass production and 118 units had been built by the time the War Production Board terminated building of passenger locomotives in February 1942.

Construction of passenger locomotives was resumed in February 1945 with the first of the "E7" series. These locomotives benefited from the experience gained from both the "E" and the "F" series freight units. Improvements included a new and larger cooling system for the engine. Externally there was a noticeable difference in that the front of the body was sloped at 80° to the horizontal, as in the "F" series, instead of 70°, as in previous "E" series bodies. Apart from this change, there were few differences in external appearance throughout the range of "E" series, and most of them concerned windows and portholes.

With locomotive fleets rundown by wartime traffic, the railroads were even more eager to acquire passenger diesels, and EMD settled down to steady production of "E7s", averaging 1 per month for four years. During this time 428 "A" units and 82 "B" units were built, so that the "E7" out-numbered the passenger diesels of all other US makers put together. In general, "E7s" were bought by roads with fast passenger services on easy gradients; for mountain work the all-adhesion "F" series was favourite.

Amongst "E7" buyers were the Pennsylvania and the New York Central. With 60 and 50 units respectively they had the largest numbers of any owner. On the NYC the most thorough comparison ever made between steam and diesel was conducted during October 1946. Two twin "E7" locomotives were tested against six of the new "Niagara" 4-8-4 steam

292

engines working between Harmon, New York, and Chicago, 928 miles (1,493km). The "E7s" averaged 28,954 miles in the month and the 4-8-4s 27,221. Average operating costs per mile were $1.11 for the "E7" and $1.22 for the 4-8-4. However, a succession of coal strikes and then some trouble with the alloy steel boilers of the "Niagaras" insured that the NYC did not allow its lingering love of steam to interpret the results in favour of the 4-8-4s. But the tests were still encouraging to steam enthusiasts in showing how small was the improvement when the best of steam locomotives, intensively used and adequately serviced, were replaced by diesels. But on most roads the margin was much wider, and there was a saving from diesels quite sufficient to offset the greater capital cost.

In 1953 the 1,125hp (840kW) 567B engine was available, and this was incorporated in the next series, the "E8". By this time most of the principal passenger services were dieselised, so the impact of the "E8" was less spectacular than that of the "E7". By the time the final version appeared, the "E9" with 1,200hp (900kW) 567C engines, the need for passenger diesels had almost been met, and only 144 units were sold between 1954 and 1963, compared with 457 "E8s".

In the 1960s the American pasenger train declined rapidly in the face of air and coach competition, and many of the later "Es" had short lives, being traded in against the purchase of new general-purpose locomotives.

The "E" series instituted the general conversion of the American passenger train to diesel operation, and they eventually saw many of the most famous trains out. In their heyday the US had an undisputed world lead in passenger train speeds. Geared for up to 117mph (188km/h), although few roads operated them above 100mph (160km/h), the "Es" were the fastest diesel locomotives in the world, and yet their construction was rugged and straightforward. In particular they had nose-suspended traction motors, which the heavy North American rails with their close spaced sleepers seemed able to accept without distress.

In 1980 Amtrak operated the last run of "E" locomotives in multiple and the ranks were very thin by this time. Fortunately the body of the first B&O unit is preserved.

Below: An early "F"-series "A" or "cab" diesel-electric unit as supplied to the Atchison, Topeka & Santa Fe Railway in 1936.

Below: A Gulf, Mobile & Ohio passenger train headed by an unusual mixed diesel-electric locomotive set consisting of an "E" series "cab" unit and an "F" series "booster" unit.

141R Liberation 2-8-2

Origin: France: French National Railways (SNCF), 1945. **Type:** General-purpose main line steam locomotive. **Gauge:** 4ft 8$^{1}/_{2}$in (1,435mm). **Propulsion:** Coal fire with a grate area of 55.5sq ft (5.2m^2) generating steam at 200psi (14kg/cm^2) in a fire-tube boiler, and supplying it via a superheater to two 23$^{1}/_{2}$ x 28in (596 x 711 mm) cylinders, driving the main wheels by means of connecting and coupling rods. **Weight:** 176,400lb (80t) adhesive, 413,800lb (187.7t) total. **Axleload:** 48,510lb (22t). **Overall length:** 79ft 3$^{1}/_{4}$in (24,161mm). **Tractive effort:** 44,500lb (20,191kg). **Max speed:** 75mph (120km/h).

Of all the different schools of steam locomotive engineering in the world, no two were further apart than the American and the French. Most French main line locomotives were complex four-cylinder compounds of an arrangement developed by Alfred de Glehn (in spite of his name and his place of work, de Glehn was an Englishman) in the early-1900s. Between the wars, when there was no money for new construction, that genius amongst locomotive engineers, André Chapelon, had modernised many of the de Glehn compounds with startling effect, giving both a thermal efficiency and a power-to-ratio unmatched elsewhere at any time.

For such outstanding performance there was, however, a price to pay in high maintenance costs. Furthermore, the men who drove French locomotives were not promoted from firemen but instead had first to qualify as skilled mechanics; in short, French drivers had also to be engineers. Thus they had the understanding to enable them to run compound locomotives with complex controls – two reversers and two throttles, for example.

Towards the end of World War II, even before the Allies had landed in France, the French government took steps to solve the urgent problem of replacing the large number of locomotives destroyed, which would amount to 80 per cent of the fleet. Orders were placed in the USA and Canada for 1,340 2-8-2s based on (but slightly smaller than) the standard USRA light Mikado design.

For use in France the builders fitted buffers and screw couplings,

Top, right: No. 141R 1043, fitted for oil-firing, pilots a "141C" on a freight train at Angers on French National Railways in 1967.

Centre, right: Even as late in the steam age as 1968, coal-fired examples of the "141R" fleet were hard at work in north-east France. Here No. 141R641 rolls a freight train near Boulogne.

Below: Few concessions were made to French principles when the "141R" design was on the drawing board in the USA towards the end of the war. But it out-lasted the native product in the end.

squeaky high-pitched whistles, left-hand drive and oil lubrication instead of
grease. Lima supplied 280, Baldwin and Alco 460 each, Montreal Loco
Works l00 and Canadian Loco Co 40. The number series ran from 141R1 to
141R1340 and all were shipped between August 1945 and the end of 1947.
Seventeen went down with the vessel *Belpamela* which foundered in a mid-
Atlantic storm, but the others survived to do great things.

Later examples of the "141Rs" were more up-to-date than the first ones
to be delivered. Delta cast rear trucks replaced the built-up Cole pattern,
Boxpok wheels replaced spoked ones, cast locomotive beds replaced
separate frames and cylinders, and roller bearings were fitted. Many of the
later locomotives were delivered as oil burners and others were converted
to combat a severe shortage of coal which developed in France as
reconstruction progressed.

US principles of design were totally vindicated by the excellent
performance and overall economy of *les Americains* and it says enough that
the "141Rs" outlasted compound 4-6-2s and 2-8-2s and eventually became
the last main line steam locomotives in normal service on SNCF. Several
have been preserved.

**Right: Plenty of black smoke as an American-built "141R" 2-8-2 of
French National Railways heads a long freight train.**

242 A1 4-8-4

Origin: France: French National Railways (SNCF), 1946. **Type:** Express
passenger steam locomotive. **Gauge:** 4ft 8^{1}/2in (1,435mm). **Propulsion:**
Coal fire with a grate area of 54sq ft (5m^{2}) generating steam at 290psi
(20.4kg/cm^{2}) in a fire-tube boiler, and supplying it via a superheater to three
cylinders, one high-pressure 23.6 x 28.3in (600 x 720mm) and two low-
pressure 27 x 29.9in (680 x 760mm), the high-pressure cylinder mounted
inside and driving the leading main axle, and the two low-pressure cylinders
outside driving the second main axle. **Weight:** 185,50lb (84t) adhesive
496,000lb (225t) total. **Axleload:** 46,500lb (21t). **Overall length:** 58ft 3^{1}/2in
(17,765mm). **Tractive effort:** 65,679lb (29,800kg). **Max speed:** 80mph
(130km/h). **Service entry:** 1946.

By every competent authority it is agreed that André Chapelon should be
included in the shortest of short lists of candidates to be considered as the
greatest locomotive engineer of all. And this magnificent locomotive was his
greatest work.

What later became the Western Region of French National Railways had
had a bad experience in 1932 with a large 4-8-2 locomotive designed by a
government-appointed central design committee. It was a three-cylinder
simple, but with poppet valve gear intended to give an expansion ratio

equivalent to a compound. Alas, the mechanism never managed to achieve this, and moreover, there were other defects in the engine which caused bad riding and a tendency to derail. No.241101 was laid aside after tests, an embarrassment to all, particularly as it had been announced with a tremendous fanfare as marking a new era in steam locomotive construction

Chapelon had long wished to get his hands on this machine and to do to it what he had done before to the Paris-Orleans 4-6-2s. Official opposition took some years to overcome, but in 1942 his plans were agreed to, with a view to building a prototype for express passenger locomotives to be constructed when the war was over. The work was put in hand by the Société des Forges et Acieres de la Marine et d'Homecourt.

The chassis needed substantial strengthening, and the extra weight involved in this and other modifications meant the need for an extra carrying wheel – hence France's first 4-8-4 tender locomotive. The de Glehn arrangement with two low-pressure cylinders inside would have involved a crank axle with two cranks and rather thin webs (since there was no room for thick ones) and it was admitted that this was a source of maintenance problems. So the new engine was to have a single high-pressure cylinder inside driving the leading main axle and two low-pressure

Below: The magnificent 4-8-4 created by André Chapelon, the most powerful steam locomotive ever to be used in Europe, but one which irked French rail authorities.

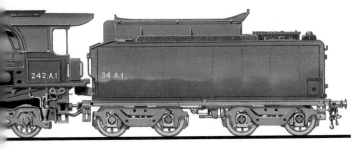

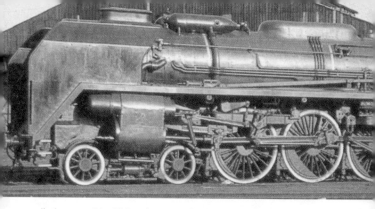

cylinders outside driving the second axle. All were in line between the bogie wheels.

Chapelon also moved away from poppet valves and used double piston valves to give adequate port openings, as in his last batch of 4-6-2 rebuilds. The outside cranks were set at 90 degrees to one another, as in a two-cylinder engine; the inside crank bisected the obtuse angle between the other two cylinders, being set at 135 degrees to each. The Walschaert's valve gear for the inside cylinder was mounted partly outside – the eccentric rod was attached to a return crank on the second left-hand driving wheel. The bad riding was tackled with a roller centring device for the front bogie, as well as Franklin's automatic wedges to take up wear in the axlebox guides. Both were of US origin.

The boiler had two thermic syphons in the firebox, concentric (Houlet's) superheater elements and a mechanical stoker. A triple Kylchap chimney and exhaust system was provided. When completed in 1946, the rebuilt locomotive (now No.242A1) indicated under test that it was by far the most powerful locomotive existing outside North America the omission of the word steam is deliberate. It could develop a maximum of 5,500hp in the cylinders, compared with 2,800hp before rebuilding. This power output is similar to that of which a typical US 4-8-4, perhaps 50 per cent heavier than No.242A1, was capable of as a maximum when driven hard.

This sort of power output enabled then unheard-of things to be achieved. A typical performance was to haul a 15-car train of 740 tons up a steady gradient of 1-in-125 (0.8 per cent), at a minimum speed of 71mph (114km/h). A 700-ton train was hauled from Paris to Lille in 140 minutes for the 161 miles (258km), while the electrified line from Paris to Le Mans (131 miles – 210km) was covered in 109 minutes with a test train of 810 tons; well under the electric timings even with this huge train. On another occasion a speed of 94mph (150km/h) was reached; this was also on a special test, as there was a 120km/h (75mph) legal speed limit for public trains in France at that time.

Alas for the future of No.242A1, the railway top brass of France were even more embarrassed by its outstanding success than they were by its previous failure. They were engaged in trying to persuade the French government, at a time when resources were at a premium, to underwrite a vast programme of electrification; and here comes a young man (Chapelon was only 58!) with a steam engine which could outperform any electric locomotive so far built, and was so economical in fuel consumption as to nullify any potential coal saving through electrification. And both of these factors were corner-stones of the railways' case for electrification.

So it is not hard to understand why this great locomotive was never duplicated. In fact it was quietly shunted away to Le Mans depot where, turn and turn-about with lesser engines, it took over express trains arriving from Paris by electric traction. The potential of the 4-8-4 was still appreciated by its crews. When such trains were delayed they could use its great performance in earning themselves large sums in bonus payments for the time regained.

Left: A view of Chapelon's masterpiece, French National Railways' magnificent three-cylinder compound 4-8-4 No.242A1, rebuilt from a pre-war 4-8-2.

Below: 4-8-4 No.242A1, a steam locomotive which could out perform any electric or diesel engine in existence in 1946, the year it went into service, and for some time afterwards.

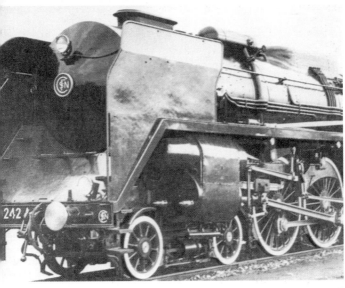

There was another potential question mark standing over a future for a production version of No.242A1. The rugged American 2-8-2s showed an overall economy over the compounds because low maintenance costs more than balanced the cost of the extra coal burnt. Ironically, some of this was due to Chapelon himself, who had improved the valve events and reduced the cylinder clearances of the 141R so that the amount of this extra coal used was reduced from some 20 per cent to 10.

So it should really be no surprise that, as revealed by Baron Gerard Vuillet in his authoritative *Railway Reminiscences of Three Continents*, there was an alternative proposal in the form of a two-cylinder simple 4-6-4 with cast-steel locomotive frame, roller bearings, mechanical stoker and a grate area of 67sq ft (6.2m²). Vuillet remarks, "this 147-ton locomotive would not have been much more powerful at the drawbar than the best French Pacifics weighing 104 tons, but would have had a higher availability."

Chapelon was countering with proposals for three-cylinder compound 4-6-4s and 4-8-4s for express passenger work. He also had in mind a triple-expansion compound 4-8-4 with four cylinders, using steam at 584psi (41kg/cm²) generated in a boiler with tube firebox. The locomotive was intended to be capable of developing 8,000hp. Confidently with the former, and it was hoped with the latter, Chapelon expected that maintenance costs of these modern compounds could be brought down close to those of simple locomotives. Alas, all this was academic – the great 4-8-4 was withdrawn in 1960 and quietly broken up.

Class WP 4-6-2

Origin: India/USA: Indian Railways (IR), 1946. **Type:** Express passenger steam locomotive. **Gauge:** 5ft 6in (1,676mm). **Propulsion:** Coal fire with a grate area of 46sq ft (4.3m²) generating steam at 210psi (14.7kg/cm²) in a fire-tube boiler, and supplying it via a superheater to two 20¹/₄ x 28in (514 x 511mm) cylinders, driving the main wheels direct by means of connecting and coupling rods. **Weight:** 121,500lb (55t) adhesive, 380,000lb (172.5t) total. **Axleload:** 45,000lb (20.7t). **Overall length:** 78ft 4in (23,876mm). **Tractive effort:** 30,600lb (13,884kg). **Max speed:** 62mph (100km/h).

Of only a few classes of steam locomotive amongst those described in this book can it be said (with much pleasure) that some remain in service, doing the job for which they were built. One of them is this massive 5ft 6in (1,676mm) gauge American-style 4-6-2, the standard express passenger locomotive of Indian Railways. Class "WP" comprised 755 locomotives built between 1947 and 1967, with running numbers 7000 to 7754.

The prototypes were a batch of 16 ordered from Baldwin of Philadelphia in 1946, before Independence, so the decision to go American was not connected with the political changes. It was taken as a result of satisfactory experience with American locomotives supplied to India during the war coupled with unsatisfactory experience with Indian standard designs of the 1920s and 1930s.

Naturally, the locomotives supplied were built to the usual rugged simple, basic US standards. Provision of vacuum brakes, standard in India made them even simpler, because a vacuum ejector is a vastly less complicated device than a steam air-pump. An air-smoothed exterior was provided for aesthetic rather than aerodynamic reasons, giving a solid dependable look to solid dependable locomotives. The original batch were designated "WP/P" (P for prototypes) and the production version differed in minor details. During the next ten years further members of the class were

Below: A commendably clean Indian Railways 4-6-2 Class "WP" brings a passenger train into a station on the Eastern Railway system. Note the broad gauge, the "cow-catcher", the side buffers with screw couplings and the high platforms set at coach-floor level.

Above: One of the standard Class "WP" 4-6-2 passenger locomotives of Indian Railways at Khurda Road, South Eastern Railway.

supplied from foreign countries as follows:

USA – Baldwin	100
Canada – Canadian Locomotive Co	100
Canada – Montreal Locomotive Works	120
Poland – Fabryka Locomotywim, Chrzanow	30
Austria – Vienna Lokomotiv Fabrik	30

There was then a pause until 1963, when India's own new Chitteranjan locomotive building plant began production of the remainder. Some further small modifications to the design were made to facilitate production.

The fleet of "WPs" worked on all parts of the broad gauge network and still found employment on many important express passenger trains in the 990s, although they were displaced from the top assignments by diesel and electrics, also Indian-built. Enormous trains, packed with humanity, moved steadily across the Indian plains each headed by one of these excellent locomotives. A crew of four was carried (driver, two firemen and coal trimmer) but even with two observers on board as well there was ample room in the commodious cab.

Class A1 4-6-2

Origin: United Kingdom: British Railways (BR), 1948. **Type:** Express passenger steam locomotive. **Gauge:** 4ft 8$\frac{1}{2}$in (1,435mm) **Propulsion** Coal fire with a grate area of 50sq ft (4.6m²) generating steam at 250psi (17.61kg/cm²) in a fire-tube boiler, and supplying it via a superheater to three 19 x 26in (482 x 660mm) cylinders, driving the main wheels by means of connecting and coupling rods. **Weight:** 148,000lb (67t) adhesive, 369,000lb (167t) total. **Axleload:** 49,500lb (22.5t). **Overall length:** 73ft 0in (22,250mm). **Tractive effort:** 37,400lb (16,900kg). **Max speed:** 100mph (160km/h).

When Sir Nigel Gresley died suddenly in office in 1941, the London & North Eastern Railway had 115 Pacifics and some 600 other three-cylinder engines of his design, all fitted with his derived motion, in which the inside valve took its drive from the two outside valve gears.

The opportunity to build a Pacific incorporating his ideas arose from the poor availability of Gresley's "P2" class 2-8-2 locomotives, one of whose troubles was heavy wear of axleboxes due to the long rigid wheelbase on the sharp curves of the Edinburgh-Aberdeen line. By rebuilding these as Pacifics he hoped to improve their performance, and also to gain experience for further new construction. Elimination of the Gresley gear involved arranging the inside cylinder to drive the leading axle, and as Thompson insisted on all the connecting rods being of the same length, an awkward layout was arrived at, with the leading bogie ahead of the outside cylinders.

Trouble was experienced with flexing of the frame, and loosening and breakage of steam pipes, but nevertheless the arrangement was applied to the "P2s" and to a further 19 mixed-traffic Pacifics with 74in (1,880mm) driving wheels. Before this programme was completed, Thompson also took in hand Gresley's original Pacific, *Great Northern*, and rebuilt it similarly with separate valve gears, larger cylinders, and a grate area of 50sq ft (4.6m²), in place of the 41.3sq ft (3.8m²) grate with which all the Gresley Pacifics were fitted.

Before Thompson's retirement, his successor designate, Arthur Peppercorn, put in hand quietly in Doncaster drawing office a further revision of the Pacific layout, in which the outside cylinders were restored to their position above the middle of the bogie, and the inside connecting rod was shortened to make the front of the engine more compact. Fifteen new Pacifics with 74in wheels were built to this design, classified "A2", and then 49 more with 80in (2,032mm) wheels were ordered, classified "A1". *The Great Northern* was absorbed into this class.

These engines were not built until after nationalisation, in 1948-49, Nos. 60114-27/53-62 at Doncaster, and Nos. 60130-52 at Darlington. They all had Kylchap double blastpipes, and five of them had roller bearings to all axles.

Above: "A1" class 4-6-2 No. 60161 *Amadis* ready to leave King's Cross, London. Note "express passenger" headlamp position.

At first they had stovepipe chimneys, but these were replaced by chimneys of the normal Doncaster shape. They had assorted names, including locomotive engineers, the constituent railways of the LNER, some traditional Scottish names, some birds and some racehorses.

The "A1s" proved to be fast and economical engines, and they took a full share in East Coast locomotive workings, except for the King's Cross-Edinburgh non-stops, for which the streamlined "A4s" were preferred. Their maintenance costs were lower than those of other BR Pacifies, and they achieved notable mileages. Over a period of 12 years they averaged 202 miles per calendar day, the highest figure on BR, and the five roller bearing engines exceeded that average, with 228 miles per day. Their riding was somewhat inferior to that of the "A4", as they had a tendency to lateral lurching on straight track, but nevertheless they were timed at 100mph plus (160+ km/h) on a number of occasions.

These engines were a worthy climax to Doncaster Pacific design, but unfortunately they came too late in the day to have full economic lives. By the early 1960s dieselisation of the East Coast main line was well advanced, and the "A1s" were all withdrawn between 1962 and 1966.

Below: Class "A1" North British depicted in the experimental blue livery tried in the early days of British Rail.

Y6b 2-8-8-2

Origin: United States: Norfolk & Western Railway (N&W), 1948. **Type:** Steam locomotive for heavy freight haulage. **Gauge:** 4ft 8^1/2in (1,435mm). **Propulsion:** Coal fire with a grate area of 106sq ft (9.8m²) generating steam at 300psi (21.1kg/cm²) in a fire-tube boiler, and supplying it via a superheater to four cylinders, two high-pressure 25 x 32in (635 x 812mm) and two low-pressure 29 x 32in (746 x 812mm), each pair driving the main wheels of its respective unit direct by means of connecting and coupling rods. **Weight:** 548,500lb (248.9t) adhesive, 990,100lb (449.2t) total. **Axleload:** 75,418lb (34.2t). **Overall length:** 114ft 11in (35,026mm). **Tractive effort:** 152,206lb (69,059kg). **Max speed:** not specified.

"Of all the words of tongue and pen, the saddest are 'it might have been'." In the USA, there was one small (but prosperous) railroad that, on a long-term basis, came near to fighting off the diesel invasion. This was the Norfolk & Western Railway, with headquarters in Roanoke, Virginia, and a main line then stretching 646 miles (1,033km) from ocean piers at Norfolk, Virginia, to Columbus in Ohio. It had branches to collect coal from every mine of importance across one of the world's greatest coal fields. In the end steam lost the battle on the N&W and big-time steam railroading finally vanished from the United States – so dealing a fatal blow all over the world to the morale of those who maintained that dieselisation was wrong. But the Norfolk & Western's superb steam locomotives came close to victory; so let us see how it was done.

The principle adopted was to exploit fully all the virtues of steam while, rather obviously, seeking palliatives for its disadvantages. It was also a principle of N&W management that the maximum economy lay in maintaining the steam fleet in first-class condition, with the aid of premises, tools and equipment to match.

During the period when steam and diesel were battling for supremacy on US railroads, it was typically the case that brand new diesel locomotives were

Above: Norfolk & Western Railway "Y6b" Mallet No. 172 hauls a westbound freight at Shaffers Crossing, near Roanoke, Virginia.

being maintained in brand new depots while the steam engines with which they were being compared were worn out and looked after in tumble down sheds. Often much of the roof would be missing while equipment was also worn out and obsolete. The filth would be indescribable.

On the Norfolk & Western Railroad during the 1950s, steam locomotives were new and depots almost clinically clean, modern, well-equipped and well arranged. A "J6B" class could be fully serviced, greased, lubricated, cleared of ash, tender filled with thousands of gallons of water and many tons of coal, all in under an hour. The result was efficiency, leading to Norfolk & Western's shareholders receiving 6 per cent on their money, while those of the neighbouring and fully dieselised or electrified Pennsylvania Railroad had to be content with $1/2$ per cent.

In the end, through, the problems of being the sole United States railroad continuing with steam on any scale began to tell. Even a do-it yourself concern like N&W normally bought many components from specialists and one by one these firms were going out of business. In 1960 this and other factors necessitated the replacement of steam and the "Y6bs" plus all the other wonderful locomotives of this excellent concern were retired.

After gaining experience – some of it traumatic – with other people's Mallets for its huge coal movement, Norfolk & Western in 1918 had built in its own shops at Roanoke, Virginia, a really successful coal-mover in the form of a 2-8-8-2 compound articulated steam locomotive. This "Y2" class received wholesale recognition because, later the same year, the United States Railroad Administration based its standard 2-8-8-2 on this excellent design.

Left: The most striking feature of this view of a "Y6b" compound Mallet 2-8-8-2 is the huge low-pressure cylinders at the front.

Below: The last in the long line of North American heavy steam motive power, the "Y6b" class of the Norfolk & Western Railway.

N&W was allocated 50 by USRA, which was then running the nation's railroads. The new locomotives, classified "Y3", came from Alco and Baldwin. In 1923 they were augmented by 30 more, designated "Y3a", and a further 10 in 1927, Class "Y4". The "Y4s" were the last new steam locomotives not to be built by N&W at Roanoke; they came from Alco's Richmond Works.

N&W policy was to move forward slowly, not forgetting to consolidate the gains already made. So the successive improvements made between the "Y2", "Y3", "Y3a" and "Y4" classes were modest. For example, provision of feed-water heaters began with the "Y3as", but earlier locomotives were altered to bring them into line, so that operationally the group of classes could be regarded as one.

In 1930 the first of an enlarged version, Class "Y5", was produced. Thus was founded a dynasty of coal-moving and coal-consuming power which would bring the science of steam locomotive operation to a never-to-be-repeated peak. Over the next 22 years modern developments were successively introduced through classes "Y6", "Y6a" and "Y6b" and, as before, the earlier locomotives were rebuilt to bring them into line so that the fleet was kept uniformly up-to-date. The last "Y6b", completed in 1952, was the last main-line steam locomotive to be built in the USA.

This time, some of the improvements passed on were not so minor. The introduction of cast-steel locomotive beds with integrally-cast cylinders on the "Y6s" was followed by rebuilding of the "Y5s" to match. The old "Y5" frames were then passed on to the "Y3"/"Y4" group, by now relegated to local mine runs. One problem with the older Mallets was that they tended to choke themselves with the large volume of low-pressure steam because of inadequately-sized valves, ports, passageways and pipes. This was corrected in the "Y5" design and these locomotives then had the freedom to run and pull at speeds up to 50mph (80km/h), which can be considered an exceptional figure for a compound Mallet.

Roller bearings came on the "Y6s" of 1936, and with the "Y6bs" of 1948 was booster equipment for extra power, whereby a modicum of live steam, controlled by a reducing valve, could be introduced to the low-pressure cylinders while still running as a compound. It was quite separate from the conventional simpling valve used for starting. An interesting feature was the

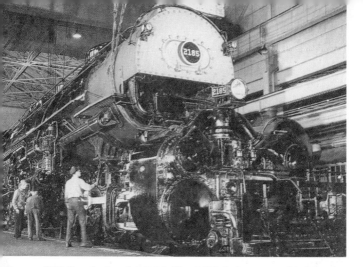

Above: "Y6b" articulated 2-8-8-2 No. 2185 being assembled in the Roanoke Shops of the Norfolk & Western Railway on May 21, 1949.

coupling of auxiliary tenders behind locomotives in order to reduce the number of water stops.

It says enough of the efficiency of these engines that following a line relocation they displaced in 1948 N&W's pioneer electrification in the Allegheny Mountains. In due time though, Norfolk & Western became the only railroad which saw a long-term future for steam, but this position became untenable in the later 1950s. With reluctance, then, the Company was forced to follow the crowd and the last "Y6" set out on the last mine run in the month of April 1960. One is preserved in the National Museum of Transportation at St Louis.

Below: The Class "A" articulated simple Mallet 2-6-6-4, here depicted hauling a coal drag, intended for fast freight work.

GP Series B₀-B₀

Origin: United States: Electro-Motive Division, General Motors Corporation (EMD), 1949. **Type:** Diesel-electric road switcher locomotive. **Gauge:** 4ft 8¹/₂in (1,435mm). **Propulsion:** One EMD 567D2 2,000hp (1,490kW) 16-cylinder turbocharged two-stroke Vee engine and generator, supplying current to four nose-suspended traction motors geared to the axles. **Weight:** 244,000lb (108.9t) to 260,000lb (116.0t) according to fittings. **Axleload:** 61,000lb (27.2t) to 65,000lb (29.0t) according to fittings. **Overall length:** 56ft 0in (17,120mm), GP20 variant of 1959. **Tractive effort:** 61,000lb (271kN) to 65,000lb (289kN) according to weight. **Max speed:** 65mph (105km/h), 71mph (114km/h), 77mph (124km/h), 83mph (134km/h) or 89mph (143km/h) according to gear ratio fitted.

For the post-war boom in diesel sales EMD offered a range of models based on three main lines. First the "E" series of A1A-A1A express passenger locomotives, secondly the "F" series of Bo-Bo locomotives for freight work, but with optional gear ratios covering passenger work to all but the highest speeds, and thirdly a number of switchers (shunters) and transfer locomotives for work within and between marshalling yards. There was an important difference between the switchers and the other models. In the switchers the structural strength was in the underframe, on which rested the engine, generator and other equipment. The casing or "hood" was purely protective and had no structural strength. The "E" and "F" series, on the other hand, had load-bearing bodies, or "car bodies", which provided an "engine-room" in which maintenance work could be carried out whilst the train was in motion, and which were more satisfactory aesthetically than a hood.

With these models EMD captured about 70 per cent of the North American market. Its ability to do so stemmed from a combination of quality of performance and reliability in the locomotive, low maintenance costs, which were helped by the large number of parts which were common to the different types, and competitive prices made possible by assembly line manufacture. Full benefit of assembly line methods could only be achieved by limiting the number of variants offered to customers, and this in turn helped EMD's competitors to pick on omissions from, or weaknesses in, the EMD range by which to hold on to a share of the market. At first EMD's main theme in its diesel sales talk was the benefit accruing from replacing steam by diesel traction, but as its competitors achieved modest success in finding gaps in the EMD range, more and more was that firm concerned

Above: A 30-year-old "GP7" diesel-electric locomotive in service in 1982 the Algoma Central Railway in Canada.

with proclaiming the superiority of its products over those of its competitors.

To achieve this superiority some changes were made in the range, of which the most important originated in customer enquiries received before the war for a locomotive which was primarily a switcher, but which could also haul branch line trains, local freights and even local passenger trains. To meet this need a small number of locomotives were built with switcher bodies, elongated to house a steam generator, and mounted on bogies of the "F" series; these were "road switchers". Construction was resumed after the war, still on a small scale, and with the design adapted to meet individual customers' requirements.

By 1948 EMD's competitors, particularly Alco, were achieving success with a general purpose hood unit for branch line work. For this application, ability to gain access to the working parts was more important than protection for technicians to work on the equipment on the road, and the hoods also gave the driver much wider field of view In 1948, therefore, EMD offered a branch line diesel, designated "BL", incorporating the 1,500hp (1,120kW) 567B engine, and other equipment including traction motors from the "F" series. These were accommodated in a small semi-

Below: "GP38-2" standard diesel-electric road-switcher locomotive as supplied to Canadian Pacific by General Motors (Canada).

streamlined casing, whose main advantage compared with a carbody was the improved view from the cab. There was, however, a serious snag: the "BL" was too expensive.

EMD then designed a true hood for general purpose duties, designated "GP", Richard Dilworth, EMD's Chief Engineer, said that his aim was to produce a locomotive that was so ugly that railroads would be glad to send it to the remotest corners of the system (where a market for diesels to replace steam still existed!), and to make it so simple that the price would be materially below standard freight locomotives.

Although the "GP" was offered as a radically new design, many parts were common to the contemporary "F7" series. The power plant was the classic 567 engine, which like all EMD engines was a two-stroke Vee design; this was simpler than a four-stroke but slightly less efficient. Much development work was devoted over the years to improving the efficiency of the EMD engines to meet the competition of four-stroke engines. The bogies were of the Blomberg type, a fairly simple design with swing-link bolsters, which were introduced in the "FT" series in 1939 and were still, with changes in the springing system, standard in EMD Bo-Bo models in the 1980s. EMD's success with this long-running design is in contrast to the radical changes which have been made in bogie design in other countries over that period.

The cab afforded a good view in both directions, the hood gave easy access to the equipment, and, despite the designer's intentions, EMD's stylists produced a pleasing outline. Electrical equipment was simplified from the "F" series, but nevertheless it gave the driver tighter control over the tractive effort at starting, and a more comprehensive overall control to suit the wide range of speeds envisaged.

First production series of the new design was the "GP7", launched in 1949. It was an immediate success, and 2,610 units were supplied to US roads between 1949 and 1953, plus 112 to Canada and two to Mexico.

In 1954 the next development of the 567 engine, the C series of 1,750hp (1,305kW), was introduced into the range, giving the "GP9". This differed in detail from the "GP7", mainly to bring still further reductions in maintenance. By this time the hood unit was widely accepted, and sales of the "GP" at 4,157 established another record. It was America's (and

Above: The "GP" series of standard diesel-electric locomotives offered by the Electro-Motive Division of General Motors were used all over North America. Here are two "GP9s" of Canadian National.

therefore the world's) best selling diesel locomotive.

So far the EMD engines had been pressure-charged by a Roots blower driven mechanically from the engine, but with its competitors offering engines of higher power, EMD now produced a turbocharged version of the 567 engine, 567D2, giving 2,000hp (1,490kW). For customers for whom the extra power did not justify the expense of the turbo-blower, the 567D1 at 1,800hp (1,340kW) was available. Both these models had a higher compression than their predecessors, which, combined with improvements in the fuel injectors, gave a fuel saving of 5 per cent. These engines were incorporated in the "GP20" and "GP18" series, respectively.

By this time US railroads were fully dieselised, and this, combined with a decline in industrial activity, reduced the demand for diesels. EMD therefore launched its Locomotive Replacement Plan. The company claimed that three "GP20s" could do the work of four "F3s", so it offered terms under which a road traded in four "F3s" against the purchase of three "GP20s", parts being re-used where possible. It was claimed that the cost of the transaction could be recovered in three to four years, and the railroad then had three almost new units in place of four older ones with much higher maintenance costs. Despite this, only 260 "GP20s" and 390 "GP18s" were sold over 4 years.

The final phase of "GP" development with the 567 engine came in 1961 with the 567D3 of 2,250hp (1,680kW) in the "GP30". The designation "30" was a sales gimmick, based on there being 30 improvements in the new model; it was claimed that maintenance was reduced by 60 per cent compared with earlier types. The "GP30" was in turn succeeded by the "GP35" of 2,500hp (1,870kW). With trade reviving, and many more early diesels in need of replacement, these models achieved sales of 2,281. At this stage the 567 engine was replaced by the 645 with which the "GP" series remained in full production in the early 1980s, while 1984 saw introduction of the 710 engine in the new "60" series locomotives.

Class YP 4-6-2

Origin: India: Indian Railways (IR), 1949. **Type:** Express passenger steam locomotive. **Gauge:** 3ft 3³/₈in (1,000mm). **Propulsion:** Coal fire with a grate area of 28sq ft (2.6m²) generating steam at 210psi (14.8kg/cm²) in a fire-tube boiler, and supplying it via a superheater to two 15¹/₄ x 24in (387 x 610mm) cylinders, driving the main wheels direct by means of connecting and coupling rods. **Weight:** 69,000lb (31.5t) adhesive, 218,500 (99t) total. **Axleload:** 23,500lb (10.7t). **Overall length:** 62ft 7¹/₂in (19,088mm). **Tractive effort:** 18,450lb (8,731kg). **Max speed:** 45mph (72km/h).

A total of 871 of these beautifully proportioned and capable locomotives were built between 1949 and 1970 for the metre-gauge network of Indian Railways. The newest members of the class were the last express passenger locomotives to be built, and many were still at work in the 1990s.

It could be said that whilst Britain's principal achievement in India was construction of the railway network, the greatest fault in what was done was the division of the system into broad and metre gauge networks of not far off equal size. Even so, 15,940 miles (25,500km) of metre-gauge railways, including many long-distance lines, had to be worked and power was needed to do it. Strictures rightly applied to the standard "XA", "XB" and "XC" 4-6-2s of the 1920s and 1930s were not deserved by their metre-gauge counterparts, the handsome "YB" 4-6-2s supplied between 1928

Above: A "YP" 4-6-2 at the head of a Southern Railway express train spreads a pall of black smoke over the Indian countryside.

Below: Indian Railways' metre-gauge Class "YP" 4-6-2, the last steam express locomotive class to be built anywhere in the world.

Above: A "YP" class Pacific takes a passenger train across a typical river bridge on the metre-gauge system of Indian Railways.

and 1950. Nevertheless Indian Railways decided to do what it had done on the broad gauge and go American. Jodhpur, one of the princely states, in those days still had its own railway, and it had received ten neat 4-6-2s from Baldwin of Philadelphia in 1948. Baldwin was asked to produce 20 prototypes of Class "YP" similar to those locomotives but slightly enlarged. The new locomotives were also a little simpler, with plain instead of roller bearings and eight-wheel instead of high-capacity 12-wheel tenders.

Production orders for the "YP" were placed overseas. Krauss-Maffei of Munich and North British Locomotive of Glasgow received production orders for 200 and 100 respectively over the next five years, but the remainder were built by the Tata Engineering & Locomotive Co of Jamshedpur, India. Running numbers were 2000 to 2870, but not in chronological order. The engines could be regarded as two-thirds full-size models of a standard USA 4-6-2. If one multiplies linear measurements by 1.5, areas by 1.52 or 2.25, weights and volumes by 1.53 or 3.375 the correspondence is very close. Non-American features include vacuum brakes, chopper type automatic centre couplers in place of the buckeye type, slatted screens to the cab side openings and the absence of a bell.

With so many available, these locomotives could be found in all areas of the metre-gauge system; this stretched far and wide from Trivandrum, almost the southernmost point of the Indian railways, to well north of Delhi, while both the easternmost and westernmost points were served by metre-gauge lines.

Diesel locomotives are now running throughout the metre-gauge network, but the extent of metre-gauge lines diminished in the 1990s as many busier routes were converted to broad gauge.

Class CC7100 C$_o$-C$_o$

Origin: France: French National Railways (SNCF), 1952. **Type:** Electric express passenger locomotive. **Gauge:** 4ft 8½in (1,435mm). **Propulsion:** Direct current at 1,500V from overhead catenary fed to six bogie-mounted traction motors geared to the axles through Alsthom spring drive. **Weight:** 235,830lb (107t). **Axleload:** 39,230lb (17.8t). **Overall length:** 62ft 1in (18,922mm). **Tractive effort:** 50,700lb (225kN). **Max speed:** 100mph (160km/h). .

French locomotive design has always been distinctive, and much of the distinctiveness has been purely French in origin, but from time to time a foreign influence has been seen. Thus in the development of express passenger locomotives for the main line electrification of the Paris-Orleans Railway (PO), adoption of the Swiss Buchli drive led to a notable series of 2-Do-2 locomotives, which bore an external likeness to contemporary Swiss designs. The last 2-Do-2 type, the "9100", was introduced by SNCF as the principal passenger locomotive for the electrification of the former PLM main line to Lyons. However, before those locomotives had been built in the quantity originally intended, another Swiss influence changed the course of French locomotive design.

   Until this time, end bogies or pony trucks had been thought essential for fast passenger work, not only to support part of the weight of the locomotive but also to guide it into curves. All-adhesion Bo-Bo locomotives, which constituted the majority of French electrics, were considered suitable only for medium-speed work. Two notable Swiss designs changed the status of the all-adhesion locomotive. In 1946 Swiss Federal Railways introduced the 56 "Re4/4I" Bo-Bo, designed for speeds up to 78mph (125km/h). This class soon attracted attention by its ability to haul trains of 400t at its maximum permitted speed, while two years earlier the Loetschberg railway had introduced its 80t Bo-Bo, classified "Ae4/4". The success of these classes established the respectability of the double-bogie locomotive for express work, and SNCF commissioned two Bo-Bo machines from Swiss makers, based on the Loetschberg design, together with two Bo-Bo and two Co-Co units from French builders.

Above, right: French National Railways' Class "CC7100" Co-Co 1,500V dc electric locomotive at Paris (Gare de Lyon) in 1979.

Below: No. CC7107; one of these "CC1500" Co-Co electric locomotives broke the world speed record in 1954 and held it for many years.

The Co-Co was produced by Alsthom to a specification based on the requirements of the PLM electrification. This called for speeds up to 100mph 160km/h) on the level with 600t, 87mph (140km/h) on the level with 850t, and the ability to start a 600t train on a 1-in-125 (0.8 per cent) gradient and haul t at 75mph (120km/h) on that gradient.

The locomotive had a motor for each axle mounted in the bogie frame, with Alsthom spring drive. The novelty in the bogie was in the pivoting and in the axle guides. The pivots are of Alsthom design, and comprise two vertical links situated mid-way between the pairs of axles on the centre line of the bogie, with their ends resting in conical rubber seatings. Lateral movement of each ink is controlled by two horizontal springs. The springs have two effects: when the body of the locomotive swings outward on curves, they provide a restoring force resisting centrifugal action; and when the bogie rotates, the inks swing in opposite directions and exert forces tending to restore the bogie to the straight line. Thus, if the bogie rotates on straight track due to irregularities in the permanent way, the springs tend to damp this motion and

discourage the flanges from striking the rails.

Each axlebox is restrained by two horizontal links, which allow vertical movement but not fore-and-aft movement, and they eliminate the wearing surfaces of traditional steam-type axleboxes. End movement of the axles is controlled by stiff springs fitted between the ends of the axles and the axlebox cover plates. These springs reduce the shocks transmitted to the bogie frame when the flanges strike the rails. Extensive use was made of rubber in the pivots of the suspension system.

The electrical equipment was notable for the large number of running notches, made possible by the large amount of field weakening. The external lines were enhanced by the two-tone blue livery, set off by light metal beading of the window frames and of the horizontal flashing.

The two locomotives, Nos. CC7001-2, were delivered in 1949 and were subjected to intensive testing on the Paris-Bordeaux main line, which was then the longest electrified route in France. Early in these tests, No. 7001 hauled a train of 170t from Paris to Bordeaux at an average speed of 81.4mph (131km/h), reaching a maximum of 105.6mph (170km/h) which was a world record performance for an electric locomotive.

After three years of testing, orders were placed for 35 locomotives differing in detail from Nos.7001-2. They were delivered in 1952, and numbered from 7101 to 7135. A further order for 23 brought the class to a total of 60. Compared with Nos. 7001-2, the production units had an increase in maximum power from 4,000hp (2,980kW) to 4,740hp (3,540kW) and the weight increased from 96t to 107t. Compared with the "9100" class 2-Do-2, the adhesive weight had increased from 88t to 107t, but the axleload had fallen from 22t to 17.8t, so that the locomotive was much kinder to the track. Six of the locomotives were fitted with collecting shoes for working on the former PLM line from Chambery to Modane (the Mont Cenis route), which was at that time equipped with third rail current collection.

Electrification from Paris to Lyons was completed in 1952, and the "7100" class then shared with the "9100" 2-Do-2s the heaviest and fastest runs. By the summer of 1954 there were three runs between Paris and Dijon or Paris and Lyons booked at 77.1mph (124km/h) start-to-stop with permissible loads of 650t. Another run from Paris to Dijon was booked at 76.1mph (122.4km/h) with 730t. These were the outstanding speed exploits in Europe at the time – on a railway which 10 years before was devastated by war.

In February 1954, the very first high-speed tests were made with No

CC7121 on a level stretch between Dijon and Beaune. The purpose of the tests was to investigate the effect of high speed on various parameters, including the forces exerted on the rails and the behaviour of the pantograph. With a train of 111t a speed of 151mph (243km/h) was reached, which was a world record for any type of traction, beating the 143mph (230km/h) attained in 1931 in Germany by a propeller-driven railcar.

Testing then moved to the former PO railway, where a long stretch of almost straight line was available south of Bordeaux. First the problem of picking up a very heavy current was investigated with two "7100" class locomotives double-heading. With the line voltage boosted by 25 per cent, these two reached 121mph (195km/h) with 714t and 125mph (201km/h) with 617t.

The next target was a speed of 185mph (300km/h), for which purpose No. CC7107 was fitted with gears of higher ratio than normal. The train comprised three coaches weighing l00t, with a streamlined tail attached to the rear vehicle. The target of 185mph was reached in 13 miles (21km) from the start. and was maintained for 7^1/$_2$ miles (12km), but, very remarkably, speed rose to (205.6mph (330.8km/h) for 1^1/$_4$ miles (2km), which required an output of 12,000hp (8,950kW). Equally remarkable, the performance was repeated exactly on the following day by an 81t Bo-Bo, No. BB9004, one of the French-built experimental locomotives mentioned earlier. The two locomotives thus became joint world record holders, and as subsequent developments in very high-speed trains have been with trainsets, it is likely that this record for locomotives will stand.

The achievement of No. BB9004 was significant; a locomotive costing little more than half a "7100" had produced the same performance. Such was the pace of locomotive development at this time. French activity was then concentrated on four-axle machines, and no more six-axle electric locomotives were built until 1964, by which time design had changed greatly with introduction of the monomotor bogie.

Although the Co-Co locomotives were soon overshadowed by their smaller successors, they took a full share in express work on the former PLM for many years, and in 1982 No. CC7001 became the first French locomotive to cover 4.97 million miles (8 million km), at an average of 409 miles (658km) per day.

Below: A "CC7000" Co-Co electric locomotive of French National Railways rides the turntable in the roundhouse at Avignon.

Class 8 4-6-2

Origin: Great Britain: British Railways (BR), 1953. **Type:** Express passenger steam locomotive. **Gauge:** 4ft 8$\frac{1}{2}$in (1,435mm). **Propulsion:** Coal fire with a grate area of 48.5sq ft (4.5m²) generating steam at 250psi (17.6kg/cm²) in a fire-tube boiler, and supplying it via a superheater to three 18 x 28in (457 x 711mm) cylinders, driving the main wheels by means of connecting and coupling rods. **Weight:** 148,000lb (67.5t) adhesive, 347,000lb (157.5t) total. **Axleload:** 49,500lb (22.5t). **Overall length:** 70ft 0in (21,336mm). **Tractive effort:** 39,080lb (17,731kg). **Max speed:** 100mph (160km/h).

The railways of Britain became British Railways on January 1, 1948 and naturally there was much speculation concerning the kind of locomotive that would succeed the "Duchess", "King", "Merchant Navy" and "A4" classes of BR's illustrious predecessors. In early 1951 it was announced that none was planned, but instead the first full-size Pacific for any British railway to have only two cylinders was unveiled. This locomotive class was intended to displace such second-eleven power as the "Royal Scot", "Castle" and "West Country" classes rather than the largest types.

"Britannia" was a simple, rugged 4-6-2 with Belpaire firebox and roller bearings on all axles, as well as many other aids to cheap and easy maintenance. It was designated Class "7", and had a capacity to produce some 2,200hp in the cylinders, at a very fair consumption of coal amounting to some 5,000lb/h (2,270kg/h). This was well above the rate at which a normal man could shovel coal on to the fire but the large firebox enabled a big fire to be built up in advance when some big effort of short duration was required.

A total of 55 "Britannias" were built between 1951 and 1953. They met their designers' goal of a locomotive that was easy to maintain, and also showed that they were master of any express passenger task in Britain at that time. They were allocated to all the regions, but it was the Eastern that made the best use of the new engines. Their "Britannias" were allocated to one line and put to work on a new high-speed train service specifically designed round their abilities. During the 1950s in most of Britain it could be said that 20 years' progress had meant journey times some 20 per cent longer. On the other hand the new 4-6-2s working this improved timetable between London and Norwich meant a 20 per cent acceleration on pre-war timings, in terms of the service in general.

In spite of being simple engines in both senses of the world, the "Britannias" displayed economy in the use of steam. In fact they were right in the front rank, yet there was always the nagging thought that the great Chapelon compounds across the Channel could on test do about 10 per cent better. This figure would be diluted in service by various factors

Above: "Britannia" 4-6-2 No.70039 *Sir Christopher Wren* hauling a Liverpool-Glasgow express at grips with the climb to Shap in 1965.

but even so it was considerable, especially as within almost exactly the same weight limits they could develop nearly 1,500 more cylinder horsepower. There was, however, a certain reluctance in Britain to go compound, because for one thing there was no counterpart to the French works-trained *mechanicien* drivers to handle such complex beasts. Past experience had also shown the extra maintenance costs implicit in the complexity to have over ridden economies due to the saving of fuel.

A point was perhaps missed, though, that since the upper limit of power output was a man shovelling, a more economical machine would also be a more powerful one. And since more power allowed faster running times, and faster running times produce more revenue, a more efficient locomotive might be both a money saver and a money earner. But there is another way to obtaining some of the advantages of compounding and that is to expand the steam to a greater extent in simple cylinders. This in its turn means that the point in the stroke at which the valves close to steam (known as the cut-off and expressed in terms of per cent) must be very early. However, the geometry of normal valve gears precludes cut-offs less than, say,15 to 20 per cent. This is because, if the opening to steam is limited to less of the stroke than that, the opening to exhaust (the same valve being used for both) is also limited on the return stroke. This means steam trapped in the cylinders and loss

Below: The solitary Class "8" 4-6-2 No.71000 *Duke of Gloucester*. Note the shaft which drives the rotary-cam poppet valve gear.

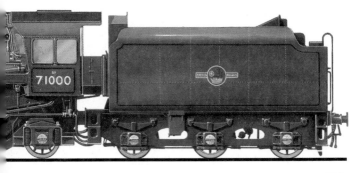

**Above: British Railways' one-and-only Class "8" 4-6-2 *Duke of
Gloucester* awaits the call to duty in Crewe station in 1961.**

of power. The solution is to have independent valves for admission and
exhaust and the simplest way of doing this is to use poppet valves
actuated by a camshaft. Alas, it cannot be too simple because the point of
cut-off has to be varied and, moreover, the engine has to be reserved.
Both these things are done by sliding the camshaft along its axis, bringing
changed cam profiles into action according to the position of the reversing
control in the cab.

Permission was obtained in 1953 to build a prototype for future BR top
link express passenger locomotives. As a two-cylinder machine, the
cylinder size came out too big to clear platform edges so, in spite of a yen
for simplicity, three cylinders had to be used. Now it is a point concerning
poppet valves that much of the mechanism is common, however many
cylinders there are. So poppet valves of the British-Caprotti pattern were
specified for this sole example of the British Railways Class "8"
locomotive. On test, No.71000 *Duke of Gloucester* showed a 9 per cent
improvement over the "Britannia" class in steam consumed for a given
amount of work done. It was a world record for a simple locomotive.

Alas, although the boiler was of impeccable lineage, being based on the
excellent one used on the LMS "Duchess" class, there was some detail
of its proportions which interfered with economical steam production at
high outputs. It would have been easy to correct the faults with a little
investigation. Unfortunately, in the words of E.S. Cox, then Chief Office
(Design) at BR headquarters, "there were some in authority at
headquarters, although not in the Chief Mechanical Engineer's
department, who were determined that there should be no more
development with steam"; so nothing was done and no more Class "8"s
were built.

So No.71000 spent its brief life as an unsatisfactory one-off locomotive.
After it was withdrawn, the valve chests and valve gear were removed for
preservation, but that did not prevent a more than usually bold
preservation society from buying the rest of the remains.

Below: *Mercury* ("Britannia" class 4-6-2 No. 70020) raises the echoes with the Cardiff-London "Capitals United Express" in 1959.

P36 Class 4-8-4

Origin: Russia: Soviet Railways (SZD), 1953. **Type:** Express passenger steam locomotive. **Gauge:** 5ft 0in (1,524mm). **Propulsion:** Coal fire with grate area of 73sq ft (6.75m²) generating steam at 213psi (15kg/cm²) in a fire-tube boiler, and supplying it via an external main steam pipe and superheater to two 22¹/₂ x 31¹/₂in (575 x 800mm) cylinders, driving the main wheels direct by means of connecting and coupling rods. **Weight:** 163,000lb (74t) adhesive, 582,000lb (264t) total. **Axleload:** 41,000lb (18.5t). **Overall length** 94ft 10in (29,809mm). **Tractive effort:** 39,686lb (18,007kg). **Max speed** 81mph (130km/h).

Having by 1930 established an excellent class of 2-6-2 passenger locomotives – the "S" class – and built about 3,000 of them, Soviet Railways could sit back and consider the future of long-distance passenger traffic at leisure. Passenger traffic had so far always taken second place to freight, but it was recognised that in due time higher speeds and more comfortable (and therefore heavier) trains would be needed for those whom the Soviet government permitted to travel.

The first prototype came in 1932 and it was a logical enlargement of the 2-6-2 into a 2-8-4, combining an extra driving axle to increase tractive effort and an extra rear carrying axle to give greater power from a larger firebox. The

lass was given the designation "JS" (standing for Josef Stalin) and some 40 were built between 1934 and 1941. None is working today but a freight quivalent with the same boiler, cab, cylinders, tender and other parts was the FD" class 2-10-2, many of which were still in service in southern China until the mid-1980s, after conversion from 5ft (1,524mm) gauge to standard.

The episode was typical of a sensible and logical attitude towards the eeds of the railway system, in respect of which the new socialist regime ardly differed from the old Czarist one. One small prestige extravagance id follow, however, with the building in 1937-38 of the first three of a class f ten high-speed streamlined 4-6-4s for the "Red Arrow" express between Moscow and Leningrad. It was hoped to raise the average speed for the 04-mile (646km) run from about 40 to 50mph (64 to 80km/h). The first two ad coupled wheels of 78³/₄in (2,000mm) diameter, but the third had them s large as 86¹/₂in (2,197mm). The latter machine again had boiler, cylinders nd much else standard with the "FD" class. Eventually the war put an end o the project, but not before the first prototype had achieved 106mph 170km/h) on test, a record for steam traction in Russia.

Below: A "P36" 4-8-4 of the USSR railway system with Train No.1 "Rossiya" awaits departure at Skovorodino, Siberia, in 1970.

Above: A Russian Class "P36" 4-8-4 express passenger locomotive waits "on shed" at an unknown location in the Soviet Union.

Right: The immense height and striking lines of the huge Russian Class "P36" 4-8-4 are best brought out in this head-on view.

World War II for the Russians may have been shorter than it was for the rest of Europe, but it was also a good deal nastier. So it was not until five years after the war ended that the first of a new class of passenger locomotive appeared from the Kolomna Works near Moscow. This prototype took the form of a tall and handsome 4-8-4, designated class "P36". The new locomotive was similar in size and capacity to the "JS" class, but the extra pair of carrying wheels enabled the axleloading to be reduced from 20 to 18 tons. This gave the engine a much wider availability, although this was never needed, as we shall see.

Whilst the class was very much in the final form of the steam locomotive, one feature which it had in common with many modern Russian engines was particularly striking and unusual. This was an external main steam pipe enclosed in a large casing running forward from dome to smokebox along the top of the boiler. This arrangement, excellent from the point of view of accessibility, was only made possible by a loading gauge which allows rolling stock to be as high as 17ft 4in (5,280mm) above rail level. Roller bearings were fitted to all axles – for the first time on any Russian locomotive – and there was a cab totally enclosed against the Russian winter, as well as a mechanical stoker for coal-fired examples of the class. Many of the 4-8-4s, however, were oil-burning, particularly those running in the west of the country.

After a cautious period of testing, production began at Kolomna and between 1954 and 1956 at least 249 were built, making them the world's most numerous class of 4-8-4. Of course, compared with other classes in Russia, which numbered from more than 10,000 examples downward, the size of the class was minuscule.

In contrast, though, their impact upon Western observers was considerable because they were to be found on lines visited by foreigners.

such as Moscow-Leningrad and between Moscow and the Polish frontier. Some of the class were even finished in a blue livery similar to the streamlined 4-6-4s, but most looked smart enough in the light green passenger colours with cream stripes and red wheel centres.

For some 15 years the "P36s" handled the famous Trans-Siberian express, the legendary "Rossiya", after the changeover from electric traction through to the Pacific Ocean shore. The run took 70 hours and there were 19 changes of steam locomotive, so Siberia was paradise to at least one class of humanity. Steam enthusiasts had to show some subtlety in recording the objects of their love on film; the use of miniature cameras was very dangerous, but some success was achieved by people who set up a a a huge plate camera on its tripod, marched up to the nearest policeman and demanded that the platform end be cleared.

Steam enthusiasm was not without its dangers for those at home. In 1956 Lazar Kaganovitch, Commisar for Transportation and Heavy Industry, who had long advocated the retention of steam traction with such words as "I am for the steam locomotive and against those who imagine that we will not have any in the future – this machine is sturdy, stubborn and will not give up", was summarily deposed and disappeared. Steam construction immediately came to an end in the Soviet Union. Some twenty years later steam operation of passenger trains also ended and with it the lives of these superb locomotives.

Class 12000 B$_o$-B$_o$

Origin: France: French National Railways (SNCF), 1954. **Type:** Mixed-traffic electric locomotive. **Gauge:** 4ft 8^1/2in (1,435mm). **Propulsion:** Alternating current at 25,000V 50Hz passed through transformer and mercury arc rectifier to four 830hp (620kW) bogie-mounted traction motors with flexible drives to axles; axles of each bogie geared together. **Weight:** 188,660lb (85.6t). **Axleload:** 47,170lb (21.4t). **Overall length:** 49ft 10^3/8in (15,200mm). **Tractive effort:** 54,000lb (240kN). **Max speed:** 75mph (120km/h).

At the end of World War II the standard system for main-line electrification in France was 1,500V dc, but French engineers, like those of a number of other countries, were interested in the possibility of using alternating current at the standard industrial frequency of 50Hz. This offered a number of advantages: 50Hz current could be taken from the public supply at any convenient point and only a small transformer would be needed to reduce the voltage to that required for the overhead wires. As alternating current could be reduced on the locomotives by transformer, the supply could be taken from the overhead at high voltage; the higher the voltage, the smaller the current, and the lighter the overhead wires and their supports. With high voltage, the supply points could be spaced more widely, because voltage drops in the line would be proportionately smaller than with a lower-voltage system.

The second most comprehensive test thus far made with electric traction at 50Hz was on the Hollenthal line in West Germany, which happened to be in the French zone of occupation after the war. French engineers thus had an opportunity to study this line closely and the results of ten years' operation of it. They formed a favourable opinion of the system, particularly as a means of electrifying lines with lower traffic densities than had previously been considered economic for electrification. SNCF therefore chose for an experimental ac system the line from Aix-les-Bains to La Roche-sur-Foron in Savoy. This was mainly single track without complicated track layouts, but it had gradients sufficiently severe to test the equipment thoroughly. French and Swiss manufacturers supplied a number of locomotives and motor coaches for this conversion, some to work on ac only and some on both ac and dc.

Success of the Savoy scheme led to a bold step forward – conversion of 188 miles (303km) of the Thionville to Valenciennes route in northern France

Above: A 25,000V ac Class "12000" Bo-Bo electric locomotive moves freight in Alsace-Lorraine. French trains take the left-hand track except here where Germany had sometimes ruled.

Below: A central cab, enabling the same control console to be used for both directions of running, was a feature of these SCNF Class "12000" high-voltage industrial-frequency electric locomotives.

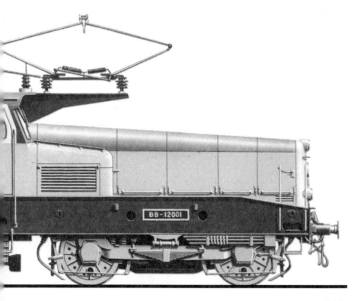

to electric working at 25,000V 50Hz. Although a secondary route, it carried three express passenger trains and up to 100 freight trains in each direction daily, and it had gradients of up to 1-in-90 (1.1 per cent). The ac traction system in West Germany and Switzerland used current specially generated at 16²/₃Hz. A normal type of electric motor as used on dc will operate on ac, but each time the current reverses there are induced effects which tend to upset the working of the commutator. These effects are proportional to the square of the frequency. At 16²/₃Hz they can be coped with, but 50Hz is a different proposition, and up to and including the Hollenthal line experiment satisfactory traction motors for this frequency had not been produced, but the target was worth striving for.

Two main alternatives were available in a 50Hz system: to persevere with 50Hz motors or to convert the supply to some other form on the locomotive for supply to the traction motors. In fact SNCF decided to test four arrangements, conversion to dc by static converter, direct use of the 50Hz supply, conversion to dc by rotary converter, and conversion to three-phase by rotary machines.

For this purpose four types of locomotive were designed, two B-Bs for the first two systems and two Co-Cos for the second two. Of these systems the simplest was the second, for as with the 16²/₃Hz locomotives in other countries, it involved only a transformer to step down the voltage to a value suitable for the motors, and a tap changer on the transformer to vary the voltage. For the ac to dc conversion by static converter, the ignitron was selected. This was a form of steel-tank mercury-pool rectifier developed by Westinghouse in the United States. The two types of Co-Co locomotive had heavier equipment involving one or more rotating machines. The four classes were designated "12000", "13000", "14100", and "14000" respectively.

Layout of the locomotives was unusual in that they had a centre cab, an arrangement normally found only on shunting locomotives. The main reason for this was that SNCF had found that 50 per cent of failures of equipment in electric locomotives on the road were in the control equipment. With cabs at both ends of the locomotive, remote control of equipment was unavoidable, but with a central cab, in which the driver could use the same controls for both directions of travel, some of the equipment could be controlled directly. Further advantages were the good all-round view and more protection for the driver in collisions. A conspicuous feature of the locomotives was the platform mounted on the cab roof, and protruding beyond it, to support the pantographs.

Below: Industrial frequency alternating current electrification became the standard as a result of the success of Class "12000".

Above: The lightness of the overhead wire system required for high-voltage electrification is clearly shown in this picture.

Bogies of the B-B locomotives were derived from those of the experimental high-speed B-B machines, Nos. 9003-4, with the axles geared together, but as the new locomotives were intended for lower speeds than Nos. 9003-4, the bogie was shortened and the suspension simplified. For the Thionville line it was sufficient for one of the four classes to be capable of express passenger work, so the "12000s" were geared for 75mph (120km/h), the "13000s" for 65mph (105km/h) and the two Co-Co types for 37mph (60km/h).

The first of the "12000" class, No. 12001, was delivered in July 1954 and was put to work immediately on passenger and freight trains ranging from 500t to 1,300t. Control of voltage to the motors was by a tap changer on the high-tension side of the transformer, as is common in ac practice. On test No.12006 achieved some remarkable results. It started a train of 2,424t on a gradient of 1-in-100 (1 per cent), with a maximum tractive effort of 38t, or 47 per cent of the adhesive weight. At 8.5km/h the tractive effort was still 33.7t. These were outstanding figures, and the ability of the locomotive to sustain this high tractive effort, just on the point of slipping, but without actually "losing its feet", was considered to be a notable achievement of the ignitron control in conjunction with the gearing together of the two axles on each bogie.

The other classes performed well, but not so well as the "12000s", and furthermore the "12000s" proved to be the most reliable. The other classes were not extended beyond the initial orders, but a total of 148 of Class "12000" were eventually built. The success of the Thionville-Valenciennes scheme led to a major policy decision – that future electrification, except for certain extensions of existing dc routes, would be on ac at 25,000V 50Hz. The first scheme to be affected by this decision was the main line of the former Nord Railway, and this scheme met the Thionville route at its northern extremity. The last of the "12000" class were ordered as part of the Nord scheme, and the last examples were withdrawn from the same area at the end of 1999.

Before construction of the class was complete, there was a major development in electrical equipment with introduction of the silicon diode rectifier. This was a simpler, more compact and more robust piece of equipment than the ignitron, and well suited to the rough life of equipment on a locomotive. The last 15 of the "12000s" were built with silicon rectifiers, and others have been converted over the years. As the most successful and the most numerous of the four types of locomotive for the Thionville electrification programme, these locomotives still dominate traffic on that route.

Experience with these four classes settled finally the type of traction equipment to be used on future ac lines. Once again, the direct 50Hz motors proved unsatisfactory, whilst the simplicity of the silicon rectifier ruled out decisively any system with rotating machinery.

Class 59 4-8-2+2-8-4

Origin: Kenya/UK: East African Railways (EAR), 1955. **Type:** Steam locomotive for heavy freight haulage. **Gauge:** 3ft 3³/₈in (1,000mm). **Propulsion:** Coal fire with a grate area of 72sq ft (6.7m²) generating steam at 225psi (15.8kg/cm²) in a fire-tube boiler, and supplying it via a superheater to two pairs of 20¹/₂ x 28in (521 x 711mm) cylinders, each pair driving the main wheels of its respective unit direct by means of connecting and coupling rods. **Weight:** 357,000lb (164t) adhesive, 564,000lb (256t) total. **Axleload:** 47,000lb (21t). **Overall length:** 104ft 1¹/₂in (31,737mm). **Tractive effort:** 83,350lb (38,034kg). **Max speed:** 45mph (72km/h).

In discussing locomotive performance, British inclines like Shap and Beattock are often spoken of with awe. Shap has 20 miles (32km) of 1-in-75 (1.3 percent), but what would one say about a climb of 350 miles (565km) with a ruling grade of 1-in-65 (1.5 per cent)? Such is the ascent from Mombasa to Nairobi, up which every night the legendary "Uganda Mail" made its way.

Construction of the metre-gauge Uganda Railway, begun in 1892, was a strangely reluctant piece of empire building, violently opposed at home, yet successful. One of its objectives was the suppression of the slave trade, and that was quickly achieved. The second objective was to facilitate trade, and that also was successful to a point where the railway was always struggling to move the traffic offering. By 1926 a fleet of 4-8-0s was overwhelmed by the tonnage, and the Kenya & Uganda Railway (as it then was) went to Beyer Peacock of Manchester for 4-8-2+2-8-4 Beyer-Garratts, with as many mechanical parts as possible standard with the 4-8-0s. It was the answer to mass movement on 50lb/yd (24kg/m) rail.

As the years went by, other Garratt classes followed and the K&UR became East African Railways. In 1954, with the biggest backlog of tonnage ever faced waiting movement, the administration ordered 34 of the greatest Garratt design ever built. Whilst their main role was hauling freight, these giant "59" class locomotives were regarded as sufficiently passenger train oriented to be given the names of East African mountains. Also, of course, they bore the attractive maroon livery of the system.

By British standards their statistics are very impressive – over double the tractive effort of any locomotive ever employed in passenger service back home, coupled with a grate area nearly 50 per cent larger. Oil-firing was used, but provision was made for a mechanical stoker if coal burning ever became economic in East African circumstances. There was also provision for easy conversion from metre gauge to the African standard 3ft 6in (1,067mm) gauge, as well as for fitting vacuum brake equipment, should the class ever be required to operate outside air-brake territory.

All the latest and best Beyer-Garratt features were applied, such as the self-adjusting main pivots, the streamlined ends to the tanks, and those long handsome connecting rods driving on the third coupled axle. Four sets of Walschaert's valve gear were worked by Beyer's patent Hadfield steam reverser with hydraulic locking mechanism. The virtues of the short fat

Above: Beyer-Garratt No. 5934 *Nenengai Crater* stands outside Nairobi Works in 1977 after the last steam overhaul done there.

Garratt boiler, with clear space beneath the firebox, made 14 or 15 hours continuous hard steaming no problem. Later, Giesl ejectors were fitted to the class, with results that were controversial operationally, and quite unambiguously awful aesthetically.

One feature which did not work out was the tapered axleloadings, which gave successive axleloads in tons when running forward of 15.4, 15.4, 19.0, 20.9, 20.8, 18.8, 15.3; 15.5, 19.0, 21.0, 21.0, 19.0, 15.3, 15.3. The idea was that the gradual rise in axleload should permit operation on 80lb/yd (38.6kg/m) rail north and west of Nairobi, in addition to the 95lb/yd (45.7kg/m) rail by then general between Nairobi and the coast. The results of fresh motive power were very impressive, the backlog of traffic was quickly cleared and the new engines soon found themselves the largest and most powerful steam locomotives in the world. That they remained that way for 25 years was due to the economical use of well-maintained steam power long preventing any case being made out for a change to diesel traction.

Even so the diesel did win in the end, displacing the "59s" from the mail trains quite early on and from the freights gradually between 1973 and 1980. In addition a proposed "61" class 4-8-4+4-8-4 with 27-ton axleloading, 115,000lb (52,476kg) tractive effort and 105sq ft (9.8m²) fire grate was shelved.

Below: Oil-fired Beyer-Garratt Class "59" 4-8-2+2-8-4 *Mount Kilimanjaro* depicted in former EAR's superb crimson-lake livery.

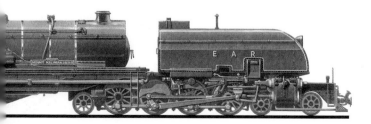

RM Class 4-6-2

Origin: China: Railways of the People's Republic of China (CR), 1958. **Type:** Express passenger steam locomotive. **Gauge:** 4ft 8¹/₂in (1,435mm). **Propulsion:** Coal fire with a grate area of 62sq ft (5.75m²) generating steam at 213psi (15kg/cm²) in a fire-tube boiler, and supplying it via a superheater to two 22¹/₂ x 26in (570 x 660m) cylinders, driving the main wheels direct by means of connecting and coupling rods. **Weight:** 137,750lb (62.5t) adhesive, 383,600lb (174t) total. **Axleload:** 46,284lb (21t). **Overall length:** 73ft 5¹/₂in (22,390mm). **Tractive effort:** 34,597lb (15,698kg). **Max speed:** 69mph (110km/h).

This unusual but neat-looking 4-6-2 is thought to be the final design of steam express passenger locomotive in the world, and the country which built it was the last in the world to have steam locomotives in production. Those built latterlyare basically freight locomotives, but like the "QJs" they are used for express passenger trains on certain mountain lines in the People's Republic.

The "RM" – "Ren Ming" or "People" class – 4-6-2s are descended from some passenger locomotives supplied by the Japanese to the railways of their puppet kingdom of Manchukuo, otherwise Manchuria. The older engines in pre-liberation days were known as Class "PF-1" ("PF" stood for "Pacific") but afterwards they became re-designated "SL" standing for "Sheng-Li" or "Victory". Locomotive construction to Chinese design did not begin for several years after the Communist victory of 1949, but by 1958 construction of the "RM" class was under way at the Szufang (Tsingtao) Works. It was an enlarged version of the "SL" class, capable of a power

Above: The world's final express passenger steam locomotive design, an "RM" or "People" class 4-6-2 near Jinan, China in 1980.

Below, left: A fine plume of steam is thrown up by "People" class 4-6-2 No. RM1019 as she heads north from Harbin, Manchuria, in 1980.

output 12½ per cent greater.

The main difference between the "RM" and "SL" class – and indeed between the "RM" class and virtually all other steam locomotives outside the USSR – was in the position of the main steam-pipe. This normally ran forward from the dome inside the boiler, but in these engines there was room for it to be situated much more accessibly in well-insulated trunking above the boiler. An interesting detail shared with other Chinese steam power, is the provision of an air horn, in addition to a normal deep-sounding steam chime whistle. In other ways, though, these fine engines followed what had been for many years the final form of the steam locomotive. Thus we find two cylinders only, using outside-admission piston-valves driven by Walschaert's valve gear, coupled with a wide firebox boiler with no frills except a big superheater and a mechanical stoker. Apart from this last feature British readers could reasonably regard the "RM" as what a Class "7" 'Britannia' 4-6-2 might have been if the designers had had similar axleload limitations, but another 3ft (914mm) of vertical height with which to play.

Visitors to China report that these engines can frequently be encountered travelling at speeds around 65mph (105km/h) on level routes hauling 600 ton passenger trains. There is reason to suppose that about 250 were built during the years 1958 to 1964 and that the numbers run from RM 1001 to RM 1250. Wide variations in the insignia and slogans which decorate present day Chinese steam locomotives introduce some variety into the plain (but always clean) black finish used. An "RM" class, specially painted in green, was used to haul the inaugural train over the great new bridge across the Yangtse River at Nanking.

Class 44 "Peak" 1-C₀-C₀-1

Origin: Great Britain: British Railways (BR), 1959. **Type:** Diesel-electric express passenger locomotive. **Gauge:** 4ft 8½in (1,435mm). **Propulsion:** 2,300hp (1,715kW) Sulzer Type 12LDA28 twin-bank turbocharged diesel engine and generator supplying current to six nose-suspended traction motors geared to the axles with resilient gearwheels. **Weight:** 255,360lb (116t) adhesive, 309,120lb (140t) total. **Axleload:** 42,560lb (19.5t). **Overall length:** 67ft 11in (20,701mm). **Tractive effort:** 70,000lb (311kN). **Max speed:** 90mph (144km/h).

The famous "Peaks" when new were the highest-powered diesel-electric locomotives supplied to British Railways. They were the first of a huge and unprecedented order for 147 express passenger locomotives (later increased to 193) with Sulzer twin-bank engines (with two parallel crank shafts in the same crankcase). Most of the latter were made under licence by Vickers Armstrong of Barrow-in-Furness, England. After the first 10 engines rated 200hp (150kW) higher were provided.

Running gear was similar to that of the Class "40" locomotives introduced in 1958. This, together with the bodywork, was built at BR's Derby and Crewe works where the locomotives were erected. Electrica

Above: British Railways' Class "46" Co-Co No. 46042 heads south from Newcastle-upon-Tyne with a relief express to London in 1978.

equipment for the first 137 engines came from Crompton Parkinson (CP) and for the remainder from Brush Engineering.

Originally the class was numbered D1 to D193, in the prime position in BR's diesel list. Later, the 10 original 2,300hp Sulzer/CP locomotives became Class "44", the 2,500hp Sulzer/CP batch Class "45" and the 2,500hp Sulzer/Brush batch Class "46". All were provided with such usual equipment as an automatic train-heating steam boiler, a vacuum exhauster for train brakes, straight air brakes for the locomotives, multiple unit control gear and a toilet. Later the locomotives were fitted for working air-braked trains and (in some cases) heating electrically-heated carriages. The first 10 were named after mountain peaks in Britain; a few others received names of regiments and other military formations.

Although there was 15 per cent more power available than on the Class "40s", the "Peaks" also had very little margin in hand when working to the best steam schedules. But even though one may criticise the design as being unenterprising, with little to offer over and above steam traction, it must be said that this slow, solid approach paid off in longevity. Finally withdrawn in the 1980s, they outlasted many of their more enterprising successors.

Left: Class "46" No. 46004 crosses the River Tyne by the King Edward VII Bridge in 1977, with a Newcastle to Liverpool express.

Below: One of the original "Peak" (later"45") class 1-Co-Co-1 diesel-electric locomotives depicted in original colour and style.

FL9 B₀-B₀-A1A

Origin: United States: New York, New Haven & Hartford RR (New Haven) 1956. **Type:** Electro-diesel passenger locomotive. **Gauge:** 4ft 8¹/₂in (1,435mm). **Propulsion:** General Motors 1,750hp (1,350kW) Type 567C V-16 two-stroke diesel engine and generator – or alternatively outside third-rail feeding current to four nose-suspended traction motors geared to both axles of the leading bogie and the outer axles of the trailing one. **Weight:** 231,937lb (105.2t) adhesive, 286,614lb (130t) total. **Axleload:** 57,984lb (26.3t). **Overall length:** 59ft 0in (17,983mm). **Tractive effort:** 58,000lb (258kN). **Max speed:** 70mph (112km/h).

These unusual and interesting machines, like a number of others, were the results of that famous ordinance of the City of New York prohibiting the use therein of locomotives which emitted fumes. It occurred like this: the New Haven railroad was is the 1950s considering abandonment of its path-finding single-phase electrification, which dated from as early as 1905, and changing over to diesel traction. The only problem was how to run into New York.

New Haven trains used both the Grand Central terminal (of the New York Central RR) and the Pennsylvania Station. Both routes were equipped with conductor rails (of different patterns) supplying low-voltage direct current. This corresponded closely to the current produced in the generator of a diesel-electric locomotive and it was suggested that a standard General Motors "FP9" passenger cab unit could be modified easily to work as an electric locomotive when required. The ac electrification could then be dismantled, yet trains could continue to run without breaking the law. In fact axleload restrictions led to one quite substantial change – substitution of a three-axle trailing bogie for the standard two-axle one; hence a unique wheel arrangement. The end product was designated "FL9" and 60 were supplied between 1956 and 1960. The most obvious evidence of their unique arrangement was the two-position retractable collecting shoes mounted on the bogies to cater for New York Central's bottom-contact conductor rail and Long Island RR's top-contact one. Otherwise the presence of additional low-voltage control gear inside the body was the principal technical difference between an "FP9" and an "FL9" locomotive.

In the event, the New Haven changed its mind over dispensing with the electrification, but the "FL9"s still found employment, surviving long enough to be taken over by the National Railroad Passenger Corporation (Amtrak) in the 1970s. Many locos of what is now a veteran class survive, a

Above: One of the New Haven's unique B-A1A electro-diesel locomotives of Class "FL9", still giving good service after more than 30 years hard work and now running under the flag of Amtrak.

few still with Amtrak, 27 on the Metro-North commuter railroad (including some rebuilt in the early-1990s), and three on the Long Island Rail Road.

While they exist, the "FL9"s represent a spark of originality in a country whose locomotives were and are much of a muchness (apart from their livery) from Oregon to Florida or Arizona to Maine.

Below: New York, New Haven & Hartford Railroad electro-diesel locomotive. As well as running as a normal diesel-electric, the "FL9"s could run on current drawn from two types of third rail.

TEP-60 C$_o$-C$_o$

Origin: Russia: Soviet Railways (SZD), 1960. **Type:** Diesel-electric express passenger locomotive. **Gauge:** 5ft 0in (1,524mm). **Propulsion:** Type D45A 3,000hp (2,240kW) turbocharged 16-cylinder two-stroke diesel engine and generator supplying current to six spring-borne 416hp (310kW) traction motors geared to the axles via flexible drives of the Alsthom floating-ring type. **Weight:** 284,316lb (129t). **Axleload:** 47,390lb (21.5t). **Overall length** 63ft 2in (19,250mm). **Tractive effort:** 55,750lb (248kN). **Max speed** 100mph (160km/h).

These powerful single-unit machines form one of the Soviet Union's principal diesel-electric passenger locomotive classes, although they have been displaced from the very top assignments by the 4,000hp "TEP-70" class. Production of the "TEP-60" continued for at least 15 years, though the total number built has not been revealed. For many years it has been the only type of Soviet diesel locomotive passed for running at speeds above 140km/h (87mph), although neither the need nor the opportunity for such fast running really exists as yet on the SZD network.

Russian experience with diesel locomotives was minimal (and, as far as it went, totally unsatisfactory) before World War II. Therefore in 1945 the mechanical engineers began with a clean sheet and the early diesels were

based very sensibly on US practice. By 1960, sufficient confidence had been attained so that original ideas could be incorporated.

A serious weakness in early adaptations of freight locomotives for passenger work was bad tracking of the bogies. Having regard to SZD aspirations towards faster passenger trains, some electric locomotives had been ordered from Alsthom of France, maker of the bogies for world rail speed record-breaker, French National Railways' Co-Co No. 7107.

Alsthom features were used in the bogies for the "TEP-60", in particular the flexible drive which enabled the traction motors to be spring-borne, and the prototype reached 118mph (189km/h) on test. This was claimed at the time to be a world record for a diesel locomotive and certainly vindicated the restrained wisdom of those responsible for the design. Other features of note in these locomotives included electric braking and the ability to cope with temperatures both hot and cold considerably more extreme than are found in conjunction on other railways.

Below: Co-Co diesel-electric locomotives of Soviet Railways' Class "TEP-60", depicted here in "ex-works" condition; these were the country's principal motive power for passenger expresses in the 1970s.

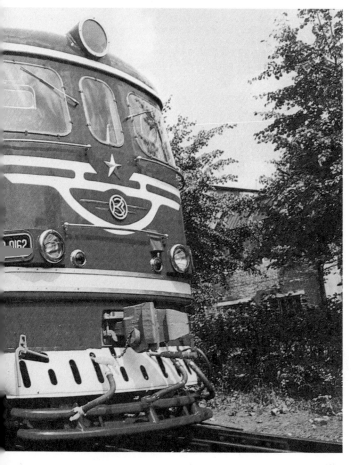

Class 060DA C$_o$-C$_o$

Origin: Romania: Romanian State Railways (CFR), 1960. **Type:** Mixed-traffic diesel electric locomotive. **Gauge:** 4ft 8^1/$_2$in (1,435mm). **Propulsion:** Sulzer Type 12LDA28 2,300hp (1,690kW) turbocharged twin-bank 12-cylinder diesel engine and generator supplying direct current to six traction motors driving the axles via resilient gearwheels. **Weight:** 257,870 (117t). **Axleload:** 42,980lb (19.5t). **Overall length:** 55ft 9in (17,000mm). **Tractive effort** 64,125lb (285kN). **Max speed:** 62mph (l00km/h).

The bulk of the diesel-electric locomotive fleet used by Romanian State Railways is based on six prototypes constructed in Switzerland during 1959. Mechanical parts were built by the Swiss Locomotive Works, the electrical equipment by Brown Boveri, and the diesel engines supplied by Sulzer. There are of the "twin bank" configuration with two parallel rows of cylinders, each driving a separate crankshaft.

The elegant bodywork is typical of Swiss locomotives and is of welded construction. No train heating equipment is included; separate heating vans are used when required.

A 550t freight train can be started by one of these locomotives on the ruling grade (1-in-40 – 2.5 per cent) of the Brasov to Bucharest main line and accelerated up to 9mph (14km/h). For heavier loads, the locomotives can be run in multiple. There is no rheostatic or regenerative braking, but the usual straight and automatic air brakes are provided. Automatic detection and correction of wheelslip is a help on these severe grades.

Production of these locomotives continued in Romania for some time and they were also offered for export. More than 300 went to China in the 1970s and 1980s as Class "ND2". Because of the severe economic situation that followed the 1989 revolution, little new motive power wa

Right and below: Three views of Romanian State Railways' Class "060DA" diesel-electric Co-Co locomotives. These multi-purpose machines are basically of Swiss origin with Sulzer twin-bank diesel engines. They have the elegantly curved bodywork and coil-spring bogies typical of that country's locomotive products. The class was produced over a long period and its members are used extensively on passenger and freight train workings all over the country. The bright grey and blue livery was an innovation – a drab green more typical of European national railway systems was the rule in Romania for many years.

purchased by CFR during the 1990s. So the ageing fleet of "060DA"s soldiers on, now divided amongst the various operating companies into which CFR was split in 1999.

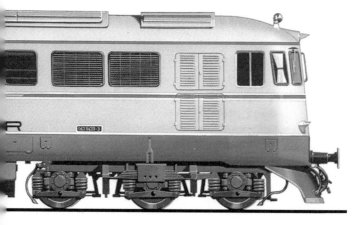

Class Dm3 1-D+D+D-1

Origin: Sweden: Swedish State Railways (SJ)1960. **Type:** Electric locomotive for heavy mineral traffic. **Gauge:** 4ft 8^1/$_2$in (1,435mm). **Propulsion:** Single-phase low-frequency current at 15,000V 16^2/$_3$Hz fed via overhead catenary and step-down transformer to six 1,609hp (1,200kW) motors, driving the wheels by gearing, jackshaft and connecting rods. **Weight:** 528,960lb (240t) adhesive, 595,080lb (270t) total. **Axleload:** 44,080lb (20t). **Overall length:** 115ft 8in (35,250mm). **Tractive effort:** 210,000lb (932kN). **Max speed:** 47mph (75km/h).

To exploit the vast deposits of iron ore found in the interior of northern Sweden, a railway was needed. It was comparatively easy work to build from the Baltic port of Lulea to the mining area around Kiruna, but the Baltic at this latitude, near to the Arctic circle, freezes over in the winter. Accordingly, the railway was continued further north still as well as westwards, crossing not only the Ofoten mountains but the Arctic circle itself, and what is now the Norwegian frontier, to reach the sheltered port of Narvik, kept free of ice year-round by the friendly Gulf Stream. The iron ore railway from Lulea to Narvik, which began operations in 1883, extends for a total of 295 miles (473km).

Steam operation was fairly traumatic, especially in winter, because of the heavy loads, the very low temperatures and the mountain gradients, not to speak of continuous darkness. Apart from the mosquitos, in summer things were more pleasant – for example, the lineside tourist hotel at Abisko (with no access except by train!) boasts a north-facing sun verandah to catch the midnight sun!

It is not surprising then that the Lappland iron ore railway was the first important line in Scandinavia to be electrified. Electric working began in 1915 and conversion was completed throughout in 1923. The low frequency single-phase system was adopted, by then well-proven in Switzerland and elsewhere.

The quality of the iron ore from Kiruna, together with the ease with which it can be won – plus, it must be said, the long-standing neutrality of Sweden, which means that customers are never refused on political grounds – always kept demand high and, in the long term, ever-rising. The problem for the railways, then, has in most years been concerned with the ability to handle the traffic offering. So far, doubling the line has been avoided by increasing the weight of the trains, and for many years they were the heaviest in Europe. Some 23 million tonnes was moved in 1996.

It is typical of the Swedish way of railroading that the motive power there today is a modest adaption of the early standard and essentially simple Class "D" locomotive. The result is this Class "Dm" locomotive of 9,650hp (7,200kW), designed to haul the now legendary ore trains. Loads of up to 5,200t are taken up 1-in-100 (1 per cent) gradients, as well as started in polar temperatures – thereby explaining the need for a tractive effort exceeding 200,000lb (900kN).

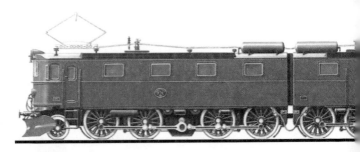

Above: A Class "Dm3" 1-D+D+D-1 electric loco hauls a massive train of iron ore through the arctic forests of Swedish Lapland.

Below: The Swedish rod-drive triple-unit Class "Dm3" electric locomotives can produce more than 200,000lb of tractive effort.

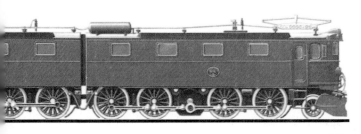

One might be puzzled why Swedish State Railways designated this mighty hauler as a sub-class (the "m" in Dm stands for *malm* or iron) of their modest and ubiquitous Class "D" 1-C-1 standard electric locomotive. The reason was that the original Class "Dm" could be said to be two "Ds" with an additional coupled axle substituted for one pony truck on each unit, which also had a cab at only one end. Two units coupled permanently back-to-back originally formed a Class "Dm" locomotive and these were introduced in the late 1940s. Eventually there were 19 twin locomotives, plus four owned by Norwegian State Railways (the NSB class is "el 12"). Both the brown Swedish engines and the green Norwegian ones operated indiscriminately over the whole line, which in 1996 was transferred to a separate organisation owned jointly by the iron ore mining company LKAB and the Swedish and Norwegian state railways.

In 1960 still more power was required and three cab-less units (also without pantographs) were built and put in the middle of three existing pairs. By 1970 all the Swedish "Dm" pairs had been converted to triples. Each individual unit bears a separate number although units are not separated in normal operation. The huge tractive effort available caused problems with the traditional screw couplings and so Russian-pattern automatic knuckle couplers have been fitted.

As a rod-drive locomotive the "Dm9" was the last of its line. Since 1970 a need for additional power has been met, and history made to repeat itself, by modifying the current standard Swedish high-power Class "Rc4" express passenger locomotive. The alterations include lower gearing, very sophisticated wheelslip control and addition of 10t of ballast, all in aid of improving tractive effort, while cabs are insulated against arctic temperatures.

Below: Swedish State Railways' Class"Dm" 1-D+D+D-1 electric locomotive as built in the 1960s for working iron ore traffic.

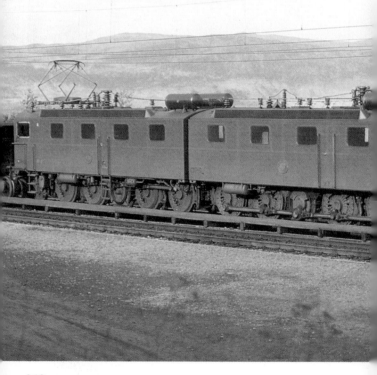

Above: These mighty haulers bring iron ore trains from Kiruna in northern Sweden to the ice-free port of Narvik.

U25B B₀-B₀

Origin: United States: General Electric Company (GE), 1960. **Type:** Diesel-electric road switcher locomotive. **Gauge:** 4ft 8$\frac{1}{2}$in (1,435mm). **Propulsion:** One GE FDL16 2,500hp (1,870kW) four-stroke 16-cylinder Vee engine and generator supplying four nose-suspended traction motors geared to the axles. **Weight:** 260,000lb (118.0t). **Axleload:** 65,000lb (29.5t). **Overall length:** 60ft 2in (18,340mm). **Tractive effort:** 81,000lb (360kN) with 65mph gear ratio. **Max speed:** 65mph (105km/h), 75mph (121km/h), 80mph (129km/h) or 92mph (148km/h) according to gear ratio fitted.

If, in the 1920s, one had said to an American locomotive engineer: "The diesel-electric locomotive seems to have great potential; which locomotive manufacturer is capable of exploiting it?" he would almost certainly have said "General Electric", for that company was then building on 30 years' experience of electric traction of all sorts by turning out diesel switchers (shunters) incorporating various makes of engine. However, the prophet would have been wrong, for it was the massive resources of General Motors Corporation thrown into its Electro-Motive Division which sparked off, and largely fuelled, the steam-to-diesel revolution in the United States.

GE was thus destined to take a minor part in the overall process, but within the 25 per cent or so of the market which did not fall to EMD, it has always had a major share. When the American Locomotive Company (Alco) embarked seriously on production of road diesels, it made an agreement with GE to use only GE electrical equipment in its products, in return for which GE agreed not to compete with Alco. From 1940 to 1953 both companies benefited from this agreement; Alco profited from the expertise of the biggest firm in the electrical traction business, and GE acquired an easy market for products which it was well qualified and equipped to supply. A second manufacturer, Fairbanks Morse, likewise offered GE equipment in its models.

By the early-1950s, total dieselisation of US railroads was certain, and although Alco was well established in the market, its sales ran a poor second to EMD and were not improving. GE then took the plunge; it quietly terminated its agreement with Alco and embarked on development of its own range of large diesels. Although most of its previous diesels had been small switchers. it had in fact built a 2,000hp (1,490kW) Sulzer-engined unit in 1936, which for 10 years was North America's most powerful single-engined diesel locomotive, and in the post-war years the company had built up an export market in road locomotives.

Above: The Rock Island Railroad is now defunct, but in 1965 one of its "U25C" diesel-electrics headed a consist at Limon, Colorado.

The essential requirement for GE to enter the home road-diesel market was a large engine. At this time its switchers were fitted with Cooper Bessemer 6-cylinder in-line and 8-cylinder Vee engines, so the company acquired the rights to develop this engine. Two versions were made, the 8-cylinder developing 1,200hp (895kW) and the 12-cylinder developing 1,800hp (1,340kW).

First outward sign of GE's new venture was a four-unit locomotive, with "cab" or totally-enclosed bodies, two units fitted with the V8 engines and two with the V12. These units were tested on the Erie Railroad from 1954 to 1959, and based on their successful performance the company launched a new series of export models in 1956, designated the "Universal" series. With the experience gained from V8 and V12 engines, GE now embarked

Below: A four-axle GE "U-boat" road-switcher depicted in the striking and unusual grey livery of the Louisville & Nashville RR.

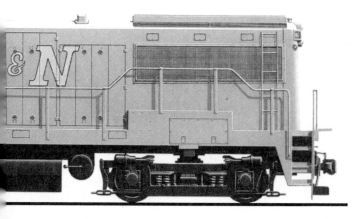

on a major step forward, a 16-cylinder version developing 2,400hp (1,790kW). Two of these engines were installed in Bo-Bo hood units, and were tested on the Erie, covering 100,000 miles (160,000km) in 11 months. Although masquerading under the designation "XR24", denoting 2,400hp export test units, these were in fact destined to be the demonstrators of a new model for the home market.

In 1960, seven years after ending its partnership with Alco, GE announced a new model, the 2,500hp (1,870kW) "Universal" Bo-Bo, denoted "U25B". Its most obvious sales point was that it had the highest horsepower of any locomotive on the US market, by 100hp (75kW); but to have any chance of breaking into the EMD/Alco markets, it had to have many attractions less obvious, but equally important to customers.

In preparing the design, GE had asked the motive power chiefs of 33 railroads what they liked and disliked in the diesels which they already operated. The costs of operating these units were also analysed, and it was found that repairs accounted for 28.7 per cent of total diesel operating costs. The designers' aim was therefore to improve performance, but at the same time to simplify equipment to make it more reliable and maintenance-free. A major cause of complaint was the air system, both for supplying the engine and for cooling. The incoming air was filtered, and in most contemporary designs the filters needed cleaning at about 2,500 miles (4,000km). Alco designed a self-cleaning mechanical filter.

In contrast to these changes, much of the electrical equipment was well tried, including the traction motors, and roads which operated Alco locomotives would already have many of the parts in stock. However, there was an electrical innovation – use of modular electronic equipment. Launching of the new model coincided with unfavourable economic conditions on the railroads, and more than a year passed before any orders came in. The first came from Union Pacific, which was always on the lookout for higher-powered locomotives, and other roads which had a specific need for higher power followed. Over a period of six years a total of 478 "U25Bs" were sold, not a great number by EMD standards, but sufficient for GE to displace Alco from second place in the US diesel sales league.

It was already established practice for a US road switcher to be offered both as a four-axle and as a six-axle unit, the latter appealed to railroads which needed more adhesive weight on a slightly lower axleload. The "U25C" therefore appeared in 1963, and added a further 113 units to GE sales. With the spread of the "U" designation, someone referred to "U-boats" and the nickname caught on.

The effect of GE competition on other manufacturers was to spur them to modify their own models. Competition was keen, particularly horse power competition. GE's 16-cylinder engine and its generator were rated

Below: A pair of GE "U25C" Co-Co units belonging to the Lake Superior & Ishpeming RR leased by the Detroit, Toledo & Ironton RR.

Above: A GE "U25B" Bo-Bo diesel-electric locomotive in the colours of the Maine Central RR at Waterville, Maine, in 1984.

modestly, so that uprating would be possible without major alterations (and more spare parts to stock!), and so in 1966 came the 2,800hp (2,090kW) engine, in the "U28B" and "U28C" models.

UP bought 16 "U25Bs", but then ordered a special model to suit the addiction of its motive power chief, D. S. Neuhart, to very powerful locomotives. Already his road was operating 8,500hp (6,340kW) GE gas turbine locomotives, and the builder now produced a 5,000hp (3,730kW) twin-engined version of the "U25B" mounted on four bogies and weighing 247t; these were the "U50Bs". Later came a simplified Co-Co version of the same power. Neither of these types was entirely successful, and with the coming of standard models of 3,000hp (2,240kW) UP was content to fall into line with other railroads and buy off-the-shelf.

The next landmark in diesel development in the US was the 3,000hp engine, produced by EMD, Alco and GE in 1965-66. The GE models, "U30B" and "U30C", appeared late in 1966, and were followed less than a year later by 3,300hp (2,460kW) versions. In 1969 yet another increase, to 3,600hp (2,690kW), was achieved. The GE decision to use a moderately-rated engine in the first "U-boats" paid good dividends at this time, for whereas GE attained these increases in power by development of the 16-cylinder engine, EMD had to move to 20 cylinders. However, the railroads soon lost their enthusiasm for engines above 3,000hp when they discovered the extra maintenance costs incurred.

In 1976 a further revision of the GE range, known as the "7-series" was accompanied by a change in designation, the 3,000hp Co-Co becoming the C30-7". These models established GE firmly in the market, to the extent that in 1983, a year of acute depression for US locomotive builders, GE built 324 units compared with EMD's 122.

By this time the railroads were again interested in high-powered locomotives, whilst increasing fuel prices made fuel economy a strong selling point. In the GE "8-series", introduced in 1983, 3,600hp (2,685kW) 6-cylinder engines were offered, and in 1984 a 3,900hp (2,910kW) "B39-8" was supplied to Santa Fe, the most powerful US four-axle diesel so far. The 12-cylinder engine was also developed to 3,150hp (2,350kW). At the same time, GE exploited the greater inherent efficiency of its four-stroke engines compared with EMD's two-stroke.

Another notable GE development was an order in 1984 for 220 locomotives for China, at the time the biggest order ever placed for US diesels, and the first for China. This was followed by a further 200 ordered in 1985.

Class 55 Deltic C_o-C_o

Origin: Great Britain: British Railways (BR)1961. **Type:** High-speed express passenger diesel-electric locomotive. **Gauge:** 4ft 8$\frac{1}{2}$in (1,435mm). **Propulsion:** Two Napier Type 18-25 18-cylinder 1,750hp (1,305kW) "Deltic" two stroke diesel engines and generators connected in series, feeding current to six nose-suspended traction motors geared to the axles of the two bogies. **Weight:** 222,600lb (101t). **Axleload:** 36,920lb (16.25t). **Overall length:** 69ft 6in (21,180mm). **Tractive effort:** 50,000lb (222kN). **Max speed:** 100mph (160km/h).

The sad thing about diesel locomotives is that, unlike steam, all the fascinating mechanism is hidden deep within. That is why it is exceptional for what they are like inside to be reflected in what they are called. But on the "Deltics" the mechanism was so very fascinating that its name spilled out into the lay world. In Greek, the capital letter "D" for delta is a triangle which, when inverted, exactly describes the layout of some diesel engines of remarkably high power for their weight and size. They were developed by English Electric's subsidiary Napier soon after World War II for fast motor gun-boats for the Royal Navy. They were to replace engines fuelled by petrol, which presented a serious fire hazard, in action and otherwise.

The advantages of an "opposed piston" engine are well known. Instead

Below: The "Deltic" Co-Co diesel-electric locomotive shown as built, when it was the world's most powerful single-unit diesel.

Above: A King's Cross to Edinburgh express passes Ouston Junction, County Durham, during 1978, hauled by "Deltic" Co-Co No. 55021.

Left: An East Coast express train rolls southward near Berwick-on-Tweed, hauled by a "Deltic" Co-Co diesel-electric.

of having one piston per cylinder, with a massive cylinder head to take the thrust, there are two pushing against one another. It is not quite two for the price of one, but part way to it. The only problem is that complications arise in making the two opposed thrusts turn a single shaft. In the "Deltic" engine, three banks of double cylinders, each with a pair of opposed pistons and arranged as three sides of a triangle, are connected to a crankshaft at each apex. Each crankshaft is then geared to the central drive shaft of the engine. The result was specific weight of only 6.2lb/hp (3.8kg/kW), some $2^{1}/_{2}$ times better than contemporary medium-speed conventional diesel engines normally used for traction. There was also perfect balance of the forces generated and of the reciprocating parts.

English Electric's Traction Division was a main supplier of locomotives to British Railways, and EE's chairman Lord Nelson realised that by putting this Napier engine on to an English Electric chassis, he had the means to double the power of a typical diesel-electric locomotive. During 1955, in

Above: Restored to its earlier green livery, No D9000 "Royal Scots Grey" was the first "Deltic" to return to main line operation, on regular summer weekend service with Virgin. *(Ken Harris)*

the teeth of opposition from the Traction Division, and at EE's own expense, a prototype was put in hand. During several years' testing the locomotive did everything that might be expected of a machine that had 3,300hp (2,462kW) available compared with the 2,000hp or so of its competitors. Moreover, it proved unexpectedly reliable.

Under BR's modernisation plan, electrification was envisaged from

London to the north of England both from Euston and from King's Cross. In the event, the former scheme was the only one put in hand at the time and the Eastern/North Eastern/Scottish Region authorities accordingly sought a stop-gap alternative which would give timings similar to those achieved with electric traction for minimal expenditure. The result was an order in 1959 for 22 of these superb locomotives, a class destined to become a legend in their own lifetime. When built they were by a considerable margin the most powerful single-unit diesel locomotives in the world.

Two separate "Deltic" engine-and-generator sets were installed,

Above: A "Deltic" diesel-electric Co-Co No. 55010 _King's Own Scottish Borderer_ under the wires at King's Cross diesel depot.

normally connected in series, but in the event of failure the crippled engine could be switched out and the locomotive could continue to pull its full load using the other one, but at reduced speed.

Auxiliary equipment on the "Deltics" included an automatic oil-fired steam generator for heating trains. The water tanks for this equipment were originally arranged so they could be filled from steam-age water cranes and also – amazingly – at speed from water troughs by means of a scoop! Later, windings were added to the generators to provide for electric heating of the train, although this abstracted several hundred horsepower from the output available for traction. Both compressors and vacuum exhauster sets for brake power were provided, as well as cooking facilities and a toilet.

The bogies were standard with the contemporary English Electric 1,750hp Type "3" locomotives (now Class "37") and automatic detection and correction of wheelslip was provided. The controls were also generally similar to other English Electric locomotives, although drivers could not run them exactly the same as other locomotives, because the low angular inertia of a "Deltic" engine precluded heavy-handed throttle movements which were liable to lead to automatic shutdown. Even so, the possibility of climbing the 1-in-200 (0.5 per cent) gradient to Stoke Summit, north of Peterborough, at a minimum speed of 90mph (144km/h) with a heavy East Coast express was something that earned the total respect of footplatemen. In the old LNER tradition, the "Deltics" were all named - some after race horses that had won their races and others after English and Scottish regiments. Originally the class was numbered D9000 to D9021; later Nos. D9001 to 21 became Nos. 55001 to 21 and D9000 became No. 55022.

One of the crucial measures in the scheme to acquire the "Deltics" was that the deal should include maintenance at an inclusive price, with penalties to be incurred if, through faults arising, the locomotives were unable to perform an agreed mileage each year. The task of keeping the "Deltic" fleet in running order was simplified because the engines were maintained on a unit replacement basis. After a few anticipated problems in the first year or so, the "Deltics" settled down to running about 170,000 miles (273,500km) a year, or about 500 miles (800km) a day, with a very low failure rate.

Above: The prototype English Electric "Deltic" Co-Co diesel-electric on trials on the East Coast main line at Markham in 1959.

After some improvements to the route, including major track realignments, the "Deltic"-hauled "Flying Scotsman" ran (for example in 1973) from King's Cross to Newcastle, 271 miles (433km) in 3hr 37min and to Edinburgh, 395 miles (632km), in 5hr 30min, average speeds of 74.9 and 71.8mph (119.8 and 114.5km/h) respectively. Such timings as these were applied not just to one or two "flag" trains but to the service as a whole; they represented substantial gains – a 1¹/2 hour acceleration compared with 12 years before between London and Edinburgh, for instance.

Fifteen years and 50 million "Deltic" miles later, electrification seemed as far away as ever, and a further stage of development without it became desirable. In the event, a possible "Super-Deltic" based on two "Deltic" engines of increased power was discarded in favour of the self-propelled High-Speed Trains (qv), with more conventional Paxman engines. It might have been hoped that the existing "Deltics" could be moved on to rejuvenate operations on less important lines, where their low axleload would permit usage. In the end, though, because their engines were expensive to maintain, it was not possible to make a case for keeping them, based on the kind of rather uninspiring arithmetic BR's accountants used in such matters.

So on January 2, 1982, the last "Deltic"-hauled train ran into King's Cross, but the high-speed exploits of these machines continue still. Amazingly for such a small class, several have been preserved, and four of them regularly haul special trains on Britain's privatised railways. Indeed, No. 55022 (carrying its original number, D9000) spent most summer Saturdays of 1999 hauling Virgin's Birmingham-Ramsgate holiday train.

As a postscript, it is worth mentioning that the plans for electrification of the East Coast route were approved at last in 1984, and the work was completed in 1991. The irony is that whereas the "Deltics" brought East Coast performance well up to the standard normally expected of electric traction, the "IC225" electrics of the 1990s barely improve on the best timings achieved by the diesel-powered HSTs which continue to run over the route on through trains to destinations beyond the wires. Nevertheless, the "IC225"s achieved Britain's fastest runs in 1999 on the now privatised Great North Eastern Railway, with the 3hr 59min of the "Scottish Pullman" being the best time ever between London and Edinburgh.

Class 52 "Western" C-C

Origin: Great Britain: British Railways, Western Region (BR), 1962. **Type:** Diesel-hydraulic express passenger locomotive. **Gauge:** 4ft 8¹/₂in (1,435mm). **Propulsion:** Two 1,350hp (1,000kW) Bristol-Siddeley/Maybach 12-cylinder Vee-type MD655 "tunnel" engines each driving the three axles of one bogie via a Voith-North British three-stage hydraulic transmission, cardan shaft, intermediate gearbox, further cardan shafts and final-drive gearboxes. **Weight:** 242,440lb (110t). **Axleload:** 40,775lb (18.5t). **Overall length:** 68ft 0in (20,726mm). **Tractive effort:** 72,600lb (323kN). **Max speed:** 90mph (144km/h).

The episode of the "Western" class diesel-hydraulics was like a glorious but futile last cavalry charge on the part of some army facing inevitable defeat. Of all the companies absorbed into British Railways on January 1, 1948, the Great Western Railway found nationalisation much the hardest to bear. Its own apparently superior standards evolved over more than a century were largely replaced by those of inferior "foreign" (non-GWR) companies. For some time the regional management at Paddington had largely to content itself with words – the General Manager even issued an instruction to the effect that no locomotive of other than GWR design should be rostered for any train on which he was due to travel!

But after a decade had passed, action became possible. BR's 1950s Modernisation Programme gave Paddington a chance to do its own thing with locomotives which followed the hallowed Great Western tradition of being as different as possible from anyone else's.

At that time the choice of hydraulic transmission as an alternative to electric for high-power diesels was less radical than it is now. BR's central management had plumped (quite correctly, seen with hindsight) for electric transmission in most of the proposed diesel locomotives. But hydraulic transmission had some great attractions, and the GWR, alone amongst the old companies, had no experience with electric traction. Since West Germany was the country in which such motive power had developed furthest, German practice was the basis of what was done. In addition to hydraulic transmission, the German locomotives had high-speed lightweight diesel engines. They revolved at speeds twice those of diesel engines used in other BR locomotives and weighed less than half as much for the same power.

The first class of importance was the 2,000hp B-B "Warship" of 1958, designed to give similar performance to BR's 1-Co-Co-1 Class "40", but weighing 40 per cent less. Sixty-six "Warships" were built, but equality with the rest of BR was not enough. What was wanted was a machine that would run BR's other diesels into the ground.

No. D1000 *Western Enterprise* appeared in late-1961, soon to be

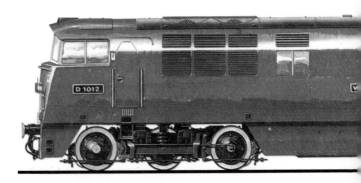

Above: A "Western" or Class "52" diesel-hydraulic C-C locomotive emerges from Harbury tunnel between Leamington and Banbury.

followed by 73 more "Western" sisters. The names chosen were mostly evocative and many, like the first, provocative to BR's headquarters at 222 Marylebone Road, London. For example, No. D1001 *Western Pathfinder*, D1019 *Western Challenger*, D1059 *Western Empire*. GWR tradition was also followed in the matter of spelling mistakes – No. D1029 *Western Legionnaire* was at first *Western Legionaire*.

Alas, the locomotives did not cover themselves with Western Glory (D1072). For one thing, the opposition did not allow their lead in power output to be held for long. In the following year came the Brush Class "47" Co-Co (described here), with a fraction more power than the ".Westerns", for only just over the some weight, and by 1967 the Class "50" diesel-electrics hired from English Electric also matched the dieselhydraulics for power. Moreover, even by 1963, central management had decided that

Below: "Western" class C-C diesel-hydraulic locomotive in the style originally adopted for these powerful units of motive power.

Above: "Westerns" still active in preservation include No D1010 "Western Campaigner", seen leaving Watchet station on the West Somerset Railway. *(Russell Ayre)*

diesel-hydraulics had no real advantage over diesel-electrics, of which it had a growing surplus. So some time before the high-speed HST125 trains took over most long-distance passenger services from Paddington in the late-1970s, the "Westerns" had been taken out of service. Withdrawal began with No. 1019 in mid-1973 and all had gone by early-1977. Several have survived in preservation. Of the rival diesel-electric classes – the "50"s were all gone by 1992, but many Class "47"s were still at work in 1999 though their numbers were likely to decline as deliveries continued of new Classes "66" and "67" to English Welsh & Scottish Railway. More will go when new trainsets start to take over Virgin's cross-country routes in 2001.

The "Westerns" had their own kind of good looks, the unusualness of their appearance being enhanced by inside bearings to the wheels. The Maybach engines were also unusual (but invisibly so) in that they were of the tunnel pattern in which the circular crank webs actually form the bearing journals of the crankshafts. Power was transmitted to the wheels via various hydraulic and mechanical transmission boxes connected by numerous cardan shafts. This mechanical complexity was a source of problems with obscure causes but unfortunate results – substitution of hydraulic fluid and mechanical components for electricity as a medium of transmission tended to lower reliability and efficiency rather than raise them as promised. Also, there were festoons of electrical circuitry serving the control systems and instrumentation, and these gave all the problems to be expected of electrics amongst the oil mist of a diesel locomotive interior.

The Western Region's mechanical department managed to solve the problems, being especially triumphant when the bad riding which had held down speeds was overcome by altering the bogies (with much simplification) to resemble in principle GWR standard ones dating from Victorian times. Such timings as a 3hr 30min schedule for the 225½ miles (363km) between Paddington and Plymouth then became possible, at last a significant improvement (of 30 minutes) over the best previously achieved with steam.

The reliability problem was eventually solved also by a long and painstaking process of diagnosis, trial and error, and finally by cure of many faults of detail in the design. Alas, by then a decision had already been taken to withdraw the diesel-hydraulic fleet from service prematurely and replace them by the Class "50" diesel-electric locomotives. It then was a case of heaping insult upon injury because (taking 1971 as an example) the "Westerns" were running 15,000 miles per failure while their diesel-electric replacements, the Class "50s", were only managing to achieve an appalling 9,000. At least British Rail gained some self-confidence in overcoming problems with a somewhat imperfect import.

Below: One of the Class "52" C-C diesel-hydraulic locomotives of British Railways Western Region brings an express train round a well-ballasted curve laid with steam-age chaired permanent way.

Class 73 B_o-B_o

Origin: Great Britain: British Railways (BR), 1967. **Type:** Electro-diesel mixed-traffic locomotive. **Gauge:** 4ft 8½in (1,435mm). **Propulsion:** Direct current at 675V fed via an outside third rail, or alternatively generated on the locomotive by an English Electric 600hp (448kW) Type 4 SRKT diesel engine, to four 395hp (295kW) nose-suspended traction motors. **Weight:** 168,000lb (76t). **Axleload:** 42,000lb (19t). **Overall length:** 53ft 8in (16,358mm) with buffers extended. **Tractive effort:** 42,000lb (187kN). **Max speed:** 90mph (145km/h).

One of the problems of an electrified railway is the need to provide for working over lines which, either permanently or temporarily, have no current supply. With third-rail systems this need is accentuated by the impossibility of providing conductor rails uninterruptedly; BR's Southern Region had solved the problem by electric locomotives which could store energy in fly-wheels to pass trains over short gaps.

As the SR's electrification became more widespread, the use of normal diesel locomotives to cover workings over shorter and shorter portions of a journey became less and less satisfactory. So a powerful electric locomotive was conceived which carried a modest (but standard) diesel generating plant for movements away from the conductor rail. The result was this versatile group of locomotives (now designated Class "73") of which 42 were built in 1967 following six prototypes of 1962.

Details of interest include provision for multiple-unit operation not only with other electro-diesels, but also with straight electric and diesel-electric trains and locomotives. The weight of the diesel engine and generator, housed at one end of the locomotive, is balanced by a massive buffer beam at the other. Both screw couplings with buffers (for coupling to freight stock) and automatic buck-eye couplers with central buffing plates (for passenger trains) are provided.

The versatility of Class "73" was demonstrated to the world in July 1981, when Charles and Diana, Prince and Princess of Wales, left London for their honeymoon at Romsey, Hampshire, behind No. 73 142 *Broadlands:* 82 miles (131km) of electrified travel down the main line was followed by 5 miles (8km) under diesel power on a lesser and non-electrified route. The locomotives took on a new role in 1984, when high-speed push-pull trains were introduced between London Victoria and Gatwick Airport. Standard formation is a Class "73" plus up to eight coaches and a driving motor luggage van. Trains run every 15 minutes throughout the day, taking 30 minutes for the 26¾ mile (43km) journey. Replacement by new Class "460" electric multiple units early in 2000 will leave few regular duties remaining for these versatile locomotives.

Above: A Class 73/2 electro-diesel in Gatwick Express livery heading a service from London Victoria to Gatwick Airport. *(Ken Harris)*

Below: A Class "73" electro-diesel locomotive passes Clapham Junction on a Victoria to Gatwick Airport push-pull express, 1984.

Below: British Railways' Southern Region Class "73" No. 73142 *Broadlands* **– an electric locomotive with auxiliary diesel power.**

Shin Kansen
Sixteen-car train

Origin: Japan: Japanese National Railways (JNR), 1964. **Type:** High-speed electric passenger train. **Gauge:** 4ft 8¹/₂in (1,435mm). **Propulsion:** Alternating current at 25,000V 50Hz fed via overhead catenary and stepdown transformers and rectifiers to sixty-four 248hp (185kW) motors each driving an axle by means of gearing and flexible drive. **Weight:** 2,031,200lb (922t). **Axleload:** 31,738lb (14.4t). **Overall length:** 1,318ft 6in (401,880mm). **Max speed:** 130mph (210km/h).

It took more than 60 years for the promise of high-speed running by electric trainsets implicit in the Zossen trials of 1903 to become reality. Public trains averaging more than 100mph (160km/h) start-to-stop, with normal running speeds 30 per cent above this, appeared first during 1965 when Japanese National Railways put into full service the new *Shin Kansen* line from Tokyo westwards to Osaka. The line had been opened in 1964, but a preliminary period of operation at more normal speeds had been deemed prudent.

In spite of the impression they give, the *Shin Kansen* (the words simply mean "New Line") trains are really quite conventional. The high speed is obtained by having plenty of power; a 16-car train has a continuously-rated installed horsepower as high as 15,870 (11,840kW), while high acceleration is achieved by having every axle motored.

No, the interesting thing is to realise how much can be achieved using existing railroad state-of-the-art if you begin with a clean sheet. Until 1964, Japanese National Railways used 3ft 6in (1,067mm) gauge exclusively, but the new line was to be totally separate even to the extent of being of different gauge. The investment involved in building a new standard-gauge (1,435mm) railway connecting some of Japan's major cities was very great, but the courage of those who promoted it was fully justified eventually, by hugely increased traffic.

The price of high speed was considerable. Not only are there land costs involved in building new lines into and out of the centres of large cities, but since very flat curves of 125 chain (2,500m) radius are required for this degree of fast running, the engineering works in open country are also very heavy. If you cannot turn quickly to avoid natural obstacles, you have to go

Below: Japanese "*Shin Kansen*" high-speed 16-car electric multiple-unit train with snow-capped Mount Fuji seen in the background.

Above: The building of an entirely new 1,435mm gauge high-speed railway was Japan's successful method of cutting journey times.

through them. Of course, with such high power in relation to weight gradients on the heavy side (1-in-66 – 1.5 per cent) are no obstacle.

The principal innovation was the self-signalling system of the trains. Acceleration and deceleration is not only automatic but is also automatically initiated when required, only the final approach to a stop being directly under the driver's control. There are no lineside signals and all relevant information about the state of the line is passed to the driving position by coded impulses running in the main conductor wires.

Originally there were 480 cars arranged in 40 12-car sets, each 12-car train being divided electrically into six two-car units, one of which would have a buffet car, with the bullet-shaped ends and driving cabs placed at the outer ends of the train.

In 1970, the 12-car trains were strengthened to 16 including two buffet cars, and train frequency increased from 120 to over 200 both ways daily. The fleet of cars had by then become 1,400 arranged in 87 16-car sets. In 1970, as soon as success was assured, a national plan was prepared to extend the high-speed passenger network from the 320 miles (515km) of the original line by some twenty-fold. So far, four *Shin Kansen* lines have been built – extending the network from Tokyo to Okayama and Hakata (Fukuoka), and from Omiya (outside Tokyo) to Nagano, Niigata, Yamagata and Akita, a total of 1,266 miles (2,037km) of standard-gauge line. New generation *Shin Kansen* trains are described in a later entry.

The scale of work involved in the mountain regions – not to speak of an 11.6 mile (18.6km) inter-island undersea tunnel – can be seen from the amount of civil engineering work needed. Of the 247 miles (398km) between Okayama and Hakata, 55 per cent is in tunnel, 11 per cent on bridges or viaducts, leaving only 14 per cent as a conventional railway built on the ground. This was partly due to the minimum radius of curvature being increased to 200 chains (4,000m), with a view to raising speed from 130mph (210km/h) to 162mph (260km/h), while at the same time reducing the gradient to l-in-65 (1.5 per cent).

The original Tokaido *Shin Kansen* continues to amaze, with its latest Series "500" trains achieving the world's fastest start-to-stop runs in 1999. Twelve Nozomi 500 expresses run the 119.3 miles (192km) between Kokura and Hiroshima in 44min, at an average speed of 162.7mph (261.8km/h).

Class X C$_o$-C$_o$

Origin: Australia: Victorian Railways (VicRail), 1966. **Type:** Diesel-electric mixed-traffic locomotive. **Gauge:** 5ft 3in (1,600mm) and 4ft 8$\frac{1}{2}$in (1,435mm). **Propulsion:** General Motors Type 16-567E 1,950hp (1,455kW) 16 cylinder two-stroke Vee diesel engine and generator supplying current to six nose-suspended traction motors geared to the axles. **Weight:** 255,665lb (116t). **Axleload:** 42,980lb (19.5t). **Overall length:** 60ft 3in (18,364mm). **Tractive effort:** 64,125lb (285kN). **Max speed:** 84mph (134km/h).

It is well known that Australia had a serious railway gauge problem, the various states having in the early days gone their own ways in this respect. The state of Victoria and its neighbour South Australia were the two which opted for a 5ft 3in (1,600mm) broad gauge. In steam days this meant different designs of locomotive, but with diesels the differences can be minimal, confined almost wholly to the appropriate wheelsets.

These Class "X" diesels of Victorian Railways (VicRail) are a case in point because, now that standard-gauge has put a tentacle into the state (notably to connect Melbourne to the Trans-Australian railway as well as over the trunk route from Sydney), they provide haulage over both gauges.

The locomotives are a typical General Motors product – like virtually all VicRail's diesel locomotives – and were assembled by GM's Australian licensee, Clyde Engineering Pty of Sydney, New South Wales. This standardisation gives an advantage in that most of the diesel fleet can be run in multiple regardless of class.

Soon after the first six "Xs" had been delivered, Clyde began offering GM's new 645 series engine and this was used for a subsequent batch of 18 supplied in 1970. The power output could thus be increased to 2,600hp (1,940kW) without weight penalty. These were then the most powerful units on the system, but subsequently axleload limits have been raised to 22.5t (24.8 US tons) on certain lines. Hence a further batch of GM Co-Co

VI80T B$_o$-B$_o$+B$_o$-B$_o$

Origin: Russia: Soviet Railways (SZD), 1967. **Type:** Electric locomotive for heavy freight haulage. **Gauge:** 5ft 0in (1,524mm). **Propulsion:** Alternating current at 25,000V 50Hz fed via overhead catenary, step-down transformer and silicon rectifiers to eight 790hp (590kW) nose-suspended dc traction motors, each geared to one axle. **Weight:** 405,535lb (184t). **Axleload:** 50,695lb (23t). **Overall length:** 107ft 9in (32,840mm). **Tractive effort:** 99,500lb (433kN). **Max speed:** 68mph (110km/h).

Soviet Railways' "VL80" series of electric locomotives, one of the most numerous in the world, was the main motive power used for moving heavy freight trains over the Russia's 13,000 mile (21,000km) network of industrial-frequency electrification. The letters VL pay tribute to Vladimir Lenin, no less, whose personal enthusiasm for railway electrification has now, many years after his death, had such impressive results.

The eight-axle locomotive has double-bogie units permanently coupled in pairs, and was a favourite for freight work in the USSR. Some 1,500 of Class "VL8" were built for the 3,000V dc lines from 1953 onwards, followed in 1961 by the start of production of the "VL10" class, also for dc lines. For ac lines, the first "VL80s", externally very similar to the "VL10s" began coming into use in 1963 with the class variant "VL80K".

The first "VL80Ks" had mercury-arc rectifiers, but it is difficult to avoid problems when (in lay terms) mercury sloshes around under the influence

Above: Victorian Railways' standard-gauge "X" class Co-Co No. X49 arrives in Melbourne with the "Southern Aurora" from Sydney.

units (the "C" class) have been supplied with an installed power of 3,300hp 2,460kW). One requirement for all Victoria's locomotives that possibly defeated General Motors' ability to supply off-the-shelf was provision of sets of pneumatically-operated token exchange equipment. Under British-style operating rules, some physical token of authority is needed to be on any particular section of single line. The token (or staff) has to be exchanged for another when passing from one block section to the next. The places where this happens often do not coincide with the train's stopping places and the exchange apparatus enables this to be done at speed. Modern electrical methods of signalling are doing away with this picturesque operation.

Above: A "VL82mm" class dual-voltage electric locomotive of Soviet Railways. This is an improved version of the "VL80T" class.

of vibration and traction shocks. Solid-state silicon rectifiers were soon substituted. The "VL80T" was a modification of the "VL80K" which had rheostatic electric braking, and this was the main production version of the "VL80" class, of which over 2,000 were built. After some years of experiment, "VL80" series-production changed to a version ("VL80R") with thyristor control and – made painlessly possible by the scope of this system – full regenerative electric braking. This is claimed to reduce current consumption by over 10 per cent.

Experiments were made on a "VL80A" version which used three-phase asynchronous induction motors supplied with variable frequency current by a solid-state conversion system. Another interesting development, which is obviously very similar to the "VL80A" arrangement theoretically, but very different practically, was to use thyristors inside each motor as a substitute for the commutator and brushes. In this way the associated problems of mechanical wear and vulnerability to flashover at the commutators can

---

Class 72000 C-C

Origin: France: French National Railways (SNCF), 1967. **Type:** Diesel electric dual purpose locomotive. **Gauge:** 4ft 8^1/2in (1,435 mm). **Propulsion:** Société Alsacienne de Construcion Mecaniques 3,550hp (2,650kW) 16-cylinder four-stroke diesel engine and alternator supplying current through silicon rectifiers to two traction motors, one on each bogie; motors connected to the axles through two-speed gearing and spring drive. **Weight:** 251,260lb (114t). **Axleload:** 41,880lb (19t). **Overal length:** 66ft 3in (20,190mm). **Tractive effort:** Low gear 81,570lb (363kN) high gear 46,300lb (206kN). **Max speed:** Low gear 53mph (85km/h), high 87mph (140km/h).

When SNCF embarked on construction of large main-line diesel locomotives in 1961, it was recognised that a more powerful unit than the 2,650hp Class "68000" would be needed eventually for the heaviest work. So two pairs of twin-engine experimental locomotives were ordered, which could develop up to 4,800hp (3,580kW). However enthusiasm for the complications of the twin-engine machines was never great, and development of new diesel engines in the range 3,500 to 4,000hp encouraged SNCF in 1964 to invite manufacturers to submit proposals for a powerful single-engine locomotive. Alsthom made a successful submission of a C-C design, based on the AG016 engine of 3,600hp (2,700kW). "A" denotes the maker, Société Alsacienne de Constructions Mecaniques of Mulhouse, "G" and "O" denote the designers, Grosshaus and Ollier. This engine was a 16-cylinder version of the 12-cylinder engine already fitted to the "68500" series of A1A+A1A locomotives.

Eighteen of the new design were ordered from Alsthom in 1966, and delivery commenced in the following year, the class being allocated numbers from 72001. SNCF was at this period developing a new family of electric locomotives incorporating monomotor bogies, and the "72000s' incorporated various parts in common with the electric units. The bogies followed closely the design recently introduced in the Class "40100" quadricurrent locomotives, with two gear ratios, the maximum speeds in the two settings being 53mph (85km/h) for freight and 87mph (140km/h) for passenger work. The traction motors are identical electrically with those of the "BB8500", "BB17000" and "BB25500" electric locomotives. SNCF estimated that the monomotor bogie saved 9t in weight compared with conventional bogies with individual axle drive, and it enabled the axleload to be kept within the stipulated limits.

Main innovation in the electrical system was use of an alternator instead of a dc generator. This delivers three-phase current which is rectified by silicon diodes for supply to the dc traction motors. The electrical equipment included Alsthom's "Superadhesion" system, in which the excitation of the field of the motors is controlled to give an almost direct relationship between motor voltage and current. By this

ossibly be avoided. A three-unit version ("VL80S") with 13,100hp 9,780kW) available for hauling 10,000t (11,000 US tons) trains has been roduced and prototypes have been built of a "VL84" version with ncreased power.

Also associated with the "VL80s" are the "VL82" series of dual-current ocomotives for 3,000V dc and 25,000V 50Hz ac, dating from 1972. Adding ogether both systems of electrification the overall picture was quite mazing – until the break-up of the USSR in 1991 more electrically hauled rail reight traffic than the whole of the rest of the world put together moved on 9,000 miles (46,800km) of electrified route.

Above: French National Railways' Class "72000" C-C diesel-electric ocomotive as constructed by Alsthom from 1967 onwards.

neans the tendency for incipient wheelslip to develop is greatly reduced, nd it is claimed that the effective starting tractive effort can be increased y 15 to 20 per cent.

The body resembles closely those of the corresponding electric classes ut has a higher roof to accommodate the engine. The treatment of the nds incorporates cab windows steeply inclined backwards to reduce lare, as introduced on the "40100" class, but the appearance was much ltered by restyling of the ends due to inclusion of massive cellular boxes 1 front of the cab to protect the driver in case of collision. They were mmediately put to work on the Paris to Brittany and Paris to Basle routes, vhere they enabled modest increases to be made in train speeds over the 68000" class, but consistent with SNCF's target of not developing full ower for more than 60 per cent of the run, compared with 67 per cent ecorded with the earlier locomotives, and also consistent with supplying lectric train heating from the engine power. The class eventually reached total of 92, and they took over the heaviest work on most non-electrified utes. Ten had modifications made to enable them to run at 100mph 160km/h). In 1973 No.72075 was fitted with an SEMT-Pielstick PA 6-280 2-cylinder engine, initially rated at 4,200hp but increased a year later to ,800hp (3,580kW), making it the most powerful diesel engine in a ocomotive (at least in the Western world).

Metroliner Two-car Trainset

Origin: United States: Pennsylvania Railroad (PER), 1967. **Type:** High-speed electric multiple-unit trainset. **Gauge:** 4ft 8¹/₂in (1,435mm) **Propulsion:** Alternating current at 11,000V 25Hz fed via overhead catenary, stepdown transformer and rectifiers to eight 300hp (224kW) nose-suspended motors one geared to each pair of wheels. **Weight:** 328,400lb (149t). **Axleload:** 41,880lb (19t). **Overall length:** 170ft 0in (51,816mm). **Max speed:** 160mph (256km/h.

In the 1960s, the United States passenger train was at a very low ebb. Most railroads were reporting massive deficits on passenger services as well as steady loss of traffic. Over long distances the jet airliner had a twenty-fold advantage in time, which hardly affected the time disadvantage between city centre and out-of-town air terminal, compared with rail. Over short distances, though, the opposite was the case and there seemed a possibility of the train continuing to compete, were it not for outdated equipment and image.

One such route was the Pennsylvania Railroad's electrified main line between New York, Philadelphia and Washington, now known as the North East Corridor. It was in order to offer better service on this route that these

Right: A "Metroliner" 11,000V 25Hz electric multiple-unit express train speed under the wires on the North East Corridor main line.

Below: The front end of a "Metroliner" electric multiple-unit two-car set. Note the driving cab window and automatic couplers.

remarkable trains came into being. Possible prototypes ("MP85") had been acquired from the Budd Company of Philadelphia in 1958 and in 1963 some cars – the Budd *Silverliners* – were acquired on behalf of Pennsy by the City of Philadelphia.

Later in the decade the railroad received some government assistance towards a $22 million scheme for new high-speed self-propelled trains plus $33 million for improvements to the permanent way 160mph (256km/h) operation was envisaged.

Orders were placed in 1966 with Budd for 50 (later increased to 61) stainless steel electric cars to be called *Metroliners*. They drove on all wheels, could attain considerably more than the specified speed and had a fantastic short-term power-to-weight ratio of 34hp per tonne. They also had dynamic braking down to 30mph (48km), automatic acceleration, deceleration, and speed control using new sophisticated techniques. Full air conditioning, airline-type catering, electrically controlled doors and a public telephone service by radio link were provided. The order included parlour cars and snack-bar coaches as well as ordinary day coaches. All had a driving cab at one end, but access between adjacent sets through a cab not in use was possible. They were marshalled semi-permanently in pairs as two-car units. An over-bold decision was taken to begin production straight from the drawing board. For once, with the Pennsylvania Railroad suffering from a terminal sickness, its officers did not insist on the usual precaution of building and testing prototypes first. As a result, faults galore again and again delayed entry into public service until after ill-fated Penn Central took over in 1968. A single round-trip daily began at the beginning of 1969 and even then a modification programme costing 50 per cent of the original price of the trains was needed to make them suitable for public service.

Amtrak took over the North East Corridor passenger service in May 1971, and a year later 14 daily *Metroliner* trips were being run and start-to-stop average speeds as high as 95mph (152km/h) were scheduled. Speeds as high as the announced 150mph were not run in public service, although 164mph (262km/h) was achieved on test; the work done on the permanent way was not sufficient for this, 110mph (176km/h) being the normal limit.

Later a programme of track work was carried out over the North East Corridor. At a cost of $2,500 million, this was 75 times as much as the original rather naive proposal, but did include the New York to Boston line. With this great work completed, 1982 saw introduction of the fastest-ever timings between New York and Washington. However, the *Metroliners*, then nearly 20 years old, were displaced from New York-Washington services by "AEM7" locomotives and trains of Amfleet coaches.

The original *Metroliner* schedule of 2½ hours for the 226 miles (362km) between New York and Washington was never achieved, but 'taking 1978 as an example) hourly trains did the run in a very respectable 3 hours (or a minute or two more) with four intermediate stops, an overall average of 75mph (120km/h). Two years later, when the engineering work was at its peak, this timing had been extended to almost 4 hours. In 1983, however, the locomotive-hauled trains, confusingly also called "Metroliners", were completing the journey in 2hr 49min with four stops, at an average speed of 79.8mph (128.4km/h).

By 1999, with further upgrading of the route completed and electrification extended northwards from New Haven to Boston, the North East Corridor

---

E50C C$_o$-C$_o$

Origin: United States: Muskingum Electric Railroad (MER), 1967. **Type** Driverless mineral-hauling electric locomotive. **Gauge:** 4ft 8$1/2$in (1,435mm) **Propulsion:** Alternating current at 25,000V 60Hz fed via overhead catenary, stepdown transformer and silicon rectifiers to six 830hp (620kW) dc traction motors geared to the driving axles. Control is by automatically generated radio received continuously at the terminals and at fixed points elsewhere. **Weight:** 390,000lb (177t). **Axleload:** 65,000lb (29.5t). **Overall length:** 65ft 7in (19,989mm). **Tractive effort:** 117,000lb (520kN). **Max speed:** 70mph (112km/h).

Railroads are a natural subject for automation but actual automatic railroads hardly exist. There is only one such in the true sense in the whole USA and it feeds the Muskingum River electric power plant near Cumberland, Ohio, now owned by the Central Ohio Coal Co. Coal is dug about 20 miles (32km) away by a huge dragline excavator known as "Big Muskie", which has to remove 120ft (36m) of over-burden before the coal seam is reached.

In 1967-68 an electric railroad was built to carry coal from the stripmine to a point from which a conveyor belt feeds the generating plant. High

Below: These two electric locomotives form the complete motive power fleet of the Muskingum Electric Railroad, Ohio, USA.

was poised once again to join the world's rail racetracks. A new fleet of 20 tilting trainsets with a maximum speed of 150mph (240km/h) was due in service in 1999, but like their predecessors had been delayed by technical problems. Also being commissioned was a batch of 15 electric locomotives geared for 125mph (200km/h). The trainsets, dubbed "Acela" by the marketing people, are intended to cut 15min from 1999's best New York-Washington timing of 2hr 59min, with some services possibly achieving the magic 2hr 30min schedule. Much depends on the success of these trains, as Amtrak has been ordered to become profitable by 2002 or be wound up.

Above: Much like any other locomotive, this Muskingum Electric RR "E50C" even has an engineer's seat-but there's no engineer!

voltage industrial frequency alternating current was connected up to a lightweight cantenary and two electric freight trains soon began moving an average of 18,000 tons of coal five days a week. Two Co-Co electric locomotives designated type "E50C" were supplied by General Electric, rather charmingly numbered 100 and 200 respectively as if the Muskingum Electric Railroad intended to have a huge fleet.

The "E50C"'s were based on the chassis and body of a standard GEC Co-Co diesel-electric road-switcher, with transformer and special control gear replacing the diesel engine and alternator. A cab is provided complete with driver's seat, which is normally vacant. The trains are controlled in the loading and unloading areas by a continuous radio signal modulated to give speed commands ranging from "stop" and "creep" to "50"mph. The processes at both ends are entirely automatic although supervised. Air operated bottom doors on each 100-ton capacity hopper wagon are controlled by a signal received via a shoe mounted on one of its bogies.

Out on the line, the locomotives encounter a fixed control location preceded by a warning marker at approximately one mile intervals. Each one of these presents a fixed coded response to a detector circuit on the locomotive as it goes by, which determines the speed of the train over the next mile. If the time taken from one control location to the next does not correspond within a reasonable margin to the speed set, then the train will make an emergency stop. This will also occur if the train has run further than a mile without encountering a control location.

The locomotives normally run at half the rated maximum speed and the 15 empty wagons of each train are propelled on the return trip. When the system was fully-operational, one train was normally loading while the other made its out-and-back trip to unload, a complete cycle taking 2hr 15 min. Six cycles were performed each weekday, making 90,000 tons weekly, hauled almost without human intervention. Sadly, only a short section of the original route remains in operation.

Class 581 Twelve-car train

Origin: Japan: Japanese National Railways (JNR), 1968. **Type:** Electric express sleeping-car train. **Gauge:** 3ft 6in (1,067mm). **Propulsion:** Alternating current at 25,000V 50Hz or 60Hz, or direct current at 3,000V, fed via overhead catenary and conversion and control equipment in two power cars to 24 traction motors of 160hp (100kW) geared to the bogie axles of six of the intermediate sleeping cars in the train. **Weight:** 638,720lb (290t) adhesive, 1,218,812lb (553t) total. **Axleload:** 26,450lb (12t). **Overall length:** 816ft 11in (249,000mm). **Max speed:** 100mph (160km/h). This is the design speed; the maximum permitted speed of the railway is 75mph (120km/h).

The worldwide trend in modern forms of motive power towards self-contained multiple-unit trains took a hold of hitherto unconquered (but not unexplored) territory when Japanese National Railways put into service these very fine electric trains. Previous examples of the provision of sleeping cars in self-propelled trains included Union Pacific's M-10001 train, various long-distance interurban electric trains in the USA and a West German set called the *Komet*, which had a brief career in the 1950s. None of these examples led in any way to the idea becoming general practice on the lines concerned.

These handsome trains, however, took over many long-distance overnight workings in Japan. Unusually for sleeping cars, all berths are longitudinal and separate accommodation is not provided for "green" (first) and "ordinary" class passengers. Instead, there is a higher charge for lower berths compared to that for middle and upper berths. Berth charges do, however include night attire and washing things, as in Japanese-style hotels. With up to 45 sleeping berths in each narrow-gauge car the designers must be admired for stating that their main objective was to create an impression of spaciousness! The 12-car set includes a dining car seating 40; the remaining 11 cars can sleep 444 or seat 656. The trains are air-conditioned throughout, and it has been said that the sound-proofing is sufficient to reduce noise levels to less than that encountered in locomotive-hauled sleeping cars.

The growth of air travel and the spread of high-speed *Shinkansen* trains dramatically reduced demand for overnight travel, and during the 1980s many Class "581" sets were converted for use on daytime local services. But a few remained in their original condition in the late-1990s, one service being JR West's overnight "Kitaguni Express" between Osaka and Niigata.

Right: The end doors of a Class "581" driving-trailer sleeping car can be opened to give communication between adjacent 12-car sets.

Below: A driving trailer car of the Japanese railways' Class "581" sleeping car train coupled to a motor non-driving sleeping car.

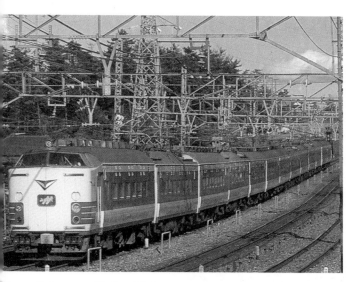

Above: A Japanese National Railways narrow-gauge sleeping car express formed of Class "581" electric multiple-unit rolling stock.

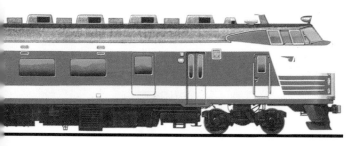

Class DD40AX
"Centennial" D₀-D₀

Origin: United States: Union Pacific Railroad (UP), 1969. **Type:** Diesel electric locomotive for heavy freight duty. **Gauge:** 4ft 8¹/₂in (1,435mm) **Propulsion:** Two supercharged two-stroke General Motors 16-cylinde Type 645 engines each of 3,300hp (2,460kW) with integral alternators feeding eight nose-suspended traction motors. **Weight:** 545,270lb (247.5t) **Axleload:** 68,324lb (31t). **Overall length:** 98ft 51n (29,997mm). **Tractive effort:** 133,766lb (603kN). **Max speed:** 90mph (144km/h).

If one were to choose the world's number one rail line, a fairly likely candidate would be the central section of the first United States transcontinental railroad, known now by the same name – Union Pacific - as it was when opened in 1869. In the days of steam, UP had the larges and most powerful locomotives in the world, the legendary "Big Boys", to haul the heavy and constant flow of freight across the continental divide Going west, this began with the famous Sherman Hill (named after Genera Sherman who was in charge of building UP) out of Cheyenne, Wyoming; consists of some 40 miles (64km) of 1-in-66 (1.5 per cent) grade.

When diesel traction took over, the power of a steam 4-8-8-4 could be matched or exceeded by coupling locomotive units in multiple, but UP management consistently made efforts to find a simpler solution by increasing the power of each unit. Extensive trials were made with locomotives propelled by gas turbines, giving a much higher power-to weight ratio; but in the end the ability to buy off-the-shelf from diese locomotive suppliers proved to have an over-riding advantage.

In the late-1960s, the UP operating authorities once again felt that there should be a better solution than having six or even eight locomotives or one train. General Motors had put together a peculiar 5,000hp (3,730kW) locomotive which they called a "DD35". This was essentially a huge booster unit with the works of two standard "GP35" road-switchers mounted on it. The locomotive ran on two four-axle bogies; these were considered to be hard on the track, but being contained in a mere booste unit could not take the leading position in a train where any bad effects o the running gear would be accentuated. Even so, no one was very keen to put the matter to the test. Only a handful of "DD35"s were sold and those only to Union Pacific and Southern Pacific. UP's track was (and is) superb however, and it was suggested to GM that a "DD35" with a normal cab hood would be useful. The result was the "DD35A", of which 27 were supplied to UP. It was not disclosed how much saving in cost, allowing fo an element of custom-building, there was between two "GP35s" and on "DD35A", but in length at least the former's 112ft 4in (34,240mm compared with the latter's 88ft 2in (26,873mm).

Above: Union Pacific No. 6900 heads a "Golden Spike" special celebrating 100 years of rail operation across the continent.

A centenary in a new country is a great event and when during the late-1960s UP's management considered how to celebrate 100 years of continuous operation, they decided to do it by ordering a class of prime mover which was the most powerful in the world on a single-unit basis. Again, virtually everything except the chassis of the locomotive came off General Motors shelves, but even so the "Centennials" (more prosaically, the "DD40AX"s) are a remarkable achievement.

In the same way that the "DD35A" was a double "GP35", the "DD40AX" was a double "GP40". The 16-cylinder engines of the "GP40" (essentially a supercharged version of those fitted to the "GP35") were uprated from 3,000 to 3,300hp (2,240 to 2460kW), thereby producing a 6,600hp (4,925kW) single-unit locomotive. This was done by permitting an increased rpm. The result was not only the most powerful but also the longest and the largest prime-mover locomotive unit in the world. Forty-seven were built between 1969 and 1971, completion of the first (appropriately No.6900) being pushed ahead to be ready on centenary day. The locomotives had a full-width cab and incorporated all the recent improvements which GM had introduced in the standard range of diesel locomotives.These included the new Type 645 engine, of uniflow two-stroke design like its long-lived predecessor the Type 567. The same

Below: Union Pacific Class "DD40X" "Centennial" diesel-electric locomotive. Note the gap between the two engines.

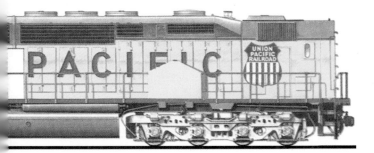

cylinder bore and stroke is common to a 1,750hp (7501kW) switcher and the 6,600hp (4,925kW) "Centennial". The generator was basically a brushless alternator, but had built-in silicon diode rectifiers to produce direct current suitable for traction motors. Naturally, the control system included dynamic braking and wheelslip correction features.

The complex electrical system common to all diesel-electric locomotives was improved in these machines by being concentrated in a series of modules which could be isolated, tested and easily replaced if found faulty. In this way, repairs, adjustments or an overhaul could be done under factory conditions. Afterwards this arrangement became standard throughout the whole range of GM locomotives, models with it becoming known as "Dash-2", for example "SD40-2" for an "SD40" with modular electrics.

It could be said that this development proved to be self-destructive to the future of monster diesel-electrics, for a principal advantage of combining two "GP40"s on one chassis was the saving of a lot of electrical control gear. So making the electrics less troublesome made inroads into this advantage, and as a result these dinosaurs have not been repeated, even for Union Pacific. Another factor was introduction of the "SD45-2" series with 20-cylinder engines rated at 3,600hp (2,685kW).

After these superb "Centennials", UP once again returned to buying diesel units off-the-shelf like virtually all US railroads and indeed the majority of railways the world over. When a train was called, required power would be calculated on a horsepower per ton basis according to the severity of the route. The most conveniently available units to make up this

Above: A pair of "Centennial" diesel-electric units at the head of a freight train at Barstow, California, in 1970.

total horsepower would then be coupled up to form the motive power: in these circumstances large special indivisible units are more of a hindrance than a help. Thus the "Big Boys" and the turbines have been superseded, and the "Centennials" submerged by more mundane motive power; even so, the pageant of freight movement up Sherman Hill and across the Divide is still one of the great railway sights of the world.

Below: Brand-new Union Pacific Class "DD40X" "Centennial" diesel-electric locomotive No. 6900, built by General Motors' Electro-Motive Division, poses for an official photograph.

Class 6E B$_o$-B$_o$

Origin: South Africa: South African Railways (SAR), 1969. **Type:** Electric mixed traffic freight locomotive. Gauge: 3ft 6in (1,067mm). **Propulsion:** Direct current at 3,000V fed via overhead catenary and rheostatic controls to four 835hp (623kW) nose-suspended motors geared to the driving axles. **Weight:** 195,935lb (88.9t). **Axleload:** 49,040lb (22.25t). **Overall length:** 50ft 10in (15,494mm). **Tractive effort:** 70,000lb (311kN). **Max speed:** 70mph (112km/h).

The first important electrification scheme in South Africa came as early as 1952, when a steeply-graded section of the Durban to Johannesburg main line between Estcourt and Ladysmith was placed under the wires. The Class "1E" locomotives supplied – the original group came from Switzerland – were direct ancestors of Class "6E" with the same wheel arrangement and mechanical configuration. Forty-four years of progress resulted in increases of 77 per cent in tractive effort, 208 per cent in power output, and 180 per cent in maximum permitted speed at a cost of only 31 per cent in weight and 16 per cent in overall length. It is typical of electric traction, though, that many of the "1Es" remained in service on humble but still arduous duties after half-a-century of work.

A country that combines prosperous development and great mineral riches with non-existent oil supplies is well-suited to electrification. Both the scale of electric operation and its rate of development in South Africa are indicated by the fact that the "6E/6E1" fleet totals 997 units, while 850 of their very similar immediate predecessors, classes "5E" and "5E1", were built between 1955 and 1969. South Africa's growing industrial capability is also shown by the fact that while the 172 "1Es" (and the similar "2Es") were wholly built in Europe, only the earlier examples of Class "51E" and none of the "6Es" were built abroad. Nearly all of both classes were still in service with SAR's successor Spoornet in the late 1990s.

All the classes mentioned, and this is especially impressive for half-a-century ago, are capable not only of regenerative braking but also of working in multiple. This whole concept or railroading, using exclusively tractors with the same two bogies as most other vehicles but coupling up as many of them as are needed to haul the train, was far ahead of its time. Five or six locomotives running in multiple can often be seen.

Below: The Class "5E/6E" locomotive design of South African Railways depicted in special "Blue Train"colours.

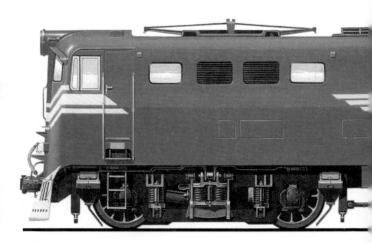

Above: Matching locomotives and cars make up the "Blue Train".

Above: South African Railways' famous luxury "Blue Train" near Pretoria hauled by two specially painted locomotives.

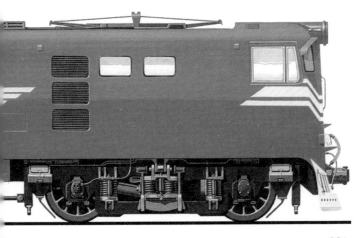

Class 103.1 C$_o$-C$_o$

Origin: Germany: German Federal Railway (DB), 1970. **Type:** Express passenger electric locomotive. **Gauge:** 4ft 8½in (1,435mm). **Propulsion:** Alternating current at 15,000V 16⅔Hz fed through a transformer to six 1,580hp (1,180kW) traction motors mounted on the bogie frames, connected to the axles through spring drive. **Weight:** 251,260lb (114t). Axleload: 41,880lb (19.0t). **Overall length:** 63ft 11½in (19,500mm). **Tractive effort:** 70,000lb (312kN). **Max speed:** 125mph (200km/h).

In 1960 the German Federal Railway (DB) began to plan a network of high-speed inter-city trains with which to meet the competition of internal air services. The fast diesel trains in pre-war Germany had operated mainly on routes radiating from Berlin, on which high speeds could be sustained for long distances. In West Germany, however, the principal routes had more frequent stops and speed restrictions, and the ability to reach high speed quickly was thus as important as the ability to sustain it. The specification which was drawn up in 1961 therefore required that a speed of 125mph (200km/h) should be maintained on a gradient of 1-in-200 (0.5 per cent) with 300t, and that the train should be accelerated to this speed in 150 seconds.

In accordance with German practice a number of companies submitted proposals. These included 1-Bo+Bo-1 and A1A+A1A schemes with four motors of 1,250kW (1,675hp), but it was considered that six motors should be fitted to keep the motor weight down, and despite some doubts about its riding qualities, the Co-Co arrangement was chosen.

Four prototypes were ordered in 1963 from Siemens Schuckert and Henschel; delivered in 1965 they were numbered E03.001-4. They made a spectacular entry into service, for in connection with an international transport exhibition in Munich that year they worked a special train twice daily from Munich to Augsburg at an average of 88mph (142km/h) with sustained 200km/h running.

The locomotives followed the pattern already established in DB standard designs, with an ac motor mounted above each axle and fully-sprung drive. Control was by tap changers on the high-tension side of the transformer. Automatic speed control was fitted, with increments of 10km/h on the driver's controller. The motors were of light weight for their power, specially designed for high speed. The one-hour rating was 6,420kW (8,600hp) at 200km/h, and the 10-minute rating was no less than 9,000kW (12,000hp). When employed on heavy expresses running at lower speeds, the locos

Above: A high-speed inter-city express train of the German Federal Railways hauled by a Class "103.1" electric locomotive.

suffered from high transformer temperatures, so larger transformers had to be fitted.

For a time, DB favoured the idea of working the inter-city network by multiple-units, but eventually it was decided that, except for any services which might in the future exceed 125mph (200km/h), locomotives would be used, and 145 more of the Co-Co units were ordered. They were delivered from 1970 onwards; under the computerised numbering system then in use they were designated Nos.103.101-245. They incorporated various improvements to the motors and control equipment which allowed them to work trains of up to 480t at 200km/h. The earlier locomotives had also developed heavy brush and commutator wear when their high-speed motors were subjected to heavy currents at low speeds, and the new machines had an additional tap-changer on the low-tension side of the transformer which made them suitable for working 600t trains at normal speed.

The body shape of the original locomotives had been determined by wind-tunnel tests, but the resultant curved ends had the effect of making the driver's cab more cramped than in other classes.

Below: German Federal Railway's standard Class "103.1" Co-Co electric locomotive introduced in 1970 for fast expresses.

Class 92 1-C$_o$-C$_o$-1

Origin: Kenya/Canada: East African Railways (EAR), 1971. **Type:** Diesel-electric mixed-traffic locomotive. **Gauge:** 3ft 3³/₈in (1,000mm). **Propulsion:** Alco Type 251F 12-cylinder four-stroke 2,550hp (1,902kW) Vee-type diesel engine and generator supplying direct current to six nose-suspended traction motors geared to the main axles. **Weight:** 218,200lb (99t) adhesive, 251,255lb (114.5t) total. **Axleload:** 36,370lb (16.5t). **Overall length:** 59ft 1in (18,015mm). **Tractive effort:** 77,000lb (342kN). **Max speed:** 45mph (72km/h).

Construction of the so-called Uganda Railway was the start of civilisation in what is now known as Kenya. Little wood-burning steam engines reached the site of Nairobi in 1895, so beginning the history of a line which for most of its existence has had to struggle to move ever-increasing traffic.

Oil-burning took over from wood in the 1930s, and traffic reached a point where articulated locomotives – the legendary Beyer-Garratts – were needed. The efficiency with which traffic was worked by these monsters made East African Railways (the former joint administration of railways in Kenya, Tanzania and Uganda) a very hard nut indeed for diesel traction to crack. Various studies over the years indicated that there was no case for change, apart from "keeping up with the Joneses" but in the 1960s the

Above: An East African Railways' (later Kenya Railways) Class "92" diesel-electric hauls an empty tank train towards Mombasa.

Below: East African Class "92" Alco-built diesel-electric locomotive. Note the pony wheels to reduce the axleoading.

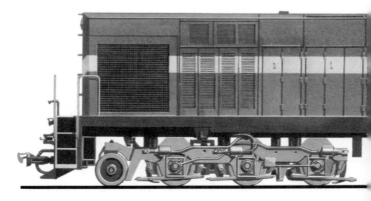

Above: A Class "92" 1-Co-Co-1 diesel-electric climbs the spiral at Mazeras near Mombasa with a freight for Nairobi.

administration began to order medium-power units from English Electric of Great Britain.

By 1970 some progress in dieselisation had been made on peripheral routes, but the main trunk route which climbed steadily from sea level at Mombasa to 9,131ft (2,783m) at Timboroa, en route to Uganda, was still a Garratt stronghold. To find a means of working this traffic economically with diesel traction, EAR went shopping outside Britain, almost for the first time. The result was this Class "92" diesel of Alco design, supplied by the Montreal Locomotive Works. It offered 38 per cent more power than the most powerful diesel then in Kenya.

The Class "92"s were based on the standard Alco product adapted for metre-gauge. To reduce the axleload to a value acceptable on the main line west of Nairobi, not only was it necessary to use six-wheel bogies but an idle pony wheel had to be attached to each bogie also. The arrangement was offered by MLW specially for low axleloads as the "African series" and EAR also ordered an even lighter lower-power version on the same chassis (Class "88") for lines with a 12 ton axleload in Tanzania.

In 1976, EAR was divided up among the owning nations, Kenya, Uganda and Tanzania. The Class "92"s went to Kenya, retaining the same classification. Since then a Class "93" Co-Co design of similar power has been imported from General Electric, followed by the 2,172hp Class "94". Advances in design have enabled axleload restrictions to be met without the pony wheels.

Class 15000 B-B

Origin: France: French National Railways (SNCF), 1971. **Type:** Express passenger electric locomotive. **Gauge:** 4ft 8½in (1,435mm). **Propulsion:** Alternating current at 25,000V 50Hz from overhead wires, rectified in diodes and thyristors, supplying two 2,960hp (2,210kW) traction motors, one mounted on each bogie and connected to the axles through gearing and spring drives. **Weight:** 198,395lb (88t). Axleload: 49,590lb (22.5t). **Overall length:** 57ft 4⅛in (17,480mm). **Tractive effort:** 64,800lb (288kN). **Max speed:** 112mph (180km/h).

Early in its experiments with 25,000V 50Hz ac traction, SNCF recognised that the combination of routes electrified on the new system with its existing network of 1,500V dc lines would make essential the use of dual-voltage locomotives capable of working on both systems. Otherwise the time consumed in changing locomotives, together with the resulting poor utilisation, would nullify much of the economy of the high-voltage system. Dual-voltage machines were therefore included in the batch of experimental ac locomotives, and this was followed by the development of "families" of locomotives, comprising ac, dc and dual-voltage machines incorporating as many common parts as possible. The numbering of these classes was a notable manifestation of Gallic logic, for it was based on the mathematical relationship: (ac +dc) = (dual voltage). Thus the "1700" ac class and the "8500" dc class combined to produce the "25500" dual-voltage class.

Successive phases in post-war development of the French electric locomotive produced successive families. Thus one group comprised the first all-adhesion four-axle locomotive with individual-axle drive. The next group, the one mentioned above, incorporated monomotor bogies with two gear ratios, and silicon rectifiers. The third group, "15000" + "7200"= Class "22200" was moved into the thyristor era, and at a nominal 5,920hp (4,420kW) they are the most powerful French B-B machines. This group was also notable in reverting to a single gear ratio. Class "15000" was intended primarily for express passenger work, and a low-speed gear was unnecessary, but it was hoped that improvements in various aspects of design since the introduction of the two-speed locomotives would enable the thyristor machines to handle the freight traffic without provision of a special gear ratio.

It is SNCF's practice to apply new technology experimentally to an existing locomotive or train, retaining as much as possible of the well-proven equipment, so as to concentrate attention on the special equipment under test. Some of the first thyristor experiments were made with one of the

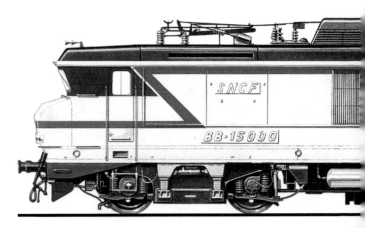

Above: French National Railways' Class "15000" 50Hz ac locomotive standard power for express trains in France.

pioneer dual-voltage locomotives, No. 20002, which retained conventional resistance control for dc operation and silicon diodes for ac traction, but had thyristors for ac regenerative braking. The first application of thyristors to control power circuits was on a multiple-unit train, and in 1971 there appeared the first production units equipped throughout with thyristors, a series of multiple-units, and the Class "15000" B-B locomotives.

Up to this time the standard method of controlling power on French ac locomotives had been by tap-changer on the high-tension side of the transformer. The thyristor offered an elegant alternative to the tap-changer, with the possibility of infinitely-variable control of the voltage applied to the traction motors.

Class "15000" was built to take over principal services on the former Est Railway main line from Paris to Strasbourg. Their introduction followed construction of the "6500" class C-C dc locomotives and the "7200" class C-C diesel-electrics; many parts were common to all three classes, including the main body structure. There is a single traction motor for each

Below: The French locomotive design depicted is produced for dc (Class "7200"), for 50Hz (Class "15000") and bi-current (Class "22200").

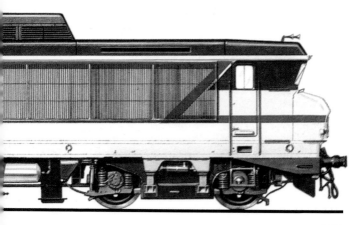

Above: A Class "7200" Bo-Bo electric locomotive (the dc version of Class "15000") at the Gare du Lyon, Paris, in 1970.

bogie, mounted rigidly on top of the bogie frame and connected to the axles through gearing and Alsthom flexible drives. The body rests on four rubber springs, two at each side of the body and close together. The springs are sandwiches of steel and rubber bonded together. They resist the vertical load by compression, whilst lateral oscillations and rotation of the bogie are resisted by shearing action. This is a remarkably simple and effective suspension.

An important innovation in the "15000"s was the control system, made possible by the comparative simplicity of thyristor circuitry. The driver has two normal methods of controlling speed, constant speed or constant current. With the former the driver sets the controller to the speed required, and also sets up the value of the current which is not to be exceeded. The control circuits accelerate the locomotive to the speed required, and then vary the current to hold it at that speed, provided that the stipulated maximum current is not exceeded. If, due to a change in gradient, the locomotive attempts to accelerate, current is reduced, and finally, if necessary, regenerative braking is set up. Alternatively the driver can isolate the speed control, and the system holds the current to the pre-selected value, observance of speed being the driver's responsibility.

The "15000"s were designed for 112½mph (180km/h), which is somewhat surprising as 124mph (200km/h) had already been permitted on some parts of SNCF when they were built, but so far on the Eastern Region the limit is 100mph (160km/h). Every effort was made to simplify the design to reduce maintenance costs, and with this in mind the traction motor was modified to make it self-ventilating and so eliminate the need for a forced-ventilation system.

They soon established an excellent reputation, and with 74 in service they dominate the Eastern Region passenger services. Work continued on chopper control for dc locomotives, and for a time C-C locomotive No.20002, with chopper equipment, ran coupled to standard B-B No.9252, No.20002 serving as a current supply to the motors of No.9252. Next No.15007 was converted to a dc machine, numbered 7003, to test the equipment for the "7200" class.

In 1976, delivery of the "7200" class began followed later in the year by the dual-voltage "22200" locomotives. These classes differ only in that the "22200" has an additional pantograph for ac operation, and a transformer and silicon rectifier for converting the ac supply to 1,500V dc. The current is then fed into the same circuits as the dc supply, so that there is only one control system. Both classes closely resemble the "15000"s, but are slightly longer in the body, and they have rheostatic braking instead of regenerative.

The "7200" and "22200" classes work over all dc lines, with the versatile

"22200"s running particularly long distances where their dual-voltage capability avoids the necessity for changing locos en route. TGVs have displaced them from the principal passenger services, but they achieve high mileages on trains such as those carrying Ford motor vehicle parts from Dagenham in East London to Valencia in Spain, hauled by a "22200" throughout between Calais and the Spanish border at Cerbere.

Although it had been hoped that Class "7200" would be suitable for heavy low-speed freight work, trouble was encountered with overheating of the motors, and the first 35 locomotives were temporarily fitted with bogies geared for 62mph (100km/h). All later locomotives have force-ventilated motors.

For nine months before its gear ratio was changed, No.7233 was transferred to the South-Western Region, and worked "L'Etendard" between Paris and Bordeaux with considerable running at 125mph (200km/h). Later No.22278 was tested similarly, thus proving that the classes were suitable for this speed, although designed for 180km/h.

A total of 210 Class "7200" locomotives and 150 of Class "22200" were built by Alsthom, and in due course the firm received an order for 48 similar locomotives for Netherlands Railways.

In 1982 No.15056 was fitted with synchronous three-phase motors, and No.15055 was selected for another series of tests with asynchronous motors. The success of the trials with No.15055 led to a decision that synchronous motors would power future batches of Bo-Bo locomotives, and in 1984 SNCF ordered 44 dual-voltage machines, designated Class "26000".

Below: Further development of the Class "15000" is in progress in France. Note the laboratory car at the head of the train.

161

RGT Four-car trainset

Origin: France: French National Railways (SNCF), 1972. **Type:** Five-car express passenger gas turbine set. **Gauge:** 4ft 8^1/$_2$in (1,435mm). **Propulsion:** One Société Française Turboméca Turmo IIIF 1,150 hp (858kW) gas turbine in each end vehicle driving the axles of the outer bogie through Voith hydraulic transmission. **Weight:** 143,040lb (64.9t) adhesive, 570,836lb (259t) total. **Axleload:** 35,760lb (16.2t). **Overall length:** 339ft 6^5/$_{16}$in (103,488mm). **Tractive effort:** 26,980lb (120kN). **Max speed:** 112mph (180km/h).

In 1966 SNCF, with no diesel locomotives able to run at more than 87mph (140km/h), studied the problem of designing railcars for non-electrified lines. The aim was to equal the performance then being achieved by electric traction, that is general running at 100mph (160km/h) with speeds of 124mph (200km/h) on suitable stretches. Non-electrified routes often had a greater number of speed restrictions than the more generously laid-out electric routes, and the performance contemplated would therefore require a much higher power-to-weight ratio than was being achieved in contemporary diesel railcars.

The French aero-engine industry has scored notable successes with small gas turbines for helicopters, and SNCF saw these turbines as a means of providing the high power required without a significant increase in weight over a diesel railcar. The first experiment was started in 1966. A Turmo 111 F engine manufactured by Société Française Turboméca was fitted to the trailer car of a standard two-car diesel set. The output shaft of this engine was connected through reduction gears to the axles of one bogie. The engine was rated at 1,500hp (1,120kW), but was de-rated to 1,150hp (858kW) for railway use, and it operated on diesel fuel, both for fuel economy and greater safety. The first trial took place on April 25, 1967, and two months later a speed of 147mph (236km/h) was recorded. The train was driven by the diesel engine below a speed of 20mph (30km/h) with the gas turbine shut down. Fuel consumption was considered acceptable.

The next step in 1968 was an order for 10 four-car trains for the Paris-Caen-Cherbourg service. In these a 440hp (330kW) diesel engine was fitted in one end coach and a Turmo III F in the other, as in the "TGS", but the coaches were appointed to main line standard with catering facilities and warm-air ventilation. The difference was that the turbine was connected to the axles through Voith hydraulic transmission, enabling the turbine to be used from rest. These sets are designated "ETG" (*Elément á Turbine á Gaz*)

In 1970 the Paris-Caen and Paris-Cherbourg services were taken over by "ETG"s, being the first full inter-city service in the world to be operated by gas turbine traction. Caen was reached in 109 minutes at 81.5mph (131km/h). Although the sets were designed for 112mph (180km/h) they have always been limited to 100mph (160km/h) in service.

Success of the "ETG"s created a demand for trains with still more and

Above: "Turbo-train" approaching Chicago. Two sets were supplied from France and several more were built in the USA.

better accommodation. This was met by building units with longer coaches which could be run in four-coach or five-coach sets with air conditioning and other appointments as in the latest locomotive-hauled coaches. The diesel engine was omitted, and there was a Turmo III power unit in each end coach. An additional small Astazou turbine was installed in each power car to provide electric power at all times, the main turbines being run only when required for traction. These trains are the "RTG"s (*Rame á Turbine á Gaz*).

"RTG"s took over the Cherbourg services in 1972 and were later introduced on cross-country routes based on Lyons. A total of 41 sets were built, of which two were later sold to Amtrak in the United States. Examples also found their way to Egypt and Iran.

Gas turbine trains were a notable success for French engineers, for not only do they perform reliably, but they are environmentally acceptable both to the passengers and to those outside the train. However, their operating costs were no longer acceptable after the 1973 oil price rises, and no further extensions have been made to these services. Nevertheless, they rank as the most successful application of gas turbines to railway passenger services.

Below: The power car of an "RTG". The power unit is in the small windowless space between the two doors at the front end.

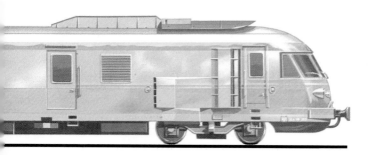

Class Re 6/6 B$_o$-B$_o$-B$_o$

Origin: Switzerland: Swiss Federal Railways (SBB),1972. **Type:** Heavy-duty mixed-traffic mountain locomotive. **Gauge:** 4ft 8^1/$_2$in (1,435mm). **Propulsion:** Low-frequency alternating current at 15,000V 16^2/$_3$Hz fed via overhead catenary and step-down transformer to six frame-mounted 1,740hp (1,300kW) motors each driving one axle through a flexible drive system. **Weight:** 26,480lb (120t). **Axleload:** 44,080lb (20t). **Overall length:** 63ft 4^1/$_2$in (19,310mm). **Tractive effort:** 88,700lb (395kN). **Max speed:** 87mph (140km/h).

Ten-thousand horsepower plus in a single locomotive! And no cheating either – all is contained in a single indivisible unit. The story of this giant amongst locomotives began with the ever increasing demands of traffic on the St Gotthard main line across the Alps.

The original heavy artillery of the Gotthard line was a famous series of rod-drive 1-C-C-1 articulated "Crocodile" locomotives, of only one-quarter the power of the "Re 6/6" engines. In all 52 were built and a few lasted into the 1980s. In 1931 two rather amazing experimental "Ae 8/14" 1-Bo-1-Bo-1 +1-Bo-1-Bo-1 twin units appeared. One of these, built by Oerlikon, brought the power available to 8,800hp (6,560kW), combined with a drawgear-breaking maximum tractive effort of 132,240lb (588kN). The other, by Brown Boveri, was slightly less powerful. These were followed in 1939 by yet another twin locomotive of the same unique wheel arrangement which did offer more than 10,000hp – 11,400hp (8,500kW) in fact – as well as 110,200lb (490kN) of tractive effort. However, it was at the cost of a total weight twice that of the "Re 6/6". Experience with these immense machines was such that they were not repeated.

The "Re 4/4" double-bogie locomotives for express passenger work came to SBB in 1946, following the example of the Bern-Lötschberg-Simplon Railway Class "Ae 4/4" of two years earlier. With hindsight it seems extraordinary that the Swiss did not simply build a lower-geared version of the "Re 4/4" and use it in multiple on the Gotthard. The fact remains, though, that they did not and instead went on seeking a single locomotive unit that would do the job. Hence in 1952 the usual firms – this time in consort – that is Brown Boveri, Oerlikon and the Swiss Locomotive Works, produced a locomotive with six driven axles and all but 1,000hp per axle, classified "Ae 6/6". They used all the know-how gained on the "Ae 4/4" and "Re 4/4" units, but adapted the design for six-wheel instead of four-wheel bogies.

Above: A Swiss Federal Railways "Re 6/6" Bo-Bo-Bo climbs up to the Gotthard tunnel with the "Barbarossa Express", in 1981.

Below: A massive 10,000hp in a single-unit locomotive! The Swiss Federal Railways' "Re 6/6" Bo-Bo-Bo mixed-traffic design.

The "Ae 6/6"s were rated at 5,750hp (4,290kW) and 120 were built between 1952 and 1966. Regenerative braking was installed and the maximum speed was 88mph (125km/h), The class ushered in the hitherto almost unheard of practice (for SBB) of naming. Naturally they began with the Swiss Cantons, but soon these ran out and it had to be important towns instead; finally, some of the much mightier successors of the "Ae 6/6"s had to make do with the names of some very small places indeed! The extra power of the "Ae 6/6"s came at the right moment, for an explosion of traffic over the line was about to occur. By the late-1960s, three times the tonnage and over twice the number of trains were passing compared with 1950.

Amongst many measures proposed to cope with the situation was provision of still more powerful locomotives. Something was done quickly by converting existing locomotives to work in multiple – a measure that the Swiss were normally reluctant to take. But in 1972, two single-unit super-power prototypes were delivered by the same consortium. There was no point in providing for haulage of trains above 850t by a single unit because European wagon couplings were not strong enough to pull heavier loads than this up the Gotthard gradients. Larger trains can be hauled, but a second locomotive has then to be cut into the centre of the load.

The first two "Re 6/6"s were articulated, but later examples and the production version had the single carbody as described. The haulage capacity was nicely balanced, for an 800t train could be taken up the 1-in-37 (2.7 per cent) at the line limit of 50mph (80km/h). One of the reasons for adopting the Bo-Bo-Bo wheel arrangement in place of Co-Co was that the length of rigid wheelbase is reduced. This is important on a line like the Gotthard, with almost continuous curvature as sharp as 15 chains (300m) radius. On the other hand, having a rigid body to the locomotive greatly simplified and reduced the cost of the centre bogie, which could align itself with the curves by being allowed sideplay.

All three bogies were pivotless and each one was made to run more

66

Above: A Class "Re 6/6" Bo-Bo-Bo electric locomotive at speed with a Swiss Federal Railways' inter-city express train.

easily over small irregularities in track alignment by giving its axles lateral movement centralised with springs.

The "Ae6/6"s (now Class "610") are still a remarkable design, but the "Re 6/6"s (now Class "620") are over 80 per cent more powerful within the same weight limitation. In addition to being an excellent freight-hauler for mountain grades, these versatile machines are also suitable for passenger trains running at the highest speeds permitted in Switzerland.

Below: A freight train is swept through a lowland forest by a Swiss Federal Class "Re 6/6" Bo-Bo-Bo electric locomotive.

SD40-2 C$_o$-C$_o$

Origin: United States: Electro-Motive Division, General Motors Corporation (EMD), 1972. **Type:** Road switcher diesel-electric locomotive. **Gauge:** 4ft 8^1/$_2$in (1,435mm). **Propulsion:** One EMD 645E3 3,000hp (2,240kW) 16-cylinder turbocharged two-stroke Vee engine and alternator supplying current through silicon rectifiers to six nose-suspended traction motors. **Weight:** 368,000lb (167t), with variations according to optional fittings. **Axleload:** 61,330lb (27.8t). **Overall length:** 68ft 10in (20,980mm). **Tractive effort:** 83,100lb (370kN). **Max speed:** 65mph (105km/h).

For 50 years the Electro-Motive Division of General Motors has dominated the US diesel market, taking 70 to 75 per cent of total orders. The remainder of the market has been shared between the former steam locomotive builders Alco and Baldwin/Lima, a few smaller firms, and latterly GE, but since 1969 only GE has survived. The effect has been that EMD has never had a monopoly, and although the company's success has been due very much to its policy of offering a limited number of off-the-shelf models, it cannot ignore specialist needs of its customers. There has thus been steady development and improvement of the EMD models over the years, directed mainly at increasing power, reducing fuel consumption and maintenance costs, and improving adhesion.

Introduction of the "hood" design "GP7" model in 1949 marked the beginning of the end for the "carbody" unit on which EMD had made its reputation. From then onwards nearly all EMD's road locomotives would be general-purpose machines. There was, however, a variant; the four-axle machines inevitably had a heavy axleload, and EMD therefore offered a six-axle version designated "SD" for "Special Duty". Although the axleload was reduced, the total weight of the locomotive was greater than that of a four-axle machine, and it thus appealed also to roads which had a need for maximum adhesion due to climatic conditions. The pattern thus became established. of offering four-axle and six-axle variants of each model.

Up to 1965, the engine used was the 567 of 567in^3 capacity, but by the time this engine was pressed to 2,500hp (1,865kW) for traction, it was reaching its limit, and a new engine was produced with the same piston stroke of 10in (254mm), but with the diameter increased from 8^1/$_2$in (216mm) to 9^1/$_{16}$in (230mm). The cylinder volume became 645in^3, thus giving the engine its designation "645". Like the 567 it is a two-stroke engine, and is available with or without turbocharger. A two-stroke engine requires some degree of pressure-charging to give effective scavenging, and if there is no turbocharger there is a Roots-type blower driven directly from the engine. There have thus been two lines of development: the

Above: An "SD40-2" diesel-electric road-switcher locomotive heads a line of Burlington Northern units of motive power.

turbocharged engine pressed to give successive increases in power, and the engines without turbochargers remaining at 2,000hp (1,490kW), but benefiting from mechanical improvements directed at reducing fuel consumption and maintenance costs.

One of the attractions of the diesels which first replaced steam on freight work was that a number of modest-sized units, working in multiple under the control of one crew, could replace the largest steam engine. These diesels were little bigger than some of the diesel switchers which the roads already operated, and their maintenance was easier than that of overworked steam locomotives which were very demanding of attention and needed good quality fuel to give of their best. The diesels could show a reduction in operating costs, even when their higher capital cost was taken into account.

However, when the possible economies from total dieselisation had been achieved, motive power officers looked for other means of effecting savings. With the problems of diesel maintenance now better understood, an attractive idea was to use a smaller number of larger units to achieve

Below: The General Motors' Model "SD40-2" Co-Co diesel-electric locomotive in the smart blue livery of Conrail

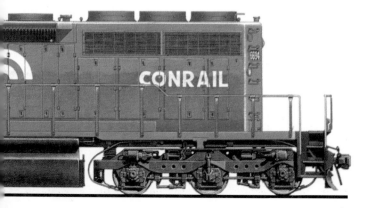

the same total power. This was found to save money both in purchase price and in operating costs. EMD's competitors were first in the field with higher horsepower as a selling point, and it was not until 1958 that EMD marketed a 2,400hp (1,790kW) engine in the "SD24" series with which to match the Fairbanks-Morse Trainmaster of 1953. In 1959 EMD produced its 2,000hp (1,490kW) four-axle model, and from then the horsepower race was on.

The 645 engine was launched in 1965 in two versions, the pressure-charged 645E and the turbocharged 645E3. The 645E was made in 8, 12 and 16 cylinder versions, and the 645E3 with 12, 16 and 20 cylinders. These engines were incorporated in a new range of nine locomotives, which included the "GP40" and "SD40" with the 16-cylinder version of the turbocharged engine, giving 3,000hp (2,240kW), and the "SD45" with the 20-cylinder engine giving 3,600hp (2,690kW). This was the first US engine with 20 cylinders, and it brought EMD firmly into the high horsepower stable, some time after Alco and GE had reached 3,000hp. The six-axle types had a new Flexicoil bogie to give improved riding, and the 3,000hp and 3,600hp engines introduced alternators, instead of generators, to the EMD range. The alternators were more compact than generators, and this assisted the designers in finding space for the larger engines.

With the railroads enthusiastic about high-power locomotives, the "SD45" was the most popular model, achieving a total of 1,260 sales in six years. The highest-powered four-axle unit in the range, the 3,000hp "GP40", achieved sales of 1,201, and for roads which required a six-axle layout, 883 of the "SD40" were supplied.

These models remained standard until the beginning of 1972 when, with competition from GE still keen, a revision was made of the whole range, which became known as "Dash-2", from the addition which was made to the class designation, for example, "SD40-2". At this stage no further increase in power was offered, and the alterations were directed at improving fuel consumption and simplifying maintenance. The most important changes were in the electrical control system, which now comprise largely plug-in modules of printed circuits which can be changed quickly from stock.

New high-adhesion bogies were offered in the six-axle models, known as "HT-W (High Traction, three axle). Adhesion was still a major concern to the railroads, and as orders came in for the "Dash-2" range, two trends became apparent: first, that the extra maintenance costs of the 20-cylinder engine and its large turbocharger and radiators were not justified for 600hp more than the 16-cylinder engine could give; and secondly, that the

Below: An "SD40-2" road-switcher belonging to Southern Pacific, fitted with special high-adhesion Type "T" bogies.

Above: Canadian National "SD40-2"s in multiple at the head of a freight. Note the modified "safety cab" of the second unit.

3,000hp four-axle locomotive, the "GP40", had given trouble with wheelslip and excessive maintenance of its highly rated traction motors. The high-power model to emerge as the most popular in the range was therefore the "SD40-2", with 3,000hp transmitted through six axles. By the late-1970s this was established as virtually the standard high-power diesel in the US, with sales approaching 4,000 by the end of the decade. The railroad with the largest number was Burlington Northern with about 900, a quarter of its total locomotive stock.

Concurrently the high cost of maintaining a turbocharger compared with a Roots blower had encouraged railroads to purchase large numbers of "GP38-2" units of 2,000hp for duties for which a 3,000hp locomotive was not required, and sales of this model passed 2,000 by 1980.

EMD now tackled the problem of improving adhesion in four-axle-locomotives by a wheelslip detector employing Doppler radar, which is sufficiently sensitive to allow an axle to work safely at the limit of adhesion. Engine development made it possible to offer a 3,500hp (2,610kW) 16-cylinder engine, and in 1980 the company launched the "GP50" with the 3,500hp engine on four axles, so that railroads once again had the choice of a high-power locomotive without the expense of six axles. This found little favour, but the corresponding six-axle unit, the "SD50", had reached 300 deliveries by late-1984. By this time also, a new larger engine, the 710, was in production, giving 3,800hp (2,835kW) in its 16-cylinder version. This was used in the "GP60" and "SD60" series, whilst the 12-cylinder version was used in the "GP59". A total of 10 of these locomotives were built in 1984-85 for extended trials.

Class Dx C₀-C₀

Origin: New Zealand: New Zealand Railways (NZR), 1972. **Type:** Diesel electric locomotive for mixed traffic. **Gauge:** 3ft 6in (1,067mm). **Propulsion** General Electric (USA) 2,750hp (2,050kW) Type 7FDL-12 twelve-cylinder diesel engine and alternator supplying current via solid-state rectifiers to six nose-suspended traction motors. **Weight:** 214, 890lb (97.5t). **Axleload** 35,925lb (16.3t). **Overall length:** 55ft 6in (16,916mm). **Tractive effort** 54,225lb (241kN). **Max speed:** 65mph (103km/h).

New Zealand may be a country with a small population as well as a small gauge railway system, but its railwaymen have always believed in big powerful locomotives. For example, the legendary New Zealand-built "K" class 4-8-4s were as powerful as anything that ran in the mother country, in spite of an axleload limit only 71 per cent of that in Britain. Similarly, these big "Dx" diesel-electrics have a power output comparable with Britain's standard Class "47"s, again within the limits of axleload in proportion as before.

Class "Dx" was the culmination of a dieselisation programme which began in the 1950s – as regards main-line traction units of, say, 750hp plus – with the 40 Class "Dg" A1A-A1A units of 1955. What was called "Commonwealth Preference" in import duties gave British manufacturers a substantial advantage in those days, and the order went to English Electric. The class was lightweight, able to run over the light rails of the South Island system, where there was an axleload of only 11t.

Between 1955 and 1967, General Motors came in in a very big way with the 74-strong 1,428hp (1,065 kW) Class "Da" as the mainstay of the North Island trunk lines. There were also the 16 lighter GM "Db" class locomotives for North Island branch lines. In 1968 and 1969 the Japanese firm Mitsubishi delivered 60 Class "Dj" Bo-Bo-Bos for the South Island; this class offered 1,045hp (780kW) for an axleload of 10.9t. As a result of these deliveries the last regular steam-hauled train ran in 1972.

It then became apparent that more powerful locomotives could be used to advantage, and the result was this "Dx" class. Very surprisingly NZR went to a fourth source for these magnificent machines. General Electric of USA-not to be confused with GEC Traction of Britain or its subsidiary General Electric (Australia) – supplied 47 of these units during 1972-75. They were used on crack trains on the North Island trunk line between Wellington and Auckland, both passenger and freight. The design is based on General Electric's standard "U26C" export model.

GEC did not capture the market though, because subsequent deliveries were from General Motors with both A1A-A1A and Co-Co versions of a similar locomotive (classes "Dc" and "Df" of 67 and 30 units respectively). This in spite of a debate then in full cry concerning the need for railways a

all in a country with such modest transport requirements. In the end the verdict was favourable to railways but not to diesels - instead New Zealand Railways embarked on a programme of electrification which would use indigenous forms of energy, but only the North Island main line between Palmerston North and Hamilton was energised.

Above: A Class "Dx" diesel-electric locomotive takes freight across a trestle viaduct typical of New Zealand Railways.

Below: General Electric (USA) supplied New Zealand Railways with the Class "Dx" Co-Co diesel-electric locomotives for both passenger and freight work on North Island lines.

Class 87 B$_o$-B$_o$

Origin: Great Britain: British Railways (BR), 1973. **Type:** Mixed-traffic electric locomotive. **Gauge:** 4ft 8½in (1,435mm). **Propulsion:** Alternating current at 25,000V 50Hz fed via overhead catenary, step-down transformer and solid-state rectifiers to four 1,250hp (923kW) fully spring-borne traction motors, driving the axles by gearing and ASEA hollow-axle flexible drives. **Weight:** 182,930lb (83t). **Axleload:** 45,735lb (20.75t). **Overall length:** 58ft 6in (17,830mm). **Tractive effort:** 58,000lb (258kN). **Max speed:** 100mph (160km/h).

Although both began almost from scratch after World War II, there could be no greater contrast than between British Rail's ac electric locomotive development story and that of its diesels. Diesel developments followed each other with the consistency of successive pictures in a kaleidoscope while ac electric locomotives moved through seven related classes all with the same appearance, maximum speed and wheel arrangement.

The first five classes were offerings on the part of five manufacturers to meet a specification for a 100mph (160km/h) locomotive capable of operation on 25,000V or 6,250V 50Hz electrification systems.

All had frame-mounted traction motors with flexible drive. Classes "81" to "84" originally had mercury-arc rectifiers, while Class "85" was fitted with solid-state rectifiers from the start and also had rheostatic braking. In the event, the need for 6,250V operation never arose, although provision was made for it. No steam heating boilers were fitted as electrically-heated sets were provided for all regular trains on the electrified lines. Separate steam-heating vans were provided for occasions when stock not fitted with electric heaters was hauled by electric locomotives in the winter.

When the complete electric service from London to Birmingham, Manchester and Liverpool was introduced in 1965-67, a further 100 locomotives were supplied. These were Class "AL6", later Class "86", which had solid-state silicon rectifiers, rheostatic braking as the prime braking system and – one major simplification – nose-suspended traction motors geared direct to the axles. Not surprisingly, this simple answer was too hard on the permanent way for such dense high-speed traffic and the class was divided into several sub-classes with different standards to suit different types of traffic. The three locomotives in Class "86.1" were 1972 rebuilds having ASEA hollow-axle flexible drive and intended as prototypes for the Class "87". Classes "86.2" and "86.3" were modified to permit

Below: British Railways' class 87 Bo-Bo standard electric locomotive design. Note a single pantograph current collector.

Above: Since privatisation of former British Rail passenger services, the Class 87s have been used by Virgin Trains on its West Coast Main Line route. *(Nic Joynson)*

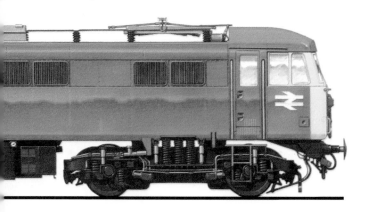

100mph (160km/h) running to continue, while the later "86.4"s and "86.6" were limited to freight hauling at up to 75mph (120km/h).

The 36 locomotives of Class "87" were supplied for the extension of electric working from Crewe to Glasgow. They were built at BR's Crewe Works with electrical equipment by GEC Traction, into which AEL English Electric, Metropolitan Vickers and British Thompson-Houston had been amalgamated. Power rating was increased 56 per cent over that of Class "81" for a 4 per cent increase of weight. The ASEA hollow-axle flexible drive, tried out on Class "86.1", was used, and multiple-unit capability was provided. At long last it had not been thought necessary to provide an exhauster for working vacuum-braked trains. All the class carried names mostly of distinguished people living or dead, and this pleasant practice also spilled over on to examples of Class "86".

The final improvement was application of thyristor control, fitted to a Class "87" locomotive redesignated as Class "87.1". No.87101 carried the honoured name of Stephenson . A successful one-off, this locomotive provided valuable experience for the thyristor technology later applied to Classes "90" and "91".

In May 1984, the maximum permitted line speed for the class was increased to 110mph (176km/h), and certain London to Glasgow trains were accelerated. As regards performance and reliability, it perhaps says enough that this can be entirely taken for granted with these locomotives. Ample power can be drawn from the contact wire for maintaining the maximum permitted speed with the usual loads, while the same locomotives are also suitable for heavier and slower freight trains.

Above, right: British Railways' Class 87 Bo-Bo *Thane of Fife* takes an express train through Stafford station in June 1981.

Right, below: Class 87 No. 87004 *Britannia* takes an express passenger train through the northern hills towards Glasgow.

Below: A British Railways' class 87 Bo-Bo electric locomotive at speed on the electrified West Coast main line.

Class 381 Nine-car train

Origin: Japan: Japanese National Railways (JNR), 1973. **Type:** Electric express passenger multiple-unit trainset with tilting mechanism. **Gauge:** 3ft 6in (1,067mm). **Propulsion:** Direct current at 1,500V or alternating current at 20,000V 50 or 60Hz, fed from overhead catenary to six motor cars, each with four 160hp (100kW) traction motors geared to the axles. **Weight:** 515,760lb (234t) adhesive, 753,802lb (342t) total. **Axleload:** 21,490lb (9.75t). **Overall length:** 628ft 11in (191,700mm). **Max speed:** 75mph (120km/h).

The concept of a tilting train arises from the fact that suitably designed trains can safely run round curves at much higher speeds than are normally comfortable for the passengers. This takes into account the superelevation (otherwise known as "cant" or "banking") applied to the track. The idea was born that a calculated amount of tilt could be added to the cant by servo mechanisms on the train, and in this way trains could be run much faster safely and comfortably without the need to build an expensive new railway. The proposition is so attractive that several railways – Switzerland, Germany, Italy amongst them – now operate tilting trains in daily service. But the development of reliable trains was a lengthy process; these JNR examples were the first to run in significant numbers.

The Japanese tilting trains (Class "381") were not for high-speed operation, intended to run, say, at 90mph (144km/h) where normal trains run at 75mph (120km/h), but instead to hold 60mph (96km/h) where a normal train would be limited to 50mph (80km/h). The tilt is limited to 5°, compared with the 9° of Britain's APT project, and the 8° of Swiss Federal Railways' "ICN" trains, and it is applied when the cars' sensors feel a certain transverse acceleration. Being intended for lines with gradients up to 1-in-40 (2.5 per cent), ample power is provided with two out of every three cars motored. One out of every two motor cars is a power car with pantographs and control/conversion equipment to cover operation on dc and 50 or 60Hz ac

Above: The tilting abilities of the Class "381" multiple-unit express trains are used to best advantage on mountain lines.

The normal formation is nine cars, with driving trailers at each end. A nine-car train has 3,200hp (2,400kW) available and this is sufficient to produce 50mph (80km/h) up a 1-in-50 (2 per cent) gradient. Dynamic braking is available for the descent. The combination of higher uphill speeds and higher speeds on sharp curves both uphill and downhill produces worthwhile savings in overall running times. Operation of the original units has been sufficiently successful for Japan's fleet of tilting cars to have risen to more than 500 in the 1990s, and Class "381" remains in service with JR West.

Below: The blunt nose and driver's raised cab are prominent features of the Japanese Class "381" tilting train.

Class Rc4 B_o-B_o

Origin: Sweden: Swedish State Railways (SJ), 1975. **Type:** Electric mixed-traffic locomotive. **Gauge:** 4ft 8^1/$_2$in (1,435mm). **Propulsion:** Alternating current at 15,000V 16^2/$_3$Hz, fed via overhead catenary, step-down transformer and a thyristor control system to four frame-mounted 1,206hp (900kM traction motors, each driving one axle by gearing and ASEA hollow-axle flexible drive. **Weight:** 171,910lb (78t). **Axleload:** 42,980lb (19.5t). **Overall length:** 50ft 11in (15,520mm). **Tractive effort:** 65,200lb (290kN). **Max speed:** 84mph (135km/h).

The "Rc" family of electric locomotives, developed by the Allmanna Svenska Elektriska Aktiebolaget (ASEA) organisation initially for Swedish State Railways, bids fair to be the world's most successful electric locomotive design. Intended for mixed traffic, the design was developed on the one hand to cope with express passenger trains at 100mph (160km/h), while on the other a version was supplied for hauling heavy iron ore trains in the Arctic regions. Abroad, such widely differing customers as Austria, Norway and the USA run "Rc" derivatives.

One of the reasons for this pre-eminence is that the "Rc1" was the world's first thyristor locomotive design, put into service in 1967; ingenuity on the part of other manufacturers is no substitute for years of experience in service.

In 1969, 100 "Rc2"s followed the 20 "Rc1"s, and they included improvements to the thyristor control system and more sophisticated electrical filters. These are needed to prevent harmonic ripples produced by the thyristor circuits feeding back into the rails and interfering with signalling currents (which also flow in the same rails) and communication circuits generally. The 10 "Rc3"s of 1970 were "Rc2"s geared for 100mph (160km/h) while 16 units, some of which have rheostatic braking, were

Below: The Swedish State Railways' Class "Rc4" "universal" mixed-traffic Bo-Bo electric locomotive equipped with a solid-state control system using thyristor devices.

Above: A Class "Rc4" electric locomotive, dwarfed by the cars it is pulling, rolls a passenger train through the snow.

supplied to Austria (Class "1043") in 1971-73.

In 1975 came the "Rc4" class, the design of which included a patent system developed by ASEA for countering wheelslip, which automatically reduces the current supplied to any driving motor which begins to creep faster than the others. There are also other improvements such as solid-state instead of rotary converters for power supply to auxiliary apparatus.

A total of 150 "Rc4"s were supplied to Swedish State Railways, plus another 15 with modifications produced for Norway (Class "el.16"), but ASEA's greatest success occurred in the USA with the fleet of "AEM7" electric locomotives supplied for Amtrak's North East Corridor operations (*qv*).

Another variant was the batch of six iron-ore haulers of 1977 (Class "Rm") which had ballasting to raise the axleload to 50,700lb (23t), automatic couplers, lower gearing, rheostatic braking and multiple-unit capability, as well as better heating and more insulation in the cab.

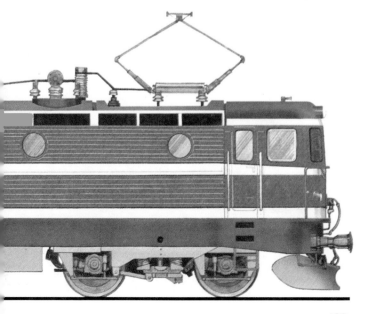

F40PH B$_o$-B$_o$

Origin: United States: Electro-Motive Division, General Motors Corporation (EMD), 1976. **Type:** Diesel-electric passenger locomotive. **Gauge:** 4ft 8½in (1,435mm). **Propulsion:** One EMD 645E3 3,000hp (2,240kW) 16-cylinder turbocharged two-stroke Vee engine and alternator supplying current through silicon rectifiers to four nose-suspended traction motors geared to the axles. **Weight:** 232,000lb (105.2t). **Axleload:** 58,000lb (26.3t). **Overall length:** 52ft 0in (15,850mm). **Tractive effort:** 68,440lb (304kN). **Max speed:** 103mph (166km/h).

The last of the EMD passenger "carbody" diesels was built at the end of 1963, and with passenger traffic declining rapidly in the USA, the need for special passenger locomotives seemed to have disappeared. Both EMD and its competitors offered a train-heating steam generator as an optional extra on certain "hood" units, and this met the needs of railroads which required replacements for ageing "E" or "F" series units.

In 1968, with the railroads' enthusiasm for high-power diesels at its climax, the Atchison, Topeka & Santa Fe Railway proposed to buy from EMD some 20-cylinder 3,660hp (2,690kW) Co-Co locomotives geared for high speed to operate its premier passenger services. The railroad asked that the locomotives should be given a more acceptable appearance for passenger work, and that the body should have less air resistance at speed than a normal hood unit. The outcome was the "cowl", a casing shaped like an angular version of the old carbody, but differing from it in that the casing does not carry any load. The cowl extends ahead of the cab, giving the front of the cab more protection against the weather than a normal hood.

The model was designated "FP45", and was very similar in its equipment to the "SD45" road switcher. Another variant had a shorter frame resulting from the omission of the steam generator; it was designated "F45".

In 1971 the National Railroad Passenger Corporation (Amtrak) took over most of the non-commuter passenger services in the US, and in 1973 took delivery of its first new locomotives to replace the old "E" and "F" series.

Right: An "F40PH" diesel-electric locomotive on commuter service with Chicago's Regional Transportation Authority.

Below: The "F40PH" Bo-Bo "cowl"-type diesel-electric unit, Amtrak's standard express passenger locomotive of the 1990s.

By this time, enthusiasm for engines above 3,000hp had declined, so the Amtrak units were similar to the "FP45" but with a 16-cylinder 3,000hp (2,240kW) engine. A total of 150 were delivered in 1973-74. They were equipped with two steam generators mounted on skids, which could easily be replaced by two diesel-alternators when steam-heated stock was replaced by electrically-heated vehicles. In view of the similarity to the "SD40"s, these locomotives were classified "SDP40F".

For a time all was well, but then an alarming series of derailments occurred to the trailing bogies of "SDP40F"s whilst negotiating curves. No explanation could be found, but it was clear that the track had been spread or rails turned over by excessive lateral forces. The bogies were only slightly different from those of other EMD "Dash-2" three-axle bogies, but it was only part of the locomotive on which any suspicion of fault could fall.

In the meantime, for shorter-distance routes on which the coaches were already electrically-heated, Amtrak had ordered a four-axle 3,000hp (2,240kW) locomotive, with an alternator for supplying three-phase current at 60Hz for on-board services driven by gearing from the engine crankshaft. This model is designated "F40PH", and deliveries began in March 1976 when the problem of the "SDP40F" derailments was acute. As the well-tried Blomberg bogie fitted to the "F40PH" had given no cause for criticism, Amtrak decided that the Co-Co locomotives should be rebuilt as "F40PH"s. The frame could be shortened by 16ft, as the steam generator was no longer needed. The "F40PH"s built new had a 500kW alternator, which drew a maximum of 710hp from the engine, but for the transcontinental "Superliner" trains an 800kW alternator and larger fuel tanks were needed, so that the "F40PH"s obtained by rebuilding are 4ft longer than the others.

In fact the rebuilding was nominal, for it cost nearly 70 per cent of the price of a new locomotive, and in effect the "SDP40F"s were scrapped when only four to five years old.

Many US commuter services are the responsibility of transit authorities, some of whom operate their own trains. A number of these operators bought a shortened version of the unhappy "SDP4OF", in which the steam generator was replaced by an alternator. This is the "F40C", and in this application this engine is uprated to 3,200hp (2,390kW). At the moderate speeds of commuter services, no trouble has been experienced with derailments, but nevertheless when further locomotives were required the transit authorities ordered the four-axle "F40PH", in some cases with the engine uprated to 3,200hp.

Below: A New Jersey Transit push-pull commuter train, in charge of a single F40PH unit, passes Harrison, New Jersey.

Above: A rake of striking double-deck cars of Ontario's GO Transit and headed by an F40PH unit, passes Scarborough, Ont.

Below: An F40PH Bo-Bo locomotive brings a short passenger train composed of "Amfleef" cars into Chicago's Union station.

Intercity 125 Ten-car train

Origin: Great Britain: British Railways (BR), 1978. **Type:** Diesel-electric high-speed train. **Gauge:** 4ft 8½in (1,435mm). **Propulsion:** One supercharged two-stroke Paxman Valenta 12RP200L Vee-type 12-cylinder engine of 2,250hp (1,680kW) with integral alternator in each of two driving motor luggage vans, each engine feeding current to sets of four traction motors mounted in the bogie frames. **Weight:** 308,560lb (140t) adhesive, 844,132lb (383t) total. **Axleload:** 38,570lb (17.5t). **Overall length:** 720ft 5in (219,584mm). **Max speed:** 125mph (200km/h).

These superb diesel-electric trains, the fastest in the world with that system of propulsion, marked a great step forward in the long history of the British express passenger train and, in addition, represented the first real original and countrywide success story of Britain's nationalised rail system in the passenger field.

As with most other success stories, the main ingredient of this triumph was the technical restraint of the trains, representing as they did a development of existing equipment rather than the result of beginning with a clean sheet of paper. The disastrous experiences with the Advanced Passenger Train (*qv*) – a clean-sheet-of-paper design if ever there was one – are a case in point.

If the technology of the High-Speed Train (HST) was just an update – except possibly for bogie suspension – then so much more impressive was the somersault in operational thinking. Ever since Liverpool & Manchester days, long-distance trains had had detachable locomotives, not only because the locomotives were liable to need more frequent (and messier) attention than the carriages, but also because they could then haul more than one type of train at different times of the day. The argument was that if the obvious disadvantages of self-propelled trains with fixed formation could be accepted, then the problems of giving them the ability to run at 125mph (200km/h) were much reduced. The power units themselves were simplified, since the need to haul other types of trains was non-existent. Things like vacuum brake equipment, slow running gear and much else were just not required and their space, cost and weight would all be saved.

As well as disadvantages, self-propelled trains have advantages. For example, HSTs can run into a terminus and leave again after a minimum interval for servicing. At the same time there is no question of trapping its locomotive against the buffer stops until another locomotive is attached at the opposite end. Annual mileages in the quarter-million region can be the rule rather than the exception. And to counter the argument that the locomotives that handled the day trains would be needed for sleeping car expresses at night, there was still the point that, for example, with

Above: A British Railways' express passenger train formed of an Intercity 125 diesel-electric ten-car set leaves town.

Below: The driving-motor-baggage van power cars which are placed at either end of each Intercity 125 ten-car set.

Above: First Great Western is one of four privatised British train operators to use HSTs: one of the FGW fleet is seen approaching Cardiff with a service from London Paddington. *(Ken Harris)*

Above, right: An Intercity 125 diesel-electric set forming a Paddington to Bristol express train, passes Reading in 1977.

Below, right: A diverted Edinburgh-London Intercity 125 express stands unexpectedly under the wires at Carlisle, 1981.

Newcastle to London then only a 3-hour ride, the need for sleeping car accommodation was eliminated.

The plan was originally for 132 HST trains intended to cover the principal non-electrified routes of British Railways with a network of 125mph (200km/h) trains. The routes in question were those between London (Paddington and King's Cross) and the West of England, South Wales, Yorkshire, the North East, Edinburgh and Aberdeen, as well as the North-East to South-West cross-country axis via Sheffield, Derby and Birmingham. Modifications to the plan reduced this number to 95, which provided a dense and comprehensive service of high speed diesel trains, christened Inter-City 125, which had no precedent nor any imitators worldwide. By 1985, the need to squeeze the maximum revenue-earning potential from these trainsets saw them extended to the London to Sheffield route, and to other important destinations on a once-daily basis.

The improvement in running time over routes where there is an adequate mileage available for running at maximum speed can approach as much as 20 per cent. For example, the shortest journey time for the 268 miles (428km) from King's Cross to Newcastle was 2hr 53min in 1985 compared with the 3hr 35min applicable during 1977 for trains hauled by the celebrated "Deltic" diesel locomotives (*qv*). Coupled with a substantial improvement in passenger comfort, this acceleration has led to a gratifyingly

increased level of patronage. A particular point is that the HSTs are not first-class only, or extra-fare trains, but available to all at the standard fare.

The design of the train was based on a pair of lightweight Paxman Valenta V-12 diesel engines each rated at 2250hp (1,680kW) and located in a motor-baggage car at each end of the train. The specific weight of these engines is about half that of other conventional diesel engines in use on Britain's railways and the design is very compact. This led to the motor cars of the units being built within 154,000lb (70t) overall weight, and it was also possible to provide baggage accommodation within the vehicle's 58ft 4in (17,792mm) length. Compare this with the "Peak" (Class "44") diesel locomotives of 20 years earlier (already described), where a unit of similar power output was so heavy it needed *eight* axles to carry it. The lower axleloads of the HST trains were also important because raising the speed of trains has a progressively destructive effect on the track.

The MkIII carriages of the trains were the result of some 10 years development from British Railways' MkI stock, standard since the 1950s. In spite of the addition of air-conditioning, sophisticated bogies, soundproofing, automatic corridor doors, and a degree of comfort hardly ever before offered to second-class passengers, the weight per seat fell by around 40 per cent. One factor was adoption of open plan seating allowing four comfortable seats across the coach instead of three – and another was

the increase in length from a standard of around 64ft (19,507mm) to 75ft 6in (23,000mm). This represented two additional bays of seating.

The concept of the HST was to provide a super train service on the existing railway, without rebuilding, replacing or even electrifying it. This meant being able to stop when required at signals within the warning distances which were built into existing signalling systems. Accordingly, the braking – with disc brakes on all wheels – includes sophisticated wheelslip correction equipment.

Particularly noticeable to the passenger was the superb ride at very high speeds over track whose quality is inevitably sometimes only fair. This was the result of the application of some sophisticated hardware evolved for the APT train, using air suspension.

A price has literally had to be paid for these advantages, however. There have been hideous maintenance costs, and many technical problems have had to be solved expensively, despite the fact that a complete prototype

Above: Unaffected by the poor visibility implicit in this wintry scene is this Intercity 125 (or Class "254") train set.

train was built and tested. This train reached 143mph (230km/h) on one occasion, a world record for diesel traction.

At the beginning of the 21st Century, the trainsets remain in front-line service on routes from London Paddington to the West of England and South Wales, on the Midland Main Line to Sheffield, and on some cross-country routes. A few continue to run under the wires on both East and West Coast main lines to destinations off the electrified network, such as Aberdeen, Inverness and Holyhead. A dozen-or-so power cars have been re-engined with the newer Paxman VP185. In their third decade of operation, sustained high-speed running is less common and many journey times less spectacular, as Britain's privatised railways concentrate more on maintaining their reliability and punctuality figures than cutting journey times.

Class 9E C₀-C₀

Origin: South Africa/UK: South African Railways (SAR), 1978. **Type:** Electric mineral-hauling locomotive. **Gauge:** 3ft 6in (1,067mm). **Propulsion:** Alternating current at 50,000V 50Hz fed via overhead catenary, step-down transformer with thyristor control to six nose-suspended 910hp (680kW) traction motors geared to the wheels. **Weight:** 370,270lb (168t). **Axleload:** 61,712lb (28t). **Overall length:** 69ft 4in (21,132mm). **Tractive effort:** 121,000lb (538kN). **Max speed:** 56mph (90km/h).

It is said that the only work of man on Earth visible from the moon is the Great Wall of China, but a further likely candidate must be the 529-mile (851km) line from Sishen in the centre of South Africa to the Atlantic port at Saldanha Bay. Not only would it have been noticed by a moon-bound earth-watcher on account of the rapidity with which it appeared, but its conspicuousness would have been enhanced by the featureless semi-desert nature of the most of the route.

Although built by the government's Iron & Steel Industrial Corporation (ISCOR) for moving iron ore for shipment, Spoornet (successor to South African Railways) operates the line, and the scale of operations is such that some unprecedented equipment was needed. In virtually uninhabited country, electric power supplies are far apart and hence a nominal voltage twice that normally used nowadays was specified. The result is that there are only six substations for the entire route, the contact wire itself acting as a main transmission line.

The 25 locomotives built for the railway (after a period of diesel operation) were designed by GEC Traction in Great Britain but built in South Africa by Union Carriage & Wagon. They normally operate in threes, so making up a 16,350hp (12,200kW) unit capable of starting as well as hauling a 20,000t load on the ruling gradient against loaded trains-of 1-in-250 (0.4 per cent). They can also operate (but at reduced speed) when the voltage drops as low as 25,000, which can happen in certain conditions, say 45 miles (70km) from the nearest substation.

One delightful feature of a harsh operation in the harshest of environments is the motor scooter provided in a special cabinet below the locomotive running board. This enables someone to inspect both sides of a 200-wagon train almost 1½ miles (2.3km) long, returning reasonably quickly to the locomotive after the round trip. Other comforts provided for the crew include full air-conditioning, a toilet and a refrigerator, as well as a hotplate for cooking. The unusual appearance is due to the roof having to be lowered

Above: One of the remarkable 50,000V 5,460 horse-power Class "9E" electric locomotives of South African Railways.

to accommodate the large insulators and switchgear needed for the high voltage.

The control system is of advanced design, using thyristors. The position of the driver's main control lever is arranged to determine not external physical things such as resistance values or transformer tapping, but instead the actual value of the traction motor currents and therefore the individual torque applied to each pair of wheels. This gives a much more direct control over the movement of the train. There are five systems of braking: straight air on the locomotive, normal air braking for the train, vacuum brakes (on some units) for occasional haulage of ordinary rolling stock, a handbrake and electrical braking. The latter, which is rheostatic rather than regenerative, can hold a full 20,000t train to 34mph (55km/h) on a 1-in-167 (0.6 per cent) downgrade. It is thought that this operation is the only one in the world where trains of this weight are worked using other than North American equipment.

Below: 16,350 horsepower moves a 20,000-tonne iron ore train on its 529 mile (851km) journey from Sishen to Saldanha Bay.

Class 120 B$_o$-B$_o$

Origin: Germany: German Federal Railway (DB), 1979. **Type:** Mixed-traffic electric locomotive. **Gauge:** 4ft 8^1/$_2$in (1,435mm). **Propulsion:** Alternating current at 115,000V 16^2/$_3$Hz from overhead wires rectified by thyristors and then inverted by thyristors to variable-frequency three-phase ac for supply to four 1,880 (1,400kW) induction traction motors with spring drive. **Weight:** 185,140lb (84t). **Axleload:** 46,280lb (21t). **Overall length:** 63ft 0in. (19,200mm). **Tractive effort:** 76,440lb (340kN). **Max speed:** 100mph (160km/h).

The relative merits of the three types of traction motors, dc, single-phase ac and three-phase ac, were well understood at the turn of the century, but the choice of motor in early electrification schemes was determined more by considerations of supply and control than by the characteristics of the motors. The commutator motors (dc and single-phase ac) proved to be the most adaptable to the control equipment available, and three-phase motors were little used. Recently, however, new control systems using thyristors have revived the three-phase motor, because it is now possible to exploit efficiently and economically its inherent qualities.

Three-phase motors are of two types: synchronous, in which the frequency is directly tied to the supply frequency, and asynchronous or induction motors. It is the latter which have excellent traction characteristics. In this motor, three-phase current is supplied to poles located round the inside of the stator, producing a "rotating" magnetic field. The rotor carries closed turns of conductors, and as the magnetic field rotates relative to the rotor, currents are induced in the rotor conductors. Due to these currents, forces act on the conductors (the normal motor effect), and these cause the rotor to turn. The torque thereby exerted on the rotor shaft depends upon the difference between the rotor speed and the speed of rotation of the field. This difference is expressed as the "slip" (not to be confused with normal wheelslip).

It can be shown that the speed of the rotor is proportional to the frequency of the current supplied to the motor, to the slip, and inversely to the number of poles. Under steady running conditions, slip is only one or two per cent of the speed, so varying the slip does not offer much scope for speed control. In early three-phase systems, the frequency of the supply to the motor was the frequency of the mains supply, and was fixed. The only way of varying the speed of the motor was thus by changing the number of poles. Even by regrouping the poles by different connections, it was only possible to get three or four steady running speeds. It was this limitation control which hindered development of three-phase traction.

Above: The Class "120" Bo-Bo electric locomotive of German Federal Railways is intended to work all types of traffic.

It was possible to vary the frequency of the current supplied to the motors only by the use of rotating machinery. This was done in several installations by a rotary converter, but the advantages of the three-phase motor were then offset by the disadvantages of an additional heavy rotating machine.

The development of thyristors opened up a new future for the induction motor. By their ability to switch current on and off quickly and very precisely, thyristors can be used to "invert" dc to ac by interrupting a dc supply. By inverting three circuits with an interval of one third of a "cycle" between each, a three-phase ac supply can be produced, and it is relatively simple to vary the frequency of this supply within wide limits. This is the key to controlling the speed of an induction motor by varying the frequency of the current supplied to it. Furthermore, this variation can be "stepless", that is, it can be varied gradually without any discontinuities.

In any motor control system the effects of "steps" or sudden changes in motor current are important because they can institute wheelslip. With thyristor control, three-phase motors can be worked much nearer to the

Below: The German Federal Railway's Class "120" design represented a fundamental step forward in locomotive control.

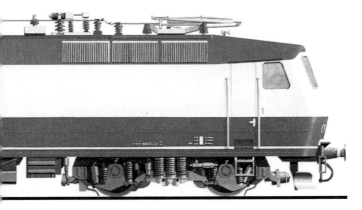

limit of adhesion than can other types because not only is wheelslip less likely to develop, but also it is self-correcting. If a pair of wheels loses its grip on the rail, it accelerates slightly, thereby reducing the slip, and, in turn, reducing the torque it transmits. This reduces the tendency for the wheels to lose their grip, so that wheelslip is self-correcting.

If the train begins to accelerate on a down gradient, the rotor accelerates, and "overtakes" the speed of the rotating field. Motor slip changes direction, and the motor exerts a braking rather than a driving torque, that is, the motor becomes a three-phase alternator. If provision is made for the current generated to be fed back into the over-head line, or to resistances, the induction motor provides electric braking quite simply.

Various experiments with induction motors were made in Europe in the 1960s and 1970s, both for electric locomotives and for diesel-electrics. Although all the systems had the common aim of supplying variable-frequency three-phase current to the traction motors by the use of thyristors, the circuitry varied between manufacturers.

In 1971, the West German locomotive builder Henschel completed, as a private venture, three 2,500hp (1,865kW) diesel locomotives with induction motors, using an electrical system produced by Brown Boveri (BBC). The basis of the BBC system is that the incoming supply is first changed to direct current at 2,800V, this voltage being closely controlled. This dc supply is fed into the inverter circuits, which feed variable-frequency three-phase ac to the traction motors. Deutsche Bundesbahn acquired the locomotives, and they were extensively tested and then put into regular service. In 1974 one of them had its diesel engine removed and replaced by ballast, and the locomotive was coupled permanently to an electric test coach equipped with pantograph, transformer and rectifier, from which direct current at 2,800V was supplied to the inverters on the locomotive.

Experience with this experimental unit encouraged DB to order five four-axle locomotives using equipment developed from the experimental work, and they appeared in 1979. The specification called for the locomotive to haul passenger trains of 700t at 100mph (160km/h), fast freights of 1,500t at 62mph (100km/h), and heavy freights of 2,700t at 50mph (80km/h); this performance was achieved in a locomotive weighing only 84t. Full advantage was taken of the good adhesion of the induction motors, for the continuous rating is 7,500hp (5,600kW), making them the most powerful four-axle locomotives in the world. The omission of commutators and

brushes from the motors enables their weight to be reduced, and in these locomotives the motors are 65 per cent lighter than corresponding DB single-phase motors. Maintenance is also simplified. The single-phase supply from the overhead is rectified to dc at 2,800V, and is then inverted to three-phase ac at a frequency which can vary from zero to 125Hz.

Early testing revealed a number of problems, and particular attention had to be given to the effect of the inverter circuits on signalling and telephone systems, and the general effect of thyristor control on the overhead supply (technically, the "harmonics" caused). Extensive tuning of the circuitry was necessary.

With these problems under control, the locomotives were tested on trains of various loads, and one of them was also subjected to high-speed trials hauling a test coach. It reached 143.5mph (231km/h), thus beating the previous world record for induction motor traction set up in 1903 in the Zossen-Marienfelde trials in Germany with high-speed motor coaches.

In their original condition the locomotives suffered unacceptably frequent failures of various electrical components, and during 1982 each of them had a major rebuild to improve reliability and simplify some of the circuitry. The locomotives were tested over a range of loads, speeds and gradients, and their performance was outstanding. At one extreme they proved capable of starting greater loads on steep gradients than the heavier Class "151" Co-Co freight locomotives, while at the other extreme they established a world record for three-phase traction of 164.6mph (256km/h).

By 1984 DB had concluded that three-phase locomotives could exploit their adhesive weight more fully and run at higher speeds than existing units, and that they were extremely efficient and easy to maintain. Approval was given for a production batch of 44, later increased to 60.

Below, left: A head-on view of the advanced and electrically very sophisticated German Class "120" Bo-Bo locomotive design.

Below, right: One of the prototype Class "120" electric locomotives at the head of a German Federal Railway express.

Class AEM7 B_o-B_o

Origin: United States: National Railroad Passenger Corporation (Amtrak), 1980. **Type:** Electric locomotive for high-speed passenger trains. **Gauge:** 4ft 8½in (1,435mm). **Propulsion:** Alternating current at 12,500V 25Hz or 60Hz, or at 25,000V 60Hz supplied via overhead catenary, a thyristor control and rectification system to four traction motors geared to each axle using ASEA hollowshaft flexible drive. **Weight:** 199,500lb (90.6t). **Axleload:** 53,300lb (24t). **Overall length:** 51ft 5¾in (15,700mm). **Tractive effort:** 53,300lb (236kN). **Max speed:** 125mph (200km/h).

The US National Railroad Passenger Corporation (better known as Amtrak) had the problem of finding motive power to replace the superb but ageing "GG1" class of 1934. New locomotives were required for use on the New York-Philadelphia-Washington main line, electrified at 11,000V 25Hz. Various substitutes fielded by US industry (which had built very few high-speed electric locomotives since the "GG1"s) and one from France were disappointing, but a modified Swedish "Rc4" (*qv*) sent over on trial – "our little Volvo" Amtrak's motive-power men called her – proved to be just what the doctor ordered. Accordingly, a fleet of 47 was proposed.

Rather than fight the "Buy American" lobby in the USA, ASEA sensibly licensed General Motors Electro-Motive Division to build, using some ASEA parts, what are known as Class "AEM7". The "AEM7"s have stronger bodies, 25 per cent more power than the demonstrator, and multi-current capability to cope with conversions to 25,000V 60Hz, with a certain amount of 12,500V 60Hz.

Maximum speed is much higher at 125mph (200km/h), while the weight has risen by 17 per cent. This is no detriment, since very high axleloads are catered for in the USA by the use of heavy rail, closely-spaced sleepers and deep ballast. Vast sums have recently been expended by Amtrak to bring the North East Corridor tracks, on which the "AEM7"s are used, up to first-

Above: The impressive front end of the standard Amtrak US-built but Swedish-designed Class "AEM7" electric locomotive.

class standards once again. This heralds replacement of the "AEM7"s from front-line service in 2000 by 150mph (240km/h) "Acela" tilting trains and a new generation of 125mph (200km/h) electric locomotives.

Below: An "AEM7" electric locomotive rolls an Amtrak express train under the wires of the North East Corridor.

TGV Ten-car trainset

Origin: France: French National Railways (SNCF), 1981 **Type:** High-speed articulated multiple-unit electric train. **Gauge:** 4ft 8¹/₂in (1,435mm) **Propulsion:** In each of two motor coaches, current taken from overhead wires at either 1,500V dc or 25,000V 50Hz (or, in a few cases 15,000V 16²/₃Hz) supplied through rectifiers and/or chopper control to six 704hp (5251kW) traction motors mounted on the coach body and geared to the axles through spring drive; two motors on each bogie of the power car and two on the adjoining end bogie of the articulated set. **Weight:** 427,575lb (194t) adhesive, 841,465lb (381.9t) total. **Axleload:** 35,480lb (16.1t). **Overall length:** 656ft 9¹/₂in (200,190mm). **Max speed:** 162mph (260km/h) initially, 186mph (300km/h) ultimately.

When, in 1955, two French electric locomotives separately established a world record of 205.7mph (331km/h) in the course of tests to measure various parameters on the locomotive and track, it seemed an esoteric exercise, far removed from everyday train running, which at that time was limited in France to 87mph (140km/h). But 21 years later two French test trains had between them exceeded 186mph (300km/h) on 233 test runs, and construction had commenced of 235 miles (380km) of new railway laid out for 300km/h running.

The main line of the former PLM railway connects the three largest cities in France, and had the heaviest long-distance passenger traffic in the country. Post-war electrification increased traffic still further, and by the 1960s congestion was severe. In an effort to overcome the problem of interleaving fast passenger trains and slower freights, traffic was arranged in "flights", with a succession of passenger trains at certain times of day and a succession of freights at others. The case for additional line capacity was very strong, and in 1966 serious study of a possible new route began. This line would not only relieve the existing route, but by taking advantage of French research into higher speeds, it would win traffic from air and road.

It was clear that a great advantage would accrue if the line could be dedicated solely to passenger traffic. The canting of curves on a line carrying mixed traffic at different speeds is always a compromise, and technology had reached a stage at which considerable increases in passenger train speeds were possible, but not those of freight trains. The axleloads of freight vehicles reach 20t and those of electric locomotives 23t, but if the axleloading on the new line could be limited to about 17t, it would be much easier to maintain the track in a suitable condition for very high speeds.

One outcome of the 1955 test running was that in 1967 limited running at 124mph (200km/h) was introduced on the Paris-Bordeaux line and further testing beyond that speed was made by railcar sets. The first experimental gas turbine train (*qv*) was run up to 147mph (236km/h), and one of the production gas turbine sets made 10 runs above 155mph (250km/h), but it

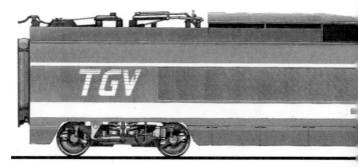

Above: Two TGV (*Train á Grande Vitesse* or High-speed Train) ten-car sets await departure from Paris Gare de Lyon station.

was the experimental very-high-speed gas turbine set which pointed the way ahead. Designated at first TGV001 (but later change to TGS when TGV was applied to the electric version), this was the first French train specifically designed to run at 186mph (300km/h), and it made 175 runs in which 300km/h was exceeded, with a maximum of 197mph (317km/h). A special high-speed electric motor coach was also built, and this reached 192mph (309km/h).

The project for a new line (known as Paris-Sud-Est) to relieve traffic on the Paris-Lyons section was initially based on using gas turbine trains similar to TGV001. To avoid the tremendous expense of a new entry into Paris, the existing route from Paris Gare de Lyon would be used for 18.6 miles (30km), and from there to the outskirts of Lyons there would be a completely new line, connected to existing lines at two intermediate points to give access to Dijon and to routes to Lausanne and Geneva in Switzerland. Substantial state aid would be needed to finance the project, but it was predicted that both SNCF and the state would reap a satisfactory return on the investment.

Before the project received ministerial approval, the oil crisis of 1973 caused a radical change of plan, and gas turbine propulsion was abandoned in favour of electrification at 25,000V 50Hz. As the new route would be used solely by very fast passenger trains, it was possible to have much steeper gradients than on a conventional railway. The "kinetic energy" or energy of movement of a vehicle depends on the square of the speed, and the faster a train is travelling, the smaller is the loss of speed due to "rushing" a given

Below: A power car of a TGV train. All wheels, including those of the adjacent bogie of the next coach, are powered.

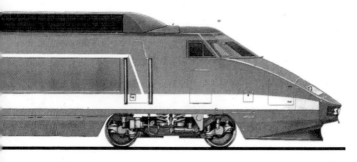

gradient. On the new line, maximum gradient is 1-in-28.5 (3.5 per cent), o four times as steep as the gradients on the existing route. By adoption o steep gradients the cost of the line was reduced by about 30 per cen compared with a conventional railway. The longest gradient on the new line reduces speed from 162mph (260km/h) to 137mph (220km/h).

Orders for the electric version of the TGV (*Train á Grande Vitesse*) were placed in 1976, and delivery began two years later. Although the design o the train follows that of the gas turbine version, the equipment is completely different, but it incorporates well proven parts wherever possible. Each train comprises two end power cars flanking an eight-car articulated rake o trailers; that is, the adjoining ends of coaches are carried on a common bogie. To transmit the maximum power of 8,450hp (6,300kW) requires 12 motored axles, so in addition to the four axles of the motor coach, the enc bogie of the articulated set also has motors. As the existing lines on which the trains work are electrified at 1,500V dc, the sets can operate on this system also, and six are equipped to work on 15,000V $16^2/3$Hz ir Switzerland. For ac working there is one transformer in each motor coach with a separate thyristor rectifier for each motor, to reduce the risk of more than one motor being out of action at once. The same thyristors work as choppers for control of the motor voltage on dc.

The sets have a bogie developed directly from that of the gas turbine train. As the new line is used only by TGVs, the curves are canted to sui these trains, and no tilting of the coach bodies on curves is needed. The traction motors are mounted on the body of the motor coach, with a flexible drive to the axles. By this means the unsprung mass of the bogie is unusually low, and the forces exerted on the track at 300km/h are less than with an electric locomotive at 200km/h.

There are no lineside signals on the new line, the driver receiving signa indications in the cab. The permitted speed is displayed continuously in front of the driver, who sets the controller to the speed required. The contro system maintains speed automatically. There are three braking systems, al of which are controlled by the one driver's brake valve: dynamic, disc anc wheel tread. The dynamic brake uses the traction motors as generators feeding energy into resistances. During braking the motors are excited from a battery, so that failure of the overhead supply does not affect the braking The dynamic brake is effective from full speed down to 3km/h. In norma service applications the disc brakes are half applied, and wheel tread brakes are applied lightly to clean the wheel treads. For emergency braking al systems are used fully. The braking distance from 162mph (260km/h) is 3,829 yards (3,500m).

The trains were built by Alsthom, the motor coaches at Belfort and the trailers at La Rochelle. Initial testing was done on the Strasbourg-Belfort line, where 162mph (260km/h) was possible over a distance. As soon as the first

Below: Banking at speed, the TGV gives a comfortable ride.

Above: The original French TGVs are permitted to run at 167mph (267.2km/h) and offer start-to-stop speeds of over 130mph (208km/h), both world records.

part of the new line was ready, testing was transferred, and one of the sets was fitted with larger wheels than standard to allow tests above the normal speeds. On February 26, 1981, a new world record of 236mph (380km/h) was established.

Services over the southern section of the new line began in September 1981, and passenger carryings soon showed an increase of 70 per cent. The northern section was opened in September 1983, with a scheduled time of 2 hours for the 266 miles (426km) from Paris to Lyons. In 1983 also the maximum speed was raised from 260km/h to 270km/h (168mph).

Apart from some trouble with damage to the overhead wires at maximum speed the new trains have worked very well. Riding on the new line is very good, but the sets are not so smooth when running on conventional lines.

The Paris-Sud-Est line is a remarkable achievement, for which the detailed planning and construction required only 10 years, and was completed to schedule. It immediately attracted so much new business that Paris-Lyons flights were curtailed. It was the forerunner of the high-speed railways that now extend northwards from Paris to the Channel Tunnel, and south-west towards Brittany and the Atlantic Coast, and which will reach the Mediterranean early in the new century. Later generations of TGV trainsets (qv) now run to the extremities of France and into Belgium and Switzerland over existing tracks, with journey times unimaginable 20 years ago.

SD-50 C$_o$-C$_o$

Origin: United States: Electro-Motive Division, General Motors Corporation (EMD), 1981. **Type:** High-power multi-purpose diesel-electric locomotive **Gauge:** 4ft 8^1/$_2$in (1,435mm). **Propulsion:** One EMD 645F3 3,800bhp (2,840kW) 16-cylinder turbocharged twostroke Vee diesel engine supplying current through silicon rectifiers to six nose-suspended traction motors geared to the axles. **Weight:** 368,000lb (167t). **Axleload:** 61,340lb (27.9t) **Overall length:** 71ft 2in (21,692mm). **Max speed:** 70mph (112km/h).

The most prolific locomotive manufacturer the world has ever known? Well, it will not be long now, because although Baldwin produced almost 60,000 in 125 years of locomotive building, General Motors' Electro-Motive Division's score even in 1999 stood just beyond the 50,000 mark. Of course EMD is well ahead as regards horsepower, while Baldwin certainly offered greater variety with steam of many wheel arrangements, rack-and-pinion and turbine, as well as straight electric and diesel-electric locomotives of the two normal Bo-Bo and Co-Co types, amongst others. EMD is not only the main supplier in the USA, having built some 70 per cent of locomotives now running on US Class I railroads, but also the biggest exporter. Most countries outside the former communist world, except for those few with a domestic industry to protect, use General Motors' locomotives.

For just three years the "SD-50" 3,800hp (2,840kW) unit, driven by the 16-cylinder series 645F3 engine, was king of the EMD range. This engine is an improved version of that fitted to the "SD40-2" locomotive already described. The "SD40-2" series was a bestseller during the 1970s but it appears that the "SD-45" series, which gave high horsepowers by using a 20-cylinder version of the 645 series engines, involved their users in high maintenance costs. The "SD-50" series was based on an alternative policy of strengthening and uprating the 16-cylinder engine.

The 12-wheel "SD-50" (the "dash 2" designation, meaning modular electrics, is now taken as read) was also offered as an eight-wheeler called the "GP-50". An axleload only 6 per cent greater than that of the "SID-50" did not pose too serious a problem as regards damage to the track, but the reduced weight on the drivers meant a 30 per cent lower tractive effort, so that the "GP-50" was more suited to less heavily-graded lines upon which high power output is more significant than maximum tractive effort.

In this connection, EMD in 1981 introduced a considerably more sophisticated anti-wheelslip device than hitherto offered. This was known as

Below: Model "SD-50" road-switcher diesel-electric locomotives of the Kansas City Southern Railroad working in multiple.

Above: Mass coal movement is now a feature of US railroads operation. Here three "SD-50"s head a massive coal drag.

the Super Series Adhesion Control System and used radar to check the ground speed against the speed of revolution of individual pairs of wheels. The torque of each motor was automatically adjusted to keep the rate of wheel creep to a minimal amount. It was claimed that one-third more tractive effort can be produced by a unit which uses this device than one which does not.

In 1984, EMD announced the "60" range of locomotives with a new 710 engine having a longer piston stroke. The new range made a much greater use of solid-state devices (including three microprocessors) in the control system. The number of relays, for example, came down from 51 to 15. Amongst many other advantages, the microprocessors enable engine control settings to be matched much more precisely to variable power demands. This range was succeeded in the 1990s by the "70s", using a refined version of the 645F3 engine, and with the first full application of ac traction technology to US freight diesels. Higher-rated "SD-80" and "SD-90" versions followed.

Class 370 APT-P Train

Origin: Great Britain: British Railways (BR). **Type:** High-speed electric passenger train. Gauge: 4ft 8¹/₂in (1,435mm). **Propulsion:** Alternating current at 25,000V 50Hz fed via overhead catenary, step-down transformer and thyristor-based control system to four body-mounted 1,000hp motors in two power cars, driving the wheels through longitudinal shafts and gearing. **Weight:** 297,540lb (135t) adhesive, 1,014,942lb (460.6t) total. **Axleload:** 37,2481lb (16.9t). **Overall length:** 963ft 6in (293,675mm). **Max speed:** 150mph (240km/h).

Nearly two decades have passed since the painful abandonment of Britain's first far-sighted attempt at developing a tilting train. The saga began in the 1960s when British Railways set its much-enlarged Research Department at Derby to do a thorough study of their most fundamental problem, the riding of flanged wheels on rails. Out of this emerged the possibility of designing vehicles which could run smoothly at higher speeds than previously permitted over sharply-curved track with the usual imperfections. To keep the passengers comfortable, the trains would tilt automatically when negotiating curves which would have to stay canted or banked only for normal speeds.

Several railways have done or are doing this, notably those of Japan, Italy and Canada. The Canadian LRC train (qv) is the only one which approaches the

Below: During trial public running, a shortened prototype Advanced Passenger Train set enters Euston station, London.

ambitiousness of the British scheme-in the others the body tilt is purely a passive response to the sideways forces encountered. In the APT, body-tilting is achieved in a much more sophisticated and positive manner, each coach adjusting its tilt response to curvature by sensing movement of the coach ahead. The amount of body tilt can rise to as much as 9°, which means that at full tilt one side of the car can be 16in (400mm) higher than the other. The result would be a train which could provide the high average speeds that the future would seem to demand if railways are to remain in business for journeys over 200 miles, without the huge capital investment involved in building new lines for them. For example, 105mph (167km/h) or 3h 50min between London and Glasgow is very close to 103mph (165km/h) envisaged in France over a similar distance from Paris to Marseilles, using the new purpose-built railway between Paris and Lyons. Put another way, the British solution-if it had succeeded-would have equalled the French for a cost of only one-fifth.

At this point one must say that the body-tilting is only part of this advanced concept-a new and fundamentally improved suspension system with self-steering bogies contributed even more to a package which looked like being a winner. A formal submission for funds to develop the project was made in December 1967. In 1973, after some delay, a four-car experimental prototype powered by a gas turbine was authorised and in 1975 was brought out into the world after early testing in secret on BR's test track near Nottingham. APT-E as it was called managed 151mph (242km/h) running between Reading and Swindon and, more impressive, ran from London to Leicester (99 miles-

158km) in just under the hour. These favourable experiences led to the authorising of three 14-car" production prototype- trains, the two central cars of each train being non-tilting and non-driving power cars, providing 8,000hp (5,970kW) for traction. The two halves of the train were isolated from one another and each had to have its own buffet/restaurant car, 72 first-class and 195 second-class seats were provided in each half.

Electric propulsion was chosen because there was no diesel engine available with a suitable power-to-weight ratio, and gas turbine was now considered too extravagant in fuel consumption after the then recent trebling in the price of oil. Moreover, the envisaged first use for APT trains was now on the longer electric journeys out of Euston to Glasgow, Liverpool and Manchester. One innovation was the solution to the problem of braking from very high speeds above 155mph (250km/h). The hydro-kinetic (water turbine) brake was adopted, giving a reasonable braking distance of 2,500yd (2,286m) from full speed, with 2,000yd (1,828m) possible in emergency. Disc brakes provided braking force at speeds too low for the hydro-kinetic brakes to be effective.

The first APT-P train was completed in 1978, but there was a series of tiresome small defects including one that caused a derailment at over 100mph (160km/h). This meant that, although the 4hr 15min Glasgow to London service (average speed 94mph 151km/h), which it was intended to provide at first, had been printed in the public timetables for several years, it was not until late1981 that public service actually began. Even then, only one complete Glasgow-to- London and back public run was made. A combination of further small defects, unprecedently severe weather and impending serious industrial action, led BR to take the train out of advertised public service, although tests continued. It all happened in a blaze of unfortunate publicity, which mattered less than the fact that authorisation of a series-production version (APT-S) was deferred and later abandoned.

But tilting remained attractive in a country with little space, money or inclination to build TGV-style high-speed railways. When the East Coast line was being electrified in the late-1980s, the MkIV coaches developed for the route were built to a profile suitable for tilting, but were not equipped to do so. Now, at the beginning of the 21st Century, Britain is at last to have tilting trains on the West Coast line for which APT was conceived, but using Italian rather

Above: British Rail's Advanced Passenger Train demonstrates its celebrated tilting capability during test running in 1981.

than home-grown technology. A major upgrade of the route will be accompanied by introduction of 54 eight-car trainsets being built for franchise-holder Virgin Trains by Alstom and Fiat. With a projected top speed of 140mph (225km/h), these trains should bring Glasgow to within 4hr of London by 2005. It is also possible that the next generation of trains for the East Coast route will have tilting capability.

Below: BR's Advanced Passenger Train was intended to run on existing lines faster than normal trains with no tilting devices.

Class 26 2-D-2

Origin: South Africa: South African Transport Services (SATS), 1982. **Type:** Mixed-traffic steam locomotive. **Gauge:** 3ft 6in (1,067mm). **Propulsion:** Coal-fired gas-producer firebox with grate area of 70sq ft (6.5m^2) generating superheated steam at 225psi (15.7kg/cm^2) in a fire-tube boiler and supplying it to two 24x28in (610x711mm) cylinders, driving the four main axles direct by means of connecting and coupling rods. **Weight:** 167,505lb (76t) adhesive, 506,920lb (230t) total. **Axleload:** 43,640lb (19.8t). **Overall length:** 91ft 6^1/$_2$in (27,904mm). **Tractive effort:** 47,025lb (209kN). **Max speed:** 60mph (96km/h).

Many people regard steam locomotives as the only proper motive power, any other kind being ersatz to some degree. Yet at the same time we are aware of steam's drawbacks – its low thermal efficiency, its labour intensiveness and its dirtiness. Of course, the low thermal efficiency can be countered by use of less costly fuels – in some countries oil costs four (or more) times coal for the same heat content and this more than cancels out the better efficiency of diesel vis-a-vis steam. At the same time the amount of fuel wasted by a steam locomotive can be reduced by relatively small improvements, and since the dirt connected with steam operation represents waste, less waste automatically means less pollution too.

This "Red Devil" of Class "26" (named *L.D. Porta* after the Argentinian engineer who was responsible for the basics of the system) is an attempt to produce a steam locomotive for the 21st Century by rebuilding a "25NC" 4-8-4, a class built by Henschel and North British in 1953. The principal change is in the method of burning the coal, which is now gasified before being burnt; the other alterations are more in the nature of fine tuning. All were carried out in South African Transport Services' Salt River Workshops at Cape Town, at very modest cost.

The first big change is that now less than half the air needed for combustion enters the firebox through the fire itself, the amount of reduction being set by smaller and exactly calculated openings between the bars of the grate. This change cuts down waste by eliminating fire-throwing when the locomotive is working hard.

Steam is also fed into the hot firebed from the sides. This comes from the auxiliaries and from the exhaust side of the main cylinders. It reacts chemically with the hot coal to produce cleanly combustible water gas, while at the same time the reaction is one which absorbs rather than produces heat. So the temperature of the firebed does not reach the level at which fusion takes place and clinker forms. The air passing through the hot (but not too hot) firebed makes producer gas and it is this mixture of gases which burns cleanly, using the air entering through openings in the side of the firebox. The existing mechanical stoker is retained; the hard labour of running steam power is reduced both when putting the fuel in and when taking the residues out.

Other improvements made include increased superheat (with

Above: Too Late? South African Railways' "Red Devil", steam's eleventh-hour answer to the diesel-electric onslaught.

consequent provision of improved cylinder lubrication), better draughting and a feed-water heater, all of which contribute to a further improvement in thermal efficiency. Adding this to the contribution made by the avoidance of unburnt fuel in the residues of combustion gives the startling result of one-third less fuel burnt for a given output. The maximum power output is increased, whilst both the quantity and the difficulty of disposal of the residues is considerably reduced. The result is a machine that can really look its diesel brethren in the eye in respect of such important matters as availability and cleanliness, and really wipe the floor with them when it comes to fuel costs in South African conditions.

Unfortunately, the current recession in South Africa has left the railways there with ample diesel-electric motive power for their non-electrified lines, and this situation leaves SATS understandably reluctant to undertake a major restoration of steam traction. However, these simple and cheap transformations of existing steam locomotives have been undertaken by several railways, including the famous Festiniog Railway in Wales.

Below: The new South African Railways' steam locomotive with gas-producer firebox. It was rebuilt from a Class "25" 4-8-4.

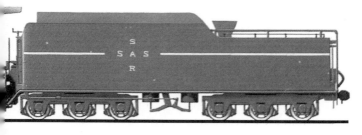

LRC B$_o$-B$_o$

Origin: Canada: VIA Rail Canada, 1982. **Type:** High-speed diesel-electric locomotive for matching train with tilting mechanism. **Gauge:** 4ft 8^1/2in (1,435mm). **Propulsion:** Alco Type 251 16-cylinder 3,900hp (2,910kW) turbocharged four-stroke diesel engine and alternator feeding via rectifiers four nose-suspended direct current traction motors geared to the axles. **Weight:** 185,135lb (84t). **Axleload:** 46,285lb (21t). **Overall length:** 66ft 5in (202,692mm). **Max speed:** 125mph (200km/h), but limited to 80mph (128km/h) by track conditions.

Having as its designation carefully chosen letters that read the same in English or French-Light, Rapid, Comfortable or *Leger, Rapide Confortable* respectively- the designers had to have pointed out to them the letter L might in French just as well stand for *Lourd* or "heavy"! The fact that an LRC passenger car weighs "only" 57 per cent more than, for example an HST car of the same capacity in Britain does lend some sharpness to the point made. Similarly the LRC locomotive weighs 20 per cent more than the HST power car. Even so, LRC is an impressive creation, although the many years which passed in development saw as many (or more) setbacks and premature entries into service as Britain's APT. Even so, the new trains went into service between Montreal and Toronto in 1982. A scheduled time of 3hr 40min was originally intended for the 337 miles (539km), 45 minutes better than that offered by their best predecessors, the lightweight "Turbo-trains" in the late-1970s. But the best offered in the 1982 timetable was 4hr 25min, with an ominous note "Timings subject to alterations, journeys may be extended by up to 55 minutes", indicating a possible need to substitute conventional equipment. In 1984, the best time was eased further to 4hr 30min, but the footnote had vanished.

This note reflected the fact that the LRC trains had to be withdrawn during the Canadian winter of 1981-82, having suffered from fine dry powdery snow getting inside sophisticated equipment. That the improvement in timings was so relatively modest is due to the effects of heavy freight traffic on the existing track and the speed limits consequently imposed on the LRC. Two sets leased by the USA operator Amtrak also failed to give satisfaction, and they were returned to the makers. Since then, problems have continued with maintenance of these trains, resulting in occasional poor availability. In the late-1990s the trains were still running and still tilting. The summer 1999 timetable showed an evening peak-hour sprint of 3hr 59min in both directions between Montreal and Toronto, though the trains are now often hauled by conventional diesel locomotives rather than the LRC power cars.

Even so, LRC was a well thought out concept. An "active- tilting system allowing 8^1/2° of tilt, ^{1}/2° less than BR's APT, is combined with an advanced

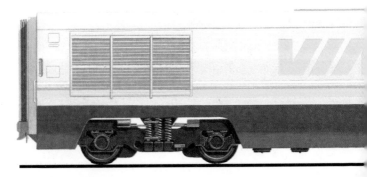

Above: The head end of a VIA Rail Canada diesel-electric locomotive for the LRC (Light, Rapid, Comfortable) train.

level of comfort for passengers. Ample power is available from the locomotives (which, incidentally, do not tilt) for both traction and substantial heating/air conditioning requirements.

Below: The Canadian-built LRC Bo-Bo diesel-electric locomotive decked out in the handsome livery adopted by VIA Rail Canada for these futuristic tilting trains.

GF6C C$_o$-C$_o$

Origin: Canada: British Columbia Railway (BCR), 1983. **Type:** Heavy duty mineral-hauling electric locomotive for Arctic use. **Gauge:** 4ft 8¹/₂in (1,435mm). **Propulsion:** Alternating current at 50,000V 60Hz fed via overhead catenary and thyristor control system to six traction motors geared to the axles. **Weight:** 330,000lb (150t). **Axleload:** 82,500lb (37.5t). **Overall length:** 68ft 10m (20,980mm). **Tractive effort:** 95,180lb (421kN). **Max speed:** 68mph (109km/h).

The early-1980s were years when the nuts-and-bolts of North American railroading were undergoing few physical changes. For many lines it was not a case of how many new diesel units to order but how many to put away in storage lines. There were even rumours that General Motors Electro-Motive Division's main plant at LaGrange, Illinois, would have to shut down for a time. Of course, when it came to placing locomotives in store, it was the interesting and unusual ones that were put away.

However, significant moves that had been distant dreams or mere ideas in the 1970s were in the 1980s becoming possibilities. If any were to happen, the technical face of railroading in North America would change almost overnight and almost out of recognition. Behind all these possibilities lay the huge change in the relative cost of energy obtained from coal compared with energy from oil. And the message was – put railroads under the wires because electrification is the best way to use coal for transportation power.

Below: A 50,000V "GF6C" Co-Co electric locomotive of British Columbia Railway's new Tumbler Ridge line on test.

Above: Three of these "GF6C" Co-Co electric locomotives are used in multiple on massive 98-wagon coal trains.

All sorts of other conditions might also have been favourable to electrification. First, government assistance might even be made available. The Department of Transportation had issued tentative construction timetables and schedules for suitable electrification projects. Secondly, the main locomotive builders – not surprisingly since diesel can reasonably be regarded as electric locos of the self-generating type – are able to supply suitable power. Thirdly, the risk that heavy additional local taxes might have to be paid on the fixed electrical equipment seemed no longer to be valid. Fourthly, the rationalisation which followed the mergers and relaxation of other restraints meant there was freedom to concentrate flows of traffic on fewer routes – and electrification needs dense traffic to justify the cost of fixed equipment. Fifthly, with profitability improving, schemes involving big capital investment might no longer be so difficult to finance. Lastly, there was now no argument as to the type of electric current to be supplied to moving trains – that is, it should be the same single-phase 60Hz alternating current that we are supplied with in our own houses.

So far, it is true, electrification has been the biggest non-event in American railroad history. The former USSR worked nearly 60 per cent of its

Above: Tumbler Ridge line electrically powered coal train hauled by two Class "GF6C" electric locomotives. Trains requiring three of these powerful machines now run.

tonne-km electrically whereas the figure for the USA is only 0.1 or even 0.01 per cent. Even 90 years ago, one could read almost the same arguments as appear above. But coming events cast their shadow before, and one notes with pleasure that General Motors (Canada) supplied a batch of ac electric locomotives, designated "GF6C" for an 80-mile (129km,) branch of the British Columbia Railway opened for traffic in 1983. This was built to bring out coal from a place called Tumbler Ridge in the northeastern corner of the province, far into the depths of the Canadian north. It was the first main-line electric railway in Canada outside the suburbs of Montreal.

The "GF6C" locomotive has a similar chassis and bogies to a standard diesel-electric road-switcher. There is a full width carbody with a depressed roof in the centre to accommodate the 50kV switchgear, and a transformer and thyristor control system replace the diesel engine and generator assembly. Three locomotives are used on each 98-wagon train.

ACE 3000 4-8-2

Origin: United States: American Coal Enterprises Inc. **Type:** Coal-burning freight locomotive. Gauge: 4ft 8½in (1,435mm). **Propulsion:** Coal-fired gas-producer firebox generating superheated steam at 300psi (21.1kg/cm²) in a fire-tube boiler and supplying it first to two high-pressure and then to two low-pressure cylinders, driving the four main axles direct by means of connecting and coupling rods. **Adhesive weight:** 240,000lb (109t). **Axleload:** 60,000lb (27.25t). **Overall length:** 458ft 6in (48,312mm). **Max speed:** 70mph (112km/h).

A most startling change in railroad motive power could be just around the corner – steam itself might be on the way back. Of course, most electric railroading is in a sense steam traction, because generators in power stations – even nuclear ones – are usually driven by steam, but the project in question is for a real steam locomotive burning coal directly. The key to the idea is the relative cost of different energy sources. In the 1940s and 1950s, when US railroads changed from steam traction to diesel, diesel fuel cost around one-fifteenth of today's price. Coal, on the other hand then cost only about a quarter of what it does today. Put another way, a dollar spent on coal now buys nearly four times as much energy as the same sum spent on diesel fuel. It is granted that the steam locomotive will be less thermally-efficient, but there will still be a handsome margin of saving.

The idea that steam traction might have substantially lower costs than diesel is one that takes a little getting used to. Even the most rabid steam fan never claims more than that the diesel takeover battle was a much closer one than the victors ever admit. The big hurdle is to produce a machine that is less labour intensive and polluting than its predecessors but which at the same time retains the simplicity and reliability which was steam's greatest asset.

The original proposer of the "ACE 3000" project (ACE stands for American Coal Enterprises) was a man named Ross E. Rowland. He and his design team bore all these things well and truly in mind because Rowland, a commodities broker, had had experience in running conventional steam locomotives on diesel-worked railroads. He was the man who put a Nickel Plate 2-8-4, a Reading 4-8-4 and a Chesapeake & Ohio 4-8-4 back on the rails, and naturally most of the original features of the new project were orientated towards solving the problems of servicing. For example, run-of-the-mine coal used as fuel would be supplied ready packaged in 11-ton modules. The locomotive-type boiler and direct-drive compound double-acting cylinders corresponded to conventional principles, although the layout proposed has not previously been successful.

An important technical feature was one that had been developed in Argentina and more recently in South Africa. The coal was to be converted to a mixture of water and producer gas before being burnt, by introducing

steam into the firebed. The reaction takes place at a modest temperature; consequently clinker does not form. There are two advantages. First, the coal is consumed more thoroughly and so the process is more efficient. Secondly, since the air for combustion is introduced above the firebed, unpleasant emissions of unburnt fuel in the form of smoke and ash are virtually eliminated, thereby making steam traction acceptable to people who object to black smoke.

To give the machine a long range between water stops, a bulky condensing tender was planned. A sophisticated electronic control system would enable the locomotive to run in multiple with diesel locomotives or another "ACE 3000", and it could be driven from a cab at either end or from another "ACE 3000". The four driving axles were rigidly mounted on the same chassis; the two inner ones had crankshafts and were coupled together by a pair of internal connecting rods. This arrangement allowed for perfect balance to be achieved.

A totally new feature is that a microprocessor would look after combustion of the fuel as well as setting the precise steam thrust on the pistons at every point during each revolution of the wheels. This would cover dynamic braking as well as normal traction, thereby opening a totally new concept of locomotive control. Trials of the computer equipment were carried out on the preserved Chesepeake & Ohio Greenbriar 4-8-4 No.614, owned and adapted by Rowland to test his theories. This locomotive hauled 3,500-ton coal trains on Chessie System's line between Huntington and Hinton, West Virginia, in January 1985.

Finance was raised to build a pair of "ACE 3000" prototypes, but the project foundered. It would have been interesting to see the actual hardware of "new steam", for this design involved much complexity, and complexity has never mixed well with steam traction.

Below: This is how the steam loco of the future could look, if ever the visionary American COALS project reaches fruition.

X-2000 Tilting express train

Origin: Sweden: Swedish State Railways (SJ), 1990. **Type:** High-speed electric train. **Gauge:** 4ft 8^1/$_2$in (1,435mm). **Propulsion:** AC at 15000V 16^2/$_3$Hz fed via overhead catenary, step-down transformer and a thyristor control system to four frame-mounted 750hp (1000kW) traction motors each driving one axle by a hollow-axle flexible drive. **Weight:** 160,850lb (73t) adhesive, 804,450lb (365t) total. **Axleload:** 40,223lb (18.25t). **Overall length:** (Motor coach): 57ft 9in (17.6m). **Overall length:** Complete train 541ft 5in (165m). **Max speed:** 131mph (210km/h).

Like the inhabitants of other nations, the Swedes have felt that their trains must go faster to maintain competitiveness into the 21st Century, but being a small country (in population terms!), those concerned seem to have made up their minds what to do about it more quickly and more definitely than others. In Sweden, the hilly countryside made the building of new lines too expensive and so tilting won the day. The ASEA company, now then amalgamated with Brown Boveri of Baden, Switzerland, to form ABB (now Adtranz), began work on a prototype tilting train, which by 1986 had reached a point where the naturally cautious railway company felt confident enough to place an order. In the event, the first of 20 such trains began public service in 1990.

A train is formed from a power car (which does not tilt) and up to six "business" and "touring" cars – the equivalent of "1st" and "2nd" class. One touring car has a buffet/restaurant section and another at the other end of the train has a driving compartment. A double-length train is possible, using two power cars and up to twelve carriages, though this has not yet been found necessary. The new trains plus track realignments and

Below: The "X-2000" awaiting departure at Stockholm Central Railway Station.

**Above: The "X-2000" Tilting Express Train at Skovde on the
Stockholm-Gothenburg line.**

upgrading. have reduced the total running time between Stockholm and
Gothenburg from just over four hours to less than three and the service of
"X-2000" trains is now hourly on this line; the resulting increase of traffic
is 37 per cent. Other less frequent services are run by these trainsets
northwards from Stockholm as well south-west to Malmo.

The tilting mechanism is controlled by an accelerometer at whichever
end is the front of the train at the time and measured at one bogie of each
coach. The amount of tilt is dependent on the speed and radius but is
limited to an amount where a passenger sitting on a corner seat on one
side of a coach is about one foot or 300mm higher or lower than a
passenger on the other, in addition to any difference in height due to the
super-elevation of the rails. Below 28mph (45km/h) the system does not
operate.

An interesting feature is that, as well as the tilting mechanism, there is
the "steerability" of the axles in each bogie. Each axle has an independent
movement to enable it to assume a radial position on curves, which are
almost continuous in hilly Sweden. This reduces substantially the forces
between wheels and rail, thereby reducing the power required as well as
wear on both.

During 1993 one of these trains was taken to North America and
demonstrated between New York and Washington under its own power
and working public train services. As well, the "X-2000" ran experimental
trains on the Boston line and elsewhere, using Amtrak diesels. It is
rumoured that the Americans liked what they saw and that an order might
eventually follow. Of course, the good experiences which the Americans
had already had with Swedish electric motive power also counted. Some
"X-2000" coaches have also been demonstrated in Australia, for a Sydney
to Brisbane tilting train.

Class 401 "Intercity Express"

Origin: Germany: German Federal Railways (DB), 1991. **Type:** High-speed electric train. **Gauge:** 4ft 8^1/$_2$in (1,435mm). **Propulsion:** AC at 15,000V 16^2/$_3$Hz fed via overhead catenary, step-down transformers and thyristor control systems to frame-mounted 895hp (1,200kW) traction motors, each driving one of the four axles in each of two motor cars. **Weight:** 352,640lb (160t) adhesive, 1,608,920lb (730t) total. **Axleload:** 44,080lb (20t) **Overall length:** 1,174ft 3in (358m). **Max speed:** 175mph (280km/h).

The German "Intercity Express" trains began public service in 1991, with an hourly service from Hamburg to Munich via Frankfurt. The trains were first ordered in 1987 and in all 60 sets were produced. Later came the direct service from Hamburg to Munich via Wurzburg and also the Hamburg-Frankfurt-Basel service, extended to Lucerne and Interlaken on certain runs. In addition, there are services to and from Berlin. The formation of each trainset was originally intended to be variable, but this was very soon abandoned and most regular trains consist of the following 14 cars:

Motor coach – 1st – 1st – 1st – Restaurant+Buffet – Service+2nd – 2nd – 2nd – 2nd – 2nd – 2nd – 2nd – 2nd – Motor coach.

Both compartments and open accommodation are provided in second-class as well as in first-class carriages. The first class in particular is very comfortable, partly because the width of loft 10^3/$_4$in (3.07m) was greater than the normal European standard of 9ft 6^1/$_2$in (2.91m); this prohibited running these sets outside Germany although the Swiss railways have made an exception. The same will apply to the new ICE 2/1 sets, now beginning to be delivered.

This handicap will be altered when the new version of the ICE train, ICE 2/2, is built to the standard European width, ready for general international train services. It is intended that these sets will carry the traction equipment along the train, with four cars out of the eight in each set having motored axles. Both domestic and fully-equipped international versions of the sets will be built.

Below: The Class "401" *Intercity Express* which is capable of 175mph (280km/h).

Above: The ICE speeds the German rail network into the 21st century.

The lines on which these new trains are currently operating are on the whole neither new nor rebuilt, exceptions being Hanover south to Wurzburg on the line from Hamburg to Munich and also from Mannheim to Stuttgart on the route from Frankfurt to Munich. In Germany two factors delay projects of this kind; first, a natural reaction to the bad old days has meant an excessive attention paid to trivial objectors and, second, a noisy group was making the point that the railway's day was over and attention should be given instead to a new guided transport system based on magnetic levitation. A scheme of this particular kind from Berlin to Hamburg is a case in point.

In spite of these difficulties a new line running from the outskirts of Berlin east to Wolfsburg, plus upgrading from Wolfsburg to Hanover, was opened in 1997. About the same time construction of the new line from Cologne to Frankfurt began, for completion during the year 2000. The route will be for ICE high-speed trains only, with gradients up to 1 in 40; the mileage is shortened from the present 140m (225 km) to 112m (180km) but the running time will be reduced from 2h 13m to a mere one hour. Of course, the lovely ride along the picturesque River Rhine will be lost, replaced by a run which is admittedly much shorter but also uncomfortably close to the autobahn. It seems that there is always a price to pay for progress!

"Eurostar" International Train

Origin: Belgium, Britain and France,1994. **Type:** High-speed electric train. **Gauge:** 4ft 8^1/2in (1,435mm). **Propulsion:** In each of two motor coaches alternating current at 25,000V 50Hz or direct current at 3,000V from overhead wires, or direct current at 750V from a third rail, is transformed and fed to six asynchronous traction motors, four on each motor coach and two on the adjoining end bogie of the articulated set. **Weight:** 899,232lb (408t) adhesive, 1,734,550lb (787t) total. **Axleload:** 37,468lb (17t). **Overall length:** Complete train, 1,292ft 6in (394m). **Max speed:** 186mph (300km/h).

A starting point for the design of these remarkable sets was a pair of the French TGV 10-car (8 passenger cars) trainsets and neither the Belgian nor the British railwaymen on the committee of design could offer any better starting point. The first point was the smaller loading gauge in Britain which meant that the maximum width had to be reduced from 9ft 6^1/2in (2,910mm) to 9ft 2^3/4in (2,814mm); the height, too, but that was less important.

Next was the demand of the tunnel safety authorities that traction power supplies to the trains should be confined to each end, and no train-mounted high-voltage cabling would be permitted. The original TGV sets had had six conventional traction motors at either end of each set, two being carried on the bogie of the coach next to each power car; in the new sets the use of 12 asynchronous variable-frequency motors now available meant that adequate power was available for high-speed running with only two power cars, one at each end, as follows:

At 25,000V ac in France and in the tunnel: 12,000kW
At 3,000V dc in Belgium: 5,700kW
At 750V dc from conductor rail in England: 3,400kW

In addition to pantographs, each motor coach is provided with retractable conductor rail collecting shoes. A point was that the contact wire in the tunnel is at a greater height than the maximum in the open line in France and this had also to be provided for. In the event of a train coming to an unscheduled halt in the tunnel, it should be possible to move the passengers into the workable half, divide the train and draw the good half out of the tunnel. Failing that, protruding retractable footboards are provided to enable passengers to reach transport out via the central service tunnel.

Speaking for once on a personal note, it was a notable occasion in my life when in November 1994 I took my seat early one morning at Waterloo with the intention of going all the way to Paris and back. On many other occasions since the 1920s the pleasure of travelling by train was marred by the thought of the horrors of the sea-crossing to come, but this time it was different. It was just wonderful! We had reserved seats in the 18 passenger cars in each set, which provide seats for 210 first-class (with meals, glasses of champagne etc, brought to each seat) and 584 second-class. There are also two buffet cars, as well as provision of space for a nursery and for handicapped passengers, luggage and telephones, as well as police and customs, with even a prison compartment. Returning in the evening from Paris with wine and pleasant company the tunnel itself was no darker than the rest of the journey!

A new terminal was built as part of Waterloo station, there not being sufficient room at the old Victoria where the Continental Expresses used to begin and end their journeys, while a depot was built alongside the Great Western main line at Wormwood Scrubs, accessible from Waterloo via the West London line. A new curved viaduct was built in Battersea, where the old Boat Train route from Victoria crosses the main line from Waterloo, and numerous curve improvements were made, notably at Tonbridge, Kent. Further down, Ashford station has been rebuilt to provide two Channel

Above: "Eurostar" No 3004 makes its first daylight visit to London Waterloo International Station in February 1994.

Tunnel platforms in the centre of what amounts to a new station. Once the tunnel is gained it is a case of a new railway through to within a few miles of Paris, where the old Continental platforms at the Gare du Nord have easily been adapted for the new service.

A brilliant technical success, "Eurostar" has been less successful commercially. Trains to Paris are popular enough, and there are good connections at Lille Europe station with TGVs to other parts of France, bringing Avignon for example to little more than 7hr from London. A winter through train to ski resorts in the French Alps has been well-used, too. But customs, immigration and safety regulations mean that "Eurostar" cannot be part of the national networks of the countries served, and it is not easy to book tickets to places off the "Eurostar" network. The Brussels service continued to disappoint even after opening of Belgian Railways' high-speed link cut the best journey time to under 2hr 40 min. In 1999, after five years' operation, "Eurostar" was carrying 6.6 million passengers annually, barely half the originally projected figure.

Another criticism has been the pedestrian progress of "Eurostar" on the congested route from London to the Tunnel – upgraded for 100mph (160km/h) running but slow by comparison with the top speed of 186mph (300km/h) on the French side. Now, after years of vacillation, construction of Britain's first high-speed railway is at last under way. Engineering and financial considerations have dictated that the line be built in two sections, the first being the more straightforward 46 miles (74km) from the Tunnel to Fawkham Junction near Swanley, in Kent, whence "Eurostars" will run on existing tracks to Waterloo. This largely 186mph (300km/h) railway should open in late-2003. The more difficult section onwards to a new Channel Tunnel terminal at London's St Pancras station, which includes extensive tunnelling beneath the River Thames and through the East London suburbs, will be built later.

A sad postscript must be added to this story of technical achievement. The new St Pancras terminal will be well placed for "Eurostars" to run through to destinations beyond London, a facility that was promised when government approved the Channel Tunnel project in the 1980s. But for the present, the operators of "Eurostar" see no commercial case for such services. So, somewhere in deepest rural England, more than 200 brand-new coaches lie unwanted, quietly decaying. These are the "Eurostars" and sleeping cars which were to provide those promised services to the north of England, Wales and Scotland, and which would have helped make the Channel Tunnel much more of a "national" asset. Built at huge cost, they have never turned a wheel in revenue service.

Below: "Eurostar" at Waterloo International London, which is a new terminal especially built for the Channel Tunnel service The train is modelled in part on the French TGV.

Above: "Eurostar" on arrival in Brussels from London Waterloo in October 1994. A new high-speed line connecting London with the Channel Tunnel will open in the early part of the 21st Century.

Class ETR 460 Pendolino tilting high-speed trainset

Origin: Italy: Italian Railways (FS), 1993. **Type:** Electric high-speed tilting trainset. **Gauge:** 4ft 8¹/₂in (1,435mm). **Propulsion:** 3kV DC, fed via overhead catenary, traction converter and chopper control to 16,820hp (12,550kW) body-mounted three-phase asynchronous traction motors. **Weight:** 1,83,847lb (483.8t). **Axleload:** 30,244lb (13.5t). **Overall length:** 776ft 3in (236,600mm). **Max speed:** 155mph (250km/h).

The tilting train came of age in the 1990s. While purpose-built but highly-expensive new high-speed lines could be financially justified for corridors generating the heaviest traffic flows, a more affordable means of cutting journey times to improve the competitiveness of rail was needed for less busy but still important routes. This was recognised early in Italy, where a two-tier approach has been taken to the development of high-speed services: new lines, such as that which will link Milan, Florence, Rome and Naples, will be primarily served by true high-speed trainsets; on other routes, where much use is made of existing infrastructure, Pendolino tilting trains are being deployed, utilising their capacity to negotiate curves at speeds up to 35 per cent higher than conventional equipment to reduce point- to-point timings.

Much pioneering work on tilting train design was carried out by the Italian company whose name has become synonymous with the technology, Fiat Ferroviaria. After many years of research and prototype testing, this firm delivered a series of 15 nine-car Class "ETR 450" 'Pendolino' electric trainsets to the national rail operator, FS, in 1987. The success of these led to a subsequent order for the much-refined Class "ETR 460" featured here.

First entering service in 1995, the "ETR 460" is also a nine-car unit, with a top speed of 155mph (250km/h). Unlike the "ETR 450", in which the hydraulic active tilting mechanism was located within the bodyshell, the "ETR 460" incorporates this equipment within the bogie, freeing potential passenger space and simplifying maintenance. As with most tilting train designs, the maximum angle of tilt is 8deg. Other features include microprocessor-controlled active lateral suspension, which ensures the body is centred over the bogies at all times, and body-mounted traction motors. The trainset formation is arranged in three groups comprising two power cars and one trailer. Seating is provided for 480 passengers in two classes.

Fiat supplied 10 "ETR 460"s to FS, deliveries commencing in 1993. Initially all were equipped only to operate from the standard FS 3kV DC system, but three have subsequently been adapted also to accept the French 1.5kV DC supply, allowing them to operate Milan-Turin-Lyons services. Two derivatives of the "ETR 460" are also now at work in Italy: in 1995 Fiat handed over to FS the first of 15 "ETR 480" units, which are essentially similar to their predecessors but are prepared for subsequent operation from the 25kV AC power supply system to be adopted for future high-speed lines in Italy; and two years earlier nine examples of the lower-geared "ETR 470" Cisalpino were supplied for cross-border services between Italy and Switzerland. Since then, Fiat has contributed tilting train technology to new-build programmes for the Czech Republic, Finland, Germany, Portugal, Spain and Switzerland. In 1997 a two-car ATR 410 diesel-electric version was completed.

Left: Three ETR 460 Pendolinos, including this example at St Jeanne de Maurienne, have been modified to operate from the French 1.5kV DC system to enable them to work Milan-Turin-Lyons services.
(Mick Alderman)

Type P40B/P42B (AMD-103) passenger locomotive

Origin: United States: GE Transportation Systems, 1993. **Type:** Diesel-electric passenger locomotive. **Gauge:** 4ft 8½in (1,435mm). **Propulsion:** GE 7FDL16 engine developing 4,000hp (2,985kW) (P40B) or 4,200hp (3,135kW) (P42B) with inverter control of fully-suspended DC traction motors. **Weight:** 250,911lb (112t). **Axleload:** 62,729lb (28t). **Overall length:** 69ft 6in (21,184mm). **Tractive effort:** 60,000lb (267kN) maximum. **Max speed:** 102mph (165km/h).

Amtrak continues to provide a network of long-distance passenger services across much of the USA, with most trains diesel-operated over the tracks of the major railfreight companies. Until the late 1990s, many of these were powered by the EMD-built 3,000hp (2,240kW) "F40PH" four-axle passenger type, dating from the mid-1970s. However, when it came to acquiring a replacement for this workhorse, Amtrak turned to EMD's competitor, GE Transportation Systems, which developed the stylish machines featured here.

Designated the "Genesis" model by GE and also known as the "AMD-103" by Amtrak, the "P40B" and "P42B" locomotives are powered by a 16-cylinder turbocharged version of this manufacturer's 7FDL engine series. The locomotives are members of GE's "Dash 8" and "Dash 9" families respectively, meaning that they employ DC traction motors supplied by rectified three-phase traction alternators. Adhesion is computer-regulated and microprocessors monitor all sub-systems, including fuel supply. Head-end power facilities are also provided, delivering electric power for train functions such as lighting, heating and air-conditioning.

It is, however, their streamlined external appearance that sets the "P40B"s and their sisters apart on a US traction scene that is dominated by "hood-style" freight locomotives. Unlike the EMD "F40PH", which is essentially a freight locomotive adapted for passenger work, the "P40B/P42B" was designed specifically for its task. The full width monocoque carbody and high-speed bogie have their origins in European practice, and were designed in cooperation with Krupp of Germany. Access to equipment is via roof hatches, making these the first Amtrak diesel locomotives not to offer side access to the engine compartment.

Amtrak initially ordered 44 locomotives of the 4,000hp (2,985kW) "P40B" "Dash 8" version; they were delivered between mid-1993 and 1994. During tests with one of the first-built examples, a speed of 115.2mph (185.5km/h) was achieved, although in service a top speed of 102mph (165km/h) applies. Subsequently, an additional 121 4,200hp (3,135kW) "P42B" "Dash 9" machines were supplied in 1996-97. The type is now used throughout the Amtrak network, usually in multiple-unit formations with other class members or with earlier locomotive types.

Amtrak also operates a lower-powered derivative of the "P42B". Equipped with AC rather than DC traction motors, the 3,200hp (2,390kW) "PC32ACDM", or "AMD-110", is fitted with 600V DC third rail current collectors, allowing it to operate as a straight electric locomotive in the vicinity of New York's Penn station, where diesel operation is restricted. Amtrak owns 16 of these machines, supplied in 1995-98, while 12 similar locomotives have been acquired by Metro-North, one of the operating divisions of New York's Metropolitan Transportation Authority.

Left: Two Amtrak P42Bs and a General Motors F40PH lead the Los Angeles-bound "Coast Starlight" out of Seattle King Street station. (John Turner)

Class 460 B₀-B₀

Origin: Switzerland: Swiss Federal Railways, 1993. **Type:** Electric all-purpose locomotive. **Gauge:** 4ft 8½in (1,435mm). **Propulsion:** AC at 15,000V 16⅔Hz fed via overhead catenary, two thyristor control systems to four frame-mounted 1140hp (1525kW) traction motors each driving one axle by a flexible drive. **Weight:** 185,136lb (84t). **Axleload:** 46,284lb (21t). **Overall length:** 60ft 8in (18.5m). **Max. speed:** 144mph (230km/h).

One part of the Swiss Federal Railways' ambitious RAIL 2000 plan are these remarkable locomotives, which were designed and built, as is the usual way in Switzerland, by a consortium of two companies, Schweizerische Locomotiv & Maschinenfabrik and Asea Brown Boveri. They were intended to be capable not only of very high speeds on the flatter sections of the Swiss network, but also of sharing the haulage of the heaviest freight trains up the great climbs to the Gotthard and Lötschberg tunnels; in fact, to be a universal locomotive, appropriate to the RAIL 2000 plan, plus the possibilities of export. At the same time, their design includes many interesting features, both mechanical and electrical, as well as a remarkably fine appearance due to styling by Italian consultant Pininfarina.

Foremost on the mechanical side is the "steerability" of the wheelsets in each bogie, whereby the axles are capable of independent movement which enables them to take up positions at right angles to the track on curves. This makes a big reduction in the forces involved, leading to less wear on wheels and rail. The cabs have lightweight bodies of glass-fibre sandwich construction, permitting an aerodynamic and attractive shape. Front windows are reinforced and, to avoid pressure changes running in and out of tunnels, the cabs are sealed and air-conditioned. Because there is no looking out, special retractable heated rear-view mirrors are provided at each corner of the locomotive.

The control system is based on micro-processors; two thyristor groups each feed the two three-phase traction motors on each bogie with variable frequency current when running. When braking is required, a regenerative current is produced plus, if required, air-brake power and, as a last resort, a magnetic track brake. The best combination is produced without the driver intervening. Incidentally, the regenerated current is "clean", with current

Above: Two "460" Bo-Bo locomotives in tandem hauling a train of motor vehicles.

and voltage cycles in phase with one another; regenerated currents obtained from locomotives braking have not usually been in phase in the past, a fact which has always discouraged use of this property.

In service, the locomotives have had a few problems, notably in the computer systems. In fact, they had to be taken off the top assignments in 1993, after a number of express trains were seriously delayed by false applications of the magnetic rail brake. For about a year the "460"s were confined to local passenger trains and running in multiple over the Gotthard line.

Swiss Federal Railways have ordered a total of 250 of these remarkable machines, over half of which have already been delivered, including some examples for running also on 25,000V 50Hz at Basel and Geneva and also at 3,000V DC for operating in Italy. The Bern Lötschberg Simplon railway also

received some of 18 slightly different locomotives between 1994 and 1997. These are a more powerful version, the Class "465", and are in fact the most powerful eight-wheel locomotives in the world, with an installed power of 7,000kW The export potential has also begun to be strongly demonstrated, with an order from Finland for 20 broad-gauge examples for 25,000V 50Hz. Later came an order from Norway for 22, following the loan of two Swiss examples – now named *Lille-Hammer* and *Olympia* – to help out during the 1993 winter Olympic Games. Incidentally, many others of the class are named, some after Swiss towns and regions but others, following substantial payment, as painted advertisements for products and services, e.g. No.460 015 is "AGFA". One stipulation is that the colours used should be as vivid as the red of the standard examples.

Left: Swiss Universal Locomotive Class "460" Bo-Bo.

Class 92 Co-Co electric locomotive

Origin: Great Britain: British Rail (BR), 1994. **Type:** Dual-voltage electric locomotive. **Gauge:** 4ft 8$^{1}/_{2}$in (1,435mm). **Propulsion:** 25kV AC 50Hz overhead catenary/750V DC third rail with thyristor chopper control of six 1,115hp (840kW) three-phase AC traction motors. **Weight:** 282,275lb (126t). **Axleload:** 47,049lb (21t). **Overall length:** 69ft 4in (21,340mm). **Tractive effort:** 90,000lb (400 kN) maximum. **Max speed:** 87mph (140km/h).

The most powerful locomotive to operate on Britain's rail network is the dual-voltage Class "92" electric unit, built from 1993 primarily to handle freight traffic to and through the Channel Tunnel linking Britain and France. With a rated output of 6,700hp (5,000kW) on an AC power supply and a starting tractive effort of 90,000lb (400kN), these are very capable but complex machines, although in the first years of their service lives their potential was not fully realised due to a combination of technical constraints and British railway politics.

The Class 92 is a dual-voltage machine, equipped for the 25kV AC power supply systems of the Channel Tunnel and routes north of London and for the 750V DC third rail system which equips lines between the capital and the tunnel. Initially, the class was confined to working conventional freight traffic – as opposed to Eurotunnel vehicle shuttles – through the Channel Tunnel shortly after its opening in 1994. This restricted their sphere of operation to the short section between Dollands Moor, near Folkestone in England, and Calais on the French side. Subsequently the class was authorised to work between Dollands Moor and Wembley, London, but only over two routes immunised against possible track circuit interference from the locomotives' power electronics. For this same reason, it was not until 1999 that the Class "92"s were permitted to undertake one of the main tasks for which they were constructed – the movement of continental

freight between the tunnel and northern England and Scotland. Since then, though, the scope of their operations has expanded to encompass a wider range of domestic freight activity on the electrified West Coast Main Line between London and Scotland.

Outwardly, the Class "92" presents a typically British appearance. Its thyristor traction control system is, however, of Swiss design and is based on that of the Swiss Federal's Class "460", which is covered elsewhere in this book. Construction of the fleet of 46 machines was undertaken by Brush Traction, whose traction motors provide the propulsion. Both rheostatic and regenerative braking is provided and the class is fitted for multiple-unit operation, a facility which is frequently used on heavier trains through the tunnel. The class is also equipped with the TVM 430 cab-signalling system used to control traffic in the Channel Tunnel.

Because railfreight operations through the Channel Tunnel were viewed as a joint initiative between the rail companies of Britain and France, nine of the locomotives were funded and are notionally owned by French National Railways (SNCF). They carry symbols confirming this, although they are operated as an integral part of the British-based fleet. A further seven were originally ordered to haul planned but subsequently cancelled overnight trains between Britain and mainland Europe. The remaining 30 machines were acquired by British Rail's Railfreight Distribution (RfD) division, becoming the property of English Welsh and Scottish Railway on privatisation of RfD in 1997.

Below: Operating from the 750V DC third rail power supply, the first Class 92, No 92001, heads a Channel Tunnel-bound freight. *(Ken Harris)*

Class 152 electric freight locomotive

Origin: Germany: German Rail (DB Cargo), 1997. **Type:** Electric freight locomotive. **Gauge:** 4ft 8^1/$_2$in (1,435mm). **Propulsion:** 15kV AC 16 2/3Hz overhead catenary with GTO thyristor chopper control of four 2,150hp (1,600kW) three-phase AC traction motors. **Weight:** 192,664lb (86t). **Axleload:** 48,166lb (21.5t). **Overall length:** 64ft 3in (19,580mm). **Tractive effort:** 67,500lb (300 kN) maximum. **Max speed:** 87mph (140km/h).

Much of Germany's railfreight is handled by electric traction, and high-powered locomotives designed specifically for this purpose traditionally featured in the fleets of both East and West German railways in the pre-unification era. One of the latest types to continue this tradition is the Class "152" 8,600hp (6,400kW) three-phase design supplied by Siemens Transportation Systems and Krauss Maffei to the freight division of German Rail, DB Cargo. An initial large order was placed for 195 of these machines, the first of four "pre-production machines" being rolled out in December 1996. These were handed over to DB Cargo in September 1997, while first deliveries from the series production commenced in 1998. They are progressively replacing older DB Cargo types, principally the Class "150" Co-Cos dating from the 1950s, with the first-built put to work in the Nuremberg area on freight services to Regensburg and Munich.

A four-axle machine, the Class "152" represents the second generation of development of the EuroSprinter modular electric locomotive concept developed by Siemens, which supplies the electrical equipment, and Krauss Maffei, which is responsible for the mechanical portion. Examples have been sold to Greece, Portugal and Spain. Today in Germany, requirements

are for speed as well as haulage capabilities, and the Class "152" has a top speed of 87mph (140km/h), compared with the 62mph (100km/h) of the Class "150" it replaces.

Traction control is by GTO thyristors, and three-phase AC traction motors are employed with individual axle control to optimise the transmission of tractive effort. One example from the series build, No 152 190-5, has been equipped with insulated gate bipolar transistor (IGBT) converters, claimed by its builders to be the world's first high- performance production rail vehicle to incorporate this traction system. Other features of the class include regenerative braking power of 5.83MW, lower energy consumption costs and the use of materials intended to encourage their environmentally responsible disposal at the end of the locomotives' working lives.

DB Cargo's initial order for 195 Class "152"s included an option on 100 more. The second-generation EuroSprinter concept has also found applications in Austria, where 50 Class "1016" and 25 Class "1116" versions were due to be delivered by 2002, in South Korea, where a Siemens-equipped prototype preceded local series production, and in China, where 40 twin-section EuroSprinter-based freight machines were ordered under a joint-venture scheme to equip the Baoji-Chengdu line. A six-axle variant has been supplied to Danish State Railways, forming Class "EG".

The commencement of deliveries of Class "152" coincided with a move heralding a major restructuring in the European railfreight industry, with DB Cargo in 1998 announcing plans to merge with its Dutch counterpart, NS Cargo. The branding adopted for the new joint company is "Railion", and this was expected progressively to feature in the new locomotives' livery.

Left: The clean lines of DB Cargo's Class 152 electric locomotive still betray a distinctive German appearance.

SD90MAC Co-Co freight locomotive

Origin: United States: Electro-Motive Division, General Motos Corporation (EMD), 1998. **Type:** Diesel-electric freight locomotive. **Gauge:** 4ft 8^1/$_2$in (1,435mm). **Propulsion:** General Motors GM16V265H 16-cylinder turbocharged engine rated at 6,000hp (4,476kW) at 1,000rpm, with traction alternator, twin inverters and six axle-hung three-phase AC traction motors. **Weight:** 426,773lb (190.5t). **Axleload:** 71,129lb (31.75t). **Overall length** 80ft 2in (24,434mm). **Tractive effort:** 200,000lb (890kN) maximum. **Max speed:** 75mph (120km/h).

The two major US diesel locomotive builders, GE Transportation Systems and General Motors (EMD), have continued to develop and refine the products to meet railroad demands for increased performance and reliability. The response to these demands from GM, the 6,000hp (4,475kW) SD90MAC, already looks set to become another classic design from this famous builder.

The use of AC traction motors has been increasingly prevalent in new US freight locomotives since the mid-1990s. In the case of GM, this is the result of a long collaboration with Siemens AG of Germany, whose traction equipment has been incorporated in the successful "SD70MAC" and "SD80MAC" types. These were respectively powered by GM's 710 series two-stroke engine developing 4,000hp (2,984kW) and 5,000hp (3,730kW) respectively. However, GM foresaw that North American freight operators would in future demand even higher horsepower, especially as the need arose to replace the "SD40-2"s, of which it had supplied more than 4,700 from the 1970s. With a 6,000hp machine, there would be an opportunity to

replace these older locomotives on a one-for-two basis, offering railroads substantial operating economies. However, the 710 series engine was felt to be at the limit of its development, and in a major departure from its long-established two-stroke practice, GM designed and produced a new four-stroke engine, the H-Engine, to power the "SD90MAC".

In the "SD90MAC", a 16-cylinder twin-turbocharger version of the H-Engine is installed. Coupled with a new-design traction alternator and a heavy-duty two-inverter system, this delivers a starting tractive effort of 200,000lb and a continuous tractive effort of 170,000lb. In tests, an SD90MAC has sustained an average speed of 65mph (104km/h) with a trailing load of 11,400t. Significant gains in fuel efficiency have also been achieved, with a 16 per cent improvement compared with the "SD40-2".

Other significant characteristics include design features intended to optimise reliability and serviceability, resulting in a claim by GM of a 25 per cent reduction in time out of traffic for maintenance compared with earlier models, and improvements to the HTCR II radial bogie.

GM's first customer for the "SD90MAC" was Union Pacific, which has also acquired examples of the competing "C60AC" model from GE. By 1999, UP had ordered 65 of the GM design in its 6,000hp configuration. Constructed in 1997, the first six UP machines were delivered in 1998. They were initially put to use on soda ash and manifest freight traffic in Wyoming and Nebraska, while others have operated intermodal services between Los Angeles and Chicago. In addition to the 6,000hp units, UP has since 1995 procured no fewer than 300 of a 4,300hp (3,207kW) version, the "SD90/43MAC", which has been designed to be retrofitted with the more powerful engine.

Left: Union Pacific was the first US railroad to order the 6,000hp SD90MAC.

Class 66 Co-Co freight locomotive

Origin: Great Britain: English Welsh & Scottish Railway (EWS), 1998. **Type:** Diesel-electric general-purpose freight hauler. **Gauge:** 4ft 8$\frac{1}{2}$in (1,435mm). **Propulsion:** General Motors 12N-710-3GB-EC engine developing 3,300hp (2,460kW) at 900rpm powering six axle- hung traction motors. **Weight:** 284,516lb (127t). **Axle load:** 47,494lb (21.2t). **Overall length:** 70ft 2in (21,390mm). **Tractive effort:** 89,800lb (399kN) maximum. **Max speed:** 75mph (120km/h).

When a private consortium led by US-based Wisconsin Central Transportation Corporation took over most of British Rail's bulk freight operations in 1996 to create English Welsh & Scottish Railway (EWS), the new company inherited a traction fleet containing many machines dating from the 1960s. The stock of life-expired equipment was further increased in 1997, when EWS acquired the international and automotive business of Railfreight Distribution, which operated a large fleet of ageing Class 47 machines. As well as delivering poor levels of availability and reliability, these older locomotives were also proving increasingly expensive to maintain, and their replacement was regarded as a matter of urgency.

With no domestically designed candidate considered suitable for its traffic requirements, EWS turned to a locomotive based on the General Motors-built Class "59", 15 of which had been acquired and successfully operated from 1985 by UK private sector quarrying and power generation companies for heavy haul work. For EWS this was an attractive option – combining the Class "59" mechanical design, which had been specially developed to meet the tight restrictions of the British Rail loading gauge, and the latest well-proven General Motors propulsion equipment. Indeed, EWS felt sufficiently confident in this concept to order no fewer than 250 examples of the type,

to be designated Class "66". This major order, the largest ever received by GM from a customer outside North America, was intended both to eliminate life-expired locomotives and to position EWS to handle the considerable traffic growth it foresaw. Construction of the fleet was entrusted to General Motors' London, Ontario, plant in Canada, where production started in 1998.

While outwardly the Class "66" closely resembles its Class "59" cousins, there are several important differences. In place of the 16-cylinder 645 series engine of the Class "59", the Class "66" employs the newer 710 engine in a 12- cylinder configuration which still develops the 3,300hp (2,460kW) of its predecessor. State-of-the-art microprocessor control and the latest traction equipment is used and the locomotive rides on radial steering bogies. And because the Class "66" is intended as a general-purpose workhorse rather than a heavy hauler, it is geared for 75mph (120km/h) rather than the 60mph (96km/h) of most of the Class "59"s.

Deliveries from Canada of Class "66"s began during the second half of 1998, with batches of 10 to 15 locomotives at a time arriving at Newport docks, in South Wales. After initial type testing, it became routine for the new locomotives to enter service virtually straight off the ship. The impact of this large influx of new equipment on the stock of older types was dramatic: by mid-1999, most examples of the once numerous EWS Classes "31", "33" and "47" had been retired and numbers of the ubiquitous Class "37" Co-Cos had been drastically reduced. Class "66"s can now be seen on most parts of the British network, hauling all but the heaviest trains.

Below: A Class 66 heads a train of new Land Rover cars for export via the Channel Tunnel. *(Ken Harris)*

Series 700 Shin Kansen high-speed trainset

Origin: Japan: JR Central/JR West, 1999. **Type:** High-speed electric trainset. **Gauge:** 4ft 8^1/$_2$in (1,435mm). **Propulsion:** AC at 25,000V 60Hz, fed via overhead catenary, traction converter and VVVF inverter control to 48 370hp (275kW) frame-suspended three-phase asynchronous traction motors. **Weight:** 1,586,118lb (708t). **Overall length:** 1,303ft 1in (39,720mm). **Max speed:** 177mph (285km/h).

Since pioneering the modern high-speed train in the 1960s, Japanese railway engineers have continued to develop and refine rolling stock for the country's Shin Kansen high-speed rail network. One of the most recent types to emerge from this process is the Series "700 trainset", which has been jointly developed by two of Japan's private sector rail companies, JR Central and JR West. Intended to replace older trainsets on the Tokaido and Sanyo Shin Kansen lines and to provide a response to increasing airline competition, the Series "700" draws on experience gained with the earlier Series "300" and "500" trainsets, creating new design offering the highest standards of performance and comfort while achieving demanding levels of reliability and maintainability.

The Series "700" train formation comprises 16 cars which in terms of equipment are of four different types; this means that in effect each train consists of four four-car sections, each with its own traction transformer and traction converter and inverter sets. Leading edge traction technology is employed, with control via a variable voltage, variable frequency (VVVF) inverter system. Twelve of the cars are motored, a total of 48 three-phase

asynchronous traction motors developing 17,700hp (13,200kW). On JR Central's Tokaido line, Series "700" is permitted to operate at 168mph (270km/h), while on the Sanyo Shin Kansen of JR West speeds of up to 177mph (285km/h) are authorised.

With 16 cars, these are high-capacity trains: each provides seating for 1,323 passengers in a mixture of first and second class accommodation. Comfort improvements include an increased ceiling height compared with earlier Shin Kansen trainsets and changes to seat mounting and geometry. Also contributing to increased comfort is a semi- active damping control system, which senses vehicle body vibration and controls it using computer technology, and inter-car longitudinal dampers. In addition, various design features of the Series "700" have been conceived to minimise both internal and external noise. Damping material fills the space in the hollow double-skin aluminium alloy body structure and is also used in the floor area to reduce the transmission of traction equipment noise. Externally, steps have been taken to reduce aerodynamic noise, such as the wind tunnel-tested styling of the rather bulbous "nose" which characterises these trains and the adoption of a low-noise pantograph.

JR Central was the first of the two railways to adopt the design, placing an order for 17 units in 1998. The first of these entered revenue-earning service in March 1999. This followed a year of extensive trials on both Tokaido and Sanyo Shin Kansen lines using a 1997-built prototype which amassed over 155,250 miles (250,000km) of test running.

Left: The first Series 700 trainsets were deployed on JR Central's Tokaido line, where they were intended to replace older equipment.

ICE 3 High-speed trainset

Origin: Germany/Holland: German Railways (DB AG), 2000. **Type:** Electric high-speed trainset. **Gauge:** 4ft 8¹/₂in (1,435mm). **Propulsion:** 15kV AC or four-voltage (additionally 25kV AC 50Hz, 3kV DC and 1.5kV DC), fed via overhead catenary and GTO traction converters to eight 1,340hp (1,000kW) fully suspended three-phase asynchronous traction motors. **Weight:** 907,313lb (405t) (15kV units); 940,918lb (420t) (four-voltage units). **Axleload:** 38,085lb (17t). **Overall length:** 656ft 2in (200,000mm). **Max speed:** 205mph (330km/h).

The German ICE high-speed train, the subject of an earlier entry, has proved an undoubted commercial and technical success. However, a handicap restricting its use as the basis for a design for future cross-border services in Europe has been the 20t axleload of its Class "401" (ICE 1) and "402" (ICE 2) power cars. This compares with 17t for France's TGV family, and was one of several factors that led to adoption of multiple-unit concept, with traction power distributed throughout the train, for German Rail's (DB) new-generation ICE 3 high-speed train. German Rail (DB) was also looking for increased performance, and ICE 3 delivers this, with a top speed of 205mph (330km/h) compared with the 174mph (280km/h) of ICE 1 and ICE 2, and an ability to tackle gradients of 4 per cent.

Designated Class 406 by DB, each ICE 3 consists of eight aluminium-bodied cars which, unlike TGV, are not articulated. Eight of the train's 16 bogies are powered, providing acceleration which is far superior to that of earlier ICEs. Effective braking systems are a particular feature of the train, with a regenerative brake capacity that at 8.2MW exceeds the traction power, as well

as innovative eddy-current electric and conventional disc brakes.

Train formation comprises three first and four second class cars, plus a restaurant/bistro car. Seating is provided for 391 passengers, including 24 in the restaurant car. That represents an increase in capacity of around 10 per cent compared with an ICE 1 of the same length. Like the earlier trains, ICE 3s can also work in multiple as two coupled sets when passenger demand is at its highest. ICEs are renowned for their high-quality passenger accommodation, and this latest addition to the family is no exception. Its quiet, comfortable and spacious interior also includes passenger information displays and a family compartment. However, the best part of ICE 3 in which to travel is the passenger saloon behind the cab, where a glass screen provides a driver's eye view of the track ahead.

Construction of ICE 3 was entrusted to a Siemens-led consortium that also includes Adtranz. Initial orders were for 54 trainsets: 37 single-voltage sets for DB domestic traffic and services into Austria and Switzerland, where the same power supply system is used; 13 four-voltage trains for services to Amsterdam, Brussels and Paris; and four four- voltage units for Netherlands Railways (NS), which were to use them in a pool with DB ICE 3s on the Amsterdam- Cologne route. Construction was well under way in 1999, and the first units in traffic were to be the NS examples, with revenue-earning services due to begin on the Amsterdam-Cologne-Frankfurt route in 2000.

As a passenger-winning concept, ICE has been very successful, and the ICE 3 is not the only addition to this family of trains: also now in service on DB's "classic" lines is a 143mph (230km/h) tilting version, ICT , and a 125mph (200km/h) tilting diesel derivative, Class "605".

Left: The first ICE 3 cars were unveiled to the public at the 1998 Eurailspeed Congress in Berlin.

Pendolino Tilting high-speed trainset

Origin: Great Britain: Virgin Trains, 2001. **Type:** Electric high-speed tilting trainset. **Gauge:** 4ft 8^{1}/$_{2}$in (1,435mm). **Propulsion:** AC at 25,000V 50Hz, fed via overhead catenary, traction converter and IGBT inverter control to 12 570hp (425kW) frame-suspended three-phase asynchronous traction motors. **Weight:** 851,306lb (380t). **Axleload:** 14.7t. **Overall length:** 634ft 10in (19,350mm). **Max speed:** 140mph (225km/h).

An earlier entry in this book provides details of the Class "87" 25kV AC electric locomotives which for more than 20 years have provided front-line traction for passenger services on Britain's West Coast Main Line. Linking London with Birmingham, Liverpool, Manchester, Glasgow and Edinburgh, the WCML is generally reckoned to be the country's most important route. Since electrification was completed in the 1970s, though, little investment had taken place either in infrastructure or rolling stock. With privatisation of the former British Rail, this has changed. The line's main passenger operator, Virgin Trains, and infrastructure owner Railtrack have teamed up to develop a ú2.1bn scheme to share the benefits of a major capacity-enhancing upgrade of track, power supply and signalling systems and a complete renewal of the rolling stock fleet. The centrepiece of is this project is to be this fleet of 54 high-speed tilting trainsets.

In northern England and the southern Scottish uplands especially, the WCML features many speed-restricting curves and tilt has long been identified as the obvious path to reduced WCML journey times. By the time Virgin Trains took over its West Coast franchise in 1997 the technology was well established and a joint venture of Alstom and Fiat Ferroviaria was named in 1998 as the winning bidder to supply the new trains. The order was part of a complex deal that included provision of 54 eight-car trainsets,

their routine maintenance and servicing of existing rolling stock until the new trains arrived.

The division of construction work between the two consortium members was to see aluminium bodyshells fabricated at Fiat's plant in Savigliano, Italy, before shipment to the Alstom UK facility at Birmingham for fitting out, including installation of underframe and roof-mounted equipment. Bogie manufacture was assigned to Fiat SIG in Switzerland, using a design based on that of Swiss Federal Railways ICN 2000 trainset. The same company's electrically actuated tilting system is also used, giving a maximum tilt angle of 8 , and a tilt-compensated pantograph maintains correct overhead line contact in curves.

Under the terms of the agreement worked out between Virgin Trains and Railtrack, the WCML upgrade is to take place in two phases: Phase 1, to be completed by 2002, will allow Virgin's Pendolinos to run at 125mph (200km/h). This will cut one hour from the 5hr 20min best Class "87"-hauled timing for the 401 miles (646km) between London and Glasgow and 30min from the 2 hr 30min London-Manchester 189-mile (304km) schedule. Phase 2, to be completed by 2005, will permit 140mph (225km/h) running, slicing a further 30min from the London-Glasgow journey time and bringing Manchester 15min closer to the capital. Increased service frequencies also form part of Virgin's tilting train strategy, with plans virtually to double the number of arrivals and departures at London's Euston station to 11 an hour.

Implementing these plans has called for a very challenging construction and delivery timetable. Delivery of a first pre-series train for acceptance testing was due in 2000, to be followed by the first series train early in 2001. All 54 are due to be in service by May 2002.

Left: Scenes like this are due to greet passengers arriving at London's Euston station to travel on Virgin Trains' Pendolino tilting trainsets.

Class NGG16 1-C-1+1-C-1

Origin: South Africa/Wales: Welsh Highland Railway, 1958/1997. **Type:** Beyer-Garratt locomotive for tourist railway. **Gauge:** 2ft ⁵/₈in (600mm) **Propulsion:** Atomised oil burnt in the firebox, generating steam at 180ps (12.6kg/cm) is fed to two engine units with twin cylinders 12 x 16in (305 × 406mm) driving the wheels directly by connecting and coupling rods. **Weight:** 93,780lb (42.55t) adhesive, 137,530lb (62.4t) total. **Axleload:** 15,456lb (7.1t). **Overall length:** 48ft 5in (14.75m). **Tractive effort:** 21,363lb (94.9kN). **Max speed:** 25mph (40km/h).

At the end of the 1990s, "Millennium Grants" were approved in the United Kingdom to cover projects likely to be completed in the year 2000. One of these is covering half the cost of the building of a railway southwards leaving Caernafon on the old London & North Western Railway branch line to Afon Wen but otherwise on the route of the old Welsh Highland Railway. The grant covers half the expense of rebuilding, relaying and re-equipping the line as far as a village called Rhyd Ddu, starting point for a brisk walk to the summit of Snowdon just above. The scenery of the area is of quite outstanding grandeur, while the roads are narrow. A 3 mile (5km) section from Caernarvon to Dinas Junction was opened in 1997, and approval for reconstruction of the whole route was granted in 1999 after a long planning enquiry. The next section, to Waunfawr, was expected to open in mid-2000, with Porthmadog being reached by 2006. The intention is, during the early years of the new century, to complete the route where the original line, opened in 1923 and closed in 1936, ran through Beddgelert and the Aberglaslyn Pass to Porthmadog. A short reconstructed line already exists here, adjacent to the WHR track bed, where one of the original locomotives, 2-6-2T *Russell*, presides over a noble collection of preserved relics of similar age.

Something rather different and more attuned to present-day conditions but with rather less historic connections was indicated for the new project, and the eyes of the promoters fell on these class "NGG16" locomotives, which were built between 1937 and 1965, a number of which were available in South Africa. A deal was struck with the Alfred County Railway, near Durban, who are the present owners of both working and surplus 2ft gauge Beyer-Garratts, and five of the latter were selected for the new Welsh Highland Railway, three of which were supplied in 1996. They are the most powerful steam locomotives ever built for the gauge and suitable for handling heavy loads on 1-in-40 grades with 2.4 chain (48m) radius curves which are the standard on the new line. The locomotives were converted to oil-burning and overhauled into "as new" condition before being shipped to the UK.

The load which a single locomotive of this type can haul is 275t, equivalent to 15 carriages, which will be designed to provide good views of the landscape as well as allowing access for disabled people. Provision of full buffet and dining service will be a feature, in spite of the narrowness of the gauge. About 50 carriages will be required for full operation of the line, but 24 will be available for the opening.

Left: An artist's impression of the Welsh Highland Railway.

TGV Duplex High-speed trainset

Origin: France: French National Railways (SNCF), 1996. **Type:** Electric double-deck high-speed trainset. **Gauge:** 4ft 8^1/2in (1,435mm). **Propulsion:** Dual-voltage – AC at 25kV 50Hz/DC at 1.5kV, fed via overhead catenary traction converter and IGBT inverter control to eight 1,475hp (1,100 kW) frame-suspended three-phase synchronous traction motors. **Weight:** 949,879lb (424t). **Axleload:** 38,085lb (17t). **Overall length:** 656ft 9in (200,190mm). **Max speed:** 186mph (300km/h).

Thalys High-speed trainset

Origin: Belgium/France/Germany/The Netherlands, 1997. **Type:** Electric high-speed trainset for international service. **Gauge:** 4ft 8^1/2in (1,435mm). **Propulsion:** Four-voltage - AC at 25kV 50Hz and 1.5kV at 16 2/3Hz/DC at 3kV and 1.5kV, fed via overhead catenary, traction converter and IGBT inverter control to eight 1,475hp (1,100kW) frame-suspended three-phase synchronous traction motors. **Weight:** 949,879lb (424t). **Axleload:** 38,085lb (17t). **Overall length:** 656ft 9in (200,190mm). **Max speed:** 186mph (300 km/h).

Described earlier, France's TGV high-speed train has become a benchmark for fast rail travel, setting the highest standards for intercity journeys and providing real competition for airlines. Development of the TGV concept has continued and several important derivatives have been introduced as traffic levels have grown and Europe's network of dedicated high-speed lines has expanded.

On France's first dedicated high-speed line, the Paris Sud Est (PSE) route to Lyons and beyond, rising passenger numbers coupled with the prospect of further business growth resulting from the planned commissioning in 2000 of the TGV Méditerranée line to Marseilles led to a major reappraisal of train capacity requirements. With the use of two-set formations of the original PSE TGVs already common, any further lengthening of trains was considered impractical because of station platform constraints. Double-deck trains were already in widespread use on commuter routes in France and it was this concept which offered a solution to PSE capacity needs, in the form of TGV Duplex.

However, stepping up double-deck vehicle design from high-capacity, medium-speed stock used only for comparatively short journeys to a high-performance trainset intended for long-distance 186mph (300km/h) operation posed major challenges, both in terms of engineering requirements and passenger amenity. Prominent among these challenges was a necessity to remain within 17t axleload limit set by SNCF for its high-speed rolling stock. This was mainly achieved by the widespread use of aluminium in bodyshell construction, but also necessitated measures such as a 30 per cent reduction in the weight of each seat compared with those of the earlier TGV Atlantique vehicles and the use of thinner electrical cables. As a result, TGV Duplex is an outstanding train, providing high levels of comfort for 516 passengers – 45 per cent more than the previous generation TGV Réseau in a similar formation of two power cars and eight trailers.

To provide traction for TGV Duplex, the technical characteristics of the TGV Réseau power car were combined with new, more rounded styling intended to improve the train's aerodynamics and modernise its appearance. Each of the two power cars is equipped with four 1,475hp

Above: Two TGV Duplex sets operating in multiple form a Paris-Perpignan service at Marseillan-Plage. *(Chris Wilson)*

(1,100kW) self-commutating synchronous traction motors, giving a total trainset output of 11,800hp (8,800 kW), and provision is made to operate under 25 kV AC and 1.5 kV DC power supply systems.

Initially, SNCF ordered 30 TGV Duplex sets, construction of which was entrusted to Alstom, builders of all previous TGVs. The first unit was delivered in July 1995 and revenue-earning services began on the PSE route in December 1996. Deliveries continued until 1998. In 1999 SNCF placed an order for an additional 12 sets which were all due to be in service by the end of 2002.

Cross-border operations without a change of traction also present rail vehicle designers with a complex set of demands, of which power supply system compatibility is just one; such trains also have to interact with the signalling, driver vigilance and safety systems and the communications networks of each country through which they pass. In the third-generation TGV trainsets developed for services linking France with Belgium, Germany and the Netherlands – known as PBKA sets because they serve Paris, Brussels, Köln (Cologne) and Amsterdam – provision has been made for operation from four power supply systems: the 25kV AC used on French and Belgian high-speed lines, Belgium's domestic 3kV DC, the 1.5kV DC which is standard in the Netherlands, and the German 15kV AC.

For these trainsets, the power car developed for TGV Duplex was adapted for this international role and paired with eight Réseau-type trailer cars. Initially 27 units were ordered, but this was later cut back to 17. Ownership of these is divided between Belgian National Railways (SNCB) (nine sets), SNCF(six) and Netherlands Railways (NS) (two), with two of the Belgian trains leased to the German operator, DB AG. Deliveries of PBKA sets started in 1996, and they work alongside 10 French-owned Thalys-branded three-voltage TGV Réseau units which operate Brussels and Amsterdam services.

The Thalys name – which has no literal meaning – also indicates a trend

Above: Thalys PBKA high-speed trainset at Paris Nord station.
(Ken Harris)

in European international long-distance rail operations. It is the brand-name of Brussels-based organisation, Thalys International (formerly Westrail International), a joint venture set up in 1995 by SNCB and SNCF to manage quality, marketing and the award of onboard catering contracts of this particular group of cross- border services. DB and NS also participate in Thalys International but not as full partners.